A Matter of Time

Don Kirchner

With courage! anything possible!
Don K—

High Ground Publications
Sedona   Los Angeles

A Matter of Time

ISBN: 0-9720153-4-5

Printed in the United States of America

Dedication

To the women in my life, from whom I have learned the hardest yet most lasting lessons of love and truth—from my mother, who was first given the lump of coal, to my daughter who only saw the diamond; from the first of my lovers who added the facits, to the one with whom I now live and dance and play, who has helped me polish it and sees its true value...

To all of them, and to all women everywhere with the challenge of doing the same for the men in their lives, I dedicate this book.

Epigraph

"Life weaves its patterns in ways we little understand
...until they're complete."

– George Addair

Foreword

This is a message I never thought I would write. The events of this book center on the early 1980s. America's war on drugs was just getting into full swing and my colleagues and I were its warriors. Our attitudes were molded by the times, and they were hard. We had seen the havoc that drugs wrought. We had seen individuals destroyed by drugs, our society corrupted by its money, and whole nations come under the control of drug lords. For these wrongs, we wanted to exact a high price. We wanted not just to fix a troubled society, we wanted to exact a measure of revenge on those who had created these problems. We routinely sought the harshest possible penalties, yet it is difficult to be involved in the criminal justice system and not be aware of and moved by the human element.

What caused me to pull Don Kirchner from the fire, I cannot say. In my 21 years as a prosecutor, I did this from time to time with people who somehow struck me as redeemable, as able to atone for their wrongs in some way other than prison. There was no precise equation for those I selected; it was a very personal decision by me, and one that caused me no small measure of concern. I made efforts to follow the lives of these people from a distance to see if my decision was justified by the conduct of their lives. I lived in fear that I may have been wrong—that this person might be beyond redemption, or that they would cause some untold harm that would ultimately be my fault. I felt that it was important that these people earn the break they had been given, that they redeem me with lives that made a difference. More than 20 years later, I still hear from many of these people. I am proud that in almost every instance my gamble paid off with good and decent lives that did, in fact, make a difference.

Don Kirchner is one of these people. He was pulled from the fire on a hunch...on a vague sense of something decent in this man that would ultimately reward society. He has earned his break, and has paid the price a thousand times over.

Having watched his life from afar, and taken silent pride in his accomplishments, I feel like the adventurer in the popular movie who, on making a very difficult and critical choice, is told, "You have chosen wisely."

David L. McGee,
Chief Deputy United States Attorney
"United States of America
vs.
Yamanis, et. al.
and
Donald E. Kirchner"

Acknowledgments

Behind every good writer there are people who, each in their own unique way, contribute in some way to that writer's success. In fact, it has been my personal experience that those people can and probably do make the difference between a good writer and a great writer.

Whenever I see a particularly good movie, I feel compelled to remain in my seat afterwards and read the names of all the people who each made their contribution to the quality and substance of the film. In like manner, I invite and encourage you to do the same with the following acknowledgements once you've read the story. Keep in mind that this is a true story—an epic journey that covers nearly twenty years of a journey through the darkness of human struggle to find the light of one's soul. Without the personal as well as professional help, encouragement and moral support of each of the following, some essential part of the story would be diminished or even lost altogether. They all made it the story that it is.

To those who played a part in this story—either unwittingly or intentionally—whom I have failed to mention here, I deeply apologize and offer my humblest gratitude to you nonetheless. No doubt, as soon as this goes to print I will remember ten of you. Rest assured that in that remembrance, I will recall with fondness and respect the part you played. In that regard, know that you are no less a valued part of my memory and experience.

To all of you—either listed here or somewhere in my memory yet unrecalled, I offer my heartfelt gratitude. I may have written the story, but you lived it with me and helped make it what it is.

First of all, no writer known to me makes it to the height of literary success without someone to sift through the mountains of rhetoric and distill it down into something enjoyable to read. Nowhere could this be more true than in the writing of this book. No recognition, in my case, would be appropriate without mentioning my first real literary taskmaster in high school, Mrs. Grace Dawson, who introduced me to the rigors involved in writing with my first assignment; a 5,000 word essay on "The Poetic, Prophetic and Philosophic Aspects of Hebrew Literature". Even in her golden years of retirement, Mrs. Dawson's lethal red ink pen went to work on the first chapters of this book as I wrote them in a prison cell over twenty years later.

More than a few other people have assisted over the years as I wrote, re-read and rewrote these chapters, not the least of whom were Betty Bach Fineman, former spouse of and editor for one of my all-time favorite authors, Richard Bach; also Ron and Nancy Melmon, who sequestered themselves with me in their home for two weeks to complete the first reading and rewriting of the manuscript; Kathleen Francis; Don Abrahams; Talasteena, John Anderson, Dennis Sigman and Andràs Nevai, the latter of whom took much time from his regular business to answer the call of a brother. My greatest taskmaster, Jean Searle, performed essential major surgery on the final draft, particularly with my obsessive use of dashes, semi-colons and participle phrases. Without her keen eye and sharp pencils, this work would have remained more like a journal than a book.

Last to help me make it readable for you was my greatest editor both in writing and in life, who sifted through all of it over and over again, and gave it the sparkle that she has in my life, Nancy Sweet.

Beyond the editing were the people in my life who, despite my brash impulsiveness and numerous bull-headed attempts to rewrite the rules of life to fit my own purposes, cared enough to look more closely and in their own unique way, threw out a life line for me to grab as I found myself being swept away like the "Sorcerer's Apprentice" in a rampaging flood of my own doing. No one served that role better or more dramatically than David L. McGee, former Chief Deputy United States Attorney for the Northern District of Florida, without whose astuteness and act of personal courage, I might still be writing this from a prison cell. His former boss, the Honorable Judge Roger Vincent, I'm certain, had a significant impact, "for the record," on my eventual early release, and no less notable authorities than the late U.S. Senator Barry Goldwater and present U.S. Senator John McCain took their own personal time while in office to read my writings on juvenile justice reform, and corresponded with me while I was still just another federal prisoner serving time.

No acknowledgement in this regard could be complete without mentioning Gordon Bernell, Director of Educational Services at the Bernalillo County Detention Center in Albuquerque, NM, who first inspired me to get beyond my personal fears and extend myself to assist others less prepared and less able to cope with the difficulties of incarceration; also Don Black, Correctional Counselor with the Escambia County Jail in Pensacola, FL, who took it upon himself to bend the rules and write a letter of commendation on my behalf that may have been the catalyst for the series of events that ultimately led to my seemingly hopeless case finally turning around.

I can't imagine anyone attempting to write (and complete) a book like this without financial help. In this category, I was blessed many times over with valiant souls who believed in me enough to support me financially as I struggled not only to rebuild my life, but to cope with the "starving artist" syndrome. Without them, this book would still be in stacks of paper-clipped, unedited chapters lying in dusty heaps and rodent-ravaged cardboard boxes while I continued to wait tables, drive taxis and throw newspapers.

Most significant among this latter group of supporters are Ron and Nancy Melmon, who not only paid my bills—*all* of them—for several months, and spent weeks of their time helping edit the entire book with me, but then gave back to me the percentage of equity in the book they so richly deserve. The rest of my backers are no less dear to me, for whatever they gave and under whatever circumstances, it always came as water to a man in the desert. Among them are Leon Lunsway, Talasteena and Jack Lin, who were the first to take the leap with me; Terry Wilson, Rob Watson and Stephen and Martha Baer, who made a huge difference with substantial leaps; Melissa Winscher; Barbara Scott; my sister, Katherine; Bonnie and Doug Klein; my aunt and uncle, Vivian and John Sedlacek; Jean and Dick Searle; Jim Sweet; Don and Sandy Abrahams; Jeanne Suliere; Charles Vass; Brian Schmutz; Marc Spector, and Blair Preston—who started it all by being the first to say "I'm in." Not to be forgotten is Debra May, who supported me unselfishly throughout the journey and who helped to build the bridge back home. She never gave up on me, even when it seemed like the only reasonable thing to do. Last and certainly not least among these intrepid souls, is my own accountant, Mary "Hass" Maxson, a feisty little lady who flies a mean Cessna 182 of her own, and who was always there for me whenever I needed to make the rent or catch up on car payments.

Special recognition I offer to Barbara *Good Sky* (two words, please note), who gave when she could least afford to, in small, unmarked bills, even if it cut her short (which it always did). Her 10's and 20's, and sometimes even 50's, kept gas in my tank and enabled me to have an occasional lunch with important prospects.

Then there are those who made their contribution sometimes with a few dollars or, more importantly, with faith, trust and encouragement that I needed to keep believing that I wasn't deluding myself about the value of the story, or of the journey itself. Among those who did that most admirably, and who have won a permanent place in my heart are Candace McKena Caldwell; all four of my sisters, Katherine, Sandee, Terri and Judith, who stuck by me each in their own unique way; Brian Schmutz, Linda Bruce, Gail Berry, Frank Darling, Janet Johnson, Cliff Jackson, Suzanne Taylor, Kym Raa, Roy VandeBogart, Sal Medina, Chrissie Hollander, Candace Zipadelli, Rob and Iva Bernhagen, Karen Reider, Enocha Ryan, Don and Patricia Davison, Gene Munson, Harold Gidish, Don Dailey, Gary and Sue Mialocq, the whole Lovett tribe, Steve Negoesgo, GianCarlo Baretta, Bente Friend, Paul Simon, Lorenzo Best, Julie Brown, Lisa Law, Thomas Handloser, Tom Berndt, Linda Dean and her entire family, Joyce Black, Jerre Sears, Norm and Jeanne Richardson, and finally, a lady who became like a mother to me...as well as a best friend...Jewell Meredith.

Not to be left out are Jean Giles, who *is* my mother, and who endured more than she will ever admit, and Bill Giles...a good man who little knew when he married her the storms he would have to weather with me in the picture. Also, Myra Boeve, my grandmother, who, at 96, still keeps a prayerful light around me always; her son, my Uncle Garold and his wife, Gerri; and Joan Marie Ryan, who gave me a daughter in the depths of the journey and stuck it out with me through more chaos than most anyone else could.

To these wondrous beings who came into my life and chose to stay in spite of it all, I add my children, who, though they had little other choice, stuck behind me anyway, and enriched my life simply by having been a part of it; Jonathan, Channon, Amber, and even if he didn't have to endure their challenges...Tyler. Also, Matt Field and James "Peace" Wilbanks, who became like sons to me. Though they might think they know it well enough by now, I love them all more than I can say.

To all those people who wrote letters on my behalf, who accepted collect phone calls from jails and prisons I was in, who accepted me as their friend and brother, or who burned candles or said prayers for my well-being, I thank you eternally. With deepest appreciation in particular for Torkom Saradarian, George Addair, Bob Trask and Brugh Joy, I celebrate the realization that *anything*, no matter how dark or difficult, can be an exciting, and never-ending exploration of Life's unfolding mysteries.

Finally, I wish to honor my very closest friends who, together and individually, have done more than anyone else to help me bring this story to life and share it with you. Whoever said "never mix business and friendship," never met these three:

To Ron and Lois Thelen, and to Nancy Sweet; the Dragon and I both salute you, and pledge our eternal Friendship.

To all of the above, and to you, the reader, Blessings, Love and a Radiance of Light.

Don Kirchner
May 19, 2000

Introduction

It is assumed that the business of our lives is as natural as childbirth—that all of us should know how to design a life worth living. Our society has dug deep into the roots of what causes us to become who we are, from the very fiber of our being locked in the strands of our DNA, to what influences from our conditioned upbringing portend the future of an individual history in the making. This true-life story delves into the matter…in this case, a matter of time and how I came to spend it, squander it, reinvest it, and eventually transform with it. It is a soul-searching inquiry into the nature of one's specific self—a look at the cloaked potential that creates a Mother Teresa or a Hitler, and the knowing that a prudent thinker is painfully aware that in each of us lives both possibilities.

This is as much an inquiry into the mystery of the psyche as it is an accounting of the events of my life. On the premise that we are here to uncover the archeology of what it means to be human, and what abilities we have to intervene in the matter of our lives, my journey begins.

My Uncle Stan had a gift for saying a great deal with very few words. He wasn't well educated in the conventional sense, having spent most of his life on a sprawling ranch on the open prairie of northeastern Colorado. One of the most rewarding experiences of my childhood was the year I was able to live there. On one occasion, my impulsiveness had resulted in a calf being injured. I told my uncle that I had meant well. He shook his head and waved an arm in the air that was his unique way of letting me know how upset he was, and recited to me a time-worn adage that has remained with me ever since.

"The road to hell," he said sternly, "is paved with good intentions."

If that were true, then in the years that followed, I had a crew of multiple personalities working around the clock constructing a six-lane superhighway. And hell is right where it led.

My life has been a strange and difficult one—strange in the sense that despite my constantly gnawing wish to be "normal", there wasn't anything normal about most of the dilemmas into which I got myself. The difficult part was maintaining the respectable image ingrained in me from birth, yet living my life the way I wanted to—challenging every rule and pushing against all limits, all the time.

The image I learned to present to the world was a clean-cut, decent one. I was raised by a career military officer, and by a mother who was determined to see that my four sisters and I would fit his picture of how kids should be raised and how they should behave. Personal feelings were never as important as the image, so I learned to keep feelings to myself and said "yes, sir," and "no, ma'am" in ways that would swell the pride of an infantry commander.

I was the All-American "boy next door"—the kind you would be pleased to have out with your daughter. I was an altar boy during most of my Catholic upbringing, and as a Boy Scout I held nearly every award obtainable. I carried that image to such an extent that I would often find myself spending more time with the parents of the girls I dated than with the girls themselves.

Though I may have been trying hard to please and impress older people, part of me truly enjoyed spending time with them. Finding myself drawn to them, I could sit and listen to their stories for hours, even though part of me would fidget and squirm with restlessness. I loved the connection I felt with them, and in the process I learned how to make them feel good about me.

I had mastered the art of persuasion almost from the time I knew how to talk. Traveling with my father in his military career, I lived in three foreign countries and in a dozen states of the U.S. before graduating from high school. German was my first language, not by choice but by heredity and exposure. My first words were spoken to our German maid and to the kids in the German neighborhood where I spent my first four years. When most teen-age boys my age were playing football and basketball, I was learning the ways of the Orient—of the people of Taiwan, Okinawa and Japan. Altogether, I attended sixteen different schools, including four high schools. In the process, I became skilled at making instant best friends…or enemies.

I think my mother may have been the first to suspect that I wasn't quite like other kids my age. In many ways disconcerting to her over the years, I was different. Often the case with mothers, she sensed that things just weren't quite right with me. There was something sneaky about me, and even defiant. I couldn't understand what bothered her so much about me, because for the most part I felt like I was a pretty decent kid. When she would get upset with me, an anger would come up in her that was irate and harsh. To soften her, I would quickly shift into the "right" persona. She seemed angry with me much of the time, and I suspect now that it was because I had learned to manipulate her. She didn't know how to deal with me, but then neither did I.

My father's approach was simply a matter of doing things 'by the book'—the stricter, the better. Everyone snapped-to when he was around. To him, that was the way it was supposed to be. But he was gone a lot, which left her to enforce whatever he felt was most important in our upbringing. Children were to be "seen and not heard," and they were to "do as I *say;* not as I *do.*" When he was home, he laid down the law —*his* law—and it was enforced with a military belt. If I had muddied the waters of the home front at all, I paid dearly for it with welts on my back end. So, I learned to muddy *other* waters, while keeping the ones at home as clear as possible.

I suppose that's where the story begins, because this was the core of my biggest challenge—learning to recognize the difference in the results of my actions as reality, and my intentions and self-image as fantasy. To me, everything was a matter of image. Once I had a certain image down, I could get away with almost anything. If I did it well enough, I could even avoid the backlash. The faster I moved, the less of my own wake I had to deal with.

So, I grew up with an instinct for saying the right thing at the right time, and knowing how to read most any situation. I learned to read people, and how to present just the right image to gain their approval. I could charm them into believing most anything about me, especially since I usually believed it myself.

I wasn't greedy or malicious, nor did I ever intend to harm anyone. So, to me it was okay to do and say whatever worked to get what I wanted…as long as my intentions were good.

Perhaps the story really begins with the day I came home late from a play rehearsal in high school. I was barely sixteen. For the first time in my life, I had begun to feel as if I finally belonged somewhere. We had recently settled into an upscale suburban community in Tacoma, Washington, where I quickly became active in school and social activities. In less than a year, I had become best friends with the most popular guy in school, the varsity quarterback and shoo-in for election to Student Body President the next year. I was also dating one of the most popular cheerleaders, and had played a leading role in that year's very successful school play, "The Miracle Worker." School elections for the next year's slate of officers were scheduled in two months, and it was increasingly rumored that I stood a very strong chance of winning the office of Senior Class President.

It was January of 1964, and I was in rehearsal after school for a series of one-act plays. I was feeling very self-assured, and pleased with the fact that in such a short time I had risen to a level of social acceptance that, as a military kid, I had never known before. As I rode my bicycle home that evening, it was growing dark and drizzly outside, but that didn't matter to me. I was on top of the world.

When I rode up into the yard, I was surprised to see the house dark with no cars in the driveway. This was unusual for that time of the evening, since my father was always home by then and my mother would normally be busy making dinner. I didn't have my key, but as I stood wondering how to get in, my mother pulled up in the driveway. Surprisingly, she couldn't get the front door unlocked, so we walked around to the back of the house where I managed to crawl in through a basement window.

There was an acrid, pungent smell in the house that I will never forget. As I groped for the light switch by the basement stairway, I felt something soft and furry on the steps. Switching the light on, I discovered it was our dog. He seemed to be breathing, but it was odd for him to be lying so limply on the basement steps with the door to the main part of the house shut. We never kept him in the base-ment, much less with the door shut.

I reached down to touch him and his eyes opened only slightly. He looked very sick, and I began to sense a rising fear in my gut that something was horribly wrong. The smell in the air was nauseating, and at first I thought it had something to do with him. I quickly opened the back door for my mother, exclaiming to her my fear that something was wrong with the dog. I vaguely remember opening windows, trying to get those awful fumes out of the house while at the same time going to the phone to call a vet. The phone was mounted on the wall by the door to the garage, and as I dialed the number I felt an eerie sense of something dark and foreboding behind that door.

As I waited for the voice on the other end to answer, I opened the door slightly and another wave of nausea hit me as I felt a rush of more acrid fumes sweep over me. I sensed a weird and very scary presence in the garage, unlike anything I had ever experienced before. By then, enough windows were open that I could feel fresh air behind me, but inside was something murky and heavy with that same pungent odor. My head began to swim, and I felt dizzy as I reached around the doorway for the light switch and flipped it on.

There in the garage was my father's car. It was in its normal place, but something about it wasn't normal at all. My eyes were drawn to a garden hose which was oddly running from somewhere in the back of the car along the floor and up into the driver's vent window. I couldn't quite see inside the car until the smokiness of the garage began to clear. Only then could I begin to make out the shape of a human form in the front seat. My mind began to swim in a torrent of dizzying, unclear thoughts and impressions as I suddenly realized it was my father. So taken aback was I at the moment that my first impression was that he must be napping. But why would he be napping in the car in a darkened garage?

Deeply puzzled by this bizarre scene, I hung up the phone and stepped into the garage, oblivious to my lungs aching for fresh air. I could detect no movement at all on his part, and as I approached the driver's door I felt as if this might be some sort of demented prank. My father was known for occasional practical jokes, but he was far too serious a person for a prank of this magnitude.

My heart began beating faster, and my mind was racing as I opened the car door and felt that sickening stench of fumes again. He was slumped over in the seat and had an awful, grayish, almost ghostly pallor covering his face and hands. I reached in and touched his face. It was cold. Frighteningly, terrifyingly cold—like a figure in a wax museum, or a cadaver in a morgue. So bewildered by the bizarre nature of the whole scene, I couldn't even fathom that this might be death that I was looking at.

I was mortified. This was beyond my comprehension. Could this be my father? He couldn't actually be dead. Not like this. Not here. Not now. This couldn't be happening. This was some kind of joke, some kind of unimaginable, nightmarish prank...not real at all, and certainly not happening to me...not to us.

Suddenly, it hit me with the full force of an explosion. It *was* real, and it *was* happening to me. How could this be? He was too strong, too powerful. This *couldn't* be real. While that part of me stood there reeling in shock and disbelief, another part suddenly stepped forward and took charge. We could clear this up. Just get to the phone. Ambulances and doctors could work miracles. Explanations would come later. Just get to the damn phone. Please, God....

The ambulance and police cars came and, shortly afterwards, the military hearse. I still wouldn't believe it...could not possibly believe it—not in my darkest dreams. He was too logical, too rational for this to happen. He was *Authority,* and from him came all the belief I had about what was real and what wasn't. *He* was real, and therefore this madness couldn't be.

As the night wore on, the shock began to wear off and my brain began to process all of the images that simply could not fit the picture my eyes and my hands had experienced that day. Mental processors were working overtime well into the wee hours of the next day. By the time the news hit the school, I was a different person.

I might have seemed the same to most of the well-wishers who came up to me, but I was definitely not the same. I smiled back at them and even somewhat relished the attention they gave me, but there was a very different personality running the show. I was embarrassed to think that my father would be known as such a weak person and, therefore, that I might be, too. The Boy Scout and the Altar Boy were left in a darkened garage that I never entered again, and in charge was one who knew that authority was only conditional. It was to be acknowledged and respected when it was apparently stronger, but was most certainly something to be circumvented whenever possible.

I had never been very close to my father. I had no fond memories of endearing moments, no father-son remembrances or heart-to-heart talks with him. But as I approached manhood, I sensed a growing feeling of wanting to connect with him and to know what he knew. He had had power over me and I wanted to know what that was all about, and how it worked.

Now, that would never happen. He was gone, and with him went the secret for understanding it. Manhood had become an elusive image for me—a uniform laid out on a bed that I knelt beside and had clung to desperately that night when I felt my childhood disintegrate. He was gone, and with him my chance for acceptance as a man. I was cut adrift in a swelling green-gray ocean of endless darkness and churning, somewhere between adolescence and adulthood, but disconnected from both.

I could momentarily catch hold of either one, and work with it for a while, but I couldn't maintain either one for long. I had no basis from which to sustain myself, no foundation of trust or understanding that would carry me through the rough spots. From that point, I drifted into and out of situations that would challenge my manhood and scare the hell out of my constantly hiding, running, mischievous child.

As I look back on it now, it amazes me that I ever survived the effort of entering the arena of adulthood. For me it was one tumultuous battle after another against forces that could annihilate me, barely escaping jaws of wrath behind a cloud of boyish innocence which I could conjure up like a cloud of smoke on the magician's stage. With each close call, I would breathe a great gasp of relief, only to return again and again to do battle in arenas others seemed to live in effortlessly.

The intellectual in me would rationalize that those people were oblivious to the forces that I knew existed. They were asleep and ignorant, I felt, and so I continued my Quixotic battles without letup. Money was always the excuse to go back into the arena—the lack of money, that is. It wasn't enough to just be a good salesman, or an innovator of great ideas. I had to find the dragons wherever I could find them—real or imagined. But I had no weapon with which to fight them, no way of achieving a victory save but to be tricky enough to deceive them and then hide like a chameleon when they came after me. But how I loved to taunt them, draw them out, and see what they were made of.

Generally, they had uniforms of some sort...or at least a badge.

Chapter One

From the back seat of the U.S. Marshal's sedan, I could see it looming up ahead on a long, gently rising hill. Its stark, white walls and gun towers left no doubt in my mind as to what it was and what it meant for me.

Sprawled out over an area too big to take in all at once, it stood like a fortress with dark, brown cotton fields sloping away from it in all directions. As we drew nearer, a sense of deep foreboding rose in the pit of my stomach. Beads of sweat formed on my face and my limbs went weak. Sensing impending danger, I felt my heartbeat quicken and my breathing shallow as we slowly approached the entrance.

"LA TUNA FEDERAL CORRECTIONAL INSTITUTION." The words were starkly etched into the old metal archway over the entrance. Beyond it, perfectly manicured trees and hedges lined the long, winding asphalt roadway. Each shrub and hedge showed years of human toil and tedious labor. As far as my eyes could see were fences—high, chainlink fences with multiple coils of razor wire running along the tops *and* bottoms. My mind raced frantically to accept the fact that razor wire, once my protection in Viet Nam from the enemy outside, was now meant to keep me *in*.

Chained to two other prisoners on either side of me, I felt myself pulled deeper into an abyss of darkness. My insides twisted in knots as the chain around my waist seemed to tighten. The steel cuffs dug deeper into my wrists as I kept shifting in my seat to find a more comfortable position.

Ahead, the fortress loomed larger in the windshield as the marshals joked about the plight of prisoners out in the cotton fields now working "for nothing" for the government. Their snide comments drowned the deeper stories that hung heavily from cotton plants tilled by men living in the depths of depravity. Some deserved hard labor, but for others such meaningless toil was simply "paying one's dues" for gambles that didn't work out.

As we drew nearer the main buildings, I remembered the first time I had ever been locked up. I was just a kid of eighteen, on my way to my first "real" job in North Dakota. I was headed across Nebraska on a long and very boring stretch of Interstate 80. I was happy to be free of school for a while, and was lost in day-dreams of new adventures ahead. My car was a '59 Ford Galaxy—a big, old boat with a huge, V-8 engine that could cruise at a 100 mph with little effort. With 400 miles of Nebraska cornfields to cover, I let the old Ford lull me into a daydream as I passed cars one after another. With the trunk weighted down with all my belongings, the rearview mirror was useless until I leaned forward and bent down low to look back. When I finally did, I saw the State Patrolman right on my tail with his lights flashing.

His siren, it turned out, wasn't working, so he had "chased" me for fifteen miles before I noticed him and pulled over. He was pretty upset, and evidently felt I might learn a valuable lesson by sitting in a local jail while waiting for the bail money to be wired. Since it was late on a Friday afternoon, my wait turned out to be longer than an 18-year-old kid could possibly feel was reasonable.

It was the first I had ever seen of the inside of a real jail cell. The shock of that cell door slamming shut behind me, and the bolts locking into place, was something I've never forgotten. Gripped with panic, I paced the floor like a caged animal, searching for a release from the terror.

I shook the cell door as if it might suddenly open if I rattled it enough. After several hours of pacing and rattling that cell door, I finally slumped to the floor, tears streaming down my face. Night was coming on. Inside the cell, the growing darkness was held back only by the dim glow of a single light bulb in the hallway. Beyond the closed door at the end of the corridor, I could hear a telephone ring occasionally in the office. Each time it rang, my heart leapt with the hope that someone was calling to arrange for my release. Hours seemed to pass, and each time the phone rang my heart pounded again…but nothing followed.

I stayed slumped on the floor, half-weeping, half-nodding off until suddenly I noticed something written in tiny little words on the wall. Low to the floor and unnoticeable to anyone not in my exact position, the writing aroused my curiosi-ty enough to momentarily pull me from my self-pity. I dried my tears and looked more closely. On the smooth bead between the cinder blocks, someone had very carefully and very precisely written a message I could barely see, let alone read.

Squinting my eyes and turning my head in different directions to catch the right angle of light from the hallway, I was finally able to focus my teary eyes enough to make out the words:

BE COOL STAY CALM   IT'S ONLY A MATTER OF TIME

Back in the marshals' car, my grip on the chains loosened a little, and my breathing eased a bit as I recalled those jailhouse words again. The sedan continued on its way toward the buildings as the marshals removed their guns from the glove box and re-holstered them. On each side of me the other two prisoners fidgeted and nervously worked their wrist chains back and forth in their hands.

Out in the cotton fields, brown-clad figures straightened from their labor to peer back at us through the blinding Texas sun, their faces showing the worn and empty look of men without a purpose. Everything passed by us in slow motion as the car moved steadily onward.

As we approached the largest of the old, Gothic structures, a high, electronically controlled gate opened for us to pass through to a side entrance of the building. As the huge gate closed behind us, the marshals parked the sedan, got out and went inside. A few minutes later, they emerged with white-shirted correctional officers, and opened the trunk. Tossing our boxes of personal effects uncaringly against the wall, they opened a back door of the sedan and motioned for us to climb out. Chains rattled and scraped against the metal cage that enclosed the back seat as each of us worked our way out the door. As I straightened to relieve the stiffness from the four-hour ride, my eyes caught sight of three armed guards standing behind us with shotguns at the ready.

Papers were exchanged and initialed as the marshals went about the routine of handing us over to the officials almost as if all their small talk and shuffling of papers was more important to the process than we were. We were only incidental to the process, it seemed, as we were led through a side door into a dark and musty-smelling inner room.

In the dim light from a single, tiny window near the top of one wall of the large room, I could feel more than see what it was. Lined with flimsy, wiremesh cages, the room had the feeling of something old and heavily used. Inside the largest of the cages were rows of old wooden benches, darkened and worn from decades of use by thousands of wayward souls who had long since come and gone before us. A heaviness of heart came over me, much like one feels in the darkened home of an elderly person who has passed away. I drew in a long, deep breath once again as we were locked in the cage and left to our thoughts.

Somber stories filled my mind as I ran my fingertips over names and dates scratched and burn-scarred into the aging, tired wood, some of them dating back to before I was born. I was caught in time, it seemed, in an ancient ruin of a distant past. Ghostly faces of countless men hung eerily in wisps of smoke and dust in the dim light of the tiny window near the top of the room. I could feel the passage of time recorded in the layers of cobwebs all around it. With squinted eyes and desperate mind I probed every corner outside the cage for what might lie beyond.

Somewhere down the darkened hallway leading to another part of the building, a tinny-sounding transistor radio added to the eeriness of our situation, as familiar tunes from the Fifties echoed emptily into our unfamiliar surroundings. Across from our cage was another slightly smaller cage, in which there was a bent and twisted metal locker with a newly-purchased suit hanging from its open door. On a metal chair was a shoe box, upon which were the hastily-scribbled words, *"Good Luck, Johnson."*

Muffled voices and the sounds of shuffling feet in the dark hallway alerted me to someone coming, as my nose simultaneously caught the smell of hot food. Meal trays were served by silent inmate orderlies, and after hungrily devouring my first prison meal, I found myself staring blankly again at the empty walls and benches. Hours seemed to pass, but it was merely a taste of what was yet to come—the empty, aching monotony of waiting...

and waiting...

and waiting.

I resumed probing the darkened spaces of the room with my eyes and my mind. Suddenly, I became aware of movement in the hallway again. Very quietly, a lone inmate emerged from the darkness beyond and stepped into the smaller cage opposite ours. An older black man, he changed into the suit and shoes without saying a word, then stood there quietly waiting. The significance of the moment was not lost on me.

"Six years," he replied to my automatic question.

Six *years* he had spent inside those dingy walls and in the cotton fields outside. Now he was about to step back into the world from which I had just come—as casually, it seemed, as if he had just dropped in for a weekend visit.

We were at opposite ends of a certain hell. The irony was unbearable, him nearly a free man and me on my way *in*. It was maddening. I had to know what he knew, even if it were only some tidbit of knowledge, some hope or some insight offered in the fleeting moment of our passing. But he had none to give, nothing of any substance or value except for the one ray of hope that eventually there was an exit from this pit of human deprivation.

Six *years,* and he had nothing to show for the time he had spent waiting and watching the world go by those fences outside. He had no education, nor had he acquired a single significant skill to take with him. He had played a lot of hand-ball, he said, and had spent a lot of time lifting weights.

I was stunned. I stared at him in disbelief. Six years of his life gone, and all he had to take with him was a tough pair of hands and a strong body. He had no idea where he was going, much less how he was going to get there or what he would do when he got there.

Absorbed in thought about Johnson's plight, I lost track for the moment of where I was, and of my own dismal fate. Suddenly I was pulled from my thoughts by the sound of loud voices and heavy boot steps in the hallway. The crackling static of two-way radios and the taunting jingle of hip-slung keys announced the movement of prison guards in our direction.

The cage was opened and we were led off to another room as Johnson stood there silently watching us go. I thought I could detect an ever-so-slight smile on his face as I glanced back at him, my thoughts now riveted on the door ahead of us. Part of me clung frantically to the cage he was in until the door slammed shut behind us. In the brightly lit room, a team of officials stood ready with their files and folders. It looked and felt exactly the same as my first day at boot camp…only this time I wasn't a new recruit but a prisoner of my own country.

They stripped us of everything, then strip-searched and checked every inch of our bodies, including our mouths. De-lousing agent was sprayed in our hair and groins. After waiting the required time for the spray to take effect, we moved like cattle through a narrow passageway where we were hosed off with cold water.

Still naked, we were fingerprinted and photographed, after which triplicate forms began filling the official file folders for each of us. Standard-issue prison clothing was pushed into our arms, along with a paper cup, a small bar of soap, tooth powder and a toothbrush cut to four inches in length.

Weary, and weak from constant anxiety, we dressed in the ill fitting, reject military fatigues as the last traces of who we had once been disappeared with our now-discarded "civilian" clothes. One by one, we were called to a waiting official and instructed to sign various forms. In the upper right-hand corner of my now-bulging prison file, was a plain and unassuming, simple little number which was to become more important than my own name—Federal Register Number 19174-008.

Johnson was out, and I was in.

Chapter Two

I knew I was dreaming, yet it was so real I could smell the dirt in my face as I lay at the edge of a steep cliff. Just beyond my reach was a high chainlink fence preventing me from getting to safer ground. When I tried to grab the fence, the edge of the cliff started to crumble from under me. Panic gripped me when I glanced over my shoulder and saw the ocean far below. Terrified, I scrambled all the more to reach the fence, but the edge just crumbled faster. With a desperate lunge I reached the fence just as the cliff gave way and plunged into the churning water below. I was suspended a thousand feet above the water, my fingers in a death grip on the now-sagging fence. Just as the chainlink pulled away from the poles and I felt myself plunging through the air, I woke up.

Beads of sweat formed on my brow while I lay there in a strange room waiting for my body to calm down and my eyes to adjust to the darkness. The faintest hint of light outside the window indicated a new day was beginning. Soon I would be able to make out where I was.

The dream had been so real I could feel my fingertips still pulsing from gripping the fence. My legs were weak from scrambling and kicking, and my heart was pounding from the fall I had taken just before waking. Relieved that it had only been a dream, I lay quietly thinking, then began to vaguely recall something about a federal register number and a guy named Johnson. Had that just been another part of the dream?

Muffled noises outside the room suddenly brought me fully alert to the reality of where I was. In the gathering light from the large window behind me, I could take in the entire room in one glance. I was in a solitary cell at La Tuna. It hadn't just been part of the dream. It was real. I was in goddamn *prison!*

Another rush of panic swept over me. I quickly sat up, nearly hitting my head on the upper bunk. I reached up and pushed on it. It was empty. I put my feet on the floor and felt the grit of weeks, maybe months, of accumulated dirt, dust and grime as two cockroaches scurried for cracks in the wall behind the toilet. I stood up and felt a wave of claustrophobia sweep over me as I realized I could almost touch three walls and the ceiling without taking a step. There wasn't enough room to *pace,* let alone exercise or move about freely.

Now it was all coming back to me. I had collapsed on the lower bunk shortly after I first entered the room the night before. The small assortment of articles issued to me was still lying on the top bunk where I had placed them before spreading a sheet and a faded Army blanket across the sagging, lower bunk. Along with the bar of soap, tooth powder and stubby toothbrush was my receipt for personal effects the officers had taken. Breathing as deeply and calmly as possible, I surveyed my surroundings.

The walls were pale green, etched and marked with an assortment of graffiti, and stained with indistinguishable matter. At the foot of the bunk bed was a tall, metal locker like the one I had seen in the cage with Johnson, only bashed in and barely standing. In the opposite corner was an old porcelain toilet, the presence of which I could more easily smell than see in the dim light. In the top of the toilet, where the water tank would normally be, was a little hand sink with a tiny hole at the bottom that drained into the toilet. The stench was so bad I didn't want to look at the thing, let alone use it.

As I shifted my attention away from the toilet, my eyes came to rest on the door. Just beyond the end of the bunk bed, it was in the center of the wall between the toilet and the locker. It seemed like such a simple thing to separate me from the rest of the world. It was a rather normal looking door with a doorknob and a small, rectangular window near the top. As I ran my hands over it, however, I realized that I couldn't have dented it with a sledgehammer. It was solid steel, painted over with plain, green paint.

As I looked closely at the small window, I saw that it was thick Plexiglas with a layer of heavy-gauge wiremesh covering it on the other side. In the middle of the door was a horizontal slot, about six inches high by eighteen inches wide, covered on the other side by a solid, metal flap. I had seen doors like this before, but never from the inside. They were used for prisoners in solitary, and the slots were for passing through meal trays and linen.

A feeling of helplessness and indignation welled up in me as I sensed that I might be in that room for a while. I recalled stories from older inmates back at the detention center who told me that new "fish" were kept in isolation until the authorities felt they had adjusted enough to be allowed into the main population. It hadn't dawned on me at the time that such a thing might apply to *me.* Jail was far enough to go, I thought. Jail was a place to wait while deals were made and breaks were given to those who were fortunate enough, slick enough or rich enough to avoid more serious consequences. To me, it was a place to wait for freedom, not for further imprisonment. My mind wouldn't accept the notion of going to prison back then. Even now it searched every nook and cranny of the tiny room for a way to escape, and for relief from the pain and tightness gripping every part my body.

I stepped back from the door and looked at the wall locker. Bashed in on one side, I pictured a former resident pathetically venting his rage on the one thing in the room that was possibly breakable. Inside the locker on one side was a long, vertical space for hanging clothes, while on the other side were shelves and a rusted drawer. Inside the drawer were piles of unused packets of sugar, salt, pepper and condiments, stockpiled by some demented soul who must have thought they actually had value.

The full light of the morning finally spilled into the tiny cell, drawing my attention to its one redeeming feature—the window. It was a large window similar to the type used in old country schools that latched at the top and were pulled open from there. Looking more closely at the latch, I sensed that it might actually work. I scanned the edges of the window for bolts or screws that might prevent it from being opened, but found none. Outside the window, of course, were steel bars and, as if that weren't enough to keep me in, heavy-gauge wiremesh just outside of them. Even with the bars and the wiremesh, however, at least I could look outside and see something. It was a refreshing change from the completely walled off and sealed environment of the detention center from which I had just come.

Having spent nearly seven months in two different detention centers where the windows were small, narrow, and sealed shut, I looked with increasing anticipation at the latch. Reaching up and grasping the ring, I yanked it inwardly toward me. With surprising ease, the window opened and a rush of air swept into the room. Although it opened from the top barely six inches, it would at least let fresh air inside. Outside, below the window was a courtyard and a patch of nicely groomed grass, surrounded by old buildings and walls ten to twelve feet high. Beyond the walls was a tall, white gun tower, boarded up and abandoned. Out on the distant horizon, I could barely make out a sliver of the sun as another summer day began.

I turned and sat back on the lower bunk, once again surveying the room. It was a dingy cell, but the mere fact of having a window that even partially opened made it far more tolerable. In the corner back toward the door, the toilet stood as a testament to the depths to which I had fallen. Layers of white, crusty tooth powder and residue of spit and soap scum encrusted the sink and the sides of the toilet. Streaks of rust permanently stained the cracked and chipped, eroding porcelain. A tiny faucet in the top was activated by pushing either the "hot" or "cold" button which, I discovered, caused barely a trickle of sulfur-smelling water to flow into the sink.

I scanned the wall opposite the bunk until my eyes came to rest on an item I had completely missed. In the corner to my immediate left as I sat on the bunk, was a tiny writing desk not much bigger than a nightstand. Examining it more closely, I discovered that it had a circular steel seat that swiveled out from where it was attached to the right front leg of the desk. I pulled the seat out and carefully squeezed my legs into the tiny opening, just to try it out. Even for a small frame like mine, it was a tight fit. But it was a desk, and something I could put to good use if I had to stay there any length of time. If I could get my hands on some writing paper, I might be able to occupy my time with something useful while I waited.

I leaned back from the desk and put my hands behind me on the lower bunk. As I did, the little seat suddenly slammed back into position under the desk, dropping my body instantly to the concrete floor. I pulled myself up on the bunk and lay there painfully contemplating the risks of taking even the slightest thing for granted from that point on. Once the pain subsided, I decided to have another look at the door. I got up and peered through the tiny window into the hallway outside. I stared in disbelief at the row of similar doors across from me, as far as I could see. Each door had its own little window and horizontal slot covered with a metal flap that was not only bolted, but locked with a padlock big enough to chain an elephant.

Voices in the hallway alerted me to activity underway. I strained to see who was coming, then spotted a white-shirted officer with a clipboard working his way toward my end of the hallway. Finally he stepped in front of my door and looked right through me as if I didn't exist. Noting something on his clipboard, he moved on to the next cell then disappeared through a doorway.

The emptiness in the hallway left me cold. At least in the detention center there had been other inmates to talk to, play cards with, and build false hopes with. I lay down on the bunk and thought about what might happen next. I was finally in prison. No more fighting legal battles, or waiting and hoping for that lucky break I was certain would come if I stuck it out long enough, or found the right lawyer to make the right deal. It was all over now. The last glimmering hope of getting back on the streets had finally disintegrated with the judge's gavel and the final ride in the marshals' sedan.

After seven long months of twisting and squirming and pressuring everyone I knew to get me out, I was now in deeper than I had ever imagined I would be. I watched a cockroach make its way along the wall across from me toward the window, and felt my insides tighten. On the wall were names and dates and graffiti from previous residents, conjuring up faces and images of bygone days. Who were they? What had *they* done to land them in this hole of a prison? What were their hopes and dreams? Had any of them been like me? What had they been like as little boys? Where did they go wrong? Where did *I* go wrong? When would I get out? How long would I be in here? Could anything worthwhile come of this mess?

Each agonizing question brought another, each with no answer. All I could do was lie there and think. And, perhaps now, sleep. If I could just quiet my tortured, half-crazed mind enough to drop off for a while, maybe I could begin to make some sense of this latest development. Only two days before, I was at the detention center, still holding out for a possible break to work in my favor. Sleep back there had been impossible, even under the best of conditions. Only in the blackness of the wee hours of each morning, when all the gladiators and the yapping dogs had finally dropped off to sleep, had there been enough quiet to even think, let alone sleep restfully. A couple of hours of sleep snatched now and then between the flashlight beams in my face, afforded only the smallest hint of respite from the never-ending cacophony of shouting, yelling, blasting televisions and slamming of cell doors. The noise was deafening and constant, and induced a constant throbbing in my head. It was an exercise in sleep deprivation that was insidious and debilitating.

At least in the solitude of the prison cell there was hope that once my mind calmed down from the shock of now actually being in one, perhaps now I might get some rest. With it maybe some fresh ideas would come and, possibly, even yet a solution to this latest drama of mine.

The cell was blissfully quiet as I watched the cockroach crawl carefully along the wall and out the window. I wondered how long it would be before I, too, would crawl out to my own freedom. I thought about the events that had led me to this fate, and a blur of faces, images and impressions flashed through my mind as a wave of total exhaustion swept over me. Feeling the weakness of a battle-weary soldier in desperate need of rest, I fell into a deep sleep as the heat of a Texas summer day began to build outside.

Chapter Three

"Hey! We got a problem with a customer," one of my waiters shouted at me through my office door. "Big, fat lady on Table 12. She's yelling at Frankie in Italian. I think she's a friend of the boss."

I sighed. Whoever thought the restaurant business was fun never managed one...at least not like this one.

"I'm on it," I yelled back at him as he scurried away. I walked out to the servers' station and spotted Stephanie, as usual smoking a cigarette. Stephanie could be a major pain in the ass, but she had the owner's eye and could sometimes be useful.

"Stephanie," I warmed up to her. "Would you please look into the situation on Table 12? Seems there's an unhappy customer needing some attention, and I only have fifteen minutes to get tomorrow's food order called in."

"Why me?" she made a face.

"Because I think she's Mr. Scarpelli's friend, and he's mentioned to me a couple of times that we should consider you for night manager. This would be part of your job, if that happens."

"Oh," she primped herself automatically. "Is *Mister* Scarpelli out there?" Her emphasis on the "Mister" was not lost on me. I knew well enough by that point that she was on a first-name basis with him from her frequent visits to his office.

"No, I don't think so...but I don't think we would want him to be right now. Better to handle the problem pleasantly, and let him find out about it from the customer...don't you think?"

"Certainly," she smiled that fake, syrupy smile of hers. "I'll take care of it." She took another long drag on her cigarette, as if to savor the moment as long as she could, then put it out in the ashtray and sauntered off.

Was this my *life*? Running an Italian restaurant in Minneapolis? I knew little and cared less about Italian food. I was working from dawn 'til well past dusk every day for an owner who couldn't care less about anything but which waitress he could get into his office. At first I had relished the opportunity to manage a 300-seat dinner restaurant, but I was out of my league on this one. He had promised me "carte blanche" to manage it, but he really only needed someone to do all the work while he ran the place like he was some kind of Mafia kingpin. He was really only a "stereo shop kingpin" who happened to acquire a restaurant he knew little or nothing about. To say I was rapidly running out of enthusiasm would have been an understatement.

It was November in Minnesota, and with each passing day the air grew colder and damper—warning of the coming of another long and bleak northern winter. I had arrived in January of 1972, which meant I was coming up on my fourth winter in a place that six months out of the year became a frozen wasteland of never-ending snow, grey skies and sub-zero temperatures

As I went back into my office, I decided I needed a major change in my life. It didn't help my mood that my relationship with Barbara was drifting apart. We had met four years before that, when I was 27. I'd started a very busy little diner down the road with a couple of partners, and she was one of our first waitresses. She often came in to see everyone on her days off, always bringing along her one-year-old son, Jonathan. He was a conversation-stopper, with an eager smile, bright, beautiful eyes and that shock of black hair. He looked every inch the full-blooded Chippewa Indian that he was, and seldom did his feet hit the floor whenever she brought him around.

I always got along with children. Ever since I was eighteen, I seemed to always attract single mothers which allowed me to act out some sort of "father-figure" role for their children. While that may have been great for single moms, playing "Dad" didn't always work out well with single women. Lasting relationships for me, consequently, were hard to come by. Passionate, steamy and even intellectually stimulating affairs came easily and often, but despite my noblest and most earnest efforts, I couldn't manage to keep one going for longer than a year or two.

Barbara and I managed to become lasting friends after the diner was sold. Our relationship was built on our willingness to be honest with each other, and while that may have been disappointing to her at times, it enabled us to enjoy time together that occasionally went beyond mere friendship. Oftentimes I stayed over at her place, where we spent more than a few long, cold nights keeping each other warm. As much as I liked her, however, the spark never did get strong enough to ignite the passion for me to consider a marriage proposal.

No one could say I didn't love little Jonathan, though. He had taken his first steps toward me, and had spoken his first words to me— so as far as both of us were concerned, I was "Dad."

Barbara's love for me was strong enough to endure uncertainty with me, and being a softie for that kind of affection, I stayed around more than I expected to. One day when she happily announced that she was pregnant with our child, it was natural for me to just go along with her plans. She was bright and loving, and deserved a break more than most women I knew at the time. Trouble was, I didn't realize that "going along" with her plans might require more than I was prepared to give.

When little Channon arrived, I kept my own apartment but found myself hanging out at Barbara's more and more. Fatherhood was official for me now, and I really wanted to be there for her and the little guys. Unfortunately, my feelings for Barbara didn't change. In fact, I began to feel more trapped each day—by her, by the new restaurant job I'd found after selling the diner, and by the coming of another Minnesota winter. One day, I couldn't suppress my feelings anymore, so I went to Barbara's apartment after the kids were in bed and told her I'd be taking off soon.

"You're going to leave me with two babies?" she asked me in disbelief. She was calm outwardly, but I could tell that she was churning inside.

"C'mon, Barbara—cut me some slack." I looked her in the eye, and a wave of tenderness came over me. "*You* know I'm not like that. I just have to figure some things out."

Her face crumpled, and her eyes filled with tears. Channon was only a year old at the time.

"I gotta get on with some things I started out to do a long time ago," I explained. "Someplace where the living's cheap and I can get it together. How 'bout when I get settled wherever I'm going, you bring the boys?"

She looked up, wiping her big, soft eyes. Her anger and hopelessness seemed to diffuse. "You wanna be a family?" she asked hopefully.

"Well, actually I was thinking of keeping things the way they are now…but you could get a place near me, and I'll still help you raise the boys…"

"Where d'you think you'll be going?" Barbara asked, her expression turning suspicious. It would be hard for her to trust that I'd stay in touch.

"I was thinking Mexico." I shrugged my shoulders. "I like the people, and the culture. I want to get more fluent in Spanish. And you know I've always wanted to write a book. I could do it down there."

She rolled her eyes, but she knew I was right. We had talked about it often, so even though it went against all of her hopes and plans, I think she understood. Then she looked around the house like she was suddenly all alone. I felt like an asshole.

Barbara rolled her red-rimmed eyes up at me. "I can't take two small boys to *Mexico*," she said flatly.

"OK, OK," I said hastily. I wanted somehow to make it all right. "Maybe it won't be Mexico. If I find something better along the way, I'll get set up and let you know. Then *you* can decide if it's right."

Her expression turned stony. I'm sure the whole thing sounded half-baked.

"In the meantime, I'll leave you with as much money as I can. And I'll send some more along the way."

She turned her back to me and, without a word, went into the bedroom and closed the door behind her.

I walked out of the house and into the city park across the street, alone except for my many guilty feelings. I didn't want to hurt someone who'd tried so hard to work things out with me. But I also felt that I couldn't—wouldn't—divert from my course. I had spent five years doing things other than what I had wanted to do when I first got out of the service.

By the time the first snow began to fall, my decision had been made. Two weeks later, I'd had enough of "Mister" Scarpelli and his restaurant. It was a drizzly, overcast Tuesday morning when I struck out for the open road, a small suitcase in hand and a hundred dollars in my pocket. Barbara had taken off with the boys for an undetermined period, and all seemed as it should be for my departure.

Three days and twelve rides later, I stood at the interchange of I-40 and I-25 in the heart of Albuquerque, New Mexico. I had just had the "Hungry Cowboy" breakfast at a nearby truckstop, and was ready to get on the road again. It was a warm, sunny Friday morning, and I felt as free as the breeze that tousled my thinning blonde hair.

As I walked along the cloverleaf access ramp leading onto I-40, I fully intended to continue west toward Flagstaff and then on to Phoenix. But fate had other plans for me. A large overhead sign read "Santa Fe," with a large arrow pointed toward the north.

I had been through and around Santa Fe in my early twenties, driving trucks out of Denver, and had promised myself that someday I'd go back and visit when

I had more time.

Well, I thought, I have plenty of time right now.

Almost without thinking, I moved toward the access ramp leading in the direction of Santa Fe. As I did, I noticed a late-model Plymouth sedan slowly making its way around the curve toward the access ramp. The driver spotted me making my way toward the ramp, and slowed noticeably. I had a sense that he just might stop if I could get eye contact with him. I held out my thumb and, sure enough, he pulled over. Two hours later, I was in downtown Santa Fe.

Walking around Santa Fe, I was amazed that it was December and yet I was in shirtsleeves. With suitcase in hand, and a heavy parka over my arm, I felt more than a little conspicuous as I walked along the narrow streets and cobblestone roads that twisted and turned in every direction. Clearly this was a town that had grown up around the old horse and wagon trails that made it famous. Intending to only stay a day or two, I found myself looking at restaurants and cafes with half a mind to check out employment possibilities.

Eventually I wandered hungry into a busy little restaurant called Grand Central Station. Packed with a lively crowd of young people lunching lazily on the patio and a few people sitting at the small bar near the front door, it looked like a place where one could savor a moment's respite on a long journey. Adjoining a stretch of the Old Santa Fe Trail, and directly across from the historic 'oldest chapel' and its 'Miraculous Stairway,' it was a sweet little place that was too good to pass up.

As I waited for my lunch of blue corn chicken enchiladas, I noticed a young man and older woman at the table next to mine. They were friendly and open, and soon we were deep in a conversation about the history of the area.

They introduced themselves as Carl and Marta. He was a sculptor—evidently of some considerable repute—and she, his sister, was his manager. As we talked, I felt an urge to help them market their work. Not knowing anything about sculpting or art in general, I nevertheless felt that they could use some guidance in how to best market his work. It was an almost compulsive trait in me, always thinking that I had an "edge" on how to sell or market things. It was something I had learned at an early age, reinforced by slick, fast-talking salesmen who, at various times in my life, had convinced me that I was the "next great millionaire" because of my gift of gab.

By the time my food arrived, they'd invited me to join them at their table, where we all babbled for over an hour about how I might help them open some new markets .

After lunch, Carl and Marta invited me to stay with them until I made up my mind about whether or not to stay in the area. I couldn't believe my good fortune, but it seemed to be the way things were working out. I had had great rides all along the way, and was constantly meeting friendly people with lots to say. I was thoroughly pleased, and more and more I let things flow the way they wanted to. Now, thanks to Carl and Marta, my expenses were next to nothing, so I went back to Grand Central Station three more times, just to feel as if I belonged in the area.

As I did, I began to notice some things about the place that I felt could be improved. As I was about to pay my bill on the third visit, a woman I perceived to be the manager stepped up to the cash register.

"I've been in the restaurant business several years," I offered, "and I've noticed a few things that might be improved upon. If you're interested, I might be able to offer a few suggestions on streamlining your operation."

The corners of her mouth turned up in an odd smile. She was definitely intrigued, but probably a bit skeptical.. "If you don't mind waiting until I close out, I'd be interested to know what you think. Can I buy you a beer?"

She finished up while I drank another beer, then sat down and introduced herself. We talked for the next two hours. As it turned out, she was managing the place for the owners, who lived in New York. But she was getting married in two weeks, and was planning to be gone at least two months. She had a friend set up to take over the business, but that hadn't worked out. Now she was stuck, and getting more nervous by the day.

"Here," she finally blurted out. "I was on my way to the newspaper office this afternoon with this." Pulling a folded-up piece of notepaper from her purse, she handed it to me and sat back to watch my reaction.

WANTED: Manager for small but busy restaurant in Santa Fe. Salary commensurate with experience. References. 505-783-5806

"The job's yours if you want it," she said, smiling at my obvious surprise.

Life was falling into place so effortlessly that I felt charmed. As if that all wasn't fortuitous enough, the next day when I came in for a meeting with her, she told me she needed someone to house-sit while she was gone. After working together for a week, she let me know that her car would be available for me to use until she got back.

"There's no point in you going out and buying one until you're settled in," she said. I had come along as an answer to her prayers, she told me one day, and once she felt okay with me she was grateful to have someone she felt reliable to take over the place.

I managed Grand Central Station for the next two years, and often worked behind the bar, getting to know the more regular patrons. It wasn't long before I felt I knew everybody who was anybody in Santa Fe. The restaurant's bar and relaxed outdoor patio attracted artists and business types alike, as well as socialites, musicians and entrepreneurs.

Antonio, a particularly friendly and outgoing type, quickly became a favorite of mine. He was bright and funny, and always made me feel like a long lost brother. Often he would come in with his business partner, Bill, who was quieter and a bit more circumspect around me. Bill had been a friend of Antonio's since their college days at UCLA.

One night after closing, Antonio and I shared a few drinks at the bar. He confided that he and Bill had earned a lot of money in their earlier years smuggling pot across the border into California.

"Things were a lot easier back then," Antonio said. "We started out with a couple of dune-buggies, and drove the stuff right into our parents' garages, stuffed into picnic coolers."

Before long, Antonio and Bill had developed a string of buyers up and down the West coast and had made enough money to "retire" before they hit 30. They decided to move to safer, unknown territory, and started a legitimate business in Santa Fe. They bought a ranch north of town, where they could grow organic vegetables for health-food stores and restaurants. They had "inherited" money, the story went, and had done well in the "stock market."

The two men—both apparently well-off and handsome—were considered among the city's most eligible bachelors. Although I never quite fit into their crowd, I enjoyed my growing acceptance with them and most of their friends. Both men were always surrounded by attractive young women, eager to be seen in their company. Working at the restaurant 24/7 demanded too much of my time and attention to get out much, so being recognized as at least a part of their backdrop was a source of some satisfaction for me. Combined with being perceived as an "up and coming restaurateur," my casual association with Antonio and Bill afforded some measure of credibility about town, and an occasional opportunity to ignite some romantic fires.

My dream of writing a book was all but lost by that point, but that was okay for the time being. And I brought more than one unfinished dream to Santa Fe. By the mid-1970s, when I arrived, the town had become a refuge for visionaries and trust-fund dependents looking to show they were smarter than their fathers. I got to know a few of both, and began to feel I'd come to the right place to nurture an idea I had before I left Denver for Minneapolis.

One night I was talking with a particularly bright young man named Thomas, who frequented our bar on a regular basis. It was a slow night and Thomas was nursing a late meal and a Bloody Mary. An intense person with an advanced degree in architecture and a huge chip on his shoulder, he had just finished telling me about an "unfinished dream," he'd had, then asked me if I had one. I thought about it for a few minutes, then responded.

"Absolutely," I said. "It's a simple concept, but something no one seems to have thought up, yet."

"So, go on," his bright blue eyes fixed on me as he downed his drink and asked for another.

"There are a lot of small companies that have occasional need of a light airplane, but can't afford or don't want the expense of owning one. So my idea is to acquire a small fleet of light, twin-engine airplanes and lease them to charter operators who can rent them to those businesses. What makes this work is that there are people who buy such airplanes for the tax advantages, but in order to keep the payments and cost of operation up, they have to lease them back to charter operators. But the problem is that then they have to constantly fight with the charter companies to use their own planes whenever they want to."

"So how's that supposed to be such a good business?" he took a deep swallow of his refreshed drink.

"Easy," I said. "We buy identical airplanes, and keep them in relatively close proximity to one another so that whenever an owner wants use of his airplane, he either gets his, or one exactly like it. We could even furnish the pilot, if the owner isn't qualified to fly it."

"Hmmm," Thomas stared into his half-finished drink. "So how do you come out ahead on this deal?"

"We contract with the owner to keep a percentage of equity in the plane, and we maintain control of it the entire time it's under a purchase contract. We make our deals with the charter operators and commuter airlines, and we get a cut of whatever they bring in. As 'co-owners' of the planes, we build up our asset base with each airplane we take into the fleet."

"Sounds good," he said. "But how are you going to prove to investors that you can keep their planes productive?"

"That's the best part. With the recent deregulation of the Civil Aeronautics Board, commuter airlines are sprouting up everywhere, and people need more expedient ways of getting around than commercial airlines."

Thomas' expression became more intent, and he put down his drink. "What exactly makes it more workable?"

"New federal tax laws on capital equipment, for one. Things have been restructured to the point where investors can practically *own* an airplane for nothing—if the planes are kept busy."

Thomas was quiet for a moment. Pushing back from the table, he looked at me sharply. "You know, you should get yourself some seed capital and try to make a go of this thing," he advised.

"Yeah, when Rockefeller shows up with his wallet open, I'll be sure to mention it," I joked. I hadn't given much thought to my idea while I was earning a living in Minnesota, and had forgotten about it until I had recently read a magazine article on how new tax laws and deregulation would stimulate the economy for small businesses.

I didn't see Thomas for nearly a week, but when he came back— this time in the mid-afternoon—he called me from the back office to the bar. There he laid out pages of sketches, notes and cash flow charts for "our" aircraft-leasing company.

"Whaddya say? Wanna fly again?" he smiled.

Within a few weeks, we were deep into planning the new business. I had turned the restaurant over to the owners, who promptly sold it to someone who wanted to turn it into a gallery. A mutual friend of ours provided $15,000 in seed capital to get us started, which I used to hire a transportation expert and a CPA to help us develop our business plan. Before the year was out, I had signed our first contract with an investor…a small electronics company in Chicago, who purchased the first three airplanes and provided enough working capital to sustain our first year of operations. I was thrilled beyond description. I felt like my future was finally opening up. Perhaps *this* was why I had taken so many twists and turns in my life so far…so that once I got clear about what I wanted, it would happen. This certainly made it all seem to have been worth it.

By the summer of '79, our business was up and running. We called it "Airventure," and it employed thirteen people and operated two brand new twin-engine airplanes. Each plane was earning enough revenue to prove that the idea was truly a good one. A third plane was on order, and two new commuter operations, Zia Airlines and Mesa Air, were offering lucrative contracts if we could provide bigger, 10 and 12-passenger airplanes. To be profitable, however, we needed more than three airplanes operating daily.

Such expansion looked promising. I was working non-stop on acquiring funding, and I had two other people ready to start doing the same. We leased our own building, which made my heart swell every time I drove to work. Few people who lived in Santa Fe believed that it would support an aviation business, even though it had a thoroughly modern airport

Back in Minneapolis, Barbara was convinced after several contacts from me that the time was finally right to put "our" plan into action. Channon was four now, and Jonathan was eight. I hadn't seen them since I'd moved, and I really wanted to fulfill my responsibility as a dad before they were too big to care. I often talked about them to my new friends in Santa Fe, and I think some people were beginning to think I had just made them up.

Once I had established an actual income from the business, I bought an older model Ford Econoline van and large travel trailer, and drove up to Minneapolis to haul them all back to "The Land of Enchantment." I hadn't realized how much I missed the boys until I was around them again…now at an age where I could have more "guy time" with them. I had managed to strike up a couple of romantic relationships during my time in Santa Fe, but any thoughts anyone might have had by that point of my being another "eligible" bachelor dissipated when the boys arrived.

While Barbara looked for an apartment and work, both boys came to stay with me…which was quite a shift in routine for me. I tried bringing them to work with me, which at first was a novelty for everyone but wore off quickly. After a couple of days of that, some daycare and some time off for me was necessary. It was a kick, however, to watch them adjust to their new surroundings and new "uncles" and "aunts," as they referred to most of my friends. Life seemed good. 1979 was really shaping up to be my year.

Then came the black cloud.

By the middle of September of that year, the prime interest rate soared from its normal 8+% to near 20%, then even higher. The American economy was going south in a big way. Panicked investors took their money and ran for high ground, while bankers smiled nervously but red-lined all but the very tightest deals. Everyone seemed convinced we were headed for the next Great Depression.

With 13 people on the payroll, and little working capital by that time, inexperience in business management left me uncertain how to turn things around for Airventure. What was worse, I had signed over the controlling interest in the company to the Chicago firm, who seized the planes and the remaining operating capital. My promising young business floundered, then capsized like an overcrowded lifeboat. I was left with over $100,000 in personally guaranteed loans and numerous bills from creditors. Faced with imminent disaster and ridicule, little did I know how shallow those waters were. Our company could have survived all the better because of the economic crisis, had I only had enough confidence and skill to weather things out and convince our investors.

Within five weeks, our offices stood empty, while I lugged boxes of files to my rental house and lined them up against the living room wall. I stood alone, looking at my dream—all our months of work—tidily packed up into the moving boxes that had so recently been used to bring us to our new offices. Thomas was in L.A., presumably finding new investor prospects, and everyone who had come on board with us had scattered around town.

I was pretty down, but I wasn't out yet. I knew I could make it all work if I could just keep some semblance of order around me, and my credibility intact. I still had money in the payroll account , so I had a few months' income to work with. I still had pending contracts with the commuter airlines, who were waiting for word from me. If I could only put together the down payments for the aircraft they needed, I could at least get a trickle of cash in to show that we had a viable business.

I called Barbara that night, and she came over the next morning to help me pull some things together and act as my "office manager." Still, doing business was pretty tricky. That first day, Barbara had to field calls from the IRS about overdue quarterly reports and payroll deductions, as well as numerous calls from creditors on accounts that were beginning to fall behind. If I could just keep them inside the 30-day-late column, or better, we could make it.

Santa Fe in those days was not only a haven for artistic types and dreamers, it was a seasonal haven for rock stars and people of "independent means"—like Antonio and Bill. Although it had never been discussed outright, it was understood that my services could prove useful—with the right amount of discretion.

With unpaid bills mounting daily, I began to wonder whether Antonio and Bill might really have something to offer. I still saw Antonio around town, and his number was in my address book.

One day, after Barbara fended off calls from a bank auditor and several bill collectors, I decided it was time to find out. After a long walk, I came back and dialed Antonio at the ranch.

He wasn't there, but Bill was. He seemed unusually friendly with me.

"Hey man, how the hell are ya'?!?" he asked.

"Not particularly great, " I sighed." I've got a great little business about to go under with these interest rates. Everybody thinks the next Depression is here."

"Yeah, tell me about it. We've got *three* businesses on the edge, and I can't seem to borrow enough to keep 'em afloat until this thing breaks."

I heard him stretch, and yawn. He didn't sound all that concerned. "So what can I do for you?"

"Well, that's really my question to you. You in need of a good pilot these days?"

"Uh, right now I couldn't say for sure. But, uh….I'll check it out with Antonio. We were just talking about that a few days ago. Maybe we could work something out."

I could almost hear him thinking. "Hmm. Look, I'm on my way to San Fran for a while. Antonio's actually up there right now, taking care of some business. But, you know…you should come up to the ranch this weekend. We could talk over some ideas, and I'll run it all by Antonio when I see him next week."

"Okay," I agreed… pleased to think there was a possibility of some money on my horizon. If I could raise enough capital just to keep the bills paid, maybe by spring I could rejuvenate the business.

The next day I drove up to the ranch in the late afternoon. It was twenty miles north of town, and several miles down a long, dirt road. Right on the banks of the Rio Grande, it was a sweet little "getaway" place for them…secluded, yet elegantly furnished.

Bill was polite and attentive to me, showing me all around the property.

"Here's where we plan to do some hydroponic lettuce," he noted, touring me through their extensive greenhouses. "And out there's where we'd like to plant some pecan groves."

While Bill wasn't nearly as chummy as Antonio was, he was unusually friendly toward me. He must have noticed me looking suspiciously around one of the greenhouses, because he laughed..

"We don't grow anything out here that can't be sold in the stores," he remarked. "We'd be too easy a target for some eager-beaver local lawmen…especially with greenhouses you can see for miles from the air. We'd lose the whole ranch."

"Here," Bill said unexpectedly, pulling a glass cigar tube from a pocket of his tailored leather sport coat. "This what you were looking for?"

Inside the tube was a long, perfectly manicured bud of seedless marijuana, with little purplish fibers running through it. Motioning to me with his head, Bill walked out to the middle of a fully tiled courtyard with a hot tub sunk into it. He pulled a hand-painted porcelain pipe from a tiny leather bag in another one of his pockets, and carefully pinched a bit of the resinous bud from the tube. Pressing the leaves into the pipe like they were pure gold, he turned and handed it to me.

I hadn't smoked any pot since my time in Viet Nam, and even that was sparingly. But there was something almost seductive about the whole setup at the ranch…something that swirled around my head even before I put the pipe to my lips. These guys knew how to live, and they seemed like decent, caring people…not the sinister, back-stabbing type portrayed in drug smuggling movies and books. I felt a genuine sense of Bill wanting to be friends with me, so I eased back and went along for the ride.

Before long, we were bubbling in the relaxing water, and deep into a philosophical conversation. I could barely stay coherent, but by the time the night was over, I had agreed to go to Miami with Bill, where he planned to rekindle a relationship with a former supplier. My services as a pilot, he told me somewhat cryptically, would come in handy later, but for now all they needed was a "co-driver" to bring a relatively small quantity of "merchandise" from Miami to San Francisco in the back of a pick-up truck.

Their regular driver, Bill told me, was an older man he and Antonio had known for many years. "He'll be perfect to show you the ropes," Bill informed me. Even in that state, I knew that "showing me the ropes" was really just to demonstrate my trustworthiness and reliability.

We talked more about what might come later, which he said would most likely be for me to simply act as a private pilot for them while they conducted their "business"…not unlike any successful business having its own "corporate airplane." In fact, the more we talked about it, the more animated he became about it. The chance to come and go from any airport in the country, rather than have to deal with commercial airline security and exposure and tedium of highway driving grew more and more appealing to him as we talked.

The trip to Miami took place in early December of 1979. I flew out with Bill, where we stayed in a local motel waiting for a phone call to say the operation was coming off. Evidently, the 600-pound lot I would be co-driving was only a very small part of a much larger shipment. If it came off without a hitch, Bill would be ready and able to take on much more from future shipments that might even be brought up the west coast for delivery.

Bill's meetings in Miami meant a lot of waiting for me at the motel, where I quickly grew sick of Bob Barker and game show and soap opera circus on TV. Early one evening while Bill was gone to make some calls from a pay phone, there came a knock at the door.

I opened it to find two dark-complected men, one older, and the other much younger and very heavy-set. They had a distinctly authoritative presence. The younger one wore several heavy gold necklaces and bracelets. If I had to guess, I'd have put his weight at a minimum of 300 pounds—without the jewelry. The older one spoke first.

"We're looking for Bill, please," he said in a rather polished voice. He had a European accent that I couldn't quite place. "Have we come to the right place?"

"Yes...yes, you have," I answered, somewhat awkwardly, it felt. "Bill's out just now, but he should be back in a few minutes. Would you like to come in and wait for him?"

"Thank you," the man smiled, stepping into the room and offering his hand.

"My name is Constantine. And this is my younger brother, Michael. Bill is a business associate of ours, and we thought we would spare him the trip out to our place...if you don't mind."

"Certainly not," I replied, trying to be equally gracious. "I'm a friend of his. I happened to be in the area while he's here. Can I get you something cold to drink?"

"Anything would be fine...nothing alcoholic, though...if you please."

The two took a seat in the small room while I opened a couple of cans of soda from the tiny refrigerator.

Who could these guys be? I wondered. They were clearly no "errand boys" or even higher-level messengers—that was for sure. Just the way they sat in the room while I poured the drinks warned me to tread lightly. There was a certain power of presence with these two.

I handed the two men their sodas, and repeated my certainty that Bill would return any moment. I wasn't certain what protocol was at this point, though. Did I sit down and chat with them, or make an excuse and leave the room until Bill returned?

"Thank you," the older man said, accepting a ginger-ale. "Please sit down and join us."

"Okay, sure" I fumbled, taking a seat opposite them both.

Constantine, as he had called himself, looked to be in his early sixties, while his brother's age was anybody's guess. Michael had a youthful face and bright, steely eyes, but his weight distorted any accurate guess on age. A wild guess would have put him at 45 or so.

The Old Man, as I began to think of him, seemed intelligent and strangely attuned to what I was feeling. He quickly reassured me by his manner that he was there with the best of intentions. As he and I exchanged civilities, I felt Michael sizing up everything around the room, including me. There was definitely a sinister edge to him, and I became uneasy with the way he was eyeing me.

"So what line of work are you in?" the Old Man asked, innocuously.

"I have an aviation business in New Mexico," I said. Michael's eyes shifted quickly back from the window to me.

"Oh?" The Old Man shifted in his chair. "That must be interesting. What sort of, uh, aviation business?"

I told them what I'd tried to do with Airventure, and how I was working on salvaging the business.

"We have a ship-salvaging business off shore," the Old Man smiled. "Perhaps we can help at some point with *your* 'salvaging' operation."

I wasn't certain whether he was just making conversation or throwing me a hook. "That would be most welcome," I replied politely, then shifted the conversation back to him and his line of work.

"We're primarily in shipping," the Old Man noted. He was a former ship captain, he said, and now headed his own international business, with offices in several countries. He and his brother were both Egyptian-born Greeks, with business ties to the Persian Gulf, South Africa, the Caribbean and both Central and South America.

The Old Man was fascinating me, and I would have loved to talk with him some more....but I knew I was already stepping beyond my bounds. I didn't know their business at all—or Bill's, for that matter. I felt I was already at the point of knowing too much about them, even though they seemed to be comfortable with the exchange. Fortunately, Bill arrived and I was able to turn the conversation over to him. I excused myself and headed out the door for a long walk.

The next morning, Barbara got ahold of me through one of the contact numbers I had left her. She announced that she had just arranged to go to Peru with "a friend" and she needed someone to take care of Channon. Jonathan would go with her to Peru, where they might stay for as much as a month or two.

I needed that like a hole in the head. How could I complete the job with my four-year-old son along? It was a tricky development, but surprisingly Bill was open to the idea. Channon, he noted, would be an excellent "decoy." The driver Jessie, Channon and I could pass for an uncle, father and son on vacation.

"If we tie a canoe to the top of the camper," he mused, "and hang some fishing poles from the gun rack in the cab, it'll be perfect!" He sat back, grinning with satisfaction.

Part of me railed against such use of my child, but by that point I had little other choice. I certainly didn't know anyone with whom I could leave him in Miami, that was for certain.

Finally, on New Year's Eve, 1979, I entered the decade of the '80s as a bonafide "smuggler"— or at least an accomplice to one. Sitting in a nondescript motel in Jacksonville, Florida, while the New Year rang in and my son slept soundly beside me, I was in deep reflection over our planned trip up the East Coast. From somewhere in Tennessee or Kentucky, we would head west all the way across the country to San Francisco with a pick-up camper full of Colombian pot. Sleeping soundly, Channon was oblivious to anything but the fact that he and his Daddy and his newfound "Uncle Jessie," were off on a "vacation."

We arrived five days later in Marin County, just north of the Golden Gate Bridge. We pulled the pick-up into a large garage attached to a private home obscured by redwood trees. Bill was on hand to meet us, soon after which he paid each of us…but only half of what we'd been promised. "The rest will come later," he said, "as soon as we see how well this stuff sells."

"No way," Jessie exclaimed. "I'm not going to go through that bullshit again." Bill glared at him. His sharp features looked suddenly taunt.

"Calm down, man. You know how this business works," Bill snapped back at Jessie. "We've got to move this stuff first."

"*That* wasn't the deal," Jessie stood up. "I…I mean *we*…did our jobs. You agreed to pay us the full amount, and that's *that*. You never said anything about 'if it sells'." He ran his hands through his sweaty gray hair.. The trip had been a long one, and it was showing on him. "This is the same shit you pulled on me two years ago, and I told you then I wouldn't stand for it again."

"This isn't the same thing," Bill shot back, trying hard to stay cool in front of me.

I wondered how heated this would get. Jessie was an older man with a strong sense of fair play. Having gotten to know him a bit during the trip, I could see he was pretty well set in his ways. This job was all he did, and he did it well.

"Those were different people," Bill said calmly, "and *you* were the one who introduced them to *me*. You have to take at least *some* responsibility for the rip-off."

"Bull*shit*!" Jessie exploded, the veins sticking out on his neck.

I excused myself and went outside to make sure Channon was okay playing in the yard. I half expected to hear a gunshot or some kind of scuffle, and wanted to make sure Channon and I were out of harm's way. Bill and Jessie had known each other for many years, I told myself, and neither was new to such matters. Jessie had told me several stories of their years together, and I was sure he was being truthful. Of course, everyone in that business, I was learning, had their own version of how things went...or should have gone.

I don't know how things ever got resolved between the two of them, but I only got a little over half of what we were to be paid for the trip. It was all so illegal in the first place, I hardly had the nerve to make an issue of it at that point.

Channon and I flew back to Santa Fe, but not before Bill informed me that the Old Man had taken a liking to me. He had worked out a deal with them, he said, that would release me to work directly with the Greek brothers if I wanted.

"If you play your cards right, he said, "you can make enough money to buy all the planes you want for your business. You might even get them to invest in your business."

My wheels were already turning.

Back at home, I paid off a few of the more critical bills, left Channon with a close woman friend, and flew out to Miami to meet with the Old Man and his brother...this time on my own terms. After all, I was now a "seasoned" veteran in the business.

Chapter Four

The Old Man greeted me at the door of his room at the Miami Airport Holiday Inn. We had barely exchanged pleasantries when he nodded to Michael, who handed me a small, brown paper bag. Inside were several bundles of crisp one-hundred-dollar bills, just like you would get at a bank. I looked at the two men across the small table, surprised.

"We heard about what Bill paid you for the California trip," he shrugged. "It's all too common a practice in this business, and why a lot of people in it fail. We don't fault him for doing it, and perhaps it's even none of our business…but we want to get off on the right foot, so we thought we'd make things right between us before we work together."

I was both pleased and amazed. I didn't know how much was in the bag, but guessed it would be pretty close to what Bill owed me…$7,000. If they really wanted to impress me, it could be more. I didn't realize it at the time, but that was my first exposure to how one person is worked against another in that business, and how loyalties are created and maintained.

The meeting wasn't a long one, but it was enough for me to see the Old Man at work. He was smooth. Not "slick" or coercively smooth, like his brother appeared to be, but gracious and calm. He knew how to win a guy's loyalty by making him feel important and respected. He did most of the talking, explaining that he and Michael were negotiating to buy an air freight business in Costa Rica. They were "shipping people," he said, and didn't know the aviation business very well. They were "having some trouble," with shipments getting through to their destinations, and wanted to see if large cargo planes might solve their problem. The way he talked, he could have just as easily been talking about shipments of coffee beans or bananas. I would have to learn to be very cryptic, I realized, as he went on to explain what they hoped I might do for them. They wanted me to go down there and evaluate the business, and find more suitable aircraft and pilots.

"If you want," he said with a respectful tone in his voice, "you could stay on nd manage the business for us. But if you don't," he lifted his hands in a gesture f indifference, "you can go back to New Mexico once things are running moothly."

The Old Man smiled in a congenial way and stretched in his seat. "Maybe we ould even help restart that airline business of yours, eh?"

That got my attention. The Costa Rica thing was intriguing, certainly, but I lid have a couple of kids back in Santa Fe, and an unfinished dream I was aching o give the right kind of attention. I sat quietly for a few minutes, mulling over his roposition, but I'm sure my face must have shown my interest.

The Old Man went on. "Your work would be strictly business for us. We do a lot of business in Third World countries. There's added risk and expense you an't imagine, even as well known as we are. Occasionally we add some 'other merchandise' with our shipments to offset losses we incur that are unpredictable n such countries. You have no idea how expensive it can be. If the air freight busi-ness can help us offset some losses, we'd like to do that. It's just 'insurance' for us. We keep it real clean. Nothing like in your American movies."

It sounded plausible to me. I wanted to believe him, but glancing over at Michael with all his gold jewelry made me feel a bit skeptical. I looked back at he Old Man, and kept my focus on him instead. Him I felt I could believe.

Years later I learned that they owned seventeen ocean-going yachts and freighters, and ran multiple businesses in seven countries on three continents. Their ships were being increasingly intercepted by the U.S. Coast Guard when I met them, and they wanted to reduce their risk of being caught by moving *all* their llicit operations to the air. Their broader intention, once they had gotten to know me better, was for me to provide the means for them to do so.

I went home, paid off a few more bills and had my van set up for more long-distance travelling. I wouldn't be taking it to Costa Rica, but I could tell I'd be naking a few trips to Florida. If the boys were going to continue to be with me, 'd need to have a rolling bedroom for them. Barbara returned from Peru all azzed about new possibilities for her down there, but I managed to get her to stay with the boys until I got back from Costa Rica. Suddenly we were becoming inter-national "jet-setters."

When I met with the Greeks again, it was at one of their homes in Ft. Lauderdale a few weeks later. It wasn't a lavish place at all, which surprised me. But then I realized the Old Man wouldn't be conspicuous about his success in that business. We sat around a rather simple kitchen table and talked about my ideas for finding suitable cargo planes. I'd have to do quite a bit of flying around to different places, looking for big planes that were still flyable and reliable. I knew airplanes, but these would be monsters by comparison with what I had flown. would have to adjust my thinking big time. I was clear about what I felt my limitations might be in that regard, which didn't put the Old Man off at all. In fact he seemed relieved that I would actually tell him my weaknesses.

"We get 'cowboy' pilots all the time," he said, "who tell us they can do any thing. If we've got a jet, they can fly it. If we got helicopters, they can fly them better than anyone. We don't like 'cowboys,' son."

His use of the word "son" went right to the heart of my military upbringing Not only did that touch the family man in me, but it was the way generals addressed their subordinates...and it usually gained a lot of loyalty.

"So how much will you need to do all this 'travelling'?" he looked directly in my eyes. I was on the spot now. My heart started pounding and I'm sure I swallowed hard. I had no idea. I hadn't even thought about it. I figured they would just tell me how much they would pay me, or maybe I would submit expense receipts or something. The two of them sat quietly, waiting for me to answer. My mind started running wild. *What should I say?* Finally, I blurted out the first figure I could come up with that wouldn't seem ridiculous.

"$50,000." I hoped like hell I didn't come off too foolish or overeager, and that they wouldn't take issue with me on it. I couldn't possibly justify that figure with any logical thinking or rationale. The Old Man nodded to Michael without even blinking or hesitating, and Michael got up and went into another room. Not five minutes later, he returned with yet another brown paper bag and handed it to me. I thought that stuff only happened in the movies. I didn't open it or check it. I knew it would be correct...right to the penny.

"We'll expect to hear from you periodically," the Old Man's voice seemed just a touch more authoritative. "You find us the right planes, and make sure everything is right down there, and we'll talk again soon about your compensation." He stood up, shook my hand and showed me to the door. As I drove away I looked around at the strictly middle class suburban neighborhood and wondered where he really lived.

For the next three months I flew everywhere...down to Costa Rica a couple of times and all over the midwest and southwest, looking for old cargo planes capable of long-range flight and of carrying payloads greater than 10,000 pounds. Though relatively cheap to buy, such airplanes were expensive to refurbish.

operate and maintain.

Expense apparently didn't matter to the Greeks, though. They didn't care much about "refurbishment." Maybe they were legitimate businessmen and would really run a legitimate air freight business. But as I continued to work with them and have occasional meetings with them, it seemed that all they really needed or wanted was a few successful flights out of each plane...or even *one,* if that's how it worked out. After all, these aircraft were as dispensable to them as Hollywood props. One successful trip with a DC4 or 6, capable of flying 15,000 to 20,000 pounds of "merchandise," could be worth four to five *million* dollars to them, based on my crudest calculations.

A month after starting to work with them, the Old Man asked me to fly with him in a chartered plane to the Grand Turks and Caicos Islands, 600 miles deep into the Caribbean. Accompanying him on the flight was a man named Charlie, who I was told was also pilot and familiar both with the Caribbean and with heavy-transport planes. I wasn't told why Charlie was along, but later was told that it was because he wasn't available to work for the Old Man on a long-term basis. Charlie's boss, another Greek, had agreed to "loan" Charlie to the Old Man for a few days to help us with logistics and planning.

The trip was an easy one, and I enjoyed getting to know both the Old Man and Charlie better during the three days we spent there. While we waited for the Old Man to conduct his business, Charlie and I talked at length at the hotel bar, and out on the veranda, overlooking the most idyllic beaches with warm, turquoise waters and azure skies. The setting, had I been with the right woman, would have topped my charts for the perfect romantic interlude.

Charlie was from rural Alabama, and had a small flying operation in northern Florida flying marijuana out of Jamaica in light, twin-engine Cessna Skymasters. He did this in quick, turn-around flights from his home, north of Panama City, Florida, by flying back and forth across Cuba in the middle of the night. The thought of flying across Cuba at night, or at *any* time, chilled my bones, but Charlie said he'd done it "pretty regular" for several years. But his operation, he said, was "small 'taters" compared to the Greek brothers' operation.

"Take this trip, fer instance," he drawled amiably, scratching his nose. "I'm just here to provide some advice about flying large planes outta' Colombia."

"You've done that?" I asked curiously.

"Sure have," Charlie responded without explanation. "And these here brothers are paying me a pretty penny just for my 'consultin'," he smiled. "What they want to do is big, and they got the green ta' do it. They think big, and they act big, that's for sure."

"Why don't you work for them, then?"

"Nah," said Charlie carefully. "They're too big and too complex for me. And too powerful." He winked at me. "I'm just a lil' ol' country boy. Like to keep things simple."

Later on, I walked on the beach with the Old Man. In a moment of bonding between us, he spoke openly about his past. This island was one of his "hide-aways," and soon to be a re-fueling point for future air operations. He had discovered the place years ago in his earlier days as a ship captain. Later, when he befriended a well-known financier and close personal friend to the President of the United States, he used the connection to provide building supplies and food goods for the islanders. In fact, nearly all of the few cars on the main island he brought and gave to various officials and influential people. The native people, almost all of Jamaican, Dominican Republic and Haitian descent, loved him. Either that was his nature, or he very shrewdly had cultivated his relationship with the islanders for just this eventual purpose.

When we got back to Miami at the end of the trip, Charlie pulled me aside.

"If you ever want some *simpler* work, you c'mon up and see me. I'll make it worth your while, and you won't have ta' deal with the suit and tie crowd, if y'know what I mean." He handed me a travel brochure as the Old Man paid our bill at the air charter desk and headed back in our direction. "Here's a great place to visit someday," he said when the Old Man was within earshot. "Me and the missus had a hellofa time there for a coupla' weeks a few years back." Later that night, I opened the brochure and saw his phone number written in one of the margins.

While the prospect of flying light aircraft over Cuba day *or* night didn't exactly excite me, I kept Charlie's number for future reference. One never knows in this business when such things might come in handy.

A month passed as I worked for the Greeks, and the more I traveled back and forth to Costa Rica and to a half-dozen locations where big cargo planes were advertised for sale, the more enmeshed I became in their world. Gradually they began to invite me to other places that were more obviously "home" to them, and even though they still weren't opulent palaces, it was evident to me that they definitely had the finances to do about anything they wanted. Sometimes I'd be at one or another of their places when some of their key people would come and go, and I felt increasingly nervous that my face and name were becoming known to people I little knew or cared to know.

Some of those people I hoped I would never see again. I learned a cryptic language and lifestyle that was at times awkward because I couldn't always tell whether or not "merchandise" meant real merchandise or illicit products. So I had to assume the latter, which at times proved almost comical.

It only took about six weeks for me to realize I was in way over my head. Not only was I woefully inexperienced in the world of drug dealing, but I didn't really know enough about heavy, post-war aircraft. I increasingly felt that I was putting things at risk—not only for the operation, but for myself personally. Expediency, I was learning, was the name of the game in their business and, if circumstances arose that required expediency, I sensed that I'd very quickly find myself doing whatever they felt was necessary at any given moment. That might even include, perhaps, suddenly being at the controls of one of those planes, learning to fly it by the seat of my pants. It would no doubt be under the worst possible conditions.

I had seen it happen already several times, to some extent , but increasingly I sensed that absolute loyalty and instant adherence to suddenly changing directives from the top was demanded. Although I felt that the Old Man would always be polite and gracious, his younger brother clearly ran a significant part of the business and would, without hesitation, press me to do things I might not want to do. After another few weeks of looking at derelict, 40-year old airplanes, and sensing that the sellers knew why I was looking at them, I couldn't maintain the façade any longer.

At a meeting with the Old Man and his brother in San Antonio later that month, I hesitantly announced that I wanted out.

The Old Man, with a deeply quizzical expression on his face, spoke first. "What's the problem? Aren't we paying you enough?"

"No," I sighed, even though no clear agreement had ever been reached about exactly what I was to be paid. "The money's not really the problem. You've been decent about that. It's just…uh… parts of this operation that I don't have experience with…BIG parts. And without the proper knowledge and experience I'm …well, I feel like I'm making things too dangerous for *all* of us."

I hesitated to get a sense of their reaction.

"You're doing fine," the Old Man said, reaching over to pat me on the back in a fatherly way. "Just keep doing what you're doing. We'll let you know if there's a problem."

"You don't understand," I protested, looking sideways at Michael, who was now staring at me unpleasantly. "The 'problem' might already be happening. I'm a *pilot,* and I understand flying. But what you want me to do is way out of my league."

Neither of the brothers spoke. I felt sweat drops beginning under my armpits. Charlie had mentioned at one point that he'd heard of unloaders and other men who worked for them suddenly disappearing from their warehouses and having been "taken onboard one of their ships, never to return." I wrote the comment off back then as just over-dramatized rumor.

"I've looked at dozens of planes for you guys, and there hasn't been *one* I could honestly recommend. I mean, any one of them might be fine, but *I* wouldn't know that. What's worse is they might have some serious airframe or engine problems, and I wouldn't spot it. A lot of these planes were built before I was *born,* for God's sake."

Michael snorted. "We got people who can figure that stuff out," he said brusquely. "Your job is just to find the planes and make us good deals. We'll do the rest."

I looked at him for as long as I could, and still maintain any semblance of respect. I was beginning to see his propensity for coldness. I turned my attention to the Old Man. "Look, I'm still responsible for finding the planes and accepting them. The kind of work you're expecting requires someone who's flown these birds and knows them inside out."

"I *told* you, we can take care of that," Michael interrupted sharply, looking at me with distinct annoyance.

Perhaps I should try another angle, I thought.

"You know, when I look at these planes, I tell people I represent a collector, or I'm an operations officer for an air-freight company. They *know* I'm not! A collector or any aircraft company worth its salt wouldn't have such an inexperienced guy looking for planes like these. There's only *one* reason a guy like me would be interested in one of these planes."

The Old Man spoke up. "We understand that," he said, looking tired. "But you don't have a record, right?"

"Right."

"Never been busted?"

"Nothing major."

"Got a good military record as a pilot?"

"Yes, but only with helicopters and light planes," I reminded him. "There's a big difference."

"Maybe," he replied thoughtfully. "Makes no difference, anyway—as long as you check out clean. What you need to understand is that the sellers of these planes are businessmen like anybody else. They don't care what 'company' you represent, or what your background is. They'll take your money like they'll take anyone else's." He shrugged his shoulders as if to say, What's the problem?

"That's not what worries me," I said, feeling increasingly nervous that they might not let me out of my "deal" with them. It was beginning to appear that they didn't want to release me, so I had to shift my approach to something that might make better sense to them.

"These planes are considered high-profile aircraft. Some of them...if not all...could easily be bugged, particularly when someone approaches them who isn't the least bit sophisticated about them."

"So?" Michael snapped. "*You're* not going to be flying them." I could feel his anger building, and it was beginning to make me feel sick inside. But I held my course and this time directed my comments to him as respectfully as was possible for me to do.

"Just the same, the fact is I'm green at this. The planes are too big, the business is too complex, and I'm just...feeling more and more like a potential liability. I might say something or do something inadvertently that could create problems for you that I might not even know about." I held my eyes on him until he got that I was speaking directly to him, then shifted my gaze to the Old Man for support.

There was no sound in the hotel room except the hum of the air conditioner and the sounds of a game show on TV.

At last the Old Man nodded. "You may have a point," he said, somewhat ponderously. "I can see how this could be stressful for all of us." He took a deep breath, glanced at his brother, then looked back at me. "I appreciate that you came to us instead of trying to fake things. We've lost too much in the past when people said they could do something they couldn't."

Relief flooded through me, then a touch of fear came back as I recalled stories of men being treated respectfully just before the knifing...or the sound of a silencer.

"Now, what can we do about this?" the Old Man asked me.

"What about the money we've paid him?" Michael said, angrily. He was definitely pissed.

"Here it is," I said, taking a check out of my pocket and laying it on the table. "I put all the money in a bank account in Nassau after you gave it to me. I've been drawing against it only for travel expenses. This will cover everything you gave me, less my actual expenses. And here are the receipts for those." I laid a thick envelope on the table next to the check containing my itemized expense receipts.

Michael's eyes widened. "You're giving us a *check?*"

"It's all there," I answered as calmly as I could. I kept my hands under the table, trying to hide the trembling I felt. "If you prefer cash, I'll have to transfer funds to a local bank and then get it to you."

Michael threw up his hands, got up and sauntered over to the window.

"That won't be necessary," the Old Man said, picking up the check and ignoring his brother's temperament. "We have accounts at that bank. In fact, we had just withdrawn money from that very bank the day before we gave you that money. If I didn't know you better by now, I would say that's very ironic...even amusing, no?"

"I guess so," I hesitated, not certain if he was goading me or really amused.

He looked me straight in the eye. "You did good in coming to us." He poured himself a glass of tonic water from a large bottle on the table. "So what are you going to do now?"

I looked gratefully at the Old Man as Michael continued to stare out the window, obviously still exasperated .

"Remember that pilot from Florida who went to the Turks and Caicos Islands with us?"

"Yes. Charlie. Are you going to see him?"

"I think so. He has a small operation using planes I can handle. I'm not excited about the route he flies, but he offered me good money just to ride along with him. Then maybe I can fly a trip or two for him myself and make enough money to get my old businesses back in action again. But," I added hastily, "Charlie said I should clear it with you if I did go up there. He doesn't want any trouble or misunderstandings with you."

"It's fine," said the Old Man. "Tell him I'll remember that. His boss is an old friend of mine."

The Old Man stood up and grasped my hand warmly in both of his. "If you ever decide you want to work with us again, you can always call."

I felt in that moment I had nothing to fear from him, but I could tell Michael felt differently. Returning from the window, he, too, offered his hand and wished me well. But it rang very hollow. I could only hope that I was right about the Old Man.

All the way down in the elevator and out the hotel door, I fought back images of bullets flying out of nowhere. The feeling didn't leave me for a long time after that. With very little money left to my name, I headed north that night toward Pensacola. It was a six-hour drive from Miami, and Charlie was expecting me at his home in the morning. I hoped he would prove to be my salvation. I needed some cash—fast.

Charlie's deal was simple enough: I would fly as a co-pilot with him in his twin-engine Skymaster, and he would pay me $25,000 per trip. If I wanted to fly a second plane in tandem with him later on, he would pay me twice that.

As I drove through the swamps and endless orange groves of central Florida, I figured my profits in my head. In three trips as a co-pilot and perhaps one on my own as a pilot, I could make enough to bail myself out of debt and jump-start things back in Santa Fe. If I wanted to do a couple more flights by myself after that, I'd have enough backing me so that I'd never have to sign over controlling interest in my business to anyone again. This could be good.

I pushed on through the night air of the Everglades. It all seemed positive. But then, so had the Old Man's offer in the beginning…and so had Bill's, for that matter. Thinking back, I was supposed to have been "peripheral" when I hooked up with Bill only a few months ago. Now I was preparing to step directly into the arena as a pilot in a plane flying pot into the U.S.—directly over Cuban airspace.

I sighed. Perhaps there was a way I could be peripheral with Charlie. Maybe there were other, safer ways I could help him and still make enough to just go home with enough money to stay alive while I figured things out. Then again, a tax-free $25,000 would pay an awful lot of bills. Given that thought alone, I figured I could at least "ride along" on one trip and see how it went.

Such thoughts came and went all night long as I drove northward toward the panhandle of Florida. Every once in a while, I caught myself wondering whether Cuba still had missiles.

Chapter Five

Charlie's place was a typical suburban home in a newly developing community two hours east of Pensacola. If I hadn't met him under the circumstances I did, I would have thought upon meeting him for the first time that he was just an average guy from the Deep South. Middle-aged and portly, he looked more like a heavy equipment operator than he did a full-time drug smuggler.

His wife of twenty-some years was a gracious southern lady who welcomed me into their home as warmly as if I had been one of Charlie's army buddies. Their teenage son, Jason, was tall and lanky, and could easily pass as an average adolescent and high school athlete.

But this was not a normal American family—at least not by customary standards. Beneath the soft and gentle "All-American" image, this family had its roots in drug smuggling that went back to before Jason was born. More than a few neighbors were even involved in Charlie's work. Backyard barbecues at Charlie's house were less likely to find amiable chatter about social events and more about weather systems that might affect a night flight over Cuba, or the latest reports of a drug task force infiltrating the local scene.

As Jason grew older, he and some of his friends worked as unloaders when Charlie would come in at dawn and touch down on a nearby highway or abandoned airstrip. It was the nicest, most pleasant urban neighborhood, where many of the better cars and swimming pools were paid for with Jamaican pot.

Charlie also had a few highly placed officials looking out for him, including a supervisor with the State Fish and Game Department who, on occasion, would even block the roads for him. In Florida, Fish and Game matters could take precedence even over the Highway Patrol, giving Charlie a decided edge at times.

Raised the last of fifteen kids on a small farm in Alabama, Charlie learned the hard way that food was only slightly less scarce than money. The first chance he had, he joined the Army where he relished having a small but steady paycheck and "three squares" a day. When he got out, he went to work for a large aircraft modification plant, where he learned how to install auxiliary fuel tanks. After making the first decent money he had ever made in his life by rigging a friend's plane with long-range fuel tanks, Charlie became a very popular guy among an elite group of very affluent pilots. Before long, he had his own twin-engine airplane and a few hours of instruction under his belt. He wasted no time learning to fly and smuggle at the same time.

When I arrived on the scene, he had three twin-engine Cessna Skymasters, each in different stages of disrepair. He liked the Skymaster because it was big enough to carry a sizable load, yet it was simple to fly. With one engine in front and one in the rear, most of the hazards of flying twin-engine airplanes were minimized. Loss of power in either engine, unlike most light twins, involved no more complex emergency procedure than feathering the prop and continuing flight as if it were a single engine airplane.

Perhaps because of growing up in a poverty-stricken, rural community, Charlie's mentality was that of a shade-tree mechanic. To him, everything could be fixed with a pair of pliers, a screwdriver and duct tape. His planes, like his cars, were evidence of his ingenuity and ability to adapt anything to suit his needs. But contrary to what he had learned in the Army and at home, Charlie's skill at fixing things was second only to his ignorance of one of the most basic principles of maintaining airplanes: "Even if it doesn't need fixing, fix it anyway." He always waited until it broke to fix it.

After a week of watching Charlie try everything he could to get even one of the three planes running, and *keep* it running, I began to have some serious doubts about this "simple" operation of his. He was well liked around town, but I wasn't certain if it was because he was so likeable or because whenever he brought in a load, everyone's lifestyle improved. Either way, mine wasn't improving, and I had been away from home for far too long. I couldn't even think about the pile of bills accumulating back in New Mexico.

Finally, Charlie announced that one of the planes was flyable. After three hours of practice landings at the local airport, and a two-hour flight to Tallahassee and back, it did, indeed, seem to be okay.

Detailed planning got underway and phone calls were made. Activity picked up in the neighborhood, and seemingly ordinary people suddenly began showing up at Charlie's house looking like Army Commandos. We took off late one evening, survival gear conspicuous among the few items Charlie felt were necessary for the flight. The sight of an inflatable life raft on board was both reassuring and disconcerting, considering the condition of Charlie's planes.

A half-hour later, we were well out over the Gulf of Mexico and night had fallen to the extent that we no longer had sight of the horizon. An occasional pinpoint of light in the blackness below indicated a ship on its way to some unknown port of call. That only accentuated the absence of anything even remotely familiar or hopeful to me. Behind us, and fading fast, were the lights of Pensacola and terra firma.

Just as I was beginning to believe that the flight might go well, the rear engine suddenly began to run roughly. Charlie jolted upright in his seat, spilling coffee over his maps in the process. He tapped on the engine gages—more out of ritual than because it might affect anything—and adjusted the fuel mixture and prop setting. We waited anxiously while the engine at first appeared to smooth out. Then it coughed again, and sputtered like it was fuel-starved. With a worried expression on his face, Charlie tapped on the other gages as if that might somehow fix the problem. Meanwhile, the engine started misfiring like an old car with fouled plugs. We both fixed our eyes on the rear engine temperature gage and watched in dismay as it climbed steadily toward the red line, while the oil pressure began to drop—a classic indication of an imminent engine failure.

Charlie cussed as he advanced the fuel mixture as carefully as he could and reduced the power. The engine temperature peaked, then began to drop. But the oil pressure continued to fall, and the roughness persisted. To maintain our airspeed and altitude, more power had to be applied to the front engine, thereby increasing its temperature as well.

Things didn't look good for us.

Finally, Charlie reached up and cut the fuel flow to the rear engine and feathered the prop. The absence of the sound of that engine did nothing to reassure me that I was anywhere near the right place, or at the right time. There are very few things I can think of more unsettling than being 70 miles out over an ocean at night in an airplane with one of only two engines shut down—unless, perhaps, it's being in one of Charlie's airplanes nearing the coast of Cuba, knowing that the one remaining engine was most likely in the same condition as the rear one.

Finally, Charlie put the plane into a long and gentle left bank, and headed back to the north without saying a word. How far would we make it? Silently, we both sat transfixed with our eyes on the remaining engine gages as the temperature of the one good engine crept dangerously close to the red line. Scarcely breathing, I felt my hand unconsciously reaching for the starter and fuel flow switches of the now silent rear engine as my eyes scanned the blackness ahead for any sign of land.

With our airspeed reduced to ease the strain on the remaining engine, it was an hour before we began to see the dim glow of the lights of Pensacola and the coast. We were still miles away from safety, but I was never so relieved to see anything in my life. With jangled nerves, we finally reached a safe approach distance and began our drop to a lower altitude. Charlie eased back the power on the front engine and carefully started the rear engine, nursing it gently back to life. Prayerfully, we dropped to the surface and made our way over the black waters to the precious coastline ahead.

Early the next morning, I had my things packed and my van gassed up for the trip home. I reassured Charlie that it wasn't anything personal, and said I was sure he would be back in action in no time. With no small sense of disappointment at the loss of yet another opportunity to make some decent money, I nevertheless gratefully—even penitently—headed for the freeway and sanity.

A few months after my return from Florida, Bill contacted me with an urgent message from the Old Man. Plans to land a big load in New Mexico had fallen through, and he was desperate for another place to bring it in. A four-engine DC-6 cargo plane was ready and waiting in Colombia with a load of marijuana, but no one knew of an alternate landing site for such a large plane. The Old Man knew that I had spent time with Charlie, and that he had experience with airstrips and large aircraft. But the Old Man and Charlie didn't trust each other. It was all part of the business they were in. Seeds of distrust were constantly planted to keep people from shifting loyalties. Now the Old Man hoped I could bring about an "understanding" between them.

Reluctantly, I flew to Miami and met with Michael at the airport. It was the first time I saw him without his older brother around.

"He's in Colombia," Michael said. "We've had the plane sitting on the strip there for two weeks, and it's getting very hot...and I don't mean the climate. If we don't do something soon, we'll lose everything."

"What do you want me to do?"

"You know this 'Charlie' character very well?"

"Yes, you know I do. I told you both I was going to work with him that night when I gave you your money back."

"Oh, yes...the money. About that money. You were short about eight thousand dollars."

"What do you mean, 'short'?"

"Short. As in unpaid. That was money to buy planes and equipment, and to pay people to work with us. It wasn't for personal expenses."

"It wasn't *personal* expenses.' Those were business expenses. Everything was documented with receipts."

"I don't care about receipts. Anybody can get phony receipts. I only care about the money we gave you in good faith to get a job done, and you didn't do it. Now we want our money back, or our money's worth."

"Money's worth? How do you figure to get your money's worth at this point? I thought I made it clear to you that I don't have enough experience to be of much use to you." I was growing very uneasy with the direction this was going.

"You have a few assets we can use."

"Really...like what?"

"An airstrip. Charlie knows airstrips up there, and we need one badly."

"And you want me to get him to let you use one?"

"Yes, of course. He'll be well-paid."

"So why don't you ask him yourself? Your brother introduced him to me."

"Because he works for a friend of ours who says he thinks Charlie ripped him off a couple of times. We don't know what to believe, but until we know for sure if he did or didn't, we can't work with him."

"But you can use his airstrips. Does that make sense?"

"When you've got a DC-6 sitting on an airstrip in a jungle in Colombia, full of very expensive merchandise, you work with whatever and whoever gets the job done. We can trust him to arrange that. We just can't work with him if he's a rip-off."

"Why don't you ask him about that? See what he says. I can arrange that for you. I don't believe he's a rip-off, anyway. He might be a little slow and simple, but I think I know him well enough by now to know he's no rip-off."

"Maybe that's true. Maybe his boss just wants to keep us from taking him away. He's too small for us, anyway. His loads wouldn't pay our rent for one month. But I would like to talk with him. Can you get him down here to meet with me?"

"I'll fly up there tomorrow. If I can get him to meet with you, will that satisfy my 'debt,' as you're calling it?"

"Almost. If he gets us the strip. But there's one more thing. My brother wants you to be at the site when the plane comes in. He doesn't know Charlie's people.

You do. And they know you. They might be easier to deal with if they see someone there they know. It'll help with Bill's people from New Mexico, too. They'll be catching for us, along with some people from Texas. We don't know all those guys, but you do. And they know you."

"That's asking a lot. As I said before, those were all legitimate expenses. If I do this, I'll do it because your brother treated me decent, and so did Charlie. I think he's getting a bum rap from his boss, and I think I can help straighten it out. But I'm not wild about being involved in the landing. I'm not experienced with that sort of thing."

"You won't have to do anything but watch. Just be eyes and ears for us. My brother trusts you. What you tell him, he believes. He said to tell you that he'll take good care of you. And the debt with us will be clear."

"I told you. There IS no debt."

"*I* think there is. And make no mistake about this: You may think my brother will watch out for you, but *I* manage the day-to-day business. What I say about most things goes. There are men who work for me that don't even know my brother. They won't be checking out my instructions with him, I'll guarantee you that. You get my drift?"

"Yeah, I get it. I wondered if you would play that card."

"With you, I can almost promise you I will. You're even more a liability to us now than you were when you were with us. We don't know where you are, or who you're talking to. But, like I said, my brother likes you, and I think in some ways you're okay, too. I can't quite put my finger on it, but there's something about you I'm not comfortable with. But if you do this for us, I'll feel a whole lot better."

I flew to Tallahassee the next day, and drove to Charlie's house. When I told him the situation, he fairly jumped at the chance to play a part in the operation. He didn't want to work directly for them, but he could provide an airstrip. He knew of several no one had used in a long time. We got into one of his airplanes and flew back to Miami to meet with Michael. It actually made it all the way with no trouble.

In short order, Charlie was able to convince Michael that what his boss had been saying was untrue. It was, in fact, a ruse intended to keep the competition from stealing his people. Once the air was cleared, a deal was made and a full-scale operation swung into action with a fervor that was unreal.

As Michael had said, the load had been paid for, the pilots had been paid and protection was costing them a small fortune every day. The plane had been sitting on a remote strip in Colombia for two weeks, increasingly vulnerable to bandits or to the Colombian army—often one and the same. With each passing day, the threat increased of information leaking out that could sabotage the entire operation. Time was running out fast, and well over five *million* dollars hung in the balance.

Once an agreement was reached, Charlie located a suitable landing strip and assembled a group of everyone he had ever worked with to act as off-loaders. Wives and teenagers, and a crew of experienced off-loaders made their plans for the "catch," and a fuel truck and its crew came in from Georgia. Bill and his group from New Mexico arrived a few days later, and the group from Texas arrived to transport the load. Plans were for the entire load to go to Texas, where it would be sorted, weighed and divided. Half would stay in Texas, while Bill and his group would take the other half to New Mexico, then on to California.

My part in all of this, according to Michael, was merely to act as one of the lookouts. It was made clear to me again later by the Old Man that the other reason for my being there was to be the intermediary between all of the groups, and to report what I saw and heard. He never mentioned anything about the "debt," and I wondered just whose idea that really was.

It was amazing to watch the entire operation unfold, knowing what I knew about each of them. So few of them knew anything about me, or trusted each other. It was ironic that I was perceived by almost everyone as the Old Man's personal emissary, yet I was probably the least experienced person in the entire operation.

Complicating the situation even further was the fact that later it was decided that Charlie, who ran the local operation, would have to go to Colombia to guide the pilots in. That left the whole operation without an experienced leader until he returned. As far as almost everyone knew at the time, I was *it*...if only by default.

Chapter Six

The Allianca Airlines jetliner banked sharply to the right to avoid one of the many thunderheads that were building north of Bogotá. The rainy season was at its peak, and Charlie wondered if that would give him any problems on his return trip the next night. He would be flying back in a vintage DC-6—a four-engine prop job that was probably older than he was. But he had flown many of them, and he knew he could get it back to the states with his eyes blindfolded if he had to. Trouble was, he wouldn't be the pilot on this one. Not even the *co-pilot*. His job was to sit in the jump seat and guide the pilots to a remote strip in northern Florida that only he knew about. He would be a *navigator* on a plane he could fly in his sleep. That would be a novel experience for him.

He looked around the plush interior of the modern jetliner, took a swallow of his third Bloody Mary and closed his eyes. The last time he had entered Colombia, things were a whole lot different. He could hardly believe that he was actually coming back again after so many years. He felt a deep uneasiness as he recalled that trip into hell.

It was five years ago...or was it six, now? Didn't matter, really. Could have been twelve, for all that had happened since then. He hated to even think about it again. The mere sight of the lights of Bogotá was enough to cause him to break out in a cold sweat. That was where that slime hole of a prison was, where he had spent two miserable, godforsaken years.

For three years he had worked faithfully for the Greek—flying here, flying there—always at his beck and call at a moment's notice. He was always off on some crazy scheme for a man who seemed to care little what Charlie felt or needed. He had been well-paid, of course, which enabled him to buy a nice home in Florida, but it was hell not having a real life with his family. Eventually, he managed to save enough money to buy his own cargo airplane—an aging DC-4 that was capable of putting him on easy street, once and for all.

The Greek had gone along with it, as long as Charlie gave him first choice on all of his loads. The Greek figured Charlie would either pull it off or he would never hear from him again. Either way was okay. There were plenty of pilots around, every one of them claiming to be the greatest one that ever flew, and promising to do Charlie's work for half the price.

It had been a good business for the Greek. He had good connections and had learned the hard way whom he could trust and what losses he could sustain. Pilots were stupid, as far as he was concerned. They might be clever in some ways, which made them appear smart, but most of them were very naive and lacked common street sense. They were also swaggering drunks, most of them, and from his experience, a bunch of overgrown boys full of pride and a weakness for women.

Charlie was different. He was trustworthy and predictable, in spite of occasional problems. Charlie may have had his shortcomings, but lying and cavorting with women weren't among them. Neither was snitching. He had been busted twice for flying Quaaludes out of Nicaragua, but never said a thing. It had cost him a few years and had put a severe strain on his family relationships, but Charlie had withstood the rigors. Simple and plodding in some ways, but reliable to the max, Charlie was a stand-up guy, and had proven it several times.

Lightning flashed outside the airliner's window, startling Charlie back to the present. The night sky was dark, but in the flash of lightning he could see massive thunderheads that were even darker. It had been just like that the night he was forced back with that load, nursing four sputtering engines. God, what a night. As long as he lived, he would never forget that night.

Three years of flying that broken-down Skymaster back and forth over Cuba had aged him ten years. He was tired of working for someone else for what he considered chump-change. He had flown worse planes before, but couldn't remember when. He could land that Skymaster on a dime, though, and fly with one engine if he had to. Twice, he'd had to. All those trips made him enough money, however, not only to buy the DC-4, but also a big enough load of Colombian pot to put him in business for himself. The Greek wisely advanced him enough on the trip to pay for protection on the ground. But in all of his hurried planning, he had neglected to take precautions with the fuel.

Claiming to be ferrying the plane to a buyer in Argentina, he flew the tired old bird down the eastern coast of Mexico, then diverted to his pick-up point in Colombia. With only a few hours of protection paid for on the ground, disorientation and a late arrival gave him scant minutes for the loading. Before he had even had a chance to stretch his legs, he was off again and headed for the States.

Two hundred miles out over the Gulf of Mexico, Charlie lost the number one engine. He had replaced all the fuel lines, pumps and filters on the plane, so he knew the trouble wasn't in there. He purged the lines, brought up the fuel pressure and nursed the engine back to life. Ten minutes later, the number three engine quit.

Contaminated fuel! Even if he'd had the time to check their fuel, he had forgotten to bring his own pumps and filters. How could he have been so stupid, after all his years in the business?

"Please, God—don't let this get worse," he prayed. Again, he purged the line and brought the engine back to life. Then number two sputtered, caught, sputtered again, then quit. Then number one. His heart pounded and sweat broke out as he feverishly struggled to keep the engines running.

This couldn't be happening. There was too much at stake. The plane had cost him a hundred grand, and the load and protection about the same. He couldn't go back to Colombia, but he wasn't even a quarter of the way to the States, yet. Far below in all directions, there was nothing but ocean.

Engines number three and one were barely running, with number two showing some promise. Then number four quit. He purged the line again, but realized that if it was this bad already, it would likely get worse before it got better. Already he had lost a thousand feet of altitude. Even if he could keep purging lines and restarting engines the entire twelve-hour trip, which was virtually impossible, he would never be able to pull off the precision landing he would need to make on that tiny airstrip. Too much was going on. The engines were dropping off at an increasing rate, and keeping all of them on line seemed less and less likely.

With extreme heaviness of heart, Charlie banked the old bird into a left one-eighty just as one and two both quit. As he purged line after line, he fought to keep at least two engines running at once. Meanwhile, his Colombian helper kicked heavy bales of marijuana out of the crippled plane into the darkening ocean far below. Up ahead, ominous black thunderheads rose like angry demons, ready to smite the impudent Gringo from their skies.

Sweat dripped from his armpits and brow as he fought the controls while straining to make out the coastline far ahead. Luckily there was enough moonlight by which to see the beaches, if those thunderheads just stayed back from the coast a bit. It was a frantic race he couldn't afford to lose. There would be no search parties, no hope for rescue—not even a written note left behind for his family. He was off on a "business trip" to Miami as far as they knew. No one would ever know, save for the monkeys and the snakes of the thick Colombian rain forest ahead, or the sharks down below. He *had* to make the beach, or he would never live to tell anyone about it. All was lost by that point, but at least he could go back to work for the Greek. God, what a humbling thought.

Finally, number three and number one engines quit altogether. No amount of purging or adjusting fuel pressure or manual restarting would bring them back. He was sure he had at least a hundred miles to go, with not a sign of land anywhere. With two engines gone, his airspeed dropped dangerously low as he fought to hold altitude. Fearing imminent loss of the remaining engines, he sacrificed altitude for the airspeed he needed to make it to land. Keeping the exact right combination of airspeed and altitude during what was little more than a controlled glide was maddening to him, especially since he had no idea how far he had yet to go.

Several times he lost the moon to increasing storm clouds as he neared the coast. In the flashes of lightning he could make out towering black thunderheads that had to be 20,000 ft. or more. Finally he began to make out the faintest hint of a few flickering lights far ahead. He wasn't sure if they were campfires of native villages or an illusion, but to him at the moment he hoped they were an answer to his prayers.

Just then, number four quit for the last time. Now he might not make the beach, but at least he could get close if number two would just hold together a little longer. In the fleeting glimpses of moonlight between the thunderheads and the flashes of lightning all around him, he could make out a long, fairly straight beach up ahead. It looked close, yet he knew he could never swim that far if he had to ditch right now. That beach was at least fifteen miles away.

As he lowered the flaps and began his descent, the moon disappeared behind monstrous black clouds. Now he had to guess where the beach might be. Rain began hitting the windshield, lightly at first then in a torrent. This must be it, he thought. What a dismal end to an otherwise exciting life. He was going down with his ship.

But he had been through too much to give up now. By God, he was a *survivor.* He'd not go easily. He straightened in his seat and took a deep breath. Imagining where he was in proximity to the beach, he set up for the approach just as if he were in a crosswind headed for the runway. He had to guess how fast he was traveling over the surface. But he knew how to *fly,* goddamn it. He was not going to crash in some godforsaken jungle, or in the drink. He'd get out of this yet.

He descended carefully another few hundred feet and gradually banked right to begin a parallel course to where he imagined the beach would be. Then he set up a steady rate of descent as if on glide path for the runway, and carefully set the one remaining propeller for landing. He adjusted the fuel mixture with the care of a surgeon.

Just then, multiple flashes of lightning startled the sky from end to end. Right ahead of him was the beach. He was about to overshoot it. Lowering the flaps full down and cutting power to the one remaining engine, he banked the plane away from the beach and stepped on the opposite rudder pedal. In a severe side-slip, he dropped the big plane the remaining few hundred feet to the shallow waters of the Colombian coast. With a blinding flash, the plane smashed into the churning waters and skipped like a giant stone across a mile of blackened waters until it reached its ignominious end, hissing and bubbling as it sank in ten feet of water. Charlie and his Colombian helper swam the few hundred yards to the beach in pouring rain, and crawled like survivors of a shipwreck into the jungle.

The rest of the story Charlie hated the most. Arrested the next day by the same federales he had paid to protect his departure, he was hauled off to prison for "entering the country without a visa"—a crime in Colombia for which the penalties back then exceeded those for drug trafficking. Charlie spoke no Spanish, despite his many forays into Central and South America. In the succeeding months while he was in prison, he learned to read and write Spanish until he was able to convince a local attorney of a technicality in Colombian law that eventually got him out.

Lightning flashed again outside the modern jetliner, jolting Charlie back to the present. The plane banked sharply and began its descent into the brightly lit city below. It was hard to believe he was actually coming back to Bogotá.

It was good to see a familiar face at the airport. Heavy rain fell against the windshield of the old pickup as Pedro drove through the back streets and out to the highway north of the city. Charlie had met Pedro once in Miami when he had flown the Greek down to meet with Pedro's bosses. His bosses were the two Greek brothers he had heard so much about. One night, over several margaritas, Pedro told Charlie about some of their exploits. The brothers, evidently, ran an operation that made Charlie's boss look like an amateur.

For his part in this trip, Charlie would have a piece of the load, but by special arrangement between the three Greeks, he had to agree to sell it to his boss at a prearranged price. Once again he would be riding in the cockpit of a plane big enough to carry a cargo that, even with his minor share, would make up for everything he lost on that harrowing flight so long ago. Except, of course, for the damage to his marriage.

His wife had stayed with him in spite of the hardships he had put her through, but it was never the same after that. She was outwardly pleasant to him and respectful in her southern manner, but there was a hardness to her now that he hadn't experienced before. He really couldn't blame her. He hadn't written to her in all that time he was in the Colombian prison. But she took him back and helped him get on his feet. He admired her for that, and begrudged her nothing in her increasing need to spend the money he made. He guessed she was probably stashing it away for the future, even if it might be just for her. Given his history, he never questioned her about it.

Pedro was quiet and likeable. They exchanged pleasantries, but Pedro's loyalty to his bosses was clear. There were no margaritas to loosen his tongue that night, so nothing about the plane, the load or where they were going was mentioned. Hours later, the rain began to let up as Pedro made his way from one narrow, unpaved road to another, each one more primitive than the one before. From his time there nearly six years before, Charlie could feel more than see the thick blackness of the Colombian rain forest all around them.

After bumping along on the last and roughest road, they pulled into a clearing where there were several large buildings and a well-kept but very muddy, sod airstrip. In the flash of the pickup's headlights, Charlie saw the plane sitting in the dark, quietly awaiting her mission like a World War II bomber at the ready.

He had forgotten how big they were, these relics of the glory days of propeller driven airliners. How sad yet beautiful the old girl was. He tried to imagine how she might have been when she was in her prime. His father's generation had grown up with planes like her. More than any other plane since the war, DC-6's and 7's had brought the world to America. Now she sat in the mud and the rain of a Colombian jungle, a forlorn, aging queen of the skies somberly awaiting an uncertain fate hauling a load of marijuana to a remote airstrip in northern Florida.

Inside one of the smaller buildings Charlie met the pilots, both Costa Rican. After a lively discussion, they quickly laid to rest Charlie's concerns about the capabilities of Third-World pilots. Within the first few minutes, it was obvious that not only could they fly the plane, but also they knew enough to check the fuel *before* it went into the plane. Professional pilots, they were even wearing their flight uniforms as if they were on an overnight layover.

The night passed uneventfully and by morning the rains had abated. But Charlie knew time was running out. Clouds were building again, and even the Greeks couldn't keep protection indefinitely. Two hours before take-off time, a light, steady rain began to beat on the roof of the bunkhouse where he was waiting. The load had been on board the plane so long that even with the tightly wrapped bales, the fumes from the pot would be stifling. A hasty meeting was called among the pilots and the ground crew. A decision had to be made. They would take off—rain or no rain.

As he climbed on board, Charlie was nearly overcome by the pungent odor filling the cargo bay. Images of identical bales kicked out over the Gulf all those years ago swam in his head as a twinge of nausea gripped his insides. He strapped himself in behind the pilots, content to check fuel and engine gages as the pilots brought the engines to life, one by one. "Dejá vu," he mumbled, his eyes riveted on the fuel flow meters.

Pulling the giant bird out of the muddy grass where it had sat through torrential summer monsoons was not easy. The roar of the engines as they strained to free the plane was deafening. Suddenly it broke loose and lurched forward, catching both pilots by surprise. The captain cut power to the starboard engines, while both pilots stepped on the right pedal and brakes with all their might. The huge plane swung to the right, its wingtip missing the large building by inches. But the forward momentum plus the power of the port engines was too much. Throttles back to idle, both pilots fought to keep the huge plane on the narrow road and moving toward the strip. As they did, it skidded across the muddy surface of the hard-packed road, slipped over the edge and sank in several feet of thick, brown ooze.

No amount of the pilots' working the thrust levers and the rudder pedals could free the plane from the mire. Charlie was uncertain if even he could have handled it any better. It would take more than engine power to pull the plane out now. The pilots shut down the engines and told him to wait for them to get it out.

Back in the bunkhouse, Charlie realized that once again he had taken off without divulging his purpose to his wife. He was on another "business trip" to Miami, with no hint to anyone but his unloading crew where he was really going. At least his son was by then a seasoned member of his crew, and could break the news to her if things got worse. He pushed thoughts of his last trip to Colombia from his mind, and allowed himself to drift off for a much-needed sleep.

He awoke suddenly to the muffled sound of gunfire in the distance. There was no mistaking the sound of M-1 military rifles—the predominant weapon of the Colombian army. Charlie had heard that sound before, and knew it well from his time in the U.S. Army. Somewhere out there, a skirmish was going on, punctuated with the rapid fire of a couple of semi-automatic, low caliber pistols. He sat up and listened for indications they might be moving in his direction.

"Not now," he pleaded. "Not again." He couldn't handle another stint in that prison.

The gunfire dwindled to a few shots here and there, but was definitely getting louder and moving closer now. He grabbed his flight bag and a small survival kit he had brought with him this time, and headed for the door. Opening it, he froze in his tracks. Before him was a company of Colombian soldiers with rifles aimed at the two pilots, Pedro and a couple of helpers, their hands over their heads. Ten feet from the door, an Army officer stood pointing his .45 caliber sidearm at Charlie.

"Buenos Dias," smiled the mustachioed commandante. "Eet seems 'jou are een a leetle beet of trobble, Señor. No?"

Laughter erupted in the ranks of the ragtag soldiers as the officer waved his pistol at Charlie, signaling him to join the others.

Back in Bogotá the next morning, a burly, unshaven Army colonel received a call from his boss, a political appointee that didn't know a rifle from a squirt gun. The colonel hated the man, but could do nothing to him. He was a cousin of the President, and never let anyone forget it. Someday though, the colonel would find a way to get rid of the pest. The little snake had cost him dearly, and was the biggest pain in the ass he'd ever had to deal with.

According to the man, a flight crew from Costa Rica had been "forced down by bad weather and a faulty engine" at a remote strip near Cali. A contingent of the colonel's men had "forced themselves upon the unsuspecting crew." No mention was made of the cargo, other than the fact that it wasn't to be interfered with.

The colonel knew the pattern well enough. At least he was high enough in rank and influence to be well paid for going along with the high command's orders. As long as they let him confiscate an occasional load for himself, the colonel was content to go along with the routine.

He wondered how much this one had cost the owners, as he picked up the phone and ordered the release of the crew and the cargo. On top of that, he was instructed to provide heavy equipment to pull the plane out of the mud.

Back in the plane the next morning, Charlie was relieved to see the sun again so soon. If these Greek brothers could pull that off in such a short time, then they were certainly people to be reckoned with. They could be either the best thing or the worst thing that had ever happened to him. It was too late to think about that now anyway, given how far into this operation he had already come.

The engines roared as the pilots pulled onto the narrow strip and signaled the tractor operator to move away. Lowering the flaps for takeoff, the pilots advanced the throttle levers and the heavy bird lumbered down the narrow runway. The fact that they were a day late in their plans caused Charlie to worry. No mention was made about what had happened up in Florida. They were supposed to have come in around midnight the night before…not tonight. He wondered what had been done to re-arrange things, as the huge plane lifted off from the mud and grass of the airstrip and banked sharply to avoid the steep hills beyond. A few thousand more feet up, and they would be able to make out the blue waters of the Gulf of Mexico.

At least the engines were running smoothly and the fuel flow meters indicated everything was as it should be. The sun glinted brightly off the metallic surface of the aging airliner-turned-cargo plane, as storms of a different kind were building far to the north.

Chapter Seven

The night air was heavy with the musty odors of the surrounding swamp. In the dim light of the moon I could barely make out the eerie shapes of the Spanish moss hanging from the branches of the nearby trees. Directly in front of the bushes where I was hiding was the edge of an airstrip long abandoned and overgrown with weeds and thick foliage. Carved out of the marsh by Naval engineers decades ago, it was one of many such airstrips used to train student pilots for war in the South Pacific. Remote and long since unused, they were little known except to smugglers who found them ideal for their clandestine operations.

I glanced across the clearing to the west of me. With some difficulty I could make out the shapes of several large trucks hidden among the trees and bushes. In every part of the clearing, ears strained to hear the drone of engines from the plane that was approaching from somewhere out over the Gulf. The four-engine behemoth would soon drop out of the night sky and fill the tiny airstrip with its deafening roar, sending a crew of men and equipment into frenzied action.

Months of planning and forging back-up plans, orchestrating logistics in five countries, mis-starts and restarts, checking and double-checking every detail, and enough anxiety to last a lifetime were all about to be reduced to a few minutes on a remote landing strip right in front of me. My heart pounded so hard I could feel it against my sweat-soaked shirt. I kept imagining government agents lurking in the bushes, waiting for the right moment to pounce on us. The urge to walk—even run—from the madness was overpowering. Twice I had to grab a nearby tree to keep my body from rebelling and taking off on its own down the nearby road.

It was crazy to put myself through this for *any* amount of money. *What good is money,* I thought, *if I'm dead or in prison?* Suddenly the issue of staying alive was much more compelling than "making good" had been when I had first agreed to be a lookout for the Old Man. This was insanity, no matter how rational it may have seemed a few days earlier. Phone lines to the nearest houses had been cut. Our rental trucks had been seen moving about late that night and during the previous two days. Out at the truck stop on the freeway, an 18-wheel tractor/trailer waited to take the load west. Several of us were strangers to the area, and had drawn the attention of more than a few of the local people. Things like that didn't go unnoticed for long in those parts.

The events leading up to that moment had been nothing short of ludicrous. Only a few hours before, everything had nearly come crashing down around us. Sitting back against a tree, I wondered how we had managed to salvage anything from such a tangle of mishaps.

We had the eighteen-wheeler parked at the truck stop the previous two days, waiting for the signal to move it to the stash house—a deserted tobacco process-ing plant far from the main highway. It was miles down several different dirt roads, and situated in an ideal place for us to transfer the load from the smaller trucks to the bigger rig. The smaller trucks would off-load the plane and then the big rig could move about afterwards without drawing suspicion.

The building had high, concrete walls, and even a loading dock. Totally hidden from view in the pine trees on the backside of a small hill, the place was covered with moss, vines and overhanging branches from the trees around it. Once the rig was in and parked, we could take all the time we wanted to make the switch. We could even break the load down into smaller units and weigh them accurately. The Old Man would love that. The only problem was that no one had checked whether the rig could actually maneuver onto the narrow access road leading to the building, nor had they noticed the low-hanging power lines above the gate. The rig would have to make a tight, ninety-degree turn from an already narrow road through a gateway barely wider than a car. Too wary of being noticed in broad daylight, we had to wait for darkness to move the rig. When we did, the effort turned into a nightmare.

The driver had to maneuver the truck over a ditch and through the gate in such a way as to not disturb anything. Before he had made it even part way through, the top of his trailer snagged the telephone wire just below the power line. The two poles on either side of the truck were so rotten, they snapped like a couple of toothpicks, dropping both wires down between the cab and the trailer. The truck couldn't move forward or back until we figured out a way to lift both lines up out of harm's way. If we cut the wires, power in the area would go out and our cover would be blown.

We had to find a way to fix the two poles without tools and only a couple of flashlights, unsnag both the telephone wire and the electric wire without electrocuting ourselves, and get the rig up to the building—all without leaving any signs of having been there. Only two hours remained before we were due back at the rendezvous area.

We fought and struggled with those poles in the dark, and cussed and pried feverishly, trying to free the truck. The whole operation centered on that stash house. Twenty-some thousand pounds of pot had to be transferred from two rental trucks to the rig without being seen. If the rental trucks had aroused any suspicion, they would be hot and identifiable.

About that time, a car appeared on the road. It came up to us and very slowly made its way around us. From inside the car, four pairs of eyes stared at us and the 18-wheeler stuck halfway in a turn onto a narrow road long overgrown from lack of use. Two snapped power poles dangled from power lines hung up on a rig that belonged out on the freeway ten miles away, and a crew of very seedy-looking guys stood among the bushes looking like they had something to hide.

It was all over. There was no way those people weren't going to call the police the second they got home. The car continued slowly down the road, all eyes staring back at us in astonishment. With a final, desperate tug on both poles, the four of us managed to lift the wires high enough to free the rig to back onto the road. With no way to turn around, we had to drive in the same direction as the car was traveling. Behind us, the two wires were left sagging a few feet from the ground. I was driving a sedan just ahead of the truck. When the locals finally turned into a driveway I pulled up behind them, got out and attempted to talk with them. My effort to convince them we were lost and had only been trying to turn around was a feeble one at best, evidenced by the way they stayed in the car staring out at me with the windows rolled up tight and the doors locked. We were in big trouble, and getting more so by the minute.

In the meantime, at a rest area along the freeway a few miles to the north of us, two of the crew waited for us with the two rental trucks. One was loaded with watermelons bought earlier in the day, intended to be loaded in the back of the 18-wheeler as a cover for the load of pot. When we didn't show up, they decided to unload the watermelons and hide them in the bushes so their trucks could be used at the strip. They parked the two trucks in an area away from the main parking lot where pine trees around the buildings partially hid them from view. Working feverishly to unload the watermelons, they didn't notice they had attracted the attention of a couple of cattle truckers who had pulled up on the other side of the trees.

When I arrived in the sedan, I saw the truckers squatting down at the edge of the trees, watching. Something from my military past took hold of me as I mustered as forceful a tone as my nerves could handle.

"What are you guys doing?" I demanded in a firm half-whisper.

"Look at these guys," the older one said. "They're up to somethin' mighty strange over there. 'Bin watchin' 'em for ten, maybe fifteen minutes, now. Can't make out what they're doin', but I betch yer ass it's drugs. Lots a' that shit goin' on 'roun here, ya know."

"Yeah, I know," I said. "My partner and I have been on these guys for three weeks now. This looks like the night we finally get some action."

"You the *law?*" They both looked at me skeptically.

"No, man," I sneered. "I'm doing the fuckin' evening news. Now, you guys get in your rigs and get on down the road before you blow our cover. My partner's on the other side over there, and he's real nervous right now. These two guys are mean and desperate, and they won't give up easy."

"You shittin' me, man?"

"Look.—you stick around here, you're *gonna* be shittin'. These guys are Colombian drug runners, and they're *armed*. I don't want the responsibility for anyone getting killed. I'm calling some backup, and when I get back I want to see those exhaust stacks smoking. Now, get the hell out of here."

I did a low duck walk back to my car, reached in the window for the CB mike and muttered something official-sounding. That was all it took. The two of them went for their rigs at a pace just under a sprint, climbed in and hauled ass. As soon as they disappeared around the bend in the freeway, I hurried over to the drivers of the rental trucks.

"Jesus Christ, you guys, why don't you be a little more suspicious?"

"Fuck you, man. Where the hell have you been?" came the hostile reply. "What *else* are we supposed to do with this shit? You didn't show up, and we need the room for the load."

"They're just *watermelons*. Why not take 'em up to the truck stop? Nothing wrong with moving watermelons around. You just scared the shit out of two truck drivers who are right now probably looking for the nearest pay phone to call the cops."

"How do *you* know?"

"I pulled up right over there and saw two truckers squatting in the trees, watching you. I went up to them like I was somebody official, and they told me right off that you were some kind of drug runners. Shit, you might as well advertise."

"Well, stashing a bunch of stinking watermelons in the middle of the night felt a little weird to us, so we figured we'd better try to do it out of sight. Besides, we were supposed to meet you guys here. Where's everybody else, anyway? Did you get the rig set up okay?"

"No. We got it stuck at the entrance to the stash house. Some locals came up on us while we were there, then split. We had to clear out."

"The rig's still there?"

"No. We got it out, and it's on its way back to the truck stop."

"What the hell are we gonna do now?"

"We'll just have to use that other place…the wide spot just beyond the airstrip with all those trees around it."

"Shit. That means we'll have to handle the load *twice* in the same night. You know how much those bales weigh?"

He didn't know that I didn't know.

"We better get the hell out of here," I said, "or we're going to be explaining these watermelons to some very suspicious sheriff's deputies."

"Like where?"

"The truck stop. Park one truck at the back of the motel in town and take the other one out to the truck stop. That way, we'll be able to get the signal to all of you at the same time. You won't stand out so much there. I wouldn't recommend hanging out together, or leaving at the same time, though."

"I think we could have figured that out ourselves," he half-sneered.

"Just the same, it never hurts to cover the details," I reminded him as I got in the car and backed out.

I pulled out of the rest area and drove down to the next freeway exit, fighting back an overwhelming urge to keep going. If my boys hadn't been back at the house, I might have. As I stopped at the end of the exit ramp and began my left turn to cross under the freeway and head back in the eastbound lane, I spotted the two cattle trucks parked at a roadside cafe. Right behind them was a sheriff's patrol car.

"*Please* don't let them see me," I prayed as I made the turn. Very cautiously, I turned left again onto the eastbound entrance ramp; both eyes riveted on the rearview mirror.

It was now nearly three A.M, and we had been waiting at the strip nearly four hours. Near a mobile home just beyond the trees, a single yard light showed no activity that would indicate aroused suspicions. In a distant peanut field, the sound of diesel motors driving irrigation equipment around in circles kept sending us false signals as the sound of the motors faded then returned, hour after hour.

Along the edges of the runway, old kerosene smudgepots were lined up as backups to the two reels of electric lights ready to be rolled out along each side of the runway at the proper signal. I could barely make out the shape of the fuel truck waiting at the end of the runway to pump gas into the fuel-starved monster that would soon be upon us.

I couldn't shake the feeling that someone was on to us. I hoped that if they were, they hadn't seen me standing there alone in the dark. When they went after the plane, maybe I could take off in the other direction. It was a tough situation for me either way. If I didn't show up at the plane when it landed, it wouldn't look good to the rest of the crew. On the other hand, if there was going to be a bust, that's where it would happen.

What could I do? I couldn't leave, that was certain. The sedan I had been driving belonged to one of the crew. We were twenty miles from the nearest town, in a place where strangers didn't go strolling down remote roads in the middle of the night. I searched frantically for answers. How would I handle walking away from this? How would the Old Man deal with it?

Movement in the bushes across the airstrip startled me until I was able to recognize one of the off-loading crew taking a leak. I looked at my watch in the waning moonlight. If something was going to happen, it had to be soon or we'd be too damn close to daylight. I stretched and laid back against the tree again. I had to calm my nerves.

What the hell was I *doing?* Did I really think I could hold my own with these guys? They knew what a beginner I was. They knew what kind of liability I might become to them eventually. I even told them so myself. Michael left no doubt in my mind that he knew, and that he would most certainly eliminate any perceived threat to the operation.

It was different with the Old Man. He treated me like a grandson, always smiling warmly when I talked to him and always making sure I was okay. Maybe that was just his style. He once showed me the scars in his chest from bullet wounds I assumed he got in some revolutionary war. It was entirely possible, given his thirst for adventure and the number of languages he spoke. Sitting at his kitchen table once, I heard him speak four different languages on the telephone in less than an hour.

Later on I had learned a little more about his relationship with the wealthy international financier he had told me about, and his connections in the White House. The yacht he had captained was the flagship of the financier's fleet, and had once been stopped and boarded by the U.S. Coast Guard. Acting on a tip, they inspected every hold and discovered tons of marijuana on board. Captained at that point by a subordinate of his, the yacht was immediately confiscated and towed to the Coast Guard station in Ft. Lauderdale. The ship was placed under heavy guard by agents for U.S. Customs, the Drug Enforcement Agency and the Coast Guard itself. Undaunted, the Old Man conceived a plan to get it back.

Very early one Sunday morning shortly after the confiscation, the federal agents guarding the yacht were alerted by a tip-off to a large drug shipment about to arrive at a nearby airport. Shortly afterward, the Old Man showed up at the Coast Guard Station with a crew of his men dressed in Federal Police uniforms. With forged documents in hand, the Old Man convinced the sleepy-eyed contingent of unsuspecting Coast Guardsmen left to guard the ship that he was under orders to transfer the ship to another location. In a bold move that later became the substance of a major motion picture, the Old Man brazenly sailed away with a $26-million, ocean-going yacht…with the drugs still on board.

The Old Man, whose former boss was now "persona-non-grata" as a federal fugitive, parlayed that heist into a fleet of cargo freighters, a ship-salvaging business and homes and businesses in seven different countries. The ship-salvaging business was located on a remote island deep in the Caribbean, giving him unlimited possibilities for registration and movement of ships and planes coming and going between Colombia and the United States.

Over a period of seven years, he and his brother were responsible for shipping well over 500,000 pounds of marijuana into the United States and Canada, at a total *wholesale* value of more than $125,000,000. And that was only what was proven in later trials.

Suddenly the porch light came on over the front door of the mobile home. A moment later, the door opened and a lanky, grizzled-looking farmer stepped out, stretched, and walked over to his ancient pick-up. The tired old engine sputtered and choked as the starter spun wildly, then finally caught and brought the motor to life. After a few minutes, the truck moved forward, turned, and headed in our direction.

Everyone hit the dirt and crawled for cover. Pulling onto the strip, the farmer drove toward the other end like it was his own personal driveway. In a minute, he would see the fuel truck and unloading trucks parked at the other end.

As he reached mid-point of the strip, he suddenly slowed down, then stopped. He got out of the truck and walked over to one of the smudge pots. Nudging it warily with his boot, he straightened and peered carefully around the perimeter of the clearing with the look of someone who knew he was being watched. He climbed back into his truck and cautiously made his way further down the strip until his headlights fell on the fuel truck. He stopped, hesitated, then backed up slowly like a man facing a coiled rattler. At the midpoint of the strip, he spun around quickly and took off with tires squealing. At my end of the strip, he hit the dirt and careened across his yard and out onto the highway, red taillights disappearing fast in the billowing dust.

A small group began to form around the fuel truck. A decision had to be made, and it was a tough one. In a very short time, lawmen of every kind would descend on the area like an invading army. But somewhere up there in the blackness of night the plane was approaching with no place to go but right where we were standing. If we left, we would be abandoning them to fly right into the hands of the police. Still, we couldn't stay and risk losing everything, with everyone going to jail on top of it all.

The decision was made. All ears strained for the sounds of airplane engines overhead as the trucks pulled out one by one and scattered in all directions.

None of us could hang around town long. Agents and lawmen of every type were certain to comb the countryside for suspects. Half the crew booked immediate flights to anywhere, and the rest faded away into the backcountry from where they had come. In motels and homes from Tallahassee to Pensacola, tired and anxious men crawled into bed for a restless morning's sleep, exhausted from the night's fiasco.

Dawn came quickly, and I had a difficult phone call to make. After considerable struggle to figure out what to say, I found a pay phone I hadn't used yet and dialed the number. The Old Man's voice was distinct as always, but strained. I had only begun to tell him what had happened when he bluntly interrupted me.

"The plane got stuck in the mud in Colombia, and the whole crew was arrested," he said. "We had to get the crew out of jail, and the plane out of the mud—*after* we paid for the same merchandise all over again."

"You got them out?" I was incredulous.

"Yes, *and* had to buy the plane back," he replied rather tersely.

"So what now? Where's the plane?" I asked in suspense.

"It's on its way," answered the voice.

"What do you mean, 'on its way'? Where do they plan to land?"

"Where else?" he snapped back. "Where we arranged for it to land."

"*What?*" I couldn't believe my ears. "Do you realize what they'll be flyin
into? There'll be cops all over the place! We've stirred up a hornet's nest. They'r
not going to just go away. They'll know we didn't get the load, and they'll b
waiting for us to make a move."

"You'll just have to figure something out," he said. "We've got three time
our original investment tied up in this thing. We're not going to blow it off nov
Besides, Vinnie will be there soon. He'll be at that motel you told us about. H
knows what to do. You just do what you can to keep the crew together anothe
day."

"This is crazy," I said. "Half the crew's already gone. How much time do w
have?"

"They took off an hour ago, so with their fuel stop you'll have until aroun
midnight tonight to get into position."

"*Damn!* You don't know what you're asking."

"Yes, I do. We've been in worse situations before."

I couldn't imagine anything worse.

"Trust Vinnie. He knows what to do. And have him call me when you'v
come up with a plan. You know the number to use."

I held the receiver in my hand for a while, staring blankly at the mouthpiec
I couldn't believe what I had just heard. Moreover, I couldn't believe I was stand
ing there even thinking about going ahead with it while most of our best men wer
already gone.

What about those guys in the plane, though? We couldn't let them fly into
trap. Shortly after I got back to the house, Vinnie called.

"Hey, man," Vinnie's Bronx/Italian voice was distinct but smooth. "What'
goin' down?"

"Don't you know?"

"Yeah, Babe. It's a little sticky, eh?"

"We better meet pretty quick," I pressed him.

"Okay. I should be at the motel in an hour."

"That's a luxury right now. We haven't got a lot of time."

"Don' worry. We'll get it all straightened out. We've got plenty of time."

The meeting was held at the home of the aircraft mechanic who was the self-appointed leader of the local group until Charlie returned in the plane. Around the room sat the most unusual assortment of people likely to be planning an operation of this magnitude. The mechanic, me, two housewives, three teenagers, a few local men, a couple of cowboys from New Mexico and a three-hundred pound Italian from the Bronx, with heavy gold chains adorning his barrel chest and hairy wrists bulging out of a $300 silk shirt.

"The problem we have here," Vinnie went right to the point, "is one of favorable advantage to us. The odds are on our side."

On *our* side? What incredible bullshit was he about to lay on us?

"You see," he went on, "the authorities think they've got it all figured out. But unless someone in this room is working for them, and tips them off, they don't have a clue who we are, where we're going to be, or even if anything's going to happen now. They're in the dark. The element of surprise is on our side. Anything we do to disrupt their thinking will give us the advantage. They'll be so tensed up and ready for action that when anything happens that looks obvious to them, they'll jump on it with everything and everyone they've got."

"So, what does all that mean?" someone voiced the question in almost everyone's mind.

"It means that we can divert their attention very easily, and go in for the catch at just the right time."

"And just how do we do that?" someone else asked.

"The cops don't know how many people we've got, or who's in with us. You've got two other guys from New Mexico still hanging around out at the truck stop, right?

"Yeah," one of the men from New Mexico spoke up. "But they're getting real shaky. They think they've been spotted, and are being watched. They didn't care too much for being told to stay put."

"That's perfect," Vinnie smiled. "They can keep waiting out there until close to the plane's arrival time—the more nervous-looking, the better. At the right signal, they jump in their pickup trucks and haul ass out to some other airstrip in the opposite direction from where we'll be. If what you say is true, they'll attract the attention of every lawman on the prowl. They probably have already, so be extremely careful how you approach them."

"So far, we've only talked with them on the phone," the aircraft mechanic spoke up, now showing a bit more confidence. "We know better at this poin They showed up here looking like a couple of 'Marlboro Men'."

Nervous laughter broke out, which seemed to ease the tension in the room little.

"Fine," Vinnie went on, now intentionally directing his words to the mechanic "This is a known fact. It's *proven*—over and over again. Law enforcement peopl are hungry for action. They've been trained to 'seize the crooks,' 'shoot th moving target,' that sort of thing. They're totally action-oriented. Any suspiciou movement, they take action. The more obvious the movement, the more they' *all* want to get in on it. *I mean it.* They're totally predictable. They'll go for an reasonable diversion, while we set up for the real thing."

"And how do we know what time that 'real thing' is?" I asked.

"You're a pilot, aren't you?" he shot back at me.

"Yes, I am. So are two others here."

"Good. So we know where and when they refueled, which was about tw hours ago. You can study your aviation maps, and check all your weather report and 'winds aloft'—or whatever you call them—and you should be able to prett closely figure their arrival time. With a little luck, and some careful planning, think we can get it down to within an hour or so. It's really not so hard. It's just little bigger, but not necessarily harder. It's ironic, I know, but it may actually b easier than any of you can imagine right now. I know. I've done this before Several times. I'm still here...alive and kicking."

Vinnie paused for a moment to gauge everyone's reaction to his plan, ther continued.

"This will be a total bandit thing, real outlaw stuff. But it'll work. They're too predictable. It takes guts, but if you just focus on what you each have to do, we' all be a whole lot richer this time tomorrow."

He was masterful. The mere mention of "richer" and his emphasis on "tomor row" diverted everyone's thoughts away from "tonight," and onto their imagined secret bank accounts.

He had them in his spell. Within a few hours, he had an entire group of com mon, everyday folk, families and neighbors who had lived together in the same suburb for years, whipped into a frenzied band of "outlaws" ready to do battl with the state police, DEA, and God knows who else might get into the action.

This was no small thing we were about to do. This wasn't a little plane on a abandoned stretch of highway, like they were used to Charlie flying. This was four-engine transport plane, capable of carrying up to 20,000 pounds of Colombian pot, packed in huge, 100-pound, burlap bales. Knowing the Old Man, that would mean there would be *30,000* pounds on board, if he could do it. That would take at least the semi-trailer rig we still had in reserve, several men and a fair amount of time to off-load. And here was this Italian Mafioso from New York pumping up this formerly rational, normally sane group of adults as if they were school kids playing cops-and-robbers.

I couldn't believe it. Everyone was actually excited, talking and planning for the off-load as if they were going to a Fourth of July picnic. But what if they *did* pull it off? If I didn't stay and they managed to pull it off, it wouldn't look good for me, especially now that Vinnie was on the scene. He was the Old Man's personal "lieutenant," and Michael's right-hand man.

Besides, I had obligated myself to see it through to the end. Having now become a liaison between the Old Man and Charlie's group, as well as between the Old Man and Bill's group from New Mexico, I was caught in the middle of it all. None of them trusted one another, and now there was Vinnie. He was slick, but the spell he had them under was bound to wear off sooner or later.

With the possible exception of Michael, everyone trusted me enough to tolerate the doubts they had about each other, at least until the goods were in and money was flowing again. On top of all that, the Old Man had the other group from Texas nearby, waiting to escort the load to Texas to get their half. And then there was Ernie, the truck driver from New Mexico. It was his 18-wheeler parked at the truck stop that would be hauling the load back west. Even though I didn't know him, he knew that I was originally part of the New Mexico group, and had driven semi's. I could tell from the conversation we'd had at the truck stop that he was relieved to have something in common with someone "on the inside." I sensed that in a tight spot he would do whatever was needed if I asked him to, or if I rode with him.

At any rate, few of them knew who was working with whom. I was the only one besides Charlie who knew who all of them were, and who had a direct line to the Old Man...until Vinnie arrived.

Now, with Vinnie clearly in charge and everyone excited and seeing dollar signs, I had a moment's relief. I got into my van and drove away to calm my nerves and get my thoughts together. This was going to be one helluva night.

Chapter Eight

After driving around town for a while just to get away from the frenzy, I headed back to the house where I was staying with my boys while we were in Florida. We were "on vacation," as far as they knew, and staying at the home of neighbors of Charlie's whom I had met during my previous stay there.

It was a nice suburban home, owned by one of the nicest guys you could meet. Jim was a court reporter with a seemingly normal family, and lived across the street from Charlie. He had helped Charlie as an off-loader several times on his trips from Jamaica, and used his position as County Clerk at the district courthouse to provide Charlie with timely information about law enforcement activity. An over-zealous, talkative cousin of his on the local police force added significantly to his value in Charlie's operation. Jim had three children of his own, and a very charming wife who made it possible for me to have my two boys with me. They were having a great time with their summer vacation, while I was entangled in a Mad Hatter's tea party.

"How was work, Dad?" Jonathan asked me as I eased myself into the sagging recliner. He had just turned eight that month. Channon, now five, climbed onto my lap as I tried to maintain some sense of calm.

"Oh, fine...I guess," I replied. "How was your day?"

"It was great!" They both talked excitedly. "We went swimming, and got to ride dune buggies around. Then we went to the movie, and had spaghetti dinner."

"Sounds wonderful. I sure wish I could go with you sometime."

"Maybe tomorrow, Dad. We're going to the beach. You can come with us," Channon pleaded.

"Yeah, Dad," Jonathan chimed in. "You could go for a coupla' hours, cancha? Please?"

Visions of camouflaged faces in the moonlight came sharply to mind as I thought of the plane out there somewhere over the Gulf of Mexico, making its way toward us even at that very moment. My heart started pounding again as my mind wandered in and out of possible scenarios I might see later that night.

"No, not tomorrow, guys. I've still got lots of work to do tonight, and if I get any time off tomorrow, I'll need to sleep before we head back to New Mexico."

"When are we going, Dad? Can't we stay a little longer? Please?"

"No. My work here is almost finished. It's hot and muggy, and I want to get back home soon. Don't you guys miss all your friends back there?"

"No, we like it here," Channon exclaimed. "We've got new friends, and they've got some great toys and stuff for us to play with. Can we live here?"

"No way, guys. This country's not for me. There might be fun things to do here, but I miss the mountains and the wide-open spaces. Don't you?"

"Maybe," Jonathan pondered. "I guess we have been gone a long time."

"Well, you two get some sleep tonight, and tomorrow we'll start packing up our things. We'll be on the highway for several days, and I'll need you guys to help keep me awake while we're driving. If you do, I'll let you take turns on my lap."

In a short time they were sound asleep, leaving me with my thoughts and anxieties playing hell with my head. Why not just pack up now and get them and me out of this madness? That motley crew would either pull it off, or they wouldn't. I got them their precious airstrip. What would it matter now if I didn't show up? All I was at this point was another pair of eyes and ears out there. Vinnie was in charge, so the Old Man didn't need me to report anything to him.

Vinnie was right, though. It *was* an outlaw move...and it just might work at that. It might turn out to be so damn easy we would all laugh at the ridiculousness of it all. And none of us would have any financial worries for a long time.

I wondered about that for a while. How well did I really know these Greeks, anyway? The Old Man had gone to great lengths to show me that he needed and trusted me. Who was I to them, after all? Once the plane was unloaded, I would certainly become very dispensable—especially with Michael's already expressed distrust of me. The Old Man, despite his affections for me, could be convinced that I was a liability. Besides, everyone knows that Mafia types always feign affection for a guy just before they waste him.

These guys were cunning and shrewd. They knew every angle and how to play into a man's weakness, whether it was money, sex, ego or, in my case, misguided loyalty. They knew how to play one person against another, to keep everyone off-balance and them in control.

They were slick, all right. And I had played right into their "needing" me.

They had the money, too. Apparently unlimited amounts of it. That was their ace in the hole. No matter how disgruntled or restless the lower level people became, they always paid homage to the two at the top who held the purse strings.

What a purse it was, too. Just this trip alone would be worth a minimal $5 million, at *wholesale* prices. The whole debacle yesterday in Colombia with the plane getting stuck in the mud, had to cost them a fortune. Nobody gets a confiscated DC-6 back *and* its crew out of jail without some powerful, very expensive connections. And the *load* back, on top of that? The whole thing had to have cost them at least a half-million *on top of* their original costs. Still they stood to net around $4 million, as far as I could calculate. Four million dollars covers a lot of expenses.

Tired out from a very active day, and now snugly dreaming of their trip to the beach the next day, my boys slept soundly while I pondered long and hard over the trap I was in. I hadn't fully realized the intricacies of the Old Man's operation, nor had I fully comprehended the depth of his commitment to it. I simply went along with each day's events, feeling as if it were all just a movie being filmed. No one really did all this stuff. Besides, my role in it—as I had come to delude myself—was so minuscule at that point that it couldn't really hurt me that much if we got busted. The government had much bigger fish to fry.

Suddenly my thoughts were interrupted by the sound of footsteps on the stairs. It was Jim, carrying a couple of cups of coffee.

"Y'all about ready?" he asked.

"I guess I'm about as ready as I'll ever be."

"You scared?"

"Of course. Aren't you?"

"Sure. Scared as hell."

"Your own wife's in on this. How does she feel about it?"

"Well, she's scared too, of course. But she sat up a bunch of nights when we were catching loads for Charlie, and she's gotten used to it."

"Yeah, but that was small potatoes compared with this. And this time she'll actually be out there with you. Can't pretend innocence out there..."

"Well, the way we figure it, if we're going to take chances we might as well take a big one and be done with it, once and for all. The other way was simpler, but we always made just enough money to whet our appetites. It would always run out too soon, even though we were careful not to spend it too fast. As far as being out there tonight, she feels like being with me all the way for a change. I don't really want her to, but it feels good to know she would take that kind of chance just to be with me."

"Sounds pretty romantic, but somehow I don't think it'll go over big with the judge."

"Well, let's not worry about any ol' judges, now. We've got some good people working with us on this. I think we'll be okay. I think Vinnie's right. We've got the advantage."

"We've got the advantage only if every little detail goes smoothly. Nobody's figured out how we're going to get an eighteen-wheeler all the way out to the strip without being noticed, then into position once the plane lands. There won't be any yard lights or loading docks out there, you know. I used to drive those things, and even the best drivers need time and a lot of room to maneuver them into position. And they generally need some light to see what the hell they're doing."

"Ernie's a good driver. We'll use the headlights of the other trucks, and John's car."

"And what about the runway lights?

"You mean those electric ones? Whose were those, anyway?"

"The guys with the fuel truck. It was a package deal. When they split, the portable lights went with them."

"We've still got those smudge pots."

"Those smudge pots were only for back-up, in case the electric ones failed. You know what smudge pots look like from 5,000 ft. up? The headlights of cars on the roads and yard lights and town lights for miles around will make those smudge pots look like candles in the middle of a Boy Scout Jamboree. To us down here they may look pretty obvious, but up there they'll be damn-near impossible to see."

"They always worked for Charlie before. Besides, he knows this area pretty well by now. It may be a bigger plane, but the ground still looks the same."

"Yeah, I know. But Charlie's still going to be hard-pressed to pull this off, no matter how well our 'bandit' routine goes. We have no idea where they are right now or exactly when they'll get here. How long do we risk sitting out there on the strip waiting while the law figures out they've been had by our diversion? All they'll have to do is make a radio call, and we'll look like Custer and his band of cavalry. You guys work all that out?"

"Yeah. Enough to feel like it's still worth it. I'll put my money on Charlie finding us."

"We'll *all* be putting our money on Charlie tonight, and on those pilots. They'll be putting a four-engine cargo plane into an abandoned airstrip built for naval *carrier* practice—carriers that were built in the 1930s. You know how short those airstrips are? Not big enough for a DC-6, you can bet your ass on that. So what about the lights, anyway? You guys come up with any other ideas?"

"Yeah. We'll have two cars lined up at each end of the runway. They'll aim their lights down from each end, and at the right signal they'll flash their head-lights in alternating sequence. That ought to do the trick. There's the radio, too. Hell, we'll be *talking* them in."

"*If* it works, and *if* we get good contact. If, if, if... "

"It's always worked before with Charlie. Jeez, you sound pretty skeptical."

"Well, let's just say I'm trying to be realistic. Fine time for that now, I know, but I can't help it. I'm not that experienced at this sort of thing. I can deal with all kinds of imaginary logistics and coordinating events, but the real thing gets a little lumpy to deal with, if you know what I mean."

"Yeah, I've been through it a few times with Charlie. The feeling never really goes away. This thing tonight is so big that it's too scary to even think about. Without Vinnie, we'd never have a chance of pulling it off."

"Good ol' Vinnie. Man of the Hour. Tomorrow he'll either be everyone's hero, or he'll be the worst nightmare that ever happened to any of us."

"Well, that's the way things go in this business, I guess. I don't know much else about it, since all I've ever done is unload the little planes for Charlie. Seems like it's time to fish or cut bait. We've all chosen to fish."

"Okay. Tomorrow night we might just be singing praises to Vinnie and danc-ing on the tabletops. Who knows? If we don't go for it, we might spend the rest of our lives wondering what could have happened. Maybe the experience alone is worth it. Maybe guys like Vinnie get some sort of special thrill that's worth more than the money, from knowing they took the chance and pulled it off. But maybe that gets to be a fever—like prospecting for gold or diamonds. Maybe it's the adrenaline rush they get from the danger of it all."

"Yeah, who knows? I guess we'll find out tonight. That's why you've got to keep your mind on what you're supposed to do and not on what might go wrong."

"And what about that farmer? We won't want him driving out on the strip again."

"Well, I'm sure Vinnie'll have something figured out."

"I hope that 'something' isn't a gun. I won't use one unless it's a life-or-death situation. I won't even carry one."

"I don't think anybody wants that. Although we've always had to be ready to shoot out tires or ram a car, if need be."

"I'll settle for look-out. You guys can shoot tires or do the ramming. If anybody gets hurt in the process, I'm out of the picture. Totally. I'll get so far away from this place my mother won't even know where I am. I won't even stay in this country."

"Yeah, I hear you. Me too, probably."

"Yeah, sure...you with a nice, split-level, suburban home and three kids. What about them? What happens to them if you both get busted?"

"Her sister's coming over tonight. She adores our kids, and her husband's got parents who would be happy to have some kids around the house for a while."

"Hmmm. Could be a *long* while."

"Could be. But we're ready to gamble on it. We agree with Vinnie. Cops really are pretty predictable. I see it all the time where I work. They're bored to death...always ready to jump on every little thing. Except for the ones who are just doing it until they retire. Those can generally be paid off."

"Maybe so. Maybe I'm making much of nothing. Don't get me wrong. I'm not obsessing over the problems. Once things get underway, I'll do whatever needs to be done—except anything violent. I won't stand for it. It's never worth the money, no matter how much is involved. I've heard too many stories of people thinking big money is worth any sacrifice. It never is. I'll be okay. I just want to be able to reassure myself later that I thought it through."

"Well, I guess you have. It's time to get going. You ready?"

"That sounds like Butch Cassidy and The Sundance Kid, just before they stepped out in that Bolivian courtyard with guns blazing."

"Yeah...that was a great movie. I don't remember how it ended, exactly..."

"You don't want to know right now..."

Chapter Nine

The night was creepy…worse than the night before. My heart pounded like a drum, and the slightest hint of movement anywhere in the bushes sent chills up my spine. Our decoys—the two "cowboys" from New Mexico—had sped off from the truck stop in their pickups over an hour ago, and we were merely guessing at the plane's arrival time. Every minute that passed increased the chances of our diversion being discovered. They had definitely been followed, but it wouldn't take long for the cops to figure it out and call for backups to check out the strip where we were waiting.

Suddenly, car headlights appeared in the distance and made their way slowly toward us. Everyone crouched down in the bushes and stayed quiet. The car came closer, then seemed to slow down as it neared the turnoff into our clearing. If it was the cops, we were sunk. There was no way to get the trucks out of there, especially the 18-wheeler parked at the end of the runway. Would somebody get crazy and shoot it out with them? Probably. Too much had gone into the whole effort to let two guys blow it now, even if they *were* police.

The car came closer. My heart pounded harder. I looked around for the safest escape route if gunfire broke out. Things could get real serious, and fast. The car slowed, then turned into the clearing and stopped. The driver killed the lights and the car sat there silently. It had to be the cops. It wasn't anyone from our crew.

Now what? What the hell were we going to do? Vinnie and his goddamn "outlaw" crap. In a minute they would see the rig, and the other trucks and cars hidden among the bushes. Hell would break loose any second. They were probably on the radio right now. Shit. What a stupid, *stupid* thing for us to have tried to pull off.

Suddenly, the car door opened. Sounds of giggling came from inside the car as a young kid got out, walked around to the back, unzipped his fly and relieved himself. Afterwards he turned, stretched, looked around for a moment and then climbed back into the car. Not fifty feet from the car was a partially hidden eighteen-wheel tractor/trailer rig, a couple of pickup trucks, three cars and a crew of off-loaders waiting for a cargo plane with 20,000 pounds of marijuana on board to drop out of the blackness of night onto the decaying airstrip in front of them. In the middle of it all were a couple of kids out for a night's fun. Behind the car, three very nervous men moved silently into position, poised to stop the unwelcome intruders from bolting when the action started.

Suddenly, the car's engine started and the lights came on. As the car began to back out of the clearing, the three men dove for cover. The car backed onto the road, then continued in the direction they had been going before.

A small group of very nervous men hurriedly gathered at the rig.

"What the hell now?" I heard someone ask.

"I think it's okay," said one of the three who had dived for cover. "They didn't see a thing. He only had his eyes on the girl."

"Yeah," said another one. "And his hand up her dress."

"Are you sure?" I heard Vinnie's distinct Brooklyn accent over all the nervous chatter.

"Yeah, I'm sure," answered the first one. "You can ask Clay, here. He was watching through the window. They were drunk, and he was pawing all over her."

"Tha's right," Clay chimed in. "They couldn't a seen nothin', the way they was a grabbin' at each other."

"What about when they pulled out?" Vinnie's voice demanded. "Could they have noticed anything? *Think,* man. We might have to go after them and keep them quiet for a while."

"No. I'm telling you, man. They never noticed *nothin'.* I was watchin' so close, I could almost see her tits, myself. They only had their minds on one thing, and it wasn't outside the car. Even when they backed out, he was still pawin' all over her, and she wasn't stoppin' him."

"Okay, okay. Everybody back to your positions. Now you can see how important it is to keep cool and calm, no matter *what.*"

The night air seemed to get colder, even if it *was* July. As the waiting continued, I sat back and wondered how Vinnie would have dealt with those kids if they had seen anything. Would he really have gone after them? What then? I wondered if he had a silencer, and if he would have used it.

Yes, I thought, he would. Maybe not on them, but my sense of this "outlaw" was that if push came to shove, he would do just about anything. He could be polite, but there was a hard, desperado edge to him that didn't come from being the personable guy he had presented to everyone at the meeting.

I had met him in Miami, at the Old Man's house. He drove a big Cadillac, and when he got out of it, the whole car shifted under the change in weight. The way he sauntered up to the house, I could tell he was used to throwing his weight around. He looked at me like I was a fly on the wall, but later opened up some when he realized the Old Man liked me. I kept my distance from him about the same as I did from Michael, who was even bigger than Vinnie. The two of them could make a Mack truck sink like a low-rider. Neither of them had any great love for me. The way they talked about the people they had working for them—who was loyal and who wasn't—and hinting at what had happened to those who weren't, gave me the creeps. I saw another side of Vinnie this time, however. He still carried that no-nonsense air to him, but he was more affable, insightful and even humorous…particularly during the meeting at the mechanic's house.

The Old Man seemed different than the two of them. He seemed to care about me, and genuinely acted as if he needed me to help him make some crucial changes. He had talked about it at length when we walked together on that beach back on the Caicos Islands, and had mentioned it again when we had flown together to other places. He said he hadn't really wanted to get involved in the drug business, but he had made a deathbed pledge to their father to look after Michael. Michael was obsessed with the drug business, and was intent on being the biggest and the best in it. Once he had allowed himself to get involved with it, the Old Man couldn't pull out. There was always "one more deal" to pay off, or to cover something that had gone wrong.

It occurred to me as I got to know them, however, that it was more likely a matter of living too long in the fast lane. I think they were addicted to it—even the Old Man. Once they handled so much money and could control so many others, it was impossible to scale down, or change their ways. It's delusional to think that once one has "made it" in that business that they could then settle down to a simpler, easier lifestyle. In truth, it gets in one's blood. And the smarter one is, the harder it is to break the pattern.

I knew of a few people who had made it big in the business, but with very few exceptions, none of the ones I met ever seemed to manage it. Like the Old Man had said, there was always some reason to get back into it when the money ran out—which was always too soon. When people get used to spending that much money so fast and freely, it always runs out sooner than expected…unless you keep your hand in it.

It was the danger of it all, too. I wondered if there might be some who would do it *without* the money. Of course, money makes it all happen, but many—if not most—who get deeply involved in the drug business actually thrive on the danger. Adrenaline flows in direct proportion to the amount of danger involved. The amount of danger involved is always in direct proportion to the amount of money that changes hands.

It's like conducting your own warfare. At least, that's how it seemed to me as I watched the various groups and bosses assume their different roles as the action shifted and moved each day. The term "lieutenant" is used in organized crime for good reason. Some are like lieutenants, and some are more like generals. Rank comes mostly through intimidation, and by how many people one controls. It isn't about the money as much as it is the type and number of "soldiers" who do your bidding. The more successful you are, the bigger the stakes…and vice versa. Money is only necessary to pay the high costs involved in playing the game.

Fortunately, I had managed to keep my exposure to that world at a minimum…at least until recently. Often I would just happen to be there when others came around to see the Old Man. Then it was all business, and he was very good at it. He wasn't much for socializing. Whenever we went anywhere, he would reserve a suite on the top floor of a Holiday Inn and stay there. A telephone, a TV always turned up to minimize the chance of eavesdropping, and room service were all he needed. Club sandwiches and French fries were the staple of his diet when he was "working."

But he was also able to make himself welcome anywhere, if necessary. Wherever we went, people seemed to like and respect him, and greeted him warmly. When we arrived at the Turks & Caicos Islands, the only hotel on the tiny island was full with a scuba divers' annual gathering. We had arrived in a small plane that we had flown 600 miles over the Caribbean, and were startled to find the airport virtually closed. As we walked up to the tiny shack that served as the airport "terminal," a young black man with dreadlocks was leaning against the fender of a '57 Lincoln convertible, holding a drink.

"Weah you wahnt to go, mahn?" he asked in his distinctive Jamaican lingo. "Dees place be fuhl' up. Dey ain't no place to stay, mahn."

The Old Man slipped into the language of the Islands and talked with him as if he were an old friend. Soon the five of us were settling into bedrooms in three different homes on the island, stuffed with conch fritters and boiled crayfish.

It was hard to believe all that had happened in the short time I had been involved with them. Now I sat among the trees and bushes of the airstrip again, with half the original crew waiting to pull off something *fourteen* men would have been hard-pressed to do the night before.

Suddenly my ears caught the faint sounds of what had to be a heavy, propeller-driven aircraft. As it drew closer, I recognized the sweet, unmistakable sound of radial engines. There was no mistake about it this time. They were up there somewhere. They had their navigation lights off, so I couldn't spot them, but I could damn sure hear them. By God, they'd made it!

Someone was out on the strip, frantically trying to light the smudge pots, while on both ends of the strip, cars lined up with their headlights ready for the signal. Someone was cussing over in one of the bushes. Something about static on the radio.

The plane crossed overhead, but well off to the east, heading north. Damn! How far would they go before turning back this way? Was it even them? It had to be. Who else could it be, sounding like a World War II bomber? It HAD to be them.

Maybe they were evading someone. Were they lost? Could they even see us? *Damn* those puny little smudge pots.

Out on the strip, men were bewildered as the drone of the big engines drifted off to the north. The smudge pots were extinguished and slowly everyone went back into hiding.

A few minutes later we could hear the engines again, faint but growing louder, this time moving closer to us. The crew scrambled again, this time with greater resolve to get the pilot's attention. All caution was thrown to the wind as car headlights flashed and smudge pots were ignited again. The plane passed directly overhead, then flashed their navigation lights twice. I could see the huge silhouette of the plane as it moved against the stars. I was spellbound.

The plane continued southbound in what I knew would have to be one hell of a descent. Nervously, I took up a position between the end of the runway and the farmer's mobile home.

How could anything that big make it into such a small airstrip? And at *night*...without decent lighting? I knew this was going to be one spectacular crash, and I wasn't about to be near it. I posted myself well beyond the end of the strip, but close to some large trees that might protect me from flying debris.

The sound of the plane faded away for a few minutes as it began the outward leg of its final descent. I could hear it turn and begin its approach, the sound of the engines growing louder by the second. My heart pounded so hard I could barely stand it. The two cars flashed their headlights from each end of the half-mile long strip when I noticed the 18-wheeler parked at the far end.

"Shit!" I exclaimed under my breath. *The rig was parked right in the approach path of the plane!* With that short an airstrip, the pilot would have to come in so low the trees would scrape the plane's belly. He would have to cut power and put the plane into an extreme side-slip with full flaps to lose the last hundred feet. With that, he would drop like a rock to the threshold, and there was the goddamn rig, parked like a wall in front of it *with no marker lights on!*

All the while, I could hear the four engines thundering louder as the pilot changed pitch and enriched the mixtures. Then the pilot throttled back for the landing, and for a few seconds all went quiet. Suddenly, with blinding intensity, the landing lights came on. From where I stood, it seemed that the plane missed the rig by inches as it swooped up and over it.

It touched down within yards of the approach end of the strip, and the pilots fought to keep the huge bird on the ground. With a deafening roar, they reversed the props and slowed to a manageable speed. Still, it was moving fast. Within a few seconds it was nearly on top of me. Just as I thought he was going to overrun the strip, the pilot swung the plane into a tight one-eighty with a roar of the starboard engines. With inches to spare, and the air pungent with the smell of smoking brakes and burning tires, the plane was rolling back to the other end of the strip. Even from where I was standing, I could see its engines glowing red hot in the night.

Just then, the number three engine burst into flames.

With the other engines stopped, I could see the pilot windmilling the number three prop, trying to blow out the flames. Any second, the flames would ignite the fumes from the empty fuel tanks and blow the plane into bits of metal and smoldering bales of pot. A door on the plane flew open and two men scrambled out, desperately trying to put out the fire with two large extinguishers.

The flames kept up as the prop, still turning, blew the foam away from the engine. I watched in horror, knowing that a huge explosion was about to occur. In a last-gasp attempt, the pilot shut down the engine and the last of the foam smothered the fire. In the remaining flicker of light from the now smoldering engine, I knew that plane wouldn't be flying again that night...if ever.

Cars and trucks descended on the plane from everywhere. The rig roared to life and maneuvered into position at the cargo door. It was really happening. I was really standing there, watching the whole process unfold. I watched it all for several minutes, then realized I should be doing something. But what? I couldn't keep watching and not help, but if I waited long enough to make sure a bust wasn't going happen I might be perceived as cowardly.

I had to make my appearance. They needed every pair of hands they could get. I had to go and face it—not hide in the bushes. I could stay put and maintain the stance that someone needed to keep a steady lookout on the road, but in the end it would look suspicious. I had to get into the thick of it and earn my right to have anything to say about it later. Slowly at first, then faster, I started toward the plane. Two men were in the plane, feverishly sliding huge bales of burlap-covered pot out the door and into the rig. The road was clear, but no one cared at that point. There could have been an army convoy coming down the road and I doubt anyone would have noticed. I took a position between the plane and the rig, and hefted a few bales.

In minutes the plane was empty. The pilots had been hustled off to a waiting pickup, the rig was loaded and everyone was racing for the road. As one of the cars passed by me, a rear door opened and I was pulled onto the laps of three sweat-soaked men, their faces painted like Army commandos. We followed the rig down the road, all eyes ahead and behind. For miles we went on like that as we made our way to the nearby Georgia border and then turned westbound toward the corner of Alabama.

By the time we reached Dothan, I had managed to regain enough composure to remember my boys back at the house now forty miles behind us. I had my ride drop me at an all-night diner at the intersection of two highways just outside of town. I stood there watching the rig and its escort disappear into the hot, muggy night, feeling as if I had just stepped into a scene from *The Twilight Zone*.

Back on the Florida side of the border, the cab driver I had called from the diner stopped at the house I arbitrarily picked out, just as the dimmest of morning light could be seen breaking over the distant horizon. For forty miles—my heart still pounding—I had to listen to his endless small talk as my brain scrambled to process all I had just been through. I walked the rest of the way through several yards and parkways to Jim's house. By the time I got there, the sun was a growing sliver of light on the horizon. As I stepped quietly into the room, Channon sat up and grinned at me.

"Hi, Dad! You up already?"

"Sure," I said. "You ready for a swim?"

"Right *now?*"

"You bet. You ever swim in the sunrise?"

"Noooo."

"Well, come *on.* Last one in's a rotten egg."

Jonathan was now wide-awake, and they both bounded from the bed and were in the pool ahead of me...their swimsuits still on from the day before. I leaned against the shallow end of the pool, feeling the cool wetness soothe my aching, tension-filled body, and watched with them the splendor of the sunrise. As I felt them both clinging to me and watched the sun climb into the morning sky, I could scarcely believe what had just taken place. Suddenly it all seemed so unreal and so far away.

As the 18-wheeler and its escort made its way west, black clouds of an angry storm were forming. From the local folks counting the money they were going to get, to the men headed west and nervously watching every suspicious movement, to the Old Man waiting by his telephone in Miami, the tension of planning and orchestrating such an event shifted to tension of another sort. This was one of intense suspicion, fear and distrust. What had ultimately worked so well in the final desperate moments of chaos and confusion now became a challenge of quite another kind.

Like the *Treasure of the Sierra Madre,* we were all about to find out that getting the gold was only part of the struggle. The pilots were already on their way back home to relative safety, but for the rest of us the journey had only just begun.

Chapter Ten

That summer was one of the hottest on record in the Deep South. Across most of Texas, the mercury climbed past 115 degrees for twenty consecutive days. The temperature in the Florida panhandle, where my boys and I had loaded our van for the trip west, was already 95 degrees, with ninety percent humidity…and it was only eight o'clock in the morning.

I had just provided the cohesive force that virtually saved an operation which would net the Old Man and his brother more than $5 million. The street value of the load would ultimately be over $14 million, but in my pocket was less than twenty dollars.

With a vivid picture of the DC-6 sitting empty on the airstrip barely twenty miles away, I felt more than conspicuous as the boys and I made our way across town toward the freeway. As I drove, I was frantic to devise a plan to get us fifteen hundred miles west with no money. There could be no doubt that my 'debt' had been paid. My efforts gave the Greeks their landing strip, and had kept chaos in check long enough to result in safe delivery of the goods.

I had more than fulfilled my part of their 'deal.' In fact, if I wanted to push the issue, I would have been well within my rights to claim the whole $50,000, or more. But that would mean another trip to Miami and, knowing how they operated, more involvement with them. I had had enough. Much more than enough. Broke, paranoid and physically as well as emotionally spent, the main thing I wanted was to put as much distance between us and their operation as possible.

The only thing I had with me of any monetary value was the gold necklace around my neck. It had been given to me in a moment of deep respect by a friend of many years—a smuggler with vast experience in the 'business' who had taken a liking to me. We had met through a mutual friend, struck up an immediate friendship, and occasionally spent time together as I was anxiously learning the business. His informative stories recounted the pitfalls and dangers of that world. He dressed in khaki outfits to give him the appearance of a 'mining engineer,' and traveled to South America so frequently that he was rarely inspected. With short, curly hair, a barrel chest and wire rim glasses, he reminded me of Clyde Beatty, the famous wild animal trainer. Sitting with him one night over margaritas, I mentioned the similarity and we laughed boisterously over his new nickname, 'The Elephant Trainer.'

He grew up in the smuggling business, with grandparents who were rumrunners during Prohibition. I delighted in listening to the many stories of his adventures and those of his grandparents. He told me of a Colombian friend of his that made trips to the states so regularly that Customs officials and airport authorities at Miami assumed he was an airport employee. Dressed in gray coveralls and carrying a collapsible broom that he would pull out after disembarking the plane, he would sweep his way right past Customs inspectors and out the door.

One night when he was telling me stories of earlier days in the business, he emphasized how important it was to be prepared for any eventuality. He opened his leather satchel and pulled out a small plastic bag containing a gold chain. Not particularly ornamental, it was just a simple gold necklace.

"Here," he said, handing it to me. "Keep this, and you'll always have something of value in an emergency. It's twenty-four carat gold, and weighs exactly one ounce. When you've accumulated some cash, buy some gold chain and have necklaces made like this. Carry them with you. I always have a few with me wherever I go. It's universal money, passes for jewelry at customs inspections and can come in real handy in a tight spot."

The value of gold in those days had just reached $300 an ounce, so I pondered where I might find the most ready market. With barely half a tank of gas, I had a tough decision to make. Tallahassee was the only city of any size within range, but it was *east* of us. To get us home, I would have to go in the *opposite* direction to sell the necklace, and then pass back through a likely manhunt searching for those involved in the DC-6 landing.

I'd been seen around town for the past three weeks, and was a guest of Charlie's a few months before. Too many people knew my van and my description. By the time the boys and I would be passing back through the area, the police might have that information. My New Mexico license plates didn't help matters much, either.

Giving up the necklace was harder than I expected. It was part of a bond between two men in very different worlds. 'The Elephant Trainer' was exceptionally good at what he did, and had provided me with valuable insights and advice.

He was very real, had a great sense of humor, and showed me more respect than anyone I had met in the business.

"The trouble you're in," he once told me, "is that you're dangling your feet in a pool of sharks. You've got to get in with them or get the hell out. If you don't, they'll eat you alive."

A cold shudder ran through me as I recalled his words. He had been right, of course. But by that time, it was too late. As the clerk at the pawnshop counted out a hundred and sixty dollars for the necklace, I said a silent good-bye to the Elephant Trainer and prayed that I was getting out in time. It was nearly noon and the heat was unbearable. I had to decide on a safe course for our journey home. What seemed most logical at the moment was to sleep through the heat of the day and drive at night. I found a quiet motel with a room close to the swimming pool and dragged my tired, aching body into the room while the boys jumped into the pool. Stretched out in the cool darkness on the bed, it occurred to me only then that I hadn't slept more than a few hours in nearly two and a half days. Within seconds, all non-essential systems in my body were shut down except for one ear tuned to the sound of the boys playing outside.

When I awoke, it was growing dark outside. I could hear the boys playing in the pool, but the blaring TV indicated they had been inside at least part of the time. I looked at my watch and was glad to see that it was only 7:30. Plenty of time to put some miles behind us before dawn. We pulled out of the motel and stopped at a McDonald's just before the freeway entrance. While the boys munched on Happy Meals, I was deep in thought about what might lie ahead.

No matter what the police discovered about the plane, or who was involved, they wouldn't expect any of us to still be in the area. Certainly they wouldn't expect one of us to be coming from the *east* with a couple of kids, so I decided to drive right through the thick of their 'manhunt' as if I didn't have a care in the world.

But then I wondered about roadblocks. The police would probably have license numbers and descriptions of vehicles. As I thought about that, I agonized over how, or even if, I should prepare the boys for what could happen. Images of my impending arrest played in my head while my eyes shifted back and forth at the road ahead and the rearview mirror, searching for the least sign of suspicious activity.

By the time we drew near the area, I was a nervous wreck. Keeping a sense of humor and a casual air became a supreme effort as the boys grew increasingly restless. Loud choruses of "Row, Row, Row Your Boat" reverberated through the van as we cruised by the all-too-familiar truck stop not far from the airstrip. In the newspaper racks by the entrance, the front pages carried the story of an abandoned DC-6 found that morning on the old airstrip north of town.

On through the night I drove. Tension increased with each passing mile until we were well into Alabama. Crossing Mobile, the boys were fascinated by the vast shipyards that even at night were bustling with workers under huge canopies of lights. The night air was muggy from the day's waning heat, and around every light were frenzied swarms of bugs.

As we neared Mississippi, my concentration on the rearview mirrors lessened somewhat, and gradually reduced to occasional glances. The worst seemed to be over. There was enough going on back in Florida to keep law enforcement agencies too busy covering their asses. They'd let a big one get in, and back there next to a peanut field east of Pensacola was the proof. Worse yet, a photographer from the local paper had snapped a picture of it, and once the media published the story and the photo, it became national news.

On the seat next to me was a copy of the local newspaper I couldn't resist picking up when I had stopped for gas. Below the picture of the DC-6 on the front page, the article described the failed attempt of the night before. Mention was made of cut telephone lines, and that the operation appeared to have been the work of 'organized professionals.' Authorities had foiled the first attempt, the article said. It went on to say that the airstrip had been staked out the second night, but that the agents had been called away. That only made matters worse, because the story led people to believe that there was an inside deal that had diverted the agents from the scene.

Years later, I was told what had really happened. The agents went for coffee and returned to discover the empty plane on the runway. If that was true, we had unwittingly caught them with their pants down. We never knew for certain if it was our wildly executed diversion or drowsiness that had drawn them away. Whichever really happened, they looked pretty bad—and they were out for blood.

In plush offices of the Drug Enforcement Administration, U.S. Customs, the Department of Justice *and* the Department of Defense, stern-faced supervisors issued angry instructions to ranks of agents and investigators. As far as they were concerned, this was one that wouldn't get away—no matter how long it might take.

By morning light we were well into Louisiana, and the windshield bore proof to the boys that they had, in fact, seen "skzillions" of bugs the night before. My eyelids were losing their nightlong battle with gravity, and the temperature outside was already climbing fast. Low-lying fog and Spanish moss hanging from the trees gave me the eerie feeling that I was still in Florida. Up ahead, the bright sign of a Holiday Inn pierced the lifting fog.

Room service was a delightful new thrill for the boys. They proceeded to make a long list of things they would order once I was asleep. But the inside pool with its video arcade won out over waiting for me to shower and settle in.

Crossing Texas wasn't so easy. The boys couldn't believe that after two more nights of driving, we were *still* in Texas. But we were, mostly because I wasn't taking any chances. Paranoid that any patrolman who stopped me would be on the alert over the Florida incident, I overcame the urge to speed. At long last, the sign "Welcome to the Land of Enchantment" appeared up ahead, and the three of us cheered loudly. I wanted to get out and kiss the ground.

Home never felt so good, even with all the bills that had piled up over the months. After a few days of unwinding, I began to look for work. Knowing what I knew, it became more and more difficult for me to tolerate the mess I had made of my personal finances. Hearing that the load made it successfully to its two destinations only amplified my frustration.

A month passed, and I was in desperate straits. Bills from my once-promising business had caught up with me, and were added to my growing pile of personal debts. The business had failed, despite its many merits, and my efforts to salvage it proved futile. Creditors wanted satisfaction, even if it was simply a 'closed' file.

Occasionally I ran into someone from the Florida crew who felt it their duty to keep me informed. The Old Man let me know through the grapevine that my efforts were appreciated. There was some money for me, it was said, and some 'work' if I wanted it. I wasn't excited about diving back into something over my head again, but I was growing desperate.

Finally one day, I ran into Bill. He was responsible for the sale and distribution of half the load through his network of dealers. Now he was caught in a dilemma. Sales of the load were progressing, and he would soon be collecting the money and would have to take it to the Old Man. He anticipated no problem collecting it, but he needed help transporting it. Two million dollars in tens, twenties, fifties and hundreds took up a lot of room.

He had another problem, however, which he was reluctant to voice. Having spent considerable time with the Old Man, I knew the nature of it. In fact, one of the prime reasons the Old Man had wanted me on the scene was that they didn't trust each other. Bill had a long-standing unpaid debt with the Old Man, and was caught somewhere between greed and self-righteousness about it. He may or may not have owed the full amount claimed by the Old Man, but I believed the Old Man to be fair and reasonable.

Whatever amount was owed, Bill's poor record of payment on previous deals had left a bad taste. No doubt they each had cause to distrust one another, but now Bill was on the hook to the Old Man once again. Without voicing it, he apparently felt I could help ease the tension somewhat. It was a bit of irony that it was Bill who had introduced me to the Old Man in the first place. They had done business with each other over the years, yet I had become their go-between. Another irony was that originally he had been passed over on the DC-6 deal altogether because of the way he had handled things in the past. I convinced the Old Man that Bill deserved another chance. At the Old Man's request, I had set up a meeting between them in Houston a few weeks before I quit. A deal was cut, and Bill was back in the saddle again.

On the flight back to New Mexico after the meeting, Bill and I rode first class and toasted the occasion. In boyish exuberance, he told me he would give me two percent of what he made regardless of my cut with the Old Man. I never saw it.

Now, two months later, Bill wanted my help. Knowing I was financially strapped, he left me with a little bundle of what we would be transporting, just to help me decide. As I looked at the envelope filled with hundred dollar bills, I recalled something else the Elephant Trainer had told me.

"In this game," he said, "people dangle ropes all the time. The trick is to learn which ones are worth grabbing, and which ones to leave alone."

I wasn't certain which kind of rope this one was, but I was damn tired of being out on a limb for so little in return. I felt that my break was long overdue and well deserved. Maybe this would be my chance to earn a decent return *and* take a firmer stand with the Old Man and his brother regarding payment on the DC-6 trip. Although I was relieved to get away from it all, I also knew that it would have been a bust if I hadn't held it together until Vinnie got there. Charlie wouldn't have been in on the deal and, for that matter, neither would Bill. I was the one who kept them both in it, and now I felt it was time I got paid for it.

During our trip to California the following week, I saw Bill in his own element and got to know him a little better. I always had the impression that he was a decent guy, and most of our mutual friends seemed to think highly of him. My sense of loyalty to him grew as we traveled together, and I discovered that he was more knowledgeable in the business than I realized.

Bill told me the ranch was purchased with earnings from their earlier days, smuggling pot across the Mexican border. From there, they built a network of dealers on the west coast that eventually was capable of moving huge quantities of marijuana very quickly. Things hadn't always gone as planned, however, and payments on the land were falling behind. What was more likely the case, as I was learning, was that fast money generally went the same way it came…fast.

But I felt Bill had good intentions, and I was glad that I managed to convince the Old Man to keep him in the game. Maybe now we could develop a business and personal relationship, and get on with the more worthwhile things I assumed we had in common. At the time, however, I was unaware that cocaine was behind his financial problems. Not only was he supporting his own habit, but most likely that of everyone else's back at their ranch. Though Bill didn't tell me that, this seemed to be the crux of the problem with the Old Man. He was riding high again. The green stuff was flowing, and so was the white stuff.

We went to a house high on one of the famous hills of San Francisco where we drank champagne and counted money. Cocaine was plentiful, and acknowledgements of brotherhood and friendship filled the air. Everything was 'brother' this, and 'brother' that, as tote bags of varying shapes and sizes were stuffed with bundles of cash along with dirty clothes to discourage inspection. Traveling with Bill to collect from other houses around the Bay and then in Southern California, I learned to count money faster than a veteran bank teller. I developed a fondness for $100 bills that was more from the ease of counting them than it was for their actual worth. There were so many of them, I lost my sense of awe and respect for what they represented. After a while, I couldn't care less about them. They weren't mine anyway.

A few days later, we flew into Miami with bags slung from our shoulders and in each hand. Each bag was bulging with more money than most people could dream about. So much money was involved, in fact, that two weeks later Bill would go back and repeat the process all over again.

Chapter Eleven

The Old Man preferred to meet at Holiday Inns. Maybe it was because there was always one wherever he went. But it was also because they were consistent. For that matter, so was he. On his bedstand was the ever-present club sandwich and French fries, cold and half-eaten. It was interesting to walk in and see him and his brother each sprawled out on a queen-sized bed, fully clothed.

Michael's immense frame sank deep into the mattress. Catlike in nature, his sharp, beady eyes and quick, piercing intelligence both fascinated and bothered me. Anytime Michael was present, I instinctively kept an eye on him, much the same as I would a cat on the prowl.

Their operations affected the lives of hundreds of men and women living and working in a world of drama and intrigue that few people in the normal world could comprehend. Yet here they were lounging in a Holiday Inn like a couple of traveling salesmen, watching "The Price Is Right" on TV. On the floor lay bags stuffed with money like so much dirty laundry.

The Old Man welcomed us in his usual gracious manner and seemed genuinely interested in how things were going with each of us. Pleasantries were exchanged, then he quickly got down to business. I took a seat at a table in the corner and sat quietly while Bill spoke with them.

As they talked, I sensed the Greeks sizing Bill up, probing for any weakness or evidence of something off. We all had a common reason to be there, but I knew better than to let my guard down even for a moment. While the Old Man talked, I noticed Michael's eyes shifting back and forth from the conversation to the bags lying in a heap on the floor. Bill spoke directly, although somewhat nervously. I sensed some apprehension in his voice, most likely because he might be brought to account for past, unfinished business. But it never came up. Apparently, the Old Man didn't want to rock the boat while it was moving in a steady direction. A time for reckoning would come later.

Bill explained that there were problems on the west coast that adversely affected prices. The load was low-to-average quality, and was competing in the streets of California with high-quality Mexican sinsemilla and 'primo bud' from Humboldt County, California. The Old Man was poised and calm, but I could tell he was irritated.

"So what's this 'sinsim...' what did you call it?" he asked.

"Sin-say-mee-ya," Bill pronounced it. "It's Spanish for 'no seeds'. It's pure bud, taken from the female plants before they go to seed. Growers in Humboldt County have been perfecting it for years. You know about their stuff. It's unbeatable. Now the Mexicans have started growing it, and it's all over the west coast. However, it's too expensive for average buyers, so we'll still be able to sell your stuff. It's just going to take longer at the prices we're asking. Most of my buyers don't want average weed, but sometimes they'll buy it, mix it with better stuff and pass it off to their less discriminating customers as 'home grown.' But not at these prices."

"I see," the Old Man replied. "And what do you think we should do?"

"Lower the price enough to increase their interest. It's still marketable, but at these prices it'll take longer to sell. That makes me nervous."

"We don't seem to have that problem in Texas," the Old Man said, questioning Bill's assessment.

"Well, Texas is different," Bill replied, a bit defensively. "They'll smoke anything in Texas. Californians are used to better quality. There's probably more high-quality pot grown in *basements* in California than in all of Texas. Buyers for this Colombian stuff are mostly kids and street people."

"Street people—common or not—are *our* kind of people," the Old Man goaded Bill. "They pay the bills." He sounded like an executive at Walmart.

Bill grew even more defensive. "I didn't mean it that way. It's just that my buyers are used to better quality. Like I said, they can sell this stuff. But in California, it will take more time at these prices."

"Well, maybe our merchandise is in the wrong place," Michael snorted. "Maybe we should move it to Texas, where 'common people' can enjoy it." Bill looked at Michael, not sure whether to deal with this annoying challenge or ignore it.

"That would be an added expense," Bill replied with carefully chosen words, "and a risk I don't think you really want to take."

"We'll take it if we have to," Michael shot back at him. "And it won't be at *our* expense." Bill straightened noticeably in his chair.

"Are you *serious?*" Bill glared at Michael. "I'd have to pull the stuff in from twenty different buyers. If they have to pick up everything they've fronted to their buyers, that'll cost me a fortune! You're implying that on top of that you want *me* to pay to move it to Texas?"

"Now, now," the Old Man stepped in. "I'm sure something can be worked out. Nobody wants to interrupt anything at this point. Let's see how we can make this work out for everyone, and keep it simple."

Listening to the three of them argue their respective views was fascinating, particularly considering the fact that the sale of the merchandise was already in progress. They were discussing an operation already half complete, and the price now had to be renegotiated. Accomplishing that became a function of how much each could convince the other that his position was adversely affected by matters the *other* one was responsible for. At their level of dealing, a $10 difference in price per pound would make a difference of $70,000 to $100,000.

I saw them like kids at a Monopoly board. On the one hand, they were discounting the value of each others' property, while busily calculating in their heads how much houses and hotels would bring. It was an exercise in shrewdness and manipulation at its best. They spoke respectfully to one another, all the while working furiously to keep one step ahead of each other. It was all so ludicrous. The bags of money lying on the floor covered more than all their expenses to date for the entire operation, and there was yet another trip for Bill to make for the second half of their payment. And that was for only *half* the load. In Texas, a duplicate operation was underway with the other half.

I watched it all silently, observing this deadly game in which I had played a major role. Originally, I was to work directly for the Old Man's organization. However, nothing had been worked out about exactly how I was to be paid. Now I was in limbo, and no one wanted to deal with the issue. They all knew that my role in the operation had been crucial, but with everything now coming to completion, their appraisal of my value became a subjective matter. My 'novice' status was never openly discussed, but it was at the core of how they chose to claim—or rather *not* to claim—responsibility for paying me.

My reluctance to make my desires and intentions clear from the beginning allowed my constantly changing role to be perceived now as having had little real value. Ironically, that ultimately may have saved me from the fate that awaited them. If I had made the money I deserved for my part in the operation, I might have gotten caught up in the same vicious circle of fast money and manipulation of power that had so completely seduced each of them. On the other hand, I was odd man out at this point and financially at their mercy.

Their voices lowered noticeably whenever matters of delicacy came up. I knew their negotiations had shifted to another subject—how they were going to take care of me. I sensed rather than heard what was being said. I quietly fought back the urge to ask them to speak up. Finally, talk ceased and they looked at me.

"How much do you want?" The Old Man dropped the bomb.

"Excuse me?" I replied.

"How much do you think your, uh, 'efforts' in this are worth?"

Suddenly my own inner computer kicked into action, busily calculating what my worth had been to the operation. Outwardly, I attempted to maintain a calm, almost disinterested attitude.

"For which part?" I asked, innocently. Inside, I felt my mind racing to come up with a figure.

"For the whole thing, of course," he responded coolly. "Everything."

Now the moment had finally come for me to step onto the stage and speak my piece. I had rehearsed that script in my head for a good while, but now that my chance to speak up had arrived, I was at a loss for words. The TV program had changed appropriately into a daytime soap opera.

"To be honest with you," I began, "I'm not sure how to determine my value. There was so much to do…so much that wasn't clear to me from the beginning. I found myself constantly doing things I hadn't agreed to do. I'm not sure if any of you fully understand what I really did. Most of the time, _I_ couldn't even keep track of it all myself. A job had to be done, and even though it was confusing and unclear, I just did what I felt needed to be done."

"Just give us a figure, and we'll tell you if it's worth it," demanded Michael.

He hadn't once been out there in all the madness. He had no idea what really had taken place. None of them did. All Michael knew were the problems I'd had understanding and using his cryptic codes during our telephone calls. To him, I was just a walking liability, especially now that the worst was over and everything was finally in the hands of 'professionals.'

"I'd like to give you a figure," I half-glared at Michael, then directed my response to the Old Man, "but I'm not even sure who I was working for at any given time. I suppose that was my fault for not bringing it up long before now, but there was such urgency, and so many problems among all of you. Frankly, I don't think _any_ of this would have held together if I hadn't done what I did to keep all of you working together."

"You think *you* made this happen?" sneered Michael, nodding in the direction of the bags.

"No, of course not…not all by myself. But there were so many different factions pulling in different directions, I don't think you could have pulled it off the way it was going. Even from the beginning, you called *me* to find you an airstrip. You recall how desperately you needed me then?" I continued.

"And after the plane got stuck and our cover was blown—when everybody scattered in different directions—you wanted me to stay and keep the crew together until Vinnie got there. And Vinnie, well…he was good, and he may have masterminded the final catch, but who reassured the crew that he was trustworthy—him with his slick talk about 'outlaws' and 'bandits'? You think those housewives and country folk would listen to some slick New Yorker with gold chains and silk shirts without *someone* there that they could relate to? I lived with those people for three weeks, My kids played with their kids, and we sweated out Charlie's missed attempts together."

"Okay, okay. You did good," the Old Man played his grandfatherly role. "How much do you want?"

Something inside me rose in defiance to defend against their indifference. My mind flashed on everything that had happened since I first got their message about needing an airstrip. I recalled money-houses in California, and imagined more houses like them in Texas and New Mexico. I saw huge amounts of money changing hands over goods I knew would never have made it to their destination if I hadn't stuck it out until the very end, including delivering their goddamned money to their lazy asses in that Holiday Inn.

"$150,000," I heard myself blurt out.

"Whaaat?!?" Michael almost fell off the bed as he jolted upright. "You got to be kidding. *I* won't even make that much after this is all over," he lied.

The Old Man looked at Bill, and nodded ever so slightly. In that nod a whole silent dialog passed between them. Loyalties were a function of who held the money and who was bringing it in. At that point, emphasis had shifted to matters of immediate gain, and away from those who had made it all possible.

Forgotten was the meeting in Houston and who had pressed them to meet and set aside their differences. Forgotten was the two percent that was so happily promised to me. Forgotten was the meeting I had arranged between Charlie and Michael so they could get their precious airstrip. Forgotten, even, was the fact that half the bags sitting in the room I had carried in *myself,* without mention of payment for delivering them.

Forgotten too was the fact that not one person in northern Florida trusted the Greeks in the first place. Nor did the Greeks trust *anyone*, for that matter. I had unwittingly become their personal emissary. But to those folks in Florida, *I* was all they knew of 'Miami.' As a perceived manager in an operation of this magnitude, I was as subject to prosecution as any of them, facing the same severe penalties under recently enacted federal racketeering laws. I didn't know that at the time, but I did know that my continuing association with them was likely to prove extremely hazardous to me, physically *and* legally. This *was* racketeering, far beyond what I had originally agreed to do. Yet there I sat, forced to play out my hand with them.

I felt them squirming inside, eager to discount what I had just related. I *had* been their emissary in Florida. By default, perhaps, but nonetheless valuable *and* liable. Now I was in the awkward position of persuading them to acklowledge a course of events most of which only I was witness to. So how could they possibly understand or appreciate it?

But the fact was, they *did* understand it. They were masters at the game. They just didn't want to pay for it.

Apart from a commercial on TV declaring the softer nature of somebody's toilet paper, the room fell quiet. Just what *had* my efforts been worth to them? No matter how often I had wanted to quit, I had fulfilled my part. Now, fair and reasonable compensation was in order.

Suppressing the urge to further defend my position, I remained quiet. For a moment, nothing was said, and bodies shifted uneasily.

"We'll talk about it after the next payment," sighed the Old Man with finality. With that, the meeting came to an abrupt end and Bill and I were on our way back to New Mexico.

The flight home was heavy with silence. The deal between Bill and the Greeks had concluded without my further involvement. It was apparent they had restored a measure of mutual respect, but only as long as the money kept flowing. I was no longer needed. Once an asset, now I was a liability—and an unnecessary expense.

With no depth of experience in their world, I was of little use to them at that point. I had little status in their eyes. Greed was the basic common denominator by which people in that business could be gauged and controlled, and until my surprise demand they couldn't find that in me. Now they didn't know what to make of me. Was I a threat to them? How much would it take to keep me quiet…and content?

Of course I had my motives, only part of which was to make some money. Far more significant was a motive they couldn't measure or understand. I didn't understand it myself, but I could feel it in my heart. Strangely enough, I cared about them. Every one of them. Even Michael. Even after I had quit and later learned he was in the hospital for a gall bladder operation, I brought the Elephant Trainer to meet him and to try to cheer him up.

The Old Man felt it. It was at the core of his affection for me. The Elephant Trainer felt it. A few others may have felt it intuitively, but because it was unfamiliar to them, it placed me under suspicion. No one simply *gave* in that business, for whatever reason. Of *course* I wanted to be paid, but there was something else I wanted that was far more important to me. I wanted to feel valued and respected— to be a part of something meaningful. I had lost a father, an uncle, two best friends and my business. In their seedy world of deceit, greed and manipulation, I was looking for friendship, and a deeper sense of belonging somewhere.

There wasn't much Bill or I could say on that flight home. He was back in their good graces, and I was in the position of knowing their entire operation while having nothing more to do with its outcome. Apparently my demand, as they saw it, was too high a price to pay. But they had to find a way to keep me content *and quiet.* What they didn't know was that I would have settled for far less than they realized.

Back home at the airport, Bill and I parted company with the half-hearted reassurance that something would be worked out.

"Until it is," he said, "this should hold you over."

He handed me another thick envelope, which I quickly dropped into my bag. When I got to my van, I opened it and counted ten thousand dollars.

Chapter Twelve

Later that month, Bill called me. A plan had been worked out, he said, for how I was to be paid. We met at a local restaurant where he was a favorite customer.

"I'm real sorry about the way things have worked out for you on the Florida deal," he said. "Sales haven't gone as well as we thought they would, and I'm getting tired of waiting for everything to settle out. I've been talking to an old friend of mine about doing a couple of small trips out of Mexico. He's into something down there that sounds very good. I'm giving some serious thought to throwing in with him."

"He's real solid," he went on. "I've backed him before, and he's always come through. I haven't heard from him in a while, and now I know why. For the last couple of years, he's been working with some Mexican farmers growing sinsemilla on a farm near Mazatlán."

"So what's that have to do with me?" I was puzzled.

"You know about all the trouble the growers up in Northern California have been having lately?" he asked.

"Yeah," I replied. "There's something in the news every week, it seems. I think 'Time' or 'Newsweek' did an article on Humboldt County recently, and even 'Sixty Minutes' did a special on it last month. I've wondered how they could get so much national publicity and still keep producing."

"Well, those aren't the original growers. The guys who started it all have been doing this a long time, and they knew the heat was bound to come down eventually. So most of them sold and moved away. A few of them hooked up with growers in Mexico and gradually moved their operations down there. The people who got busted on those news programs were over-eager 'wannabees' from Southern California and Northern New Mexico who had just bought those fields. Deals were cut a year or so ago, and entire fields in Humboldt County were sold for dirt cheap prices. But all the technology went south of the border."

"Interesting. So how does your guy fit into all of this?" I inquired.

"Well, he had a good reputation with several growers who went to Mexico. Since he used to live there and speaks the language, he was able to help quite a bit. The Mexican farmers love him. He was able to get a bunch of Gringo 'hippies' to bring their know-how and teach the Mexicans the sinsemilla business. When their first crops hit the market last year, very few people could tell the difference from Humboldt County smoke. This year, as I understand it from my guy, their crop is looking better than anything that ever came out of Humboldt."

"Great. So how does all this figure into how I'm supposed to get paid from the Florida deal?"

"Well, this guy called me last week and offered me a deal. In fact, he came up from Mexico two days ago and convinced me to fly back down there with him tomorrow and have a look. Before I get into it any deeper, I wanted to run it by you and see if you're interested in getting involved."

"Are you serious? After what happened in Florida? I'm still a little shell-shocked from all that, and I've yet to see any real money come out of it. I thought you said a 'deal' for paying me had been worked out."

"I did say that, and I feel real bad about the Florida thing. But I'm working on getting you paid for what you did." I didn't have the presence of mind at that point to remind him of the two percent he promised me on the plane home that night. He continued.

"Anyway, this thing with Mike—we call him 'Iron Mike'—sounds so good and so simple, I think we can make enough to pay you a good price to fly the load. It's an easy trip, too. It's just a few hundred miles down the west coast of Mexico, a beach landing, and a quick return to a spot here in New Mexico I know several good places where we can unload you, refuel the plane and have you back in the air before anyone would know it."

"Yeah, I know about your 'good places.' Didn't the DC-6 deal fall through because you guys couldn't find a suitable landing site?"

"No, that was their fault. We had the places. They just couldn't get a DC-6 this far from Colombia. They originally planned to refuel in Costa Rica, if you recall, but couldn't make that work. That was supposed to have been part of *your* job. Besides, I'd much rather deal with smaller, simpler loads like this. The profit ratio on primo weed is so much higher, and it involves a lot fewer people."

"How 'fewer'?" I questioned.

"Just you, me, Mike and a couple of unloaders. You already know them. Aside from the loaders in Mexico, you'll never even see anyone else."

Still feeling the sting from my past experiences with unclear terms of compensation, I mustered up a little nerve.

"So, how much is my 'effort' going to be worth this time?"

Bill paused and scrunched up his face as if he were calculating the figures for the first time. I could sense in his hesitation a distinct attempt to determine how little I might be willing to settle for.

"At least twenty-five thousand," he said, pausing to gauge my reaction. Not getting any immediate read from me, he quickly added, "But I'll try to work out a little more, since you got such a bum deal in Florida." He thought about that for a second or two, then added, "If you decide to do it, I'll pay you something up front right now out of my own pocket for the Florida deal."

The "deal" between them, I learned later, was to pay me out of sales, and deduct it from his payments to the Old Man. I never did find out how much the Old Man authorized, but I knew it was more than ten thousand dollars.

"Oh?" I said. "And how much would that be?"

"Ten-thousand now, another ten before you go, and a bonus payment after we sell the load. I won't know how much of a bonus until I see how much the whole thing is going to cost, and how much comes in from sales of the Colombian load."

"What about a plane?" I pressed him. "I'm not going to be too excited about renting one, you know."

"If sales pick up with the Colombian stuff we still have on the street, I'll give you the cash and you can buy any plane you want with it…within reason, of course."

"This is getting better by the minute. Keep talking. Maybe I'll be able to hire my *own* pilot to fly the trip."

"Very funny. But don't push me. Things aren't good in California right now. The market for Colombian smoke is still down, and I have a firm price to pay in Florida. They don't believe what I'm telling them. They're calculating prices according to what's going on in Florida and Texas, not in California. I'd like to have them sitting in some of *our* buyers' houses and hear what I'm hearing. This stuff needs to be off'd *now,* not sitting around waiting for the market to dry up so we can charge higher prices."

Evidently, he still didn't realize that I knew there was more to the story than he was telling me. But I still lacked the balls to negotiate my deal. I naively believed that he and I were of like mind because we had some of the same friends and seemed to share similar philosophies. I forgot that deals made in this business weren't based on what's fair and reasonable, but on whatever you can get away with.

I remembered an earlier lesson demonstrated years before by another friend in 'the business.' His name was David, brother of a sweet young girl I was deeply in love with at the time. He was all of twenty-three, yet savvy as the sharpest street merchant. He had grown up with eight brothers, all involved in the drug business. One day I listened in amazement as he described how he had just ripped off a friend over a small amount of pot.

"Why did you do that to someone you like so much?" I asked.

"In this business, there's no room for fools," he replied, his eyes piercing the smoke he had just exhaled in my direction. "If you make a foolish mistake in this business, you deserve to be ripped off." He thought for a moment or two, then glared at me sharply. "In fact, anyone who *doesn't* rip you off is an even bigger fool for *not* taking advantage of you. You shouldn't be in this business if you're going to make stupid mistakes."

"How else do you learn?" I asked naively.

"You just have to learn fast. You have to pay attention to what others do before you get in too deep. It's real risky, and it jeopardizes too many other people. You either learn fast, or you wind up in prison —or dead. Trouble is, guys like him end up becoming DEA agents…if they don't get killed first. They make a couple of deals in college, never make it big, and think they know all about the drug world. If they get busted before they make it to law school or the police academy, they become paid informants. That's even worse."

That incident was in the early 1970s, and such was the law of the drug world. Over the succeeding years, with the proliferation of heavier drugs such as methamphetamines, acid, heroin and cocaine, things got far worse. Now I was deep in their jungle, where nothing was predictable except that you *will* get burned if you trust too much or lose your focus. It wasn't in my heart to live like that. Still, something in it appealed to me and drew me like a magnet.

Was it the action? Had the excitement of that night on the airstrip in Florida gotten into my blood? Was it the intrigue and drama? Was it the promise of big money?

I never felt it was just the money, although I couldn't deny that having a lot of money at my disposal was alluring. Yet after all I'd been through, I was sitting there with barely enough money to pay the tab while Bill was probably flush enough to buy the whole damn restaurant if he wanted to.

He was smart, but then so was I. I just didn't have his experience and confidence. I didn't want to be in his shoes, but I did want to have a fair shot at making enough money to put some life back into my old business. I had to prove to myself that I could do it. Charlie made fifty to a hundred *grand* per flight in his small planes, and had offered me the same amount of money just to be a *co-pilot* that Bill was now offering to me do the whole job.

I was so eager to prove myself worthy and loyal to this guy, I was willing to overlook all indications that he really didn't give a damn about me or about the unresolved situation in Florida. Apart from that, there was something very exciting about being able to go out and pay cash for an airplane and have it equipped the way I wanted. I longed to fly the high-performance "STOL" aircraft out of small clearings like I had seen CIA pilots do in Viet Nam. *In fact,* I thought, *I could probably find one of those planes now that the Viet Nam war was over.*

"A STOL plane!" I blurted out. Bill was caught off guard with my sudden outburst.

"What?" He looked at me quizzically.

"If you'll do what you say—let me pick out the plane and equip it the way I want, I'll do it. I know a plane that can get in and out of a postage stamp of a field, and still fly at better than two-hundred knots. I don't know what kind of range they have, but even if I can't get one of those, there are STOL kits and long-range fuel tanks you can attach to the bellies of airplanes like Charlie did with his."

"STOL kits?"

"Short Take-Off and Landing. The wing and tail surfaces are extended and the wingtips are flared for better lift at slower airspeed, plus a few other modifications. The CIA used turbine-powered STOL aircraft for their "Air America" operations in Viet Nam all the time. They could do damn near anything our helicopters could do, except hover or fly backwards. If I can't find one, I still think we can get what we need for under fifty grand. Think that'll fit into the budget?"

"Maybe," he pondered. "Like I said, it depends on how things go in California. I'll call you as soon as I get back from Mexico." He dropped a thick, brown envelope on the table, left a big tip for the waitress and walked out the door. I looked in the envelope and felt the same rush of excitement and fear that I had with the brown paper bags from the Greeks. Inside was a fat bundle of crisp hundred dollar bills. I had to admit, when push came to shove, these guys knew how to get your attention.

A few days later, my phone rang. It was Bill.

"I've got good news," he said. "Can you come over to my place?"

"Sure. Right now?"

"Yeah. I've got someone for you to meet, and some information for you."

"Okay, I'll be right over."

Bill's house was only a short drive from my place, but it was far enough away to give me time to think about what might be developing. I was sure he wanted me to meet this "Iron Mike" character, and work out a plan.

As I drove along, I wondered what position should I take. How much should I accept for the job? Who did he have to unload us, and how long would he take to pay me? Shouldn't I demand what Charlie got paid? I should *at least* expect that the plane would be mine, free and clear, for the amount Bill was willing to pay me. If I could carry a four or five hundred pound load in the plane, and this was such good smoke, it would be worth something in the range of five to six hundred thousand. I should get *at least* ten to fifteen percent for my part.

I had played things too damn weakly in the past. I wasn't comfortable with the way I was coming off, nor with how much risk I was taking. I had learned a lot, but I kept getting lost in the urgencies and complexities of Bill's personal needs. I had been foolish, just as my young friend David had said years before about the 'fools' he ripped off. I didn't intend to suffer the same fate."

I had been short-changed on the Florida deal, but rationalized that I didn't really want to be in their game in the first place. I was drawn initially by the Greeks' seemingly honorable approach toward me, but after experiencing their world, I wanted no part of it. I was glad I hadn't come out better, but still resented not being recognized for having saved their asses.

This time things would be different. After all, now I was more experienced in their world. I had been an integral part of something few successful drug dealers had ever seen. I had *been* on that airstrip, and had tossed a few hundred-pound bales myself. I had stuck it out to the end, held my own and kept quiet about it. I knew every detail of what happened. Even Bill, despite having been on the airstrip, was only on the fringes of the action. He had to be good at what he did to survive at his level, but likeable as I thought he was, there was something about him that didn't add up. I was determined to watch myself more closely this time, and make my moves more cautiously.

As I made my way up the quiet little street leading to Bill's house, visions of high-speed, low-flying STOL-equipped airplanes filled my head. I became even more excited as I thought of paying cash for a plane I could own and use for anything I wanted.

I pulled into his driveway, carefully maneuvering around construction equipment and building materials assembled there. I knocked at the old Spanish door, and looked around the yard as I waited. A major remodeling and wall-building effort was under way. I wondered where the money was coming from, and why it wasn't being used for the operation.

Bill had recently married, and his new bride greeted me warmly as she opened the heavy wooden door. "Come on in," she said with a smile that I had come to enjoy in the few times I had seen her. I stepped into the inner patio and walked towards Bill and another man who were chatting amiably. They both stood up as I approached.

"I want you to meet Mike," Bill said to me as he shook my hand, putting his other hand on his friend's burly shoulder.

"Mike, this is the pilot I told you about. I've seen him work. If anyone can get you in and out of some of those places you've told me about, he can."

Stocky and tough looking, 'Iron Mike' looked more like an overweight city boy than he did the tall, ruddy-complexioned version of the smuggler I had pictured in my mind. From his handshake alone, however, I could see why he might be called 'Iron Mike.' His casual grip nearly brought me to my knees.

He had a warm, friendly personality, and I quickly found myself at ease with him. He was confident, and I could tell right away that he was not one to cross. As he talked of his various exploits, I could tell that he was sizing me up, checking for strengths and weaknesses. There was strong eye contact between us, which gave me a good intuitive feeling about him.

He told me the Mexican farmer story much the way Bill had told it. I found it fascinating.

"Back in the seventies," he said, "you may remember that the Mexican government, backed by U.S. authorities, launched a so-called 'attack' on marijuana growers. In a staged show of cooperation, the Mexican government invited American media to film government helicopters spraying a few pre-selected pot fields with Paraquat. It was only a ruse to reassure the American public that Mexico was 'after the drug lords.' The film clips were shown on the evening news in the States for weeks. Shortly afterward, the spraying stopped and business in Mexico went on as usual."

I remembered that event well enough. Mention had been made in all the news reports that Paraquat was a chemical herbicide more commonly known in the aftermath of the Viet Nam war as "Agent Orange." The damage from the resulting hysteria alone was devastating to Mexican growers. Buyers all over the states stopped buying Mexican pot, leaving huge harvests unsold. Added to that was the destruction of legal crops in many areas where random spraying occurred.

What I didn't know, until I heard it from Mike, was that Paraquat had contaminated the food, the water and the air. For a long time, Mexican crops of all kinds were boycotted. In the meantime, Colombians seized the marijuana market and, in the several years it took for the Paraquat scare to die down, improved the quality of their notoriously low-grade pot.

"Adding to the drama," Mike went on to describe, "women and children suffered in the process. Birth deformities skyrocketed after the sprayings." Now, according to Mike, Mexican farmers were out with a vengeance to recapture the marijuana market. With the help of the highly experienced California growers, that was about to happen.

We discussed the overall plan, and how the crops were nearly ready for harvesting. It was decided I would fly to Mexico commercially the following week to get the lay of the land, and to plan the landing and takeoff. Mike and I exchanged some common pleasantries in Spanish, and I was assured that at least his conversational skills were better than mine. Humorously bastardized by his penchant for street slang, his manner of speech and brusque personality made me like him all the more. As we parted, I felt intrigued with the prospect of seeing him in action south of the border.

Everything looked great. Mike was perfect for the job. Bill was pleased with the way things were going in California, and a new plane was in the offing. At last I felt confident. Finally, I would get to participate in something that felt well-organized and profitable.

Chapter Thirteen

I don't think I will live long enough to experience another ride in a car quite like the one I had with Iron Mike in Mexico. He picked me up at the Mazatlán airport in a rented VW "Super Beetle," and took me on a ride that made a Hollywood police chase tame by comparison.

"It's the most popular car for Americans to drive down here," he said as he wove his way between two large produce trucks and a bus careening in opposite directions. By the time we had gone only a few miles out of town, we were doing seventy miles an hour and passing cars and bicycles as if we were in a high-speed chase.

"What I like most about Mexico," he yelled at me over the blaring horn of a small car that had to swerve to avoid hitting us head-on, "is that down here you get to drive any way you want. There's no highway patrol, and the Federales don't give a shit how you drive. As long as you don't hit anything, you can do whatever you damn well please."

"I know," I yelled back with some familiarity. "But I haven't seen anyone do it quite like you."

"Well, then you must know the first rule of the road down here: Whoever's the biggest gets to go first."

"Yes, I've heard that. But in case you haven't noticed, we're in a *Volkswagen*."

"Yeah, I noticed. But I *think* big. Besides, I *like* these little bugs. Down here, this is what you need. They're so damn maneuverable."

As if to demonstrate his point, he swerved around a slow-moving bus on the *right* side, well onto the shoulder still doing seventy-something. Shifting like he was driving a Ferrari, he pulled ahead of the bus and back onto the two-lane highway just in time to avoid slamming into an abandoned wreck on the side of the road. Then, without a hint of concern that we had come so close to adding ourselves to the wreck, he yelled over at me again.

"There's another rule that cancels out the first one: If you can out-bluff 'em, you get to go first."

"Sounds like 'chicken' to me."

"It IS, only down here it's not a teenybopper thing. It's the way they do things. It's machismo at its best. I *love* it!"

He pulled out to pass another car while an oncoming truck barreled down on us without a sign of slowing up. Mike held his course, grinning widely. I held my breath as I realized that he wasn't going to back down. The truck roared toward us, and with each passing second, its massive grill loomed in our tiny windshield larger by the second. Still Mike didn't budge. In the last second, it seemed, the big rig moved to the right barely enough to allow us to squeeze between it and the car we were passing.

My life had not quite flashed completely before me as I realized we were still alive and now in a full-on race with the car next to us, which had sped up to keep us from passing. The two drivers glared fiercely at each other as they raced along, oblivious to the cars, bicycles and trucks swerving to avoid us.

"See what I mean?" Mike yelled at me.

Unable to muster enough strength to answer, I smiled weakly, nodded, and gripped the seat tighter, certain that my fingerprints had become permanently etched in the fabric of the seat by then. "Viva Mexico," I thought to myself as I braced for the two-hour drive to his place on the beach. I now had my second clue about why he was called 'Iron Mike.'

I stayed three days with Mike in a small thatched hut on the beach while we waited for word from the farmers he was dealing with. We enjoyed fresh coconuts right from the trees, and a short drive to the nearby village provided fresh food at the open market. At night we drank beer in the village tavern and swapped stories of our adventures. We were on vacation 'for the fishing' we explained to anyone who asked. Most people didn't ask, however. They knew there was only one reason Gringos would be in that part of the country at that time of the year, and it wasn't for the fish.

Finally one night, the farmers came to the hut with a sample of their harvest. They spoke too fast and too quietly for me to understand much, but Mike seemed able to hold his own with them. There had been some difficulty with one of their local contacts—a town official who could make trouble for them, he explained later. Now that a deal was imminent, this guy wanted more money. They knew his game, however, and felt that a delay on their part would elicit his cooperation again. We would have to wait a bit longer, but it would cost less in the long run.

They seemed sincere and honest, so we waited. Meanwhile, they took us to another beach about an hour north of there, where I was to land to pick up the load.

I looked it over closely and tried to get my bearings from the few surrounding landmarks. It was a good area, with hard-packed sand and a fairly strong prevailing wind off the ocean from the southwest. That would mean either a takeoff to the south if it were strong, or a left-quartering tailwind if I took off to the north. Either way would consume little of the fuel that I would need for the first part of the trip, since I would be headed in a slight northeasterly direction for the first few hours. With any kind of headwind, I wouldn't have the range I would need. Fortunately, the winds at higher altitudes in that area were reported to be usually out of the south, and strong. With twelve hundred miles to cover, I would need every break I could get.

I told them I would need something on the beach to indicate the wind direction for the landing, and a way to communicate with someone on the ground. Then I realized that I really wouldn't have a choice in the matter. By the time I arrived, there would be no place else to go. I would be coming in right at dawn, low on fuel, and deep in Mexico where night flying wasn't permitted for private planes. Especially Gringo planes.

We worked out where the fuel truck would be hidden, where I would land, and how the load would be placed into the plane. A feeling of *deja vu* swept over me as I realized that once again I was standing in a remote place far from home, planning an intricate, illegal operation that could easily get out of hand. This one should be child's play compared to the Florida escapade, but it was still fraught with danger.

I could fly the plane—that much I knew. I could land it in a parking lot, if I had to. But even with this small operation, there was much to be dealt with. Different personalities, different personal agendas and very different circumstances. From the simple farmers and their problems in the fields and villages deep in the back country of Mexico, to Bill's network of buyers on the California coast eagerly awaiting an exotic new strain of tantalizing bud, there were so many details to consider. Any mistake could adversely affect the entire operation at any point.

We all shook hands, and Mike and I drove back to our beach hut. Later that night, he pulled out the sample the farmers gave us, rolled a small joint and handed it to me. I drew in a deep toke, and even before I exhaled I felt a buzz coming on. Most pot since Viet Nam had little effect on me, so I seldom smoked. The Old Man never smoked, nor did his brother or anyone else in the operation that I knew of. Except for a few times with the Elephant Trainer, or with Bill and his friends in the privacy of his home, getting high was a rarity for me. For the Old Man and his people, pot was strictly business—just like any other commodity. Money was their high.

Money was important to Bill, too—but so was the high. It was not only the pleasure that came with the high, but the perception of status. To Bill and his inner circle of friends, fine quality 'bud' on hand was as important as having a box of rare Havana cigars, or a case of Dom Perignon, or fine cognac. It was a symbol of their success in life, and their discriminating taste.

At any rate, Bill and his group would enjoy this shipment if this was any idication of the quality of the rest of the load. I didn't need another hit. Neither did Mike, who said he normally needed two or three joints just to get a buzz. We were both very pleased with the product.

Back in the states two days later, I began shopping for the airplane. I scrutinized aircraft sale publications and found several possibilities. However, the type that had my interest was in very short supply. Only two were available, but they were pretty tired and worn out. They wouldn't have the range I needed anyway. Their huge, turbine engines sucked up jet fuel as fast as a helicopter did.

I decided on a single-engine Cessna 206, with large cargo doors in back. It had a strong engine, which could be leaned back at cruise for lower fuel consumption, and wheel struts strong enough to land on rough fields. However, unretractable landing gear made for more drag, slower airspeed and less range.

After finding a few good possibilities, I thought about auxiliary fuel tanks while I waited for Bill to come up with the money. Auxiliary fuel tanks were available through normal aircraft parts outlets, but I wasn't comfortable going to a licensed commercial shop to have one installed. There was nothing illegal about having a bladder tank, but there were certifications to obtain, paperwork to sign off and reasons to be given. In the Southwest, there were very few reasons for such modifications, other than the most obvious one.

Charlie had been in the aircraft modification business, so he knew how to install bladder tanks. He could even build a new fuel tank and fabricate an aerodynamic housing for it under the belly. It crossed my mind to fly to Florida with the new plane and have him do it, but even the thought of being in northern Florida gave me the chills. I would just have to figure out a reason for why I would need such a modification. A ferry flight to Alaska? A long-range endurance test? A trip to Hawaii? Something would have to come to mind soon.

Two weeks passed. I was getting very restless. Mike was waiting in Mexico with the growers, Bill wasn't to be found, and no money had come forth for the plane. A great deal still had to be done to find the plane, make the purchase, get it equipped to suit our needs and then test fly it until I felt completely comfortable with it. Meanwhile, the remodeling at Bill's house continued full force, which began to aggravate me. It seemed that the whole damn house was being rebuilt while our little operation stumbled along without proper financing.

Finally, I got an urgent phone call from Bill asking me to meet him. When I got there, he was highly animated and anxious.

"Mike's got a load for us. It's not the load we've been waiting for, but it's in hand and ready right now. Can you do it?"

"What?!? Are you joking? We don't even have the plane."

"You can rent one. This trip will be even easier than the other one."

"Oh, really? What could possibly make it worth using a rental plane? Let me guess. It's already on this side of the border, and all I have to do is fly it to California for you, right?"

"No. It's not quite that simple. I wish it were. But it should be very easy."

"Why isn't the other plan working?"

"It *is* working. We've just run into a few more delays. In the meantime, Mike ran into another farmer he used to do business with, and the guy's got a load for us. Now, get this—they'll bring the stuff *right to the border.* All you have to do is pick up Mike in Yuma and pop over the border to pick it up."

"*Pop over?* Why is it you guys always think that just because it's an airplane, it's only a matter of *'popping over'?* It's just as much risk flying across the border one mile as it is a thousand."

"I know, but at least this way you don't have the fuel problems to deal with, or the exposure. Once you take off, your part will be over in three hours," Bill continued in his persuasive manner.

"I'm not sure I like how that sounds. *Anything* can be over in three hours."

"You know what I mean. You'll be unloaded and back here in town in less time than it takes to drive to Albuquerque and back."

"And what about the plane? You said we'd have our own to work with. I don't want to rent one, especially not from around here. A lot of rental planes this close to the border are bugged, you know."

"Yeah, I've heard that. But they can't bug *all* the planes in every big city close to the border. We'll still get our own plane, but right now there just isn't enough money for one." I fought back the strongest urge to mention his remodeling project.

"It's too much risk with a rental plane," I said quietly.

"You've been renting planes out of this area for a long time, now. Has anyone ever checked you, or even questioned you?"

"No, but then I never had reason to be checked or questioned. I was in the aircraft leasing business. Airplanes were the tools of my trade."

"Exactly my point. So, how would this be any different?"

"It wouldn't be, I guess. But I think they know by now that I don't have the business anymore."

"It's no different, really. If you know the corridor to fly in, and if radar really can't pick anyone up in there, then you'll be through it, off-loaded and back in the air without anyone ever knowing where you went or where you came from."

"Yeah, if nothing goes wrong. We don't know who this other farmer is, or where I'm landing the plane. For all I know, it's a set-up to steal the plane. Or an ambush. How would I explain bullet holes in the fuselage?"

"That's not going to happen. Mike's known this guy for years. He wouldn't get us into anything he didn't know he had complete control over. How long would it take to get the plane?" he asked confidently.

"Depends on if one's available. How much weight are we talking about?"

"Probably three hundred, maybe four hundred pounds. You might not even have to pull the back seats out to do it."

"Another 'bandit' thing, eh?" I said with resignation.

"Why not? You know how much traffic goes across that border every day?"

"Yeah, yeah. I've heard all the stories."

"Well, they're true. Someone's doing it right now, I'll bet. This won't be the quality stuff we were talking about before, so I won't be able to pay you what we first agreed. But I'll definitely make it worth your while, and you can have your precious airplane."

"*Our* precious airplane..."

"No, it'll be yours. I don't want to have anything to do with it, except use it when we need it."

"Okay, *my* precious airplane," I threw back at him, "but I'm not likely to do this again. I guarantee you that."

I called the charter company in Albuquerque and reserved a Beech Bonanza. Strong and fast, it was a fairly new, single engine airplane with room for six people—and had a conveniently large cargo door in the rear.

Chapter Fourteen

The sun was setting low in the western desert as I began my descent to the Yuma airport. As far as I could see, there was nothing but brown, arid terrain, covered with scrub brush, cactus and rugged mesas. For a hundred miles, jagged ridges and dark mountains of varying shades of gray and brown studded the vistas in all directions. Except for the muddy waters of the Colorado River and the sprinkling of scrub brush and cactus, I would have thought I was landing on the moon.

As I banked into the final approach, I set the fuel mixture and the prop and looked off to the south. I wondered where Mexico started, and how far into it I would have to go. More importantly, I wondered how difficult it would be to get back across the border. From my vantage point, it looked rather easy. The engine was running smoothly, and from the response I felt in the controls, I knew there would not likely be a problem with the plane. I had done a lot of business during the previous year with the charter service from which I had rented it. They knew me, and seldom questioned where I was going or why. The plane's rear seats were now in the back of my van at the Santa Fe airport, leaving a spacious area for cargo.

Faster and smoother than older Bonanzas, this particular model was more sensitive to fuel mixture settings at higher altitudes than most airplanes I'd flown. I made a mental note to remember the check-pilot's instructions.

"On take-off's at higher elevations," he had warned, "this particular engine *will* quit on you if you don't adjust the mixture properly on your take-off roll. It will flood just like an old car on a hot day."

With Yuma nearly at sea level, that wouldn't be a factor, but it could be when I took off from the drop site in northern New Mexico the next day. The elevation there was well over 7,000 feet.

I touched down lightly on the asphalt strip of the Yuma airport, taxied to the transient ramp, and found a tie-down spot to park the plane. I got out and looked around. In the afterglow of the sunset, I felt strange and out of place. Not a person in sight. It was as if all human life had suddenly disappeared and I was the last person alive. Finally, from the front of the deserted airport building, I could see the Denny's restaurant where Mike said he'd be waiting. As I walked toward it, I was relieved to see people eating and talking, and waitresses scurrying about like normal. Mike was sitting in the back near the pay phones.

After a quick bite, we went to his motel room. On the way there, he told me some of the details about how this deal had come together. Now that we were in the motel room, I felt a wave of lightheadedness come over me. I laid my things on one of the beds and dropped into the chair next to it.

"You a little nervous?" Mike queried.

"Not too much," I lied. "Show me where we're supposed to be landing to meet these guys." I pulled the charts from my flight bag.

"Well, like I told you," he said, "the place is within ten, maybe fifteen, minutes of here. I checked it several times, and it's a good spot. It's on a hard-packed road, which will be blocked for us during the time we're on the ground. They've got gas in a couple of drums to top us off for the trip back. We probably won't need it, but it'll be good to have just in case... "

"Just in case? In case of what?" I asked tensely.

"Whatever. In case we have to fly around looking for them and we burn too much fuel, or if we need to go to an alternate landing spot. Wouldn't you rather have full tanks on takeoff?" he reassured me.

"Of course. But I've heard about planes getting contaminated fuel in Mexico."

"I bought this stuff myself at a Mexican airport. And I brought the drums with me from up here."

"Good. I hope they have a good pump."

"Oh, shit! I forgot the pump!"

"What?!?"

"Just kidding. Stop worrying, will ya? I've done this a hundred times, and under far worse conditions. This is just a routine pick up and drop off that these guys do all the time. I wouldn't be surprised if we see some other gringo planes down there."

"At the same place?"

"No, but close enough."

"I'd think the area would be pretty hot by now, wouldn't you?"

"Well, there's talk that things are heating up a little." He sounded a bit more pensive. "But it's just too expensive for them to chase down every light plane that moves down here. There's a lot more activity in Florida and Texas for them to worry about."

"Yeah, but it's only the ones that come across the border that upset them." I thought of the DC-6 and wondered what had become of it.

"Well, it's pretty well-known that they don't have enough radar to cover this whole area. Hell, Mexican ranchers fly their airplanes into *Yuma* all the time without being checked."

"I seriously doubt that. Seems a little like wishful thinking to me."

"Doesn't matter, really. I've heard from other pilots that all we have to do on the way back is head for Yuma at low altitude below their radar, then divert to New Mexico. That way, it'll look like we took off from Yuma on a regular U.S. flight," Mike strategized.

"Well," I interrupted, "that may be true, but I have a different plan. We'll head straight east, staying well within the border of Mexico, then turn north along that corridor I told you about at Bill's place. It's just south of Douglas. I flew it with another pilot once, so I'm familiar with it. I can get low enough that if they do have any surface radar, they'll lose us in the scud they pick up on the surface."

I drew our projected course on the chart with my finger. "Right here's the Interstate. Over here are a bunch of hills, and over here is a *very* tall smoke stack in this long valley just south of the border. We'll be so low we'll be eyeball to eyeball with the cows."

"It's okay with me," Mike agreed, "as long as you're comfortable with it."

We went over the maps and plotted our course to the spot where the Mexicans would be waiting, and our route southeasterly from there to give the appearance of a normal flight of a Mexican aircraft. When we disappeared from their radar headed in that direction, they would think we were landing at a private strip in Mexico.

Flying low to the ground, we would then turn north and follow the valleys and canyons into the Douglas and Bisbee area of Arizona. The craggy terrain around Yuma was just too weird for me. Besides, the military was supposed to be experimenting with some pretty sophisticated radar in that area. It was common knowledge that the military didn't cooperate much with law enforcement, but I wasn't taking any chances on a sudden change of policy.

We talked for a while about Mike's connection with these farmers, and how he had run into one of them in a little store while waiting for the other group to get their harvest ready. Mike was bored and funds were running low. It was "average to below-average Mexican pot," Mike said, but they would pass it off as Colombian until the other group's crop was ready, which could be any day now.

What bothered me most was that marijuana crops all over Mexico were reaching their peak. If *we* knew that, certainly everyone else knew it too. I had heard horror stories about Mexican prisons. Even if we managed to bribe our way out, there was no way we would get the plane back. That was too big a plum for them to let out of their hands. Such thoughts played in my head as I lay tossing and turning until nearly dawn.

We were up before sunrise, and headed for Denny's. By the time we climbed into the plane, the sun was just beginning to show on the horizon. The air was cool and calm, and the plane climbed smoothly as we banked to the south and crossed the invisible border into Mexico.

Within minutes, we were near the landing area Mike had picked out on the chart. Throttling back, I lowered the flaps and banked into wide, lazy circles until Mike recognized some landmarks. There weren't many distinguishable features, except for the crossing of a couple of dirt roads with a hard-packed one. He felt certain of the spot, so I flew in tighter circles to get a better picture of the best approach and departure paths. As I did, an old beat-up pickup truck pulled out of the bushes. A crowd of little brown men burst out, waving hats at us.

"That's Alphonso!" Mike shouted over the drone of the engine.

I took a deep breath and began the descent to a narrow stretch of an apparently little-used road. Mike had reassured me that it was a good road, with no major potholes. As I set up for the final approach and lowered the gear, I remembered Mike's driving in Mexico and wondered just what he meant by "major." The air was still cool and the winds calm, so the approach was easy and smooth. We touched down on the road and I kept the nose off the ground as long as possible until we rolled to a stop just in front of the pick-up. Mike climbed down from the plane, and the group of men around the truck swung into action. A tarp was pulled back from the truck bed, revealing several large garbage bags. The men quickly passed them along until all of the bags were on board the plane and secured.

From the ease of his style, I could tell Mike was well experienced with this kind of work. He was in his element, I thought, as I watched him direct the men to keep things moving quickly. Within minutes, the plane was loaded, the fuel tanks were topped off, and Alphonso and his men were back in their pick-up, grinning and waiting like a bunch of kids to watch us take off.

The winds were still calm, so I advanced the throttle to full, all the while standing on the brakes to generate maximum power with the least amount of take-off roll. The flaps were set for short-field takeoff. The engine roared in our ears. Releasing the brakes, I was impressed with how hard we were pushed back in our seats. Mike waved happily at Alphonso and his men. With room to spare, we were airborne. I kept the plane low and eased the flaps up to cruise setting. As I did, the airspeed increased and we climbed southeastward into the bright morning sun, headed on our course away from Yuma.

The first part of the trip was smooth, with only a few bumps in the air to indicate thermals were beginning to build around us. We both felt the adrenaline rush from our departure. I had heard a few stories about such simple events turning into horrendous nightmares. Mike had some stories of his own, but thankfully he kept them to himself until much later. One of them, as it turned out, involved Alphonso in a shootout with Federales he owed money to.

Forty-five minutes later, we crossed a railroad, which, according to my chart, indicated we were still well within Mexico and south of Douglas. It was time to begin a gradual descent and make a wide swing to the north.

"Ready for some action?" I shouted at Mike.

"Ready as ever!" he grinned, as we both tightened our seat belts.

I turned slightly southeast toward a private airstrip indicated on my charts, and then began what would appear on radar to be a normal landing approach. When I felt certain we were below any radar coverage, I banked slowly to the north and dropped into a valley between large, sloping hills. We hugged the terrain like a high-speed roller coaster, rising and falling with it. Smoke on the ground ahead and a couple of Mexican villages rushing by gave me the feeling I was back in Viet Nam, coming in over the treetops. Only the wop-wop of the rotor blades was missing, along with the whine of the turbine and the discordant chatter of the radios.

I banked sharply to the left to avoid the outcropping of a ridge, then rolled to the right and dropped down again to hug the terrain. It flattened, rose slightly, and then dropped away from us to the north and west. As I pushed the nose down; the upward force pressed us tightly against our seat belts.

Directly ahead were the high, narrow hills of the corridor I was looking for. Relieved to see the familiar landmarks I saw on a flight with the other pilot several years before, I opened the throttle and headed for a small valley between two of the steepest hills. Banking sharply just to give Mike an added thrill, I stepped on the right rudder pedal and nosed the plane over and through the hills, then dropped down to a few feet above the ground. My heart was pumping hard as bushes and trees flashed by us on both sides.

"Over here in 'Nam, ol' buddy," I could hear my first aircraft commander shouting at me, "we fly *around* the bushes...not *over* 'em."

Careful not to lose my concentration, I glanced over at Mike for an instant. He was wild with delight.

Suddenly we were in the open again. Off to the north and east were a few low mountains that would provide cover from surface radar I heard was in place near Douglas. Ahead, the smokestack of a huge Mexican power plant I was looking for came into view, indicating our proximity to the border, and that we were on course.

"We're crossing over right now," I yelled at Mike. He gave me a thumbs-up sign, still grinning like a kid at a carnival.

We dropped down again, so low that radar would pick up the cars on the Interstate just ahead of us before they'd pick up our plane. The only difference was we were doing 180 knots across the ground. Whizzing by cows and horses on the flat desert all around us, we shot past ranch houses on both sides. At ten feet off the ground and headed north from the Mexican border, there was only one thing we could be doing. I could only hope that our sudden appearance and our high rate of speed would foil attempts to read the plane's very large tail numbers.

As we neared the Interstate on the American side of the border, I eased back on the throttle and began a gradual climb into U.S. airspace. Banking sharply to the southeast, I wanted to make it appear on radar as if we were climbing out from the Douglas airport, headed toward El Paso. That would put us on a *southeasterly* course, paralleling the Mexican border. No one would be suspicious of an aircraft heading toward El Paso from the northwest. By the time we neared Las Cruces, New Mexico, I decided the ruse should have worked well enough. Just to be sure, I set up for an approach to the Las Cruces airport.

As I began the descent, Mike leaned forward and his expression tightened.

"What are you doing?" he yelled at me. "Isn't that Las Cruces?"

"Yeah, it sure is."

"We can't go in there with a load of pot in full view!"

"Don't worry," I yelled back, "we're only making a low approach. Pilots do it all the time. On radar, it'll look like we're just practicing landings. Smugglers wouldn't be taking the time to practice landings, now would they?" Mike grinned and sat back in his seat.

I shot the approach to Las Cruces, even lowering the landing gear and throttling back to touch-down speed as we crossed the threshold of the active runway. I looked closely at the nearby hangars and ramp to see if anyone appeared alert for our arrival, but saw no signs of life. I pushed the throttle forward, raised the flaps and landing gear, and set the mixture as we climbed back into the sky headed northward. The sun was higher by then, and the rough air indicated the day's thermal activity was well underway.

Ahead were the Sandia Mountains near Albuquerque, and beyond them was the high country of Santa Fe. Two hours had passed since our departure from Alphonso's world, and we still had another hour to go. As we rounded the foothills southeast of Santa Fe, we could barely make out the ranch where we were to land.

Scanning the area for wind direction and signs of turbulence, I began the descent. As we neared the ranch, a sudden impulse came over me. Advancing the throttle to full power, I raised the nose and climbed back to our cruise altitude. We passed the ranch well above the planned approach altitude, and continued flying for several miles. Mike looked over at me, perplexed.

"*Now* what are you doing? That was the ranch back there."

"Just hang on," I said. "If someone's following us, I don't want to lead them right to the ranch. Unless they're in a helicopter, they're not likely to follow this... "

I pulled back on the throttle and banked hard to the left. Letting the nose drop slightly, I stepped on the left pedal, putting the plane into a diving half-roll that dropped us like a rock into a narrow canyon. We leveled out between the mountains to the west of us and the foothills below them as I set my course for the ranch, hugging the hills and the canyon until we were nearly there.

Up and over one last hill, we raced above the ranch barely a hundred feet off the ground. Throttling back to idle, I pulled hard on the yoke, lowered the flaps and banked into a tight teardrop pattern back toward the road leading to the ranch. Two pickup trucks raced from the house to meet us as we touched down just outside the heavy iron gate.

Braking the plane to walk speed, I spun it around quickly to see if anyone had followed us. Relieved to see nothing behind us, I shut the engine down and followed Mike out the door. The plane hardly had time to cool off before Mike and the ground crew had the plane unloaded and refueled enough to get me home. Waving at me from the back of the truck, Mike disappeared in a cloud of dust and dirt along the road to the ranch house. I taxied back to my touchdown spot, set the flaps for a short-field takeoff and the fuel mixture for the high altitude, and advanced the throttle to full power. With faces grinning and hats waving, the crew disappeared behind me as I roared back into the air again, banking smoothly in the direction of the mountains and Santa Fe.

I had finally completed a mission of my own. I had seen a load through from beginning to end. There could be no question about my loyalty or ability now. I had come through with the goods, and had kept my end of the bargain—even if it wasn't the load we had planned.

Suddenly the rush of satisfaction dissipated as a wave of paranoia swept over me. What if those ranchers back at the border had gotten my tail number? What if a chase plane had picked me up and was at that moment following me? Even now, the police could be moving in on the ranch, and others waiting for me in Santa Fe. My heart started pounding as I tried to think of an alternate airport.

But the plane's back seats were in my van at the Santa Fe airport. I couldn't leave them there, and I couldn't take the plane back without them. The plane was reserved for early the next morning, and the company wanted it back that evening. Fear overwhelmed me. I felt disoriented and uncertain of what to do or what to think. Or even where to go. After several minutes agonizing over every possibility, I realized that I had no other choice. I had to go on to Santa Fe and take my chances. There wasn't time to land somewhere else and transport the seats back to the plane. I had to return the plane before the charter company closed that night. I silently cursed Bill and his damned remodeling project.

The aspens and towering spruce trees on the mountain slopes passed in slow motion beneath the plane as I finally pulled on the yoke to avoid them. The trees and jagged rocks fell away beneath me as the plane climbed gracefully toward the clouds gathering above the peaks of the mountain. I would at least have a moment of freedom before heading in.

Minutes later I was soaring effortlessly among towering columns of iridescent clouds. Turning, climbing and gliding up, over, and around them at twelve thousand feet, I marveled at the rainbow colors cascading down through the clouds and playing on the wingtips as I passed through them. I nosed the plane over, dove into a long, billowing corridor of clouds, then broke out and into the clear, blue sky again. Far below me, Santa Fe sprawled out like a miniature town in a giant model train set.

Descending through eight thousand feet, I began to make out the shape of the airport beyond the city. With no control tower there, it was up to me to pick the direction for landing. Preparing for the worst, I made a high pass over the airport, straining to see if anything looked unfamiliar or out of place. Satisfied that all appeared normal, I turned downwind and set up for the approach. I touched down midfield and taxied briskly to a tie-down spot near my van, all the while scanning every building and ramp for signs of suspicious activity. Relieved not to see anything, I rolled to a stop just over the tie-down ropes and shut the engine down. Jumping quickly down from the plane, I walked nervously to the van parked on the other side of the fence.

Just as I reached the rear of the van, a gray, four-door sedan pulled out of a nearby parking lot and drove quickly toward me. My heart raced. What would be the fastest way to escape? Glancing quickly at the plane, I realized I couldn't push it back, turn it, get in and start it before they would be on me.

I looked at the van and wondered how it would handle in a high-speed chase. I reached for the driver's door and prayed the engine would start right away. Just as I was about to leap into the driver's seat and make a mad dash for the gate, the sedan pulled alongside me and the driver's window rolled down. A kind-looking elderly man peered out at me. In the passenger seat was a young boy.

"Excuse me, sir," he said meekly as he looked up at me. "Could my grandson and I have a look at your plane?"

I wanted to kiss him and hit him at the same time. I was barely able to speak. I thought about the airplane seats stowed in the back of the van and looked back at him in disbelief. My legs felt shaky and my hands were trembling. I could hardly *breathe*, let alone carry on a casual conversation. My life was suddenly in a state of suspension, and here they were looking for a tour of an airplane.

"I promised my grandson I'd show him the inside of a real plane," he continued, not noticing my state of near-hysteria, "and yours is the only one we've seen this morning."

I looked up at the sky to reassure myself that no one else was up there. Relieved that there wasn't, I looked back at the old man, then at his wide-eyed, eager little grandson. Taking a long, deep breath to calm my nerves, I mustered a weak smile and squatted down beside the car.

"Have you ever been inside a plane before?" I asked, directing my question to the boy.

"No, sir!" he replied.

"Well, then," I said, "why don't you give me a hand getting these seats over to the plane and we'll have a look."

"Wow! All right!" he snapped back at me, and in a flash he was out of the car and at my side like an excited puppy.

With the boy happily in the pilot's seat, his grandfather and I carefully replaced the seats. He didn't ask me why I had them out. Still unable to detect any suspicious activity around the area, I fought the urge to take them for a spin around the pattern. Still shaky from the momentary scare and from the morning's flight, I thought better of it and decided not to take any more chances. I bid them farewell and climbed back in for the final jaunt to Albuquerque.

I made my way along the Sandia Mountains toward Albuquerque, feeling a sense of accomplishment. Even with the scare in Santa Fe, I felt such elation—nothing could bother me after this. The sun was high overhead as I began the approach to the small airport north of Albuquerque where the charter company had its operations. Below and ahead of me, the city teemed with life as usual, as another hot day wore on in the high desert. I wondered what lay ahead as I pulled back on the throttle and began my descent.

Chapter Fifteen

The drive from Albuquerque back to Santa Fe was uneventful. I scanned the road ahead and behind for any signs of trouble, but everything seemed normal. As the lights of Santa Fe came into view, I wondered how people in this business put up with constant paranoia and stress. Or was it just me? Some appeared to thrive on it. Others seemed numb to it, while still others worked it out of their system with high-risk sports and exotic thrills. In many ways, it seemed to me that the whole drug business was just a way for people to get their psychological 'high.' It was a way to support a need for fast action and an opportunity to control people they ran with. Of course, fast money attracted them, but it was the action that kept them in the game. I had seen plenty of action so far, but I damn sure hadn't made the kind of money that made it worth the emotional stress. Instead, I found myself dependent on others' whims and purse strings. Hopefully, the trip I had just made would bring in enough money to pay off at least some of my debts and spark some life into my old business.

As I pulled into my driveway, I half-expected to be suddenly surrounded by police cars and drug agents. I sat quietly in the van until I felt the rush of paranoia subside. The house was cold and dark. I turned on the lights and looked around, remembering how cozy it felt when I first moved in. A bit of kindling and a match under half-burnt logs brought the adobe fireplace to life. I mused over how different the temperature could be between Santa Fe and Albuquerque.

I sat back on the couch and watched a tiny flame work its way up and around the charred logs. The warmth and the glow from the fire carried me back to that earlier time when I had first dreamed of going to Mexico. Back then it was for a much different purpose. I wanted to live there, learn the language and write. Four years later, I hadn't learned much of the language but had acquired enough material for several books.

A telephone call to Barbara assured me that the boys were fine and fast asleep. They would be eager to spend some time with me the next day. I was glad she moved to Santa Fe the previous year, and that our friendship had grown since those years in Minneapolis. I stretched out on the couch, pulled a blanket over me and watched the fire until I fell fast asleep.

The next several days were somewhat quiet. Bill was 'on the road,' I was told, and would be in touch with me soon. News came to me via the grapevine that the merchandise was disappointingly inferior and would be hard to sell. Mike, in his eagerness to get something going, had evidently failed to inspect the merchandise. Maybe Alphonso had evened an old score, or maybe it had simply been an act of desperation on Mike's part that could prove to be an expensive lesson.

A few days later, Bill returned and confirmed the report. He showed me a bag of what he said had come from the load, all of it stems and moldy leaves. From the look of it, he said it wasn't even this year's harvest. Remembering my young friend David's comment about 'fools,' I considered pressing the issue with Bill to prove that it was the pot I had flown in. I couldn't believe an 'expert' like Iron Mike could make such a critical mistake. Pushing the thought from my mind, I allowed sympathy and a sense of loyalty to overrule my instincts again. Besides, unless I had inspected the load myself, how could I prove otherwise?

According to Bill, payment for my work once again would not be forthcoming, except for a small amount "for expenses." The load was virtually unsaleable according to him. It would practically have to be given away, and even *that* might prove difficult. He lost what he put up for the trip, he lamented, and would need some time to recoup. In actuality, it occurred to me, he hadn't really lost anything but some time and a little remodeling money.

Perceiving that he *had* "lost," however, he was eager to make up for it. Consequently, he made an error in judgment that jeopardized everything he had tried to accomplish to date. He turned to outside sources to sell the load. He fronted part of the load to one of the off-loaders by the name of Ron, who said he knew people in Farmington who would buy it. Located in the northwest corner of New Mexico, Farmington was home to a fast-growing population of young people eager to indulge in the pastimes of their youthful counterparts in Santa Fe and Albuquerque. Ron assured Bill that they would be happy to get anything that even *looked* like marijuana.

Relatively new to the group, Ron had been introduced to Bill in a last minute, friend-of-a-friend arrangement, and was eager to prove himself. Most likely, he also saw an opportunity to establish himself as one of Bill's dealers. Embarrassed to approach his more sophisticated contacts on the West Coast with such poor-

quality merchandise, Bill allowed Ron and his friends to attempt to salvage something from the load. By all that was logical in that business, they should have
burned or buried the stuff.

In his eagerness to build his own group of buyers, Ron let it be known to his
young friends in Farmington that what he was fronting them was just a 'test run.'
A much larger and better quality shipment would be coming soon. If they could
move the smaller amount quickly, they would be in line for some of that load.
Unbeknownst to the rest of us, several dozen pounds of Alphonso's ragweed fell
into the hands of two college kids in Farmington that none of us knew.

A few nights later, a routine traffic stop by a Farmington police officer led to
the arrest of one of those young men when a half-smoked joint was discovered in
his ashtray. A subsequent inspection of his trunk revealed a large bag of poor-
grade marijuana. Barely out of high school and highly frightened by the ensuing
interrogation, he was quick to provide information to the arresting officers.

Ordinarily, a small bust like that would be of little consequence to higher
authorities. But during the questioning, the chance presence of an expert investi-
gator with the recently formed State Police Drug Task Force suddenly made it
significant. Within minutes, he was able to obtain not only the name of the young
man's contact, but information that another shipment of greater quantity and
much better quality would be arriving soon. Pressed further, the young man
agreed to help investigators determine when, where and how the shipment would
come in. An otherwise harmless, low-level and inexperienced operative, desperate to save his own skin, had now become an effective informant...just like young
David had said to me many years before. He was set up by the experts to expose
our increasingly vulnerable operation.

At State Police Headquarters, a team of investigators took the case and care-
fully pieced together scraps of information. An alert was issued to the Federal
Drug Task Force in El Paso, the DEA and U.S. Customs, and the New Mexico
State Police officially launched a task force to track the operation.

In the meantime, Mike returned to Mexico. Two weeks passed with no word
from him. An uneasy feeling started to build up in me. A subtle restlessness
evolved into a full-blown gnawing inside to get out of this busines once and for
all. This latest fiasco was proof of the completely unpredictable and unreliable
nature of the drug trade. If I didn't get out soon, one aspect of it would be
absolutely predictable.

I had taken major risks, yet I was still in the same fix I was in six months earlier. No significant money was made, we had no plane of our own, and there was constant paranoia and distrust among us. A big part of me knew I should get out and get on with something meaningful in my life, no matter what it took. If I was going to take such high risks, I should be doing it with something over which I had more control, and with people who genuinely cared about me.

There was no real joy or happiness with anyone I'd met so far in their business. With the exception, perhaps, of the Elephant Trainer, no one seemed to really enjoy life. Bill had sold nearly half of a DC-6 load of pot in California yet, he never appeared to be genuinely happy. Happiness, as I observed those around me, was superficial and a direct function of how much cash was on hand to lavish on those closest to them at any given moment.

The rules were becoming more clear to me. You make your deals and you play hardball from start to finish. You take care of yourself first, and you do it as quickly and as often as you can. The risks and the costs are so great, a sizable nest egg is crucial. But no matter how much cash is accumulated, it never seems to be enough. Just as important, a lot of insulation is needed between you and the people who work with you. But that was the "Catch-22" for those at the top. Too *much* insulation can diffuse control and permit information to leak into the wrong hands.

In our case, the leaks were disastrous. Back in Florida and in Washington, D.C., a task force of a much larger scope was at work on their investigation of the DC-6 incident. Referring to it as "The Ghost Plane," the media had devoted considerable coverage to the issue of how such a huge plane could have entered U.S. airspace, landed and unloaded its cargo without detection.

In Tallahassee, an Assistant U.S. Attorney for the Northern District of Florida was assigned to investigate and prosecute the case. A former member of a special drug task force, he enjoyed unprecedented cooperation from state and federal law enforcement agencies. And for the first time ever, he had full cooperation from military investigators ordered to account for such a flagrant breach of the national air defense system.

Reports from federal agents and parole officers tied a network of dealers on the west coast to an operation in Texas with a link to New Mexico, but nothing solid was established that could connect them with the DC-6 incident. In the area where the DC-6 was discovered, information trickled in from local people about a Greek organization in Miami. Reports of a government official providing information to the organization began to surface and informants related that a Florida

State Fish and Game officer often blocked roads for smugglers. New Mexico State Police reported heightened activity tying a Santa Fe group with California dealers. A connection to Florida and Texas, the prosecutor surmised, was beginning to look increasingly possible.

While this was silently percolating, I continued to agonize over whether or not to get out of the business. Unpaid bills were still accumulating, and two little boys were eagerly looking forward to Christmas—now just a month away. As I sorted through boxes of files from my old business, I was inspired to find ways to resurrect the more promising ideas I had when it went under. I began to feel excitement stirring again, and for the next several days refined my plans and ideas for financing them in more conventional ways.

A few days later, the phone rang. It was Bill, with an urgent request to meet him as soon as possible. I closed my files and put everything away, then drove over to his favorite meeting place.

"The load's ready," he said flatly before I even sat down. "We've got two days to get it out there. Can you be ready by tomorrow?"

"You're joking. You're talking a rental plane again, right?"

"Of course. We haven't got time for anything else. But I'll promise you this: If we pull this off the way we did the last one, I'll give you what you need to buy whatever you want." I noticed his emphasis on 'we.' He went on. "If you can do what you did the last time, we'll make enough to buy the plane you want and pay you for *both* trips."

"Great, except this won't be one of your 'hops.' We'll have a whole lot more ground to cover, as I recall."

"Well, that's what we've been planning all along, isn't it? That's nothing new. Can you get the plane?" He was tenacious.

"You know the deal with rental planes. They might not have one available."

"How soon can you find out?"

"Well, I can call them. But you know how I feel about rental planes."

"Yeah, yeah—I know. You've made a major theme of it by now," he retorted.

"No, I haven't. Not really. I've only stated from the beginning that we're foolish to use anyone else's equipment—particularly commercial aircraft. Not only do we have some of the more obvious problems, but even little things like dirt or blades of grass or weeds in the landing gear housing could arouse suspicion. I'm not supposed to be landing their airplanes on dirt fields or unimproved airstrips, let alone *beaches*. Even if they considered us their best customers, their insurance doesn't cover operations on unimproved airstrips, *particularly* in foreign countries. They take a real dim view of that kind of use.

"So, what's your point?"

"The point, if you have to have one, is that they may have found something from that last trip. I could be under suspicion by now. It wouldn't take much for them to call someone the next time I reserve a plane."

"I think you're just being paranoid," Bill said defensively.

"Easy for you to say—you're not the one flying the plane. You won't even be in it. Look—you've been in this business a lot longer than I have, so despite what you may think, I always hesitate to push my opinions on you. In fact, I've pretty much taken a back seat to your decisions ever since we started working together. But I've seen some mistakes made, and to me this business of using rental planes is one of the worst. Maybe that 'outlaw' stuff works for guys like Vinnie, but sooner or later it's got to catch up. The law of averages applies to this stuff just like it does with everything else."

"Is this going somewhere?" he shrugged.

"Hopefully. I mean, you're pressuring me into taking a huge risk. I think you should at least hear me out."

"Okay, I'm listening." He looked at his watch.

"I just don't think you can keep making mistakes and taking short-cuts without racking up some heavy debts. Debts that some of us won't be able to pay. As far as the owners of the plane are concerned, we're actually a threat to their operation. If we're caught with one of their planes, they stand to lose their entire business—not just the plane. Don't you think the Feds have been around to see them? Don't you think they've been warned to report any suspicious activity?"

"Sure, it makes sense. But we've only used their plane once for a run," he continued to justify his reasoning.

"Yeah, but they don't know that. I used it for several trips. If there's even a hint of suspicious activity, they'll assume I'm doing something illegal every time I take a plane out. You know how easy it is to attach a transmitter to the inside of a plane?"

"Okay, so I'm convinced. I told you we'd get our own plane, but the money just hasn't come through like I expected. Just one more and I promise we'll get our own plane." Bill was determined.

"You know what that sounds like to me?"

"What?" He rolled his eyes.

"It sounds like a bank robber in one of those old Westerns saying, 'We're just gonna do one more job and then we'll buy that little spread up in Montana and go straight.' Only *you're* talking about how we can improve *future runs*. When is it enough?" I continued.

"After what we went through in Florida, it's crazy to sit here now and cry about not having enough money to go on and do more of the same thing. I think we're bordering on stupidity. There's too much risk, and too much stress. It's loony—and getting worse all the time

"Are you saying you're backing out *now*, after all this waiting? With Mike down there *sleeping* with the stuff? *The load's all paid for,* for Christ's sake." Bill's guilt trip broke into full force.

"You know, that's exactly what the Old Man said about the Colombian trip. Only that was *20,000* pounds…not the few hundred you're talking about."

"But this is *primo* bud. It's not just run-of-the-mill Colombian pot. This is like having a planeload right out of Humboldt County. It's worth *ten times* more per pound." He wasn't letting up one bit.

"Yeah, but is the actual cost you've got into it worth taking this kind of chance? Even with what you might make on the whole thing? Seriously, man…*think* about it. I don't think it's worth it, and I'm the one who can least afford to back out right now."

"I've got too much riding on this." He glared back at me as though I were some kind of traitor. "People are depending on me. I need this to work out, and I need *you* to finish it," he persisted, pushing me as far into a corner as he could. "You're the only pilot I can count on who knows how to pull it off. You can't back out now."

Money was at stake, of course, but making money had become so elusive by that point, to even be an issue. It really came down to whether or not I would go the distance for friends 'in need.' This had become a rescue mission, and Bill was playing it for all it was worth. Ghosts from Viet Nam were staring down at me. Our boys were under fire. Someone had to go in and pull them out.

From across the table Bill looked at me pleading, as if lives were at stake. They *were*. One of them was mine.

I held my eyes on him until I felt there was nothing more I could say. I was not going to alter his course. With a sigh of resignation, I got up from the table, walked to the pay phone on the far wall and made the call. I hoped none of their planes would be available. But no such luck…all three were available.

"The plane's available for three days," I said, returning to the table.

"That's great!" he replied excitedly. "I need to get to San Francisco and pick up some money for you to take to Mike. Can you fly me up and leave from there?"

"Why not?" I said. "Might as well get it all done at this point. How soon can you be ready?"

"First thing in the morning."

We made some hurried plans and agreed to work out the details on the way to California the next morning. It was December 4, 1980.

The next morning I drove to the Albuquerque airport to get the plane, then flew to Santa Fe to remove the rear seats and pick up Bill. When I arrived, he said that he couldn't go. He gave me a package to deliver to Antonio. He would give me the money, he explained, to take to Mike who had called with last minute instructions for the trip. Mike and his crew of Mexicans would be expecting me at the break of day the following morning.

It was a four-hour trip to San Francisco. I landed about noon at the Marin County airport, a few miles north of the Golden Gate Bridge. It was encouraging to see Antonio waiting for me. It seemed appropriate that the night before such a memorable trip, I would have the opportunity to spend a little time with the one man in the entire operation I completely trusted and who had originally inspired me to get involved in the first place.

After making sure the plane was ready for the trip that night, we headed for his home in the woods of nearby Mt. Tamalpais for a short rest. During the ride from the airport, I learned that although he and Bill were still involved in the ranch together, other business dealings between them had fallen apart.

"How do you feel?" he asked. I felt his genuine concern.

"To tell you the truth," I replied, "I don't feel too great right now."

"Aside from natural survival instincts, what's bothering you?"

"Well, I just don't feel confident about the way things are being handled. There hasn't been enough preparation for my part of the deal. I feel like what I'm doing is the most important aspect of the whole trip, yet it seems to have the lowest priority. Too many mistakes are being made."

"Well, from what I've been hearing, that's bothering me, too. I don't know how your end is being handled, but I'm aware of some sloppiness lately. I'm not sure what it's all about, but I don't like it much."

"Yeah, well, you're relatively safe up here, out of the action. Tomorrow, I'll be flying twelve hundred miles into Mexico with a *rental* plane, and making a run for *northern* New Mexico with several hundred pounds of Mexican sinsemilla. If I have any kind of headwind, it's going to get real tricky. And using a damn *rental* plane puts me in a hell of a dangerous position."

"I hear you, brother. It's been on my mind, too. I've talked with Bill about it several times, but he can't keep the finances together to do things the way he *knows* they should be done. It's always been that way, though. In the beginning we took some real crazy chances just to save money. But back then, we *had* to. The only money we had to work with was supposed to be for our college expenses.

"We'd go down into Mexico and buy the few pounds we could afford, then make a run for the border with a couple of dune buggies. After a few trips, we made enough money to hire a pilot and an old Beech 18 bomber to make a couple of flights. You talk about dangerous. One time we came out of Mexico low on fuel in that old bomber, and had to land at an *Air Force base*.

"With a load of *pot?*"

"Yeah. It was nuts. We rolled out all the way to the far end of the runway and kicked those bales out as fast as we could. Then we had to taxi in to their transient operations area and fill out all kinds of forms and answer a bunch of questions. We were sweatin' it out like you wouldn't believe, tryin' to keep our cool. Like what the hell would a couple of rough-looking guys in a World War II bomber be doing so close to the border in the middle of the night?"

"So, what *happened?*"

"Would you believe it? They didn't even look inside the plane."

"You're puttin' me on," I said in amazement.

"No, I'm not. They were either bored stiff or totally ignorant. They didn' check us out at all. They just had us fill out some forms, pay for the fuel, and we were on our way."

"What about the pot? Wouldn't they know you left the bales there when they found them the next day?"

"That's the greatest part of the story. We didn't leave them. We went back and got them later," Antonio exclaimed with some pride.

"No shit? How?"

"Well, luckily for us, the end of the runway was right near a highway. The base was small and nearly inactive. After we took off, we landed at Riverside called a friend and drove back to the base with his pickup truck. We pulled off the highway near the end of the runway and faked a breakdown. While our buddy pretended to work under the hood, Bill, the pilot and I crawled under the fence and snuck back to the runway."

"Jesus Christ. How the hell did you get them out of there?"

"By sheer determination, I guess. One by one, we found the bales and dragged them to the fence. As fast as we could move our butts, we got them over the fence and into the truck, then high-tailed it out of there."

"Damn. What a night that must've been."

"No shit. It was almost dawn when we got the last bale out of there. Another half-hour and we would've been sittin' ducks. If a highway patrolman had come along, it would've been all over. We'd have been nailed not only for importation and possession, but maybe spying—or even treason. At *least* criminal trespassing on an Air Force Base. They'd be so pissed, they'd have hit us with every federal charge in the book. I've never been so scared in my life."

"What a story!"

"Yeah. We've got a few of 'em, that's for sure. And you know, something that has always nagged me about that night?"

"What?"

"I don't think we got all the bales. The pilot was sure we did, but I could swear there was one missing. I've never been able to get over the thought that some airman cruising along that runway on a routine inspection may have come across that bale. From there, who knows what might have happened?"

"I'll be damned. It's a fascinating thought."

"Yeah, it is. I've always hoped that if one of those guys did find it, that he was able to do something with it. It was worth several thousand dollars in those days…more than a few months' paychecks for an airman. Can you imagine? What if the poor bastard got caught with it? He'd be prosecuted as a 'big-time' smuggler, probably accused of using the Air Base for routine stops." He paused for a minute, then went on.

"Yeah, it's a great story. But from what I've heard from Bill about the DC-6 thing, you guys have a hell of a story, too. I almost wish I'd been there myself."

"No, man…you don't. It's a can of worms that still hasn't settled out. Bill doesn't even know half the story. I wish I had time to tell you the details. It's worth telling, that's for sure. Someone like you would appreciate it."

"I think I know what you mean. Most of us have stories that make it hard to comprehend why we would take the chances we did. There are so many facets to this business. That's why I've decided to stay as clear of it as possible."

He went on to relate how things had gotten out of hand over the years, and efforts to keep a straight business together just hadn't worked out. Their earlier years of intrigue and drama had earned them enough money to go places and do things only the privileged few could do. Their activities separated them from the toils of the 'normal' world. They appeared to be lulled into a false sense of security about money. They never developed enough self-discipline to put their money and their determination into a legitimate business that prospered. Instead, they bought expensive real estate and tried to inspire the people they knew who still held onto the 'free-love' and 'free-everything' ideals of the 1960s into working the land to make it productive.

They seemed attached to an outdated vision and the hope that somehow things would just 'work out.' In their jet-set world of fast money and drama, expenses ran exceedingly high. Bundles of one hundred dollar bills disappeared quickly, and there was always a need to replenish them. In Bill's case, priorities were out of line. Cocaine had taken control of his life. He had a 'good guy' outward appearance to friends, but inside he was losing control and growing more and more desperate.

Consequently, he would spend money on his home, his ranch and his outward image, but for his business, which by its very nature had to be invisible, funds were limited. The business was his lifeblood, but it was also his nemesis. Everyone involved with him was dependent on the wisdom of his actions. Unfortunately, his inner conflict charted for him a crash course with fate...with the rest of us on board.

Chapter Sixteen

It was dark when I woke up. There was a chill in the air from the fog rolling in over the steep hills near Antonio's house. It was a little past seven in the evening and I had no time to lose. It would take at least five hours to fly to Tucson, and I wanted to be there between midnight and 2:00 AM. Antonio dropped me at the picturesque little airport, wished me well and drove off into the night. I tossed my things into the plane and walked over to the small office to call for a weather report. The fog was coming in fast over the hills to the west, so I opted for an in-flight weather report and headed for the plane.

A quick preflight assured me that all was in order, and soon I was taxiing out to the runway. The steady throb of the engine heightened my anticipation of the night's events, and a few minutes later I was climbing smoothly into the night sky above the black waters of the Bay. Below and stretching in all directions as far as I could see were the bright lights of San Francisco, Oakland and San Jose. The air was clear and calm. I felt as if I were in a spaceship, effortlessly gliding among the constellations. I set my course for the Sierra Nevada Mountains, and the blackness of the Mojave Desert beyond.

An hour later, I was high over the San Joaquin Valley, barely able to see the San Fernando Valley and Los Angeles way off to the south. Far ahead, barely distinguishable beyond the Tehachapi Mountains, was the glow of the lights of Barstow, the last visual indication that I was on course for the border of California and Arizona.

Leveling off at fifteen thousand feet, I began to make out the bright lights of Las Vegas to the north and east. They were partly obscured by desert mountains to the west of the city. On the eastern horizon, an eerie glow intensified as a tiny sliver of the full moon barely peeked into the darkness.

With the plane on automatic pilot, I studied my maps while I listened to the recorded weather report on the radio. The monotone voice reported a high-level disturbance with a low-pressure system moving across the southwestern desert. I dimmed the interior lights to reduce the reflection in the windshield, and looked closely for signs of cloud buildup. The moon had risen enough by then to illuminate the horizon, which made me feel a little more secure for the moment. Below me for miles in all directions, was the craggy, inhospitable desert mountain terrain I had flown over many times before. Even in broad daylight, I would hate to have to make an emergency landing down there.

I returned to my maps, keeping a wary eye all around me for sudden changes in the weather. I tuned one of the radios to a frequency used by commercial aircraft, and listened for pilot reports on weather activity in the Tucson area. High clouds were moving in, and reports of moderate to high turbulence indicated a weather system was moving across southern Arizona. The skies were still clear where I was, but a check with Flight Service revealed that the probability for rain was increasing in the Tucson area.

The only suitable alternate place to refuel and wait for the weather to pass was Phoenix, but if I landed there, the chance of making Tucson by midnight could be slim—and I'd have to refuel *again* when I got there. I had a very small window of time in which to take off from Tucson and make the beach in Mexico at the appointed hour.

The moon was growing noticeably fainter, sometimes disappearing behind thick, dark clouds. An occasional flash of lightning way in the distance heightened my sense of urgency, so I inched the throttle forward until the plane was near maximum cruise.

Palm Springs and the Coachella Valley faded away—Blythe started to come into view, indicating the California/Arizona border. With the moonlight diminishing, there would be very few places to land in an emergency, so my attention on the developing weather ahead intensified as I continued through the darkness.

My thoughts began to revolve around what I was about to do, and what might come of it. I was only a few hours away from taking the step that would remove any doubt about my culpability if a criminal case ensued. Until now, I could have maintained some degree of innocence. Despite my close involvement in the DC-6 landing, I could rationalize that I had only been "peripheral," and that my part in it was in response to having been threatened. Even with that last ragweed run across the border, I was still able to convince myself that it was just a "trial run." Of course, I couldn't *really* believe that, but since I was never paid for the trip, my self-delusion was reinforced.

Another hour passed slowly as the stars and the moon were sporadically obscured by the developing weather. Strobes of ominous lightning startled the distant horizon as I began to pick up the lights of Phoenix. I could relax a little now. With Tucson just a half-hour beyond Phoenix, I could make it on instruments if I had to. What concerned me most at this point weren't the landing conditions, but what the weather would be when I wanted to take off. Even more important was what kind of weather I'd be facing on the return trip the next morning.

As I pressed on to my destination, I found it hard to believe that everything would be completed in a matter of hours. The conclusion of five months of planning, waiting and worrying was less than fifteen hours away. I calculated a couple of hours on the ground at Tucson, five hours to get to the beach in Mexico, no more than half an hour there, and six hours back to the landing site. Little more than half a day's time, and I would either be free of financial worries for a long while, or I'd be in the worst situation of my life.

The landing in Tucson was smooth and uneventful. It was just after midnight, and I was pleased to have made such good time. A wind out of the north the whole way down, if it continued, could carry me to the beach in Mexico with fuel to spare. The way back would be a different story. I would be praying for winds out of the *south*.

I taxied to the transient ramp and called for the refueling truck. With a couple of hours to kill before my expected departure, I went inside to study my maps and get the latest weather report.

Bad weather was definitely moving in, and was expected to adversely affect visibility for the next twenty-four hours. Not very encouraging. The report carried with it an interesting possibility that Vinnie, I thought with amusement, would appreciate. "For someone bold enough," I could almost hear him saying, "it could work to my advantage." Drug agents might have sophisticated radar and fast airplanes, but they still had to *see* what they were chasing. A low approach to any relatively busy airport on my return could shake them off if marginal weather was a factor. Unless, that is, I had a bug on board. But I couldn't think about that now.

Studying maps of Mexico was unsettling. There were very few navigational beacons of any kind to keep me on course, and very few towns large enough to use as landmarks. Most of my flight would be in total blackness, with long stretches navigating by magnetic compass alone. With the distance I would be covering, a degree or two off course in the beginning could make a difference of a hundred miles at the other end. With no visuals or lights below me, even the coast would be hard to spot. I could end up miles out to sea before I had enough daylight to see I was off course. On the other hand, I could find myself deep in the central part of Mexico, low on fuel and far from the coast. I would be forced to land in a strange place at the wrong time of day. That could be not only a costly mistake, but a fatal one, since there were high mountains in central Mexico.

Landing at any airstrip that far south of the border at dawn with no back seats would make my intentions obvious. Not having an entry visa would wrap things up for Mexican authorities. To make matters worse, the money I had on me wouldn't be enough to bribe a dogcatcher down there, let alone a Federale or an airport "capitán." Bill's house remodeling popped into mind, and I shook my head in disgust that I was still willing to go through with this flight. "Just what," I pondered, "had I been *thinking* all this time?"

The maps were of marginal value, weather was deteriorating, and cash was short. Battle plans were drawn, and the troops were in place. At this very moment, Iron Mike and his crew were loading the pot into a beat-up old stakebed truck and preparing for the long drive to the rendezvous point on the beach. It was a hazardous trip for them too, since road traffic at night was subject to random inspections by Federales eager for a good bust and the consequent pay-off. If Mike was working from the same treasury I was, he'd be in big trouble if they were stopped.

Time dragged as I waited for the departure. A long walk around the airport did nothing to calm my nerves. My mind continued to raise more concerns. On this side of the border, there were landmarks I was familiar with, and my landing at any airport was generally unnoticed and unquestioned. In Mexico, I would stand out like a UFO if I had to land somewhere other than the beach where Mike and his men would be waiting.

Finally, my departure time arrived. I was at a decision point once more. Last chance. Abort and go home, or fly off to an unknown fate. But it was too late, really. The decision had already been made back in Santa Fe two nights before. I was only carrying out the mission like a misguided, loyal soldier. Once again, just like it was in Florida, I allowed everyone else's expectations to suck me into a maze of greed, avarice and misguided hopes. Still, I pressed on like a man with a life-or-death mission.

Hoping against hope that somehow everything would come out all right, I went into automatic like a programmed robot. I turned the Master Switch on, flipped the fuel control switch and pressed the ignition. The engine roared to life, and soon I was on the runway building airspeed to climb back into that jet-black sky. And now, somewhere deep in Mexico, my counterpart vehicle, headed by a renegade Gringo with a penchant for playing "chicken" on the highways, was making its way a hundred miles over back roads to the beach where I was headed.

A half-hour later, I could thankfully distinguish the border of Mexico, even at night. I could literally see the border running right through the middle of Nogales—the dense bright lights on the north side and the dramatically fewer lights to the south. Past the city to the east, I could barely make out the border from the yard lights of the American ranch houses and again, the scarcity of lights to the south. Beyond that, nothing but the faintest flicker of an occasional camp-fire and a smattering of tiny lights in the villages peppered the distant hills.

As I continued southward, I tried to track where exactly I would cross. Once I crossed the boarder, it would be illegal to return without a flight plan or an entry visa. Any return from that point to Tucson or any other American airport would mean an encounter with authorities for certain. If I had to turn back and land once I crossed the border, it would most definitely warrant an inspection of the aircraft. My name would go into their computers, my FAA files would be red-flagged, and the owners of the aircraft rental company would be notified.

Fifteen minutes later, it was too late to worry about it any more. I was well into Mexican airspace. To insure radio reception of American navigation signals as long as possible, I climbed as high as safety allowed. Maximum altitude would also give me a longer glide range to find a flat surface on which to make an emer-gency landing if the engine quit. An hour later, I was high over the Sonoran desert, with only the dim lights of an occasional car or a small village far below to assure me I was still over land. Another hour passed and my navigation instruments began to fluctuate, indicating that I was on my own. With nothing on the ground to confirm that I was on course, I could only hope that winds wouldn't change direction before daylight and blow me too far off course to pick up the landmarks. Another long hour, and I grew increasingly nervous. There was nothing below but an occasional cluster of dim lights. At least I wasn't over water—yet. I wondered what it was like down there, and who might be listening to me passing overhead. Who would still be awake at this hour, and what were their lives like? Mexican farmers most likely asleep, I mused, or maybe downing the last of the night's "cervezas" and tequila and boisterously carrying on? I imagined myself sitting among them and listening to their raucous laughter and staccato Spanish, trying to make out what they might be saying.

From where I sat in a snug cockpit high overhead, I might as well have been an astronaut orbiting silently in the night. In a few short hours, those nameless farmers would be up and going about their daily chores, while I would be searching for other farmers waiting on a beach with a different sort of harvest that promised to make *our* lives a whole lot better.

Soon I could detect the faintest of light on the eastern horizon. Thirty minutes more, and the morning light confirmed that I was still over land, hopefully still on course. Ahead in the gathering light was the coastline of Baja and the Gulf of California. It was six-thirty, and my fuel gage read below a quarter-tank. That meant I had about an hour's worth of fuel left, including reserve. Normally by that point, I would be charting a course for the nearest airport, but this time my only hope was an empty beach somewhere up ahead. If I couldn't find it, I'd be desperate to come up with a way to get back.

I scanned my charts of the area, closely examining every detail of the coastline to determine my position. Unable to distinguish a single feature to correlate with my charts, I feared that I could be as much as a hundred miles too far north, with nothing on the chart I was reading to let me know where I was. Finally, a large town with a small inlet came into view. There were only a few such places indicated on the map, so I prayed this was one of them.

The minutes dragged on as I searched for the slightest clue that might confirm my location. The map indicated railroad tracks just beyond the town, but it still wasn't light enough to find them. I slowed down and began a wide circle of the town for a better look. With the fuel gage showing that I was now well into my fuel reserve, I couldn't afford to waste a drop. Just as I was about to resign myself to the possibility that I was way off course, a narrow clearing in the trees beyond the town hinted of a railroad track. I turned toward it and dropped down for a closer look. Sure enough, there it was. Overgrown and apparently unused, it *was* a set of railroad tracks. If they were the ones indicated on the chart, then not only was I on course, I was nearer to my destination than I had hoped.

Finally, a distinctly familiar group of pinnacles appeared in the distance. A cross check with the chart confirmed that I was nearly on top of the beach. I didn't have fuel to circle around every familiar-looking beach, so I pulled back on the throttle and banked the plane for a spiraling look at what I prayed was my destination.

As I got closer to the ground, I could see what appeared to be the old highway where Mike and I had driven to meet the farmers. I could almost make out the cluster of houses in the distance where we met them. But still, everything looked so plain and nondescript it could have been anywhere. I dropped down for a closer look at the beach.

It was barren. Not a sign of a truck or of men eager to welcome me. Now what? Was I certain enough about the place to land and wait? What if it was the wrong place? I stopped my descent and continued circling, a wary eye on my fuel gage. The needle was pegged on "empty." I had at *most* fifteen or twenty minutes of fuel left. Maybe less. The engine could quit at any second. I checked for wind conditions and the best approach into the area. With a long sigh and no reasonable recourse, I set up for the approach.

Just then, a battered old truck sped into view and turned off the highway toward the beach where I was circling. I made a tight, diving bank in their direction, and as I did, I could see Mike standing on the running board, waving frantically. Were they just glad to see me, or were they waving me off? I couldn't tell for sure, but then, I really had no choice. If there was a convoy of Federales behind them, I *couldn't* go anywhere else. I was flying on fumes.

Throttling back to idle, I set the flaps for the slowest flight possible while setting up for the approach. Circling in a wide, slow turn to downwind, I watched them make their way over a dirt road and down to the beach. The truck skidded to a stop and Mike and his crew ran to their positions, indicating it was safe to land. With great relief, I set up for a very short base turn and landing.

Chapter Seventeen

It took less than twenty minutes to load and refuel the plane. Like a Pony Express rider, I waited while the men scrambled to get me on my way. I felt exhilarated having actually found the place with such little fuel left. Now I was pumped up and eager to be back in the air again. Keeping a wary eye on how the bags were being loaded, I scanned my charts to confirm that my planned route back was still the best of several possibilities. I noticed it was a rather large load for what I had been told would only be a few hundred pounds. As I checked the load for proper tie-down and balance, Mike came up to me, travel bag in hand.

"I need to go back with you. Think we can manage it?" I noticed his emphasis on "we."

"No way. This is supposed to be a 'cargo' flight."

"Yeah, but there's no need for me to stay here. I'd much rather be traveling with this stuff. Besides, I've got to see the look on Bill's face when he tries this shit."

"I think I know how you feel, but this load's much bigger than I expected."

"It's only a little over three hundred pounds. That's about two average-sized passengers. Shit, I don't want to drive all the goddamn way back."

"Why's it so big, then?"

"It's all *buds,* man! The sweetest, prettiest bud you've ever seen. Not a seed in the load. They don't pack this stuff with compactors." He eyed the right seat. "You can squeeze me in..."

"Squeezing's not the problem," I said. "It's your weight that bothers me."

"So? I'm only one-eighty, maybe one-ninety. You've only got three-hundred-something in the back," he continued to press me.

"Normally, there'd be no problem. But this isn't a normal flight. You know that. We'd get off the ground okay, and most of the flight would go fine. But I've got twelve hundred miles to go, and this plane's range is only a little over a thousand. I'll be praying for a tail wind. It's a marginal chance without one, and a next-to-zero chance if there's even a slight headwind."

He stared back at me the same way Bill did the night he so desperately "needed" me. In that look was a whole story, and one that I didn't have time to hear. There was more to this than simply wanting to avoid a long drive.

"Okay," I said. "But you know the chances you're taking. There's no guarantee of anything on this flight." He dropped the bag on the co-pilot's seat and jubilantly ran to shake the hands of the men he had been living with for several months.

I walked out to the water's edge and back to the point where the sand was soft. From there I paced off the distance I would need for a safe takeoff. As I did, I felt for the slightest change in the breeze that was rising across the beach. It would be a slight left tail wind, but it was worth sacrificing some lift to conserve fuel that would be required to takeoff in the opposite direction and then turn back to the north. I had plenty of beach to make a gradual, low-power climb to a decent altitude, and then a turn slightly northeast to take advantage of that tail wind during the rest of the climb.

I looked back at the plane and over at the men now pulled well back near the brush beyond the beach. Mike paced nervously by the tail, obviously anxious to get on with it. Only then did I notice the knots in my stomach. My heart was pounding. The time had finally come. This was it…time to make it all pay off for once.

I picked up a handful of sand and tossed it in the air as if to double-check the wind, but in my own way I was performing some sort of ritual I didn't fully understand at the moment. Somehow I wanted to do something that seemed significant. I reached down and took one more handful and put it in my jacket pocket and walked briskly back to the plane.

"Let's go," I said, as Mike eagerly climbed in after me.

With both of us strapped in and adrenaline rising, I flipped the Master Switch and the fuel switch to "on," and in a timeless ritual engrained in me from my first flight as a student pilot, opened the little window on my side and yelled "CLEAR!" I touched the starter button and the engine roared to life without hesitation. Taxiing back to my touchdown point for the takeoff, I spun the plane around in my best imitation of how I'd seen fighter pilots in movies do it, and set the brake. Advancing the throttle to full, I set the fuel mixture and prop, lowered the flaps for short-field takeoff, and carefully scanned the gages. Satisfied that everything was in the green, I released the brake and let her rip.

With five Mexican peasants waving as we roared past them, I held my breath as we inched off the damp surface of the beach and began the gentlest climb I could manage. The instant we were off the ground, I retracted the gear and carefully eased the flaps up. Sinking slightly with the resulting reduction in lift, we picked up a few knots of airspeed and I felt a reassuring increase in the rate of climb we would need to clear the tall palm trees ahead. As soon as our rate of climb was stable and we were clear of the trees, I reduced the throttle slightly to conserve fuel and adjusted the controls for the gentlest angle of climb possible. With the treetops of the surrounding countryside barely passing beneath us, I knew that everyone in the nearby village either saw or heard us roar directly over them. Was this a new experience for them, I wondered, or a regular event?

Glancing over at Mike, I could sense his urgency to get clear of the area.

"Are you nervous?" I yelled at him.

"Hell, yes!" he shot back at me.

"What about? We've got several hours before we get to that part."

"I don't know. I guess I just feel safer up higher."

"That's only a factor if someone's shooting at us. Do they shoot at planes down here?"

"Only Gringo planes," he grinned back at me.

"Oh, well. Life has its little tradeoffs, I guess."

"I've already 'traded off' more than I can afford on this trip," he said with a sigh.

"That seems to be the norm in this business," I yelled at him over the throb of the engine. "In this case, we need to conserve fuel. Seems we have an extra 'hundred-eighty…maybe ninety' pounds…on board."

"Very funny."

As we climbed through three thousand feet, I tried to remember something I had learned long ago in flight school about "rate of climb" versus "angle of climb," as it applied to fuel efficiency, but I couldn't remember exactly how to apply the formula. I did know that fuel efficiency was better at higher altitudes, but I didn't want to burn excessive fuel just to get there faster. At that moment, surface winds still seemed to favor our direction of flight, however we were leaving them far below. Winds can change as much as a hundred-eighty degrees within a few thousand feet, and without navigational beacons or clear landmarks on the ground to go by, calculating my ground speed was almost impossible.

An hour later, we climbed through ten thousand feet. Winds aloft in that area were supposed to favor northerly flight. I could tell from the movement of our shadow across the ground that we appeared to have a strong tail wind out of the southwest. An easterly route, in that case, appeared better, so I wouldn't waste fuel trying to keep a course due north. I pulled my chart out and looked for a route that might work better than the one I had planned.

"Take a look at this," I said to Mike as I handed him the map and explained our situation. "I can't tell for certain without radio fixes, but it seems like we'll have a good tail wind if we head slightly northeast for a while, instead of due north."

"Beats me," he shouted back, "but where would we cross the border, then?"

"Depends on the winds. I want to go in the same way we did last time, but I can't risk burning up fuel fighting winds."

"Either way," he snorted, "it seems we could have a problem...but nothing we can't handle, I'm sure. Worse comes to worse, we can put down at that spot near Yuma where we picked up that last load, and I'll hustle for some fuel."

"And leave me on the ground with a load of *pot?!*"

"You got a better idea?"

"Not yet."

"In this business, you do what you gotta do," he snorted.

"I've heard that before. I think I'll pass on that idea."

Two hours later, we were level at fifteen thousand feet and gradually swinging in a wide arc to the north. Our shadow on the ground was barely noticeable at that altitude, but I could make it out just enough to do some rough calculations based on our movement over certain identifiable terrain features. It appeared that we were making very good time.

An hour after that we started picking up El Paso's radio beacons, which shouldn't have happened for at least another hour. I checked my instruments and my radio frequencies for accurate readings, and soon had my ground speed. I couldn't believe it. I reached over and nudged Mike awake.

"According to the maps and these instruments, our groundspeed's a little over two hundred knots!

"That's great! Can I start getting nervous now?"

"Go ahead—if that gets you off."

"Good. But it won't be because it gets me off. It'll be because you're taking us right into the hottest area on the whole border. You realize that, don't you?"

"If you mean El Paso, yes. But we're not going there. I'm planning to head slightly back toward the west, and start dropping altitude. We'll save a bunch of fuel, and still make the crossing near Douglas."

I pulled out the chart for the Douglas area and realized we had nearly an hour's flight just to get back that far to the west. The strong tail wind we had enjoyed was a left-quartering tail wind, which had carried us rapidly to the north but also way east. Mike knew enough about aviation charts to realize that that part of my plan wasn't going to work out so well.

"Look," he said flatly, "we can't risk the fuel going all the way over to Douglas, right?"

"It would be a major risk at this point," I said, glancing at the fuel gage and the fuel-flow meter. "We've done great so far, but even with the reduced power for the descent, we'd eat a bunch of fuel going against this wind. We've got to have enough fuel to climb out on the other side of the border like we did last time, and then get all the way east to Raton, which is another eighty miles north of the ranch."

"Okay, so think about this. I flew with a guy from Texas once who said there was a place just to the east and south of El Paso where the terrain is rough enough to provide good coverage for a low-flying plane. It's about a hundred miles out, he said, and you can get down low enough to avoid their radar. He showed it to me, but I can't remember exactly where it is. Seemed to me like it was the Big Bend area."

We scanned the charts for an area like that, but given the lack of topographical features on them, it was hard to tell exactly what the terrain might look like. If it was the Big Bend area, it would provide some radar coverage, but I had never flown that area before. We would be flying unknown territory well outside of the routes I had considered within the plane's safety range.

I thought long and hard. At our present ground speed, we were fast approaching El Paso and had to make a decision. They most likely had us on radar already, and were probably checking their records for our flight plan. It was common for Mexican pilots to cross without a flight plan, but only if they landed at an approved airport and went immediately to a Customs checkpoint. Any deviation from that routine would be immediate grounds for an alert to chase planes and surrounding radar facilities.

We were headed directly for them, so we wouldn't be likely to arouse much attention unless we showed signs of deviation or other suspicious activity. If we dropped off their screen or made any sudden or drastic changes in course or altitude close to the border, they would no doubt swing into action.

I studied the chart for some indication of what Mike's friend said might be there, and decided to chance it. This was exactly the sort of thing I hated to do. Vinnie's "outlaw" crap again. The thought of Vinnie lingered. What would he do? I looked at the chart again and found myself staring at El Paso.

El Paso was becoming the heart of the Drug Enforcement world. It housed the headquarters for a newly-established Task Force that was increasingly able to coordinate law enforcement with independent agencies and, for the first time ever, with military operations. Supposedly, it was not fully operational yet, but recent media coverage indicated that it was well funded and poised to put the "war on drugs" into a whole new level of combat readiness. The testing of high-tech electronic tracking and monitoring systems could be underway day or night. Immediately to the north of El Paso was the immense Ft. Bliss Army Base, headquarters for the Army's Southern Region Air Defense Command, with its own air traffic control system, including area surveillance radar (ASR) and precision approach radar (PAR). El Paso's own international airport had its full array of Air Traffic Radar, including Approach and Departure Control and the El Paso Air Traffic Control Center. Rumor was that El Paso was becoming a base of operations for D.E.A. and U.S. Customs chase planes.

To the north and west of El Paso was the sprawling Alamogordo Air Force Base, home of several squadrons of U.S. Air Force jet fighters. Their primary mission was identification of unauthorized aircraft breaching United States' air space. Between the two bases and stretching out to the north and west for thousands of square miles, was the heart and nerve center of guided missiledom, White Sands Missile Range, New Mexico. With restricted airspace as tightly guarded as NORAD headquarters, even a hint of an intruder would scramble jet fighters from Alamogordo. Very soon, everyone with a radar screen would be alert to our approach.

But I thought we were still deep enough in Mexico not to be of concern to them. But if we appeared to be headed for the United States without a flight plan, they would track us until we landed somewhere. If we stayed in Mexico, they would watch us until it was certain we were *staying* there.

I stared at the map for a long time, then suddenly it hit me. Right smack in the middle on our side of the border from El Paso was Juarez, one of the largest cities in Mexico.

"Juarez!" I shouted over at Mike.

"What?!" Mike jumped in his seat, startled at my sudden outburst.

"Juarez!" I yelled again. "We'll head for Juarez."

"Are you out of your mind??! We can't go into *Juarez*. El Paso and Juarez are practically the same city!" Mike exclaimed.

"I know. Think of what they'll be expecting. Either we're smugglers, or we're headed for Juarez. But smugglers wouldn't head right for the *city*. Besides, at the speed and altitude we're showing on their radar right now they know we're not some Mexican farmer in a Piper Cub. We can't pretend we're landing at a little dirt strip. And if we drop off their radar along the border, they'll know what we're up to, and they'll be watching for us to come up somewhere nearby. They know we've got a fairly sophisticated aircraft, so anything we do that isn't the expected routine will have them all over us. We'll set up for a normal approach to Juarez, just like we did that time at Las Cruces, and once they're satisfied we're landing, they'll forget about us."

"No, they won't—not if we jump right across into El Paso. You know what kind of radar they have there?" Mike said apprehensively.

"Yes, of course—the same kind every big city has. They get distracted and pressured just like anywhere else. Besides, we won't go straight across, anyway."

"What, then?"

"We'll climb out from Juarez, and head south, again—southeast and slightly away from the border, but real slow like a Piper Cub. We'll stay low, and when we get to an area that looks safe enough, we'll cross over and head north."

"Shit. We'll be in Texas then…and deep enough to make me damn nervous." Mike was still unconvinced of my plan.

"Well, we're not going to land there."

"Let's hope not. Texas is no place to get caught with drugs."

With that, I pulled back on the throttle and set our course for an approach to Juarez. A half-hour later, we were descending over the outskirts of the city. I was surprised to see that even Juarez had its suburbs. Soon we spotted the Juarez airport and, not intending to contact the tower, we watched intently for approaching and departing aircraft. A scant few miles ahead, well within our gliding distance, was the border. Just beyond that, we could make out the traffic on Interstate 10, moving along in perfectly normal fashion.

The Juarez tower controllers could identify us visually. We were well below the normal approach path for their landing traffic. I looked at Mike and we both shrugged our shoulders as I banked hard right and headed east southeast, careful to maintain the slow airspeed of a typical Mexican aircraft. I checked the fuel gage and the fuel-flow meter. We showed slightly less than half a tank, which was phenomenal for the distance we had covered, but we were now using fuel at a rate that made me very nervous. We wouldn't be able to keep such a low altitude for long or we'd never make Raton. It was a good three hundred miles away, yet.

I headed in the direction of some small dirt strips I had seen on the map and flew lower, then higher, as we reached what I thought might be the right areas. About half an hour out, I began to see some low-lying ridges and mesas off to the east that I figured would place us inside of Texas. That would be perfect, I thought, and headed in their direction—fifty feet off the ground.

Just then, to the south of us heading due north above our flight path, emerged a big, black aircraft with a wingspan unlike anything I had ever seen in the air before.

I banked hard to the south, just in time to watch the most awesome thing I'd ever seen in flight—the unmistakable, monstrous form of a U.S. Air Force B-52 on a low-altitude run with all eight engines blazing, leaving a trail of black exhaust in front of us.

I felt like a mosquito. It was breathtaking yet fearsome to watch up so close like that. I had seen one on the ground before, but to see it in flight was spellbinding and majestic. A jolt of reality swept over me as my sense of patriotism suddenly turned into paranoia. We would be perceived as the "enemy."

"Jesus Christ!" I yelled, realizing the predicament we were facing. "We're right in the middle of their bombing range! They're doing low-level practice runs!"

Hoping against hope that there wasn't another one right behind that one, and that they hadn't gotten our tail number, we banked sharply to the left and headed north into what had to be Texas. After hugging the terrain for another half-hour, all the while scanning for more black monsters or the jet fighters that often accompanied them, I finally couldn't stand it anymore. Knowing we were well into Texas and using fuel fast, I set the controls for a steady climb and prayed that somehow we had managed to elude detection. If we had, it was sheer luck…and by the grace of God.

An hour later, we were across the New Mexico state line headed northwestward, within an hour of our destination. Back at fifteen thousand feet, we were once again making exceedingly good time. Although the rate of fuel consumption was well below normal, we were down to an eighth of a tank. There wouldn't be much left for unnecessary maneuvering or looking for alternate landing spots.

The place we were headed for was on a high mesa just south of Raton, on the New Mexico/Colorado border. It was selected for its remoteness, the unlikelihood of it being suspected as a smuggler's destination, and for the rancher's willingness to conveniently be in town whenever anyone landed there. I kept my altitude high as the area came into sight just as I had done before when I approached the ranch. I didn't feel good about the way we had crossed the border. In case we had picked up a chase plane, I sure didn't want to give away our destination by slowing down or losing altitude.

Just as before, I passed directly over the landing spot. I held my speed and altitude for five minutes or so, made certain of the landmarks I would need for our navigation, and then signaled to Mike that we were going in. I cut the throttle, banked sharply to the left and nosed the plane into a tight, spiraling dive. With our stomachs pushing against our throats, we fell like a rock. I glanced over at Mike, and could tell by the look on his face he had reached his limit of thrill rides.

In a few seconds, we were on the deck, swerving and dodging the bushes again, and headed back toward the mesa. Interstate 25 flashed beneath us as I set the prop and mixture for landing. A couple of miles ahead was the mesa. The fuel gage once again read "empty." Another mile, and I reduced power enough to lower the gear, but I held my speed in case the engine quit. If it did, I hoped my airspeed would be high enough to pull up to a height sufficient to glide the plane in for the landing. In a few seconds, we were up and over the rim, right on top of the clearing.

I cut the throttle and pulled up into a tight, left-hand bank to kill our airspeed. Lowering the flaps and the landing gear, I came around in the same teardrop pattern I had before, dropping back into the clearing for the touchdown. How I did it, I will never know. It was almost as if the wings were feathered, and we had just come in to the nest at a dead stop.

Caught off guard by our sudden arrival, the offloading crew scrambled into action. With a boyish hoot and waving of arms, Mike was out of the plane and dancing around the truck. Doors were flung open and bags were unloaded, while fuel was poured into one of the empty tanks. Within minutes, Mike, the pot, and one truck were gone, and enough fuel was in the tank to get me home. The remaining truck started to pull out, then suddenly stopped. A man I recognized as a friend of Bill's jumped out and ran to the plane, motioning for me to let him in. As I opened the door, the truck sped off and the man climbed in.

As he buckled in, I locked the door and cranked up the engine. Spinning around for the takeoff, I advanced the throttle and held the brakes while I checked the instruments and lowered the flaps for takeoff. Satisfied that all was clear, I released the brakes and started the takeoff roll as I had on the beach that morning. At sixty-five knots, I pulled back on the wheel to clear the ground, then lowered the nose to let the airspeed build. When we were safely off the ground, I raised the gear and eased up on the flaps, hopefully for the last time on this kind of flight.

Climbing through three hundred feet, I reached for the controls to adjust the prop and mixture for our climb, when suddenly, without a hint of warning, everything went silent. Without even a sputter, the engine had quit.

It was flooded...plain and simple. In my state of frenzy to get out of there, I had forgotten to set the fuel mixture for high altitude takeoff. The check pilot had warned me about this. Now I was headed for the ground with a perfectly good engine gasping for air. Stressed out from the constant tension and endless calculations and apprehensions of the previous two days, I froze. I couldn't think or do anything but pick a flat spot ahead to glide into. I didn't even attempt a restart, which would have worked easily. The prop was still windmilling, and would have restarted instantly with a two-inch adjustment of the mixture lever. As we dropped the last few feet to the ground, I felt the sickening scrape of metal against rough ground. The landing gear was still up.

We slid along the ground for a hundred feet, yawing sideways toward the end. Half-expecting an explosion of flames, I barely remembered to turn everything off as we slid to a stop. My passenger was out the door almost before we stopped, and I was right behind him. Out on the ground and well clear of the plane, I looked back and confirmed visually what my heart knew from the first contact with the ground. There would be no flight out of there today, if ever.

The two of us looked at each other in desperation. What to do now? Grab my stuff and run for it? Stay with the plane and come up with some cock-eyed story of why I had put down there...with no rear seats? I looked around as if an answer would come if I strained hard enough. This goddamn rental plane was wrecked beyond simple repair. If it had been registered under a fictitious name and address, I could have just left it, or torched it, but no—it was in my name. What reason could I possibly come up with to explain *this?*

There was snow on the ground around us. But the cold seemed to generate from inside of me as I frantically thought through the few options I had. I couldn't make sense of anything. Then I noticed a large, twin-engine airplane circling overhead. Gradually, it began to descend in slow, spiraling turns above us.

Well, there you have it, I thought. We had been discovered, which added to my deteriorating state of mind. Although I was glad to see that someone had spotted us, now I would have to come up with an explanation. At least I would have a little time before anyone could respond to his radio calls and find their way to such a remote area. I might even have the night to work on a few ideas before rescuers could reach us. Torching the plane now was not an option, because the pilot of the other plane certainly would have reported the condition of the plane and passengers by then.

I decided to let them know we were okay, so I waved at them and pointed to my passenger, who also waved. Then, thinking I would have time to gain some composure, I walked back toward the plane. Much to my dismay, the other plane's landing gear was lowering. I couldn't believe it. This guy was landing a plane twice as big as ours on a mesa even smaller than the one from which I had just departed. Already, he was turning a tight base to short final. Either this guy was some fanatic about rescuing people, or...

The plane was on us in seconds. How he got that big plane stopped in time, I'll never know. Rolling to a near stop in front of us, he was clearly one hell of a pilot. The starboard engine feathered and the door opened even as he was still rolling. This guy was nuts.

As quickly as the plane came to a stop, a tall, rugged-looking man swung out of the door and jumped to the ground. In a few bounding steps, he was on us. Even before I saw his face, I saw the gun in his hand, aimed right at my head. In his other hand was a badge.

"Looks like you boys are in a little trouble," he said. "United States Customs," he went on. "I'd appreciate it if you both would lie face down on the ground right where you are, and put your hands behind your back."

I will never forget looking out over that cold, barren mesa at those two planes. One had just carried me three thousand miles and was now bellied into the ground like a beached whale. The other had one engine running, and one of its occupants standing over me like John Wayne with his boots in my face. On the ground, face down in the dirt and snow, I heard the Customs agent talking to a crackling voice on his two-way radio. It was a sound that would become painfully familiar to me over the years to come.

Chapter Eighteen

The United States Federal Courthouse in Albuquerque occupied nearly a full square block in the central part of town. It rose several stories above old, concrete structures and even older adobe buildings built in the last century. The modern design with its glass exterior contrasted sharply with the dilapidated buildings that remained in the old downtown district. Impressive as it was, the courthouse was being rapidly overshadowed by the frenzied construction of even larger, more modern buildings that one by one were changing the shape of the city skyline.

One of these was the Bernalillo County Detention Center, where I spent two weeks before being released on my own recognizance. The next three months were spent negotiating plea agreements through my court-appointed attorney, attending pretrial hearings, and attempting to make a living at home while the wheels of justice turned ever so slowly. During that time, various state and federal agents approached me with their own agenda. They pressured me to provide information on, and even to testify against, the other members of the operation. I agreed to provide information only on what I knew about the flying part of the operation, and met with investigators twice. They were not at all pleased with the lack of more substantial information they wanted, and let me know that if I weren't more forthcoming it would not set well with the Court.

My attorney managed to negotiate a reduction of charges if I pled guilty to one count of Importation of Marijuana and one count of Possession with Intent to Distribute Marijuana. Each count carried a possible prison term of five years, however as a first offender it was likely that I would receive probation or a relatively short, combined sentence. A federal probation officer was assigned to conduct a Pre-Sentence Investigation Report, or "PSI," to determine my culpability in the case and factors in my past that might influence the Court's decision regarding my sentence. Finally, sentencing day arrived for me and all four of my co-defendants in the case who were all caught and arrested on the mesa.

There was standing room only in the spectator section of the main courtroom, where that entire day's docket was set for sentencing of various defendants in multiple cases before the court. In our case, all of us had agreed to plead guilty as part of a unified plea agreement stipulated by the prosecution. Friends, relatives and, in some cases, victims of defendants were assembled to watch the proceedings. The morning's contingency of manacled, orange-clad prisoners, along with those of us out on bail, waited for our respective cases to come before the judge.

Attorneys and probation officers moved purposefully through the courtroom as if they owned the place, while people shuffled noisily into the spectator section like a crowd at a hanging. Uniformed guards moved into strategic positions, indicating the serious nature of the day's events. In the front of the courtroom, prisoners who had not made bail or those who were already serving time, shifted nervously on a bench under the watchful eyes of the sheriff's deputies.

One by one, prisoners were called to stand before the judge for sentencing. The finality of the proceedings weighed heavily on each defendant as he or she stood beneath the judge's imposing perch above the floor of the courtroom. It was clear from the outset that the judge was in no mood for compassion or leniency, particularly with cases that involved violence or drugs. Stacks of thick files on the clerk's desk indicated the day's formidable workload, reducing even further what little allowance there might be for individual circumstances or mitigating factors. Those who tried explaining their actions or pleading for mercy were brushed off as tiresome and insincere.

The pressure to go along with established procedure without delay or deviation was immense. The weight of the court's crowded calendar bore down on each case, compounded by the peer pressure of prisoners who lived together twenty-four hours a day. Subject to intense scrutiny and manipulation by others to act according to unwritten codes of behavior, each prisoner faced the dire consequences of appearing cooperative or "weak" in the eyes of other inmates. Eyes, ears and probing minds searched constantly for any hint of deviation from exhibiting hatred and contempt for the "system."

Gradually I spotted my co-defendants sitting with their friends and families. Three had been caught after a high-speed chase across the mesa by a combined force of State Police and Drug Enforcement Agents who had staked out the area. The fourth was picked up with me at the plane. Iron Mike, not surprisingly, had made a safe escape.

My heart pounded as I watched the judge dispose of case after case without a hint of leniency toward anyone. Eight defendants were sentenced before our case came up, and each one received the maximum allowable sentence.

The clerk read our case number and each of the five names on the indictment. From the deepest reaches of my psyche, I called forth my Altar Boy and Boy Scout to step forward and deal with this most threatening situation. A deputy held the low wooden gate open as the five of us stood up and moved apprehensively through to the defendants' table. The first two, Larry and Russell, were called to stand before the bench. Their roles had been minor, with little or no say about the operation. They were young, nervous and obviously unsure of themselves. The judge scanned their files intently, read aloud the federal statutes they had admitted violating, and explained the possible consequences. He then asked if each understood what they were doing and if their pleas were of their own free will. Receiving affirmative answers from them, he then asked each one if he had anything to say.

Neither spoke up—no doubt as instructed by their attorneys as a strategy intended to give no hint of strong personalities or decision-making capability. Everyone's PSI had been completed, and deals had been worked out previously between their attorneys and the prosecution. Neither was considered a "threat to society," nor had they been involved in the operation very long. With no prior felony records, if anyone was to get probation, these two certainly would.

The judge, in an obviously well-practiced manner, lingered enough to allow the full weight of the judicial process to hang in the air and keep everyone in suspense.

"It is the decision of this court, then, that you will be remanded to the custody of the United States Attorney General for a period of five years on each count," he announced. Everyone stayed quiet while he paused to let the impact of the sentence fully hit them. Gasps and mutters of disbelief rippled through the spectator section. People were shocked, and the co-defendants turned visibly pale.

Shuffling the papers in each one's file for what seemed like minutes, he looked up and went on. "In view of the minor role you played in this offense, however, both sentences will run concurrently. I will suspend custody and place you both on probation for five years. But let me assure you that this court will not tolerate the slightest deviance from the terms of your probation. If you so much as spit on the sidewalk, I'll have you behind prison bars before you know what hit you."

A wave of relief swept over them as they attempted to mask their smiles of joy from the judge. My hopes rose slightly as the next name was read. Victor had coordinated the off-loading and the refueling operation, and had recruited the other two. He would be seen as a manager in the operation, and therefore more culpable.

Again the judge studied the file in front of him for a few minutes, then raised his head slightly and peered down over thin reading glasses at Victor.

"You consider yourself a pretty smart guy?" he goaded the defendant.

"No, Your Honor," Vic answered. "Obviously not in this business."

"So it seems," the judge retorted. "Too bad you couldn't have found some other career to which to apply your talents. It says here that you have a college degree, and have had some pretty good jobs in the past. You have a problem with working for a living?"

"No, Sir. I just get side-tracked sometimes."

"Side-tracked? Is that what you call this? It also says here that this isn't your first time. You've been caught before, and it seems likely that there've been other times that you weren't caught. You like to play 'cops and robbers'?"

"No, sir. I'm sure it looks like that, but I think I've had enough."

"I should think so. Your record isn't going very well, so far. Looks to me like you're asking for punishment. You have anything to say to convince me otherwise?"

"Well, ah, not much," Vic stammered. The judge had cleverly thrown him off what I was sure was his well-rehearsed speech. "Just that I'm sorry I did it, and that I really want to change. I know I won't do anything like this again."

"Too bad," the judge sighed. "You know, it's amazing how this courtroom seems to bring that out in everybody. They stand there just like you are now, with this great inspiration to turn their lives around and do everything right. But you know what happens? They just go right back out there and do it again, as often as they can get away with it. Funny how that works, don't you think?"

"Yes sir. I mean, no, sir. It's not funny at all."

"That's right. It's not funny. Frankly, I'm real weary of it. I don't see anything in your records, nor have I heard anything from you that indicates you're likely to be any different in the future. You are hereby remanded to the custody of the United States Attorney General for a period of two years on each count, sentences to run concurrently."

The power of the judge's words, and the silence that followed, kept us all riveted while he studied the papers in the defendant's files. Was he going to be lenient? Would he grant the precious reprieve Vic and each of the rest of us was praying for? He finally looked up, cleared his throat and went on.

"In view of the Probation Office's recommendation that you be allowed to turn yourself in, I will grant you thirty days to get your personal affairs in order. On or before the expiration of that thirty days, you are to turn yourself in to the United States Marshal's Office, or directly to your designated facility. Failure to do so will result in severe added punishment and a serious mark on your already blemished record. Do you understand?"

Vic went pale as the full impact of the sentence hit. Momentarily weakened from the shock, he was unable to speak. Finally gathering strength, he looked up at the judge.

"Yes, sir," he replied mournfully. My heart skipped a beat. As the pilot in the operation, I would be viewed as being even more culpable in the scheme than Vic. At least I didn't have any prior record. I had two kids living with me full-time, and a good standing in the community. My PSI report had to show that I had worked hard and built my own business, even if it had failed. But what I heard about this judge, together with what transpired all morning, had me on edge.

"Next," demanded the judge. The bailiff called Jack Howard.

Jack, the fourth of my codefendants, stood up. He had contracted to oversee the landing, off-loading and transporting of the load to Bill's dealers in New Mexico and California, and was considered by investigators to be the "boss" of the operation. This was not a particularly big drug case, but Jack had gotten away with a lot over the years. He had done time twice before, and had a cocky, even belligerent attitude toward the authorities. An "incorrigible" as far as they were concerned, his future now looked bleak.

"You seem to have a real problem with the law," the judge stated flatly as he peered scornfully down at Jack. "Breaking the law isn't new to you, from what I'm reading here. Not only that, but the flagrance with which you do it seems to indicate it doesn't matter to you what we do or what we stand for. Evidently, you feel that the law applies to everyone else, but not to you. You have any comments on any of that?"

"No, sir. I don't." Jack glared back at the judge with the look of a man fully prepared for the gallows.

"I didn't think so. At least I can thank you for sparing the Court empty promises or pleas for mercy. The Court accepts your plea of guilty, and hereby sentences you to five years on Count One and five years on Count Two, both counts to be served consecutively. You are hereby remanded to the custody of the

United States Attorney General."

"Consecutively" meant that Jack, in effect, had gotten a *ten* year sentence. In cases like ours, where the type and amount of drugs was relatively minor, the sentences would have been "concurrent," but Jack's attitude and history had caught up with him. Finally, the prosecutor and the police would enjoy a little payback.

Now it was my turn. A hundred inner voices jabbered incessantly, and my heart pounded wildly. I was dripping with sweat, and felt a wave of diarrhea about to overpower me. My name was called, and I forced my body up from the defendant's table.

"So, you're the pilot in this operation?" The judge seemed particularly severe as he peered down at me over his half-rim glasses.

"Yes, sir," I replied as crisply and directly as possible.

"Well, I'm sure you can understand why courts are moved to act more harshly with managers and pilots, can't you?"

I weighed my words carefully, wary of any verbal traps he might be setting for me.

"Well, Your Honor, being new to this sort of thing," I emphasized, "I can only guess at the more obvious reasons."

"Just for the record, then," he drove his point home, "so you and everyone else gets it clear, I'll sum it up for you. No matter what amount of planning and orchestrating goes into any operation, nothing happens without the pilots and the boat captains. They, in essence, make it happen. Then there is the flaunting of certain skills and expertise for which this government grants permits and licenses. To use those licenses, under which the holder is entrusted with the public welfare, to flagrantly break the law and enrich themselves, is a violation of not only public statutes but of common decency and trust.

"You used your pilot's license—a license that hundreds, perhaps thousands of young people in this country would give anything to have—to bring drugs into this country. You have no control over where those drugs end up, or who uses them. Sooner or later, they fall into the hands of young people who aren't strong enough to say no." Care to comment on that?"

"Yes, sir, I do," I heard myself say. I had no idea what I could say at that point that might make any difference, but I had to try. I could feel him ready to drop the bomb on me, but I had thought long and hard about exactly what he was saying. He was right. It may have "only been marijuana," as we had rationalized earlier in our planning, but there was far more at stake in this than what the actual crime was. It was a betrayal of the trust and self-respect I had once enjoyed by earning my license, and flying thousands of hours in the military and in civilian life. It was also a betrayal of everything my father had stood for, and what, in his own way, he had attempted to instill in me. I looked up at the judge's stern and scowling face like a kid who had just wrecked the family car.

"Somehow," I began, "I managed to convince myself what I was doing was okay. I let my fear of failure in my business, and two small boys on my hands, to cloud my judgment and scare me into justifying my actions. Instead of finding more honorable solutions, I looked for shortcuts. When I did, I discovered other people I admired who were doing the same thing. We allowed ourselves to believe that the ends justified the means, that because we were 'good guys' with good intentions, then whatever we did to accomplish those dreams was okay. It seemed like a victimless crime."

"It wasn't 'victimless'," the judge snapped back. "It never is."

"I realize that now," I said carefully, "and not just because I'm standing here. I've thought about it a lot since my arrest. Even setting aside a prison sentence, I've already lost more than I can say." I hesitated for a moment to let my thoughts catch up with the words that were coming out of my mouth. The judge seemed unmoved, but I felt inspired to continue.

"I've sat here watching others who, like me, may have used the same reasoning. I'm beginning to realize that 'right or wrong' isn't really the point. What's more important is the trust and sense of hope we have an opportunity to cultivate in younger generations. Instead, we've set an example for them that says it's okay to live by your own rules."

The judge sat back in his seat, and I thought I detected a slight shift in his scowl. It didn't matter by that point, anyway. It was more important to me at that moment to express the disgust and remorse I felt than it was to use my words to stay out of prison. The way things were going, there was little I could do to stop that from happening.

"I fought a war for this country, and saw a lot of corruption at the highest levels. We all watched a President of the United States assassinated, and in that same year, I found my father dead from suicide. Since then, there has been an endless string of political crimes that brought down another President, a Vice President and other leaders we once respected. It was easy to justify my actions, but in so doing I contributed to the corruption that's eating at the core of morality in this country. Instead of doing something positive to change things, I rationalized behavior that I detested.

"To me, that's a far worse punishment in the long run than anything else I could experience. In the Army, I *earned* my wings and my bars, and I felt like one of the heroes in the movies I watched when I was kid. I lost track of the importance of honor in my life. I got scared, and I learned to cover my fear with excuses. I gave up my integrity, and I'm only just beginning to realize how important that is."

The judge sat quietly for a moment, then, satisfied that I was finished, leaned forward and leafed through some pages in my file. I could tell he was troubled by what he had heard. He looked over at the prosecutor, and for a fleeting moment I felt that he was about to go against what had already been decided. I was trembling, and felt so light-headed I reached out and touched a corner of the table for stability. The judge cleared his throat.

"Very touching words," he said sincerely. "It's too bad you didn't think about all that before you took off on that flight. I'm sure you did give it some thought, but unfortunately not enough to influence you to make the right decision. Jails and prisons of this country are filling up with people like you, who could have made a difference in the world. Instead, they took the easy way out and sent that message you just spoke of to kids in their communities that not only are drugs okay, but that doing drugs, selling and transporting drugs, is the way to solve their personal and financial problems."

He paused again while he leafed through a few more pages in my file, then continued.

"Just like I said to your co-defendant earlier, everybody gets a new revelation standing there in front of the Court. But I can't help wonder whether you would have continued your involvement if the operation been successful. I suppose right now you would say to me that you wouldn't have gone on and done it again, but somehow I suspect that even with all your noble sentiments you *would* have, given similar circumstances. I've heard the story a thousand times. Fast money goes fast, and then it's back to the streets. In your case, it's back to the skies.

"No, I don't think I'm completely taken in by your speech, although I'm sure that right now you mean it. If you hadn't been caught, and someone came up to you with the right deal, under the right circumstances, I believe you would take it. Or you wouldn't be here now in this courtroom.

"It is the opinion of this court that this crime would not have been successful without your participation. Therefore, your role is viewed as essential to the commission of the crime, and as culpable as the highest-level managers. In fact, you *were,* by the very nature of your position in the crime, one of the managers. The Court hereby sentences you to a period of two years on Count One and two years on Count Two; sentences to be served consecutively. You are remanded to the custody of the U.S. Attorney General."

My head started spinning, and my bowels nearly exploded. His words ricocheted through every part of my brain. Voices screamed in my head. *Four years?* He couldn't have said that. Not for *me. What about probation? What about a "suspended sentence"? Surely, he'll make it a little easier on me than four goddamn years.* The judge sat there glaring down at my file while my insides twisted. *Why isn't he going on? He can't just leave it at that...*

Finally, he looked up again. My body was on fire, but for a moment I felt a reprieve, a hint of coolness to ease the burn. Now it would come. *Please, God. Please let it be probation.*

"In view of your lack of prior convictions, and your noble sentiments expressed here today, I will grant you thirty days to get your things in order. You are to turn yourself in to the U.S. Marshal's office, or to your designated facility, within that period. Failure to do so will result in added felony charges and severe penalties. Do you understand the terms presented?"

My mind screamed in protest. *What about probation?!?*

I waited to see if he was holding out, just to scare me. It was possible. Maybe he just wanted to see if I would break, or do something stupid. He *had* to know I was sincere, and that I had potential good to offer society.

He glared down at me over those damned glasses. It was all I could do to hold myself up and breathe. Finally, it was clear he had nothing more to say

"Well?" he questioned.

"Yes, sir," I replied. "I understand." Still I waited, clinging desperately to the fleeting hope he would suddenly lift the weight I felt bearing down on me, and announce a suspension of sentence.

"Court's in recess," he announced, and walked into his chambers.

The courtroom erupted in multiple conversations and handshaking between onlookers and participants. Words were muffled in my ears, and shadows of people filled my senses. People were milling about, some smiling and shaking hands, others looking grim and serious. Larry and Russ smiled and carried on as if school had just ended for the summer. They got probation, but I got *four years.* They looked at me and attempted to look sorrowful, but their own relief and elation overshadowed their attempt to show empathy.

Someone came up behind me and put a heavy hand on my shoulder. I turned and looked at him, half-heartedly thinking maybe there was a break yet to be had. He wore a suit and tie, and looked for the moment as if he really cared.

"Sorry about how it turned out for you," he said. "I'm even sorrier to have to give you this. I wish you the best of luck," he said as he pushed a thick envelope into my hands, turned and walked away.

Everything seemed so pointless, I couldn't bring myself to open the envelope just then. I made my way through the crowded hallway outside the courtroom, and found my way to the lot where my van was parked. When I reached into my pocket for the keys, I still had the envelope in my hand. I got in the van and sat for a moment behind the wheel, then tore the envelope open. What could be so damned important it had to be handed to me at that particular moment?

I unfolded the official looking documents and found a summons to appear before yet another court to answer a civil lawsuit filed by an insurance company. Through the tears now filling my eyes, I noticed something about damage to an airplane in the amount of $30,000. There was something else about "punitive damages," and an amount I couldn't even fathom at that moment.

I shoved the papers into my suit coat pocket and drove across town and onto the freeway towards Santa Fe. How could I possibly deal with this? How would I break the news to the boys?

I had never driven as slowly as I did going home that day. A few miles north of Albuquerque, I pulled off the freeway and drove to a grove of Cottonwood trees and sat by the edge of the Rio Grande. How peacefully the water flowed, and how simple life seemed there in that moment. The trees swayed gently in the light breeze as I sat quietly mourning the death of something essential to me.

Freedom to choose my destiny had just been ripped away from me…for good.

Chapter Nineteen

A week passed. Still reeling from the shock of knowing I was actually going to prison, I grew steadily more bitter and angry. Angry with Bill, angry with the judge, angry with life, angry with myself.

Resigned to my fate, I began to wind up my personal affairs and started packing my things for storage. I arranged for the boys to go with Barbara to Taos, while I "went away for a while." She and I had remained on good terms throughout the ordeal, and I knew she would provide a loving home for them in my absence.

In the meantime, fate delivered an ironic twist. Right after the Florida trip, a relationship had developed with a young woman I had met in Colorado. With the advance money Bill had given me for the Mexico deal, I had taken a camping trip to the alpine country of Aspen for a few weeks to recover some sanity and give my nerves a rest. Joan was a radiant beauty. Almost like a storybook princess, she had appeared in the pine forest where I was camping and took my breath away. Not only was she tanned and healthy from a summer of cutting firewood for the condominiums and resorts of Aspen, but she also ran a successful white-water rafting company with her soon-to-be-former husband. We hit it off right away. The chemistry was definitely right, and after a couple of weeks of blissful time together, she announced that she wanted to come to New Mexico with me.

Although she gradually became aware of my involvement with Bill, she kept herself "removed" from all of it. But clearly she wanted to be close to me. Even taking on my two kids didn't dampen her tenacious spirit in the months that passed before my arrest. In fact, she treated them as if they were her own. After my arrest, she let me know that she intended to stick with me all the way through the legal process. She said she'd even stay connected with the boys from time to time, and would help with their upbringing.

Now it was time to face the trial of separation. I arranged for her to keep my van and an old Airstream travel trailer we had bought by pooling our few assets and available cash. While I prepared for my journey, she worked at two jobs to save enough money to travel during my "settling in" period. Then, if she still felt strongly enough to stay with me, she could move to wherever I was. I understood that my designated facility was the La Tuna Federal Correctional Institution near El Paso, which wouldn't be too difficult for her. Work and affordable housing in a community that size wouldn't be difficult. But neither of us expected or planned for anything specific. There were too many variables, and life would not be easy for either of us for a while.

One day while I was packing and Joan was at work, I was startled by the door bell. As I worked my way through the assortment of partially filled boxes toward the front door, I wondered who would be visiting me at this point. Most of my friends had suddenly become "too busy" to spend time with me. Perhaps one of them had finally decided to drop by to offer some encouragement

When I opened the door, I was startled to see the face of the New Mexico State Police lieutenant that had been in charge of the investigation of my case.

"Hello," I said hesitatingly.

"May I come in?" he asked. My curiosity was aroused by a hint of respectfulness in his manner.

"Is this an official visit?" I inquired.

"Yes...and no," he replied.

"Well, which part is 'yes', and which is 'no'?"

"I think I could explain that a little better inside, if you care to listen. I have a few questions to ask you, and perhaps a bit of helpful information for you."

I remembered the Elephant Trainer's warning. I distinctly felt the rope dangling. But I also detected enough sincerity in his voice to feel there was no harm in finding out what he wanted.

"You've already been sentenced," he went on with a bit more urgency. "It can't hurt you to listen. I might even be able to help you some."

"Okay, come in," I said, as I backed away from the door. "You'll have to excuse the boxes and the clutter. As you can see, I'm packing."

"Yes, I see." He noted the sarcasm in my voice as he found a place to sit on the couch. I took a dining room chair and placed it opposite him, sitting so that the back of it was between us.

"I've been reading over your files," he said ponderously. "And I'll be damned if I can understand why you have to go through all this. You have a good record You didn't really need to do any time."

"We've been through all this before," I cut him off with some exasperation. After my arrest, he and his colleagues had grilled me at length about what I knew, and if I would be willing to testify against the bigger players in the operation.

"Yes, but we thought you may have had a chance to reconsider."

"I told you all I knew about the flight routes, and I gave you information that might be useful in other cases. I told you I didn't really know Jack and his group that well. In fact, you know far more about them than I ever did. I purposefully stayed as far away from them as possible."

"Let's say for the moment that that's true," he went on. "Someone hired you and financed the deal. We know it wasn't Jack. As crafty as he is, he's not smart enough to handle the kind of money and logistics this operation required. From what I've read in your files, and from what I've learned about you from background checks, I can't picture you mixed up with Jack and his kind. You guys had a money man behind this deal. One who had deep connections in Mexico, as well as buyers for what I'm told is some pretty high-quality stuff. This stuff is way out of Jack's league. We're pretty sure we know who the guy is. If it's who we think it is, he's an even worse scumbag than Jack. He may appear like a decent guy, but it's guys like him that keep Jack and his kind in business. They set these things up, rake the cream off the top, and let guys like you do their dirty work for them...*and* do their time on top of it."

"So, what do you want from me? You want me to make up a name to give you?"

"No, of course not. We know you were working with someone else. We also know that there was another guy that came up from Mexico with you. We want to know who they are, and where we can find them. If you cooperate with us, I'm sure we could get the judge to reconsider your sentence."

"Reconsider? Exactly what does that mean?"

"Well, it means we might get your sentence reduced. We could probably get you out earlier, or at least into a decent facility with some privileges."

"Might? Probably? Those are very tricky words. Neither one sounds too solid to me."

"That's the best I'm allowed to offer you right now. It's up to the judge, once you're sentenced. Even the prosecutor can't guarantee anything, but he does swing a lot of weight."

"A 'reduced sentence', eh? I guess you guys don't read the papers. Or maybe you don't really give a damn what happens to guys once they cooperate and then have to do time anyway. They don't live too long, you know."

"Well, that happens sometimes—but only at much higher levels, and when there's a lot more at stake. In your case, it could go *much* easier for you than you might think."

"I told you I would be willing to work with you on something I didn't have a prior agreement on. Some people out there need to be locked up because of sheer greed and malice. I was willing to consider setting up some kind of 'sting' oper- ation, but not just to save my own skin," I said. In any case, I can't stomach rolling over on someone on the mere hope it 'might' set well with the judge. It's hard enough living with the fact that I'm now a convicted criminal, but I'd have a hard time rolling over on someone just to save myself."

"Well, which do you prefer: *having* a hard time, or *doing* hard time?"

"Neither one, of course. I felt that I had offered a plausible option for you. We could have worked something out that would have served both of our purposes.'

"Doesn't work that way. That's for the movies and television. It won't hold water with the people I work for. Besides, the judge likes to see good faith. Anyway, you think it over and give me a call. I can get you a break, but you've got to come clean."

He got up, left his card on one of the boxes, and headed for the door. Pausing for a moment, he turned and said, "Remember, 'concurrent' is a whole lot better than 'consecutive'. That much I know I can do. It can get better, but you'll have to show good faith. How, or even *if,* you do your time depends entirely on you."

He left me to my unpacked boxes and a lot to think about. He was dangling a rope, but there was no certainty it wouldn't be yanked away. Even if it wasn't, weighing what was the "right" thing to do in a situation where everything went wrong plagued my reasoning. Playing ball with the authorities would hardly set well with the motley crew hidden in the wings. A few days later, the phone rang. I picked up the receiver.

"Hello?" I said.

Nothing.

"Hello?" I repeated.

Not a sound.

"Hello? Who's there?" I asked again.

Still only silence. I hung up the phone and continued packing. A few minutes later the phone rang again. This time, I heard a sinister voice, muffled so I couldn't recognize it.

"We know you've been talking. Keep it up, and you won't be talking long. Consider this a 'courtesy warning'. But it's also a promise." A click, and the voice was gone.

I was thrown off by the call. Evidently, someone had been watching my house when the lieutenant was there. God, how stupid of these cops to think they can just drive right up to a newly convicted felon's house in their unmarked cars and think nothing about it. And *he* assured *me* of protection!

Two nights later, a trusted old friend showed up at my back door. The last person I expected to see was the Elephant Trainer. At first I was delighted to see him again. Then I was taken aback by his brusque, commando-like manner as he scanned the kitchen closely before he said anything.

"What the hell are you *doing?*" he demanded in a hushed but forceful tone. "You can't be talking to these cops. Don't you know they don't give a shit about you? Why the hell would you want to talk to them at this point?"

"I'm not talking," I said. "Not about anything significant. They've tried twice to get names and information from me, but I haven't given them anything. Why do you suppose I got *four years?*" I was suddenly on the defensive.

"That's what everyone thought, at first. Now it seems that was only to get you to talk. Now they'll offer you deals on their terms. Once they've got you by the balls, like they do now, they'll squeeze until you talk. Now's when the *real* shit starts to fly. You'll be smart to keep your mouth shut. Go do your time like the rest of us have done, and you'll come out better for it in the long run."

"That's what I'm doing. Look around here. Can't you see I'm packing? I didn't invite the guy here."

"You didn't have to let him in," he said pointedly.

"I wanted to see what he wanted. Besides, it's *my* goddamn house. It's my business who I open my door to. If you're so concerned about the people I'm entertaining, then *you* can pay my rent. And while you're at it, you can hire me a decent attorney, and get me an appeal." I was losing it, and I didn't care.

"I'm not the one who's nervous. I could care less who you talk to. I'd just like to spare you some grief before you create a bigger problem for yourself." His tone was sobering.

"You think I want more grief than I already have?"

"No. Stay cool. Things always work out for the better, eventually, if you keep to yourself from this point. Things will never work out by talking to cops. They'll make it seem like it will, but they'll only take your information and leave you hanging by your balls. They don't care about you." Our eyes locked.

"And you do?"

"Yes, of course. That's why I'm here. It's the *only* reason I'm here. Nobody sent me. I heard you were in trouble, and I came to see if I could help. I'm just letting you know that you've gotta be more careful. You'll get help. Keep quiet, do your time, and it'll all be over before you know it. When you get out, and even while you're in, things will start to happen for you. You'll survive—but not if people think you're a snitch. That's no way to do time, I can assure you. I've been there. I did most of my time in solitary because I wouldn't kiss up to anyone, and I'm doing fine now.

"Anyway, I can't risk coming here again. It's too hot. You know you're being watched all the time, don't you?"

"Yeah, I see them coming and going a lot."

"Well, you might as well know that one of their people, a *federal* parole officer, told a couple of his parolees that you've talked already, and that you've been talking all along."

"Bullshit! I met with investigators a couple of times, like I said. I gave them some vague information about routes and places to land...stuff that anybody can figure out. But I never gave them any names, or what they really wanted. They were pissed off. *That's* probably why their guy is leaking information." My frustrations mounted.

"Well, *I* believe you, but there are a couple of guys we both know who might not believe it much longer. They're watching what's going on, and they're *real* nervous. You're a prime candidate for the Witness Protection Program, and they don't want to see you suddenly disappear."

"Oh? Seems like that's *exactly* what they'd like to have happen."

"Not if they don't know where you've gone."

"Well, that's too damn bad. I've been in this mess up to my neck right from the start, and haven't had a grain of help from anyone yet. Now, all of sudden, they're concerned about what's happening to me? Not likely. All they're concerned with is their own necks."

"That may be true, but right now the spotlight's on you. If anything you do looks the least bit suspicious, there are people who might see that you *do* disappear."

"Is that a threat?"

"Not from *me*. I'm just giving a friend a warning, nothing more."

"Well, I wish I could be more convincing, but right now it's *my* ass on the line—not theirs."

"Yeah, well it might be more than your *ass,* if you're not real careful. I'm serious about this," he said quietly.

"Thanks for the warning. How about getting the message back to them that I'm not doing anything but getting ready to do my time. You see all these boxes being packed? That's not for the 'Witness Protection Program'."

"Yes, but the point is, you could go either way right now. That's what's making them nervous. "

"Well, where was everyone when I was in court? And what about financial help? Someone left a duffle bag of shit weed in my yard. Was that their idea of a 'legal defense fund'? What the hell was I supposed to do with that shit? Even if it was pure *bud,* I wouldn't have been able to do anything with it. Especially now. I don't have any contacts. That was so stupid. Such a low-life thing to do, dropping a duffle bag like that in my front yard."

"I don't know about that, or who's idea it was. It sounds like something Jack's guys might do. But you told everyone from the start you didn't want any legal help."

"Not from some high-powered drug attorney, no. I wanted to be seen as someone who was basically decent, who made a mistake. But some help with my personal expenses would have made it easier for me. This whole damn thing was poor-boyed from the start. I warned Bill over and over. None of this had to happen."

"Well, *you* know that and *I* know that," he said, "but that comes with the territory. I told you when you first got into the Florida thing, there are always wild cards in this business. You live through it, and you learn. Sometimes you're dealt a great hand, other times a rotten one. You try to average 'em out. I did three years in a *Mexican* prison. Try *that* before you get too self-righteous."

"Anyway," he went on, "I've got a lot to do tonight, and I have a plane to catch in the morning. I just wanted you to know that it's never as bad as it looks. But if you run scared and start making deals with the government, you'll wish you hadn't."

"Yes, I'm getting the picture. I've already seen the way they've handled their 'deal making' with me so far. What's hard is the lack of support from our side, the people I put my ass on the line for. It's like nobody gives a damn."

"Yeah, I know. But things will work out. They always do, if you keep your wits about you. The cops'll put heavy pressure on you until they figure you're not going to give in. If you show any weakness, they'll be on you until you break. Some of them can come off as the nicest guys, too. You'd think you could move in and live with 'em, they'll be so nice. But it only lasts 'til they get what they want."

"Okay, okay. I got it. Now how about telling the guys to back off and stop thinking I've become an informant?"

"I'll do my best, but it's what *you do* that counts. I won't be seeing you for a while, but it won't be because I don't care. It's just the way things are for now. I can't let myself get dragged into this. I've got a record, and they can still yank the old chain. I wish you the best. And I *mean* that. Good Luck."

He stood up, gave me a hug, and was out the door. For the brief time I had known him, I felt like he was my closest, most trusted friend. Now he was gone, and since that day, I've never seen him again.

Two nights later, as I was packing the last of the boxes, I was startled by a loud crash in the front part of the house. I ran into the living room and there in the middle of shattered glass from the window it came through, I found a piece of broken brick on the floor with a note wrapped around it. I couldn't believe it. It was just like something in a movie. I looked out the window. There was nothing. No car squealing away, no dark, sinister figures running in the night. I bent over and picked up the piece of brick, removed the note and read it.

Talk any more, asshole, and you won't make it to the joint. We're watching you. Meet with those pricks again and child support will be one less thing you'll need to worry about.

My blood ran cold. I looked around at the nearly empty house and tried to imagine who might be out there watching me. I went into the bedroom, picked up the phone, and called another friend of mine—one I knew I could still trust.

Ron was a successful building contractor who had taken a liking to my innovative ideas for marketing new business ventures. He was a well-educated world traveler, intensely involved in life. He was also a former high-level agent for the CIA.

Thankfully, he was home and agreed to meet with me later that night. Aware of the legal problems I was having, he suggested an obscure little bar, far from the places we generally frequented. It was good to feel his genuine concern as I told him what was happening, and to know that at least this was a person who had well-placed contacts that could advise me. After reassuring me that he would look into the matter, he left and I went home.

Joan had gone out of town for a few days. While I waited for Ron to get back to me, I kept a low profile in the house. Finally, he called and asked me to meet him outside of town on a remote road near the airport. His apparent need for such secrecy was unnerving.

His car was well hidden in a stand of piñon trees when I arrived. The remote location, and the way he hid himself, gave me the creeps. Had I not known him so well, I would have turned around and made a run for it. I pulled up next to him, uncertain of his intentions. He motioned for me to get in.

"I'll get right to the point," he stated flatly. "You're in far worse trouble than you realize. You've been designated for a prison camp at La Tuna, which normally would be no big deal. It's outside the walls of the main joint, where inmates generally do pretty easy time. But evidently you've pissed off some local brass and they've got a federal task force on you. They're trying to connect you with some big-time operation in Florida.

"Whether or not you *are* connected, I don't know. I don't even want to know. But right now, you're their main target, buddy boy. They think you might be their link to another operation in California, and they think it's big. Once they get their hooks into you, they won't let go. I can guarantee you, they're not going to let you do your time on a tennis court at La Tuna."

"What, then?" I asked. "What will they do?"

"They'll force you to cooperate, now that you're their property. They won't play games with you, or be nice to you. They'll put you inside the main joint, just to scare the shit out of you while they leak information that you're a snitch. You know what that's like?"

"No, but I suppose I could guess."

"It's like dangling a piece of raw meat in a tigers' cage. They'll let you dangle until you beg them for "protection." If you don't talk, you'll end up either dead or maimed. They could also take you on their 'bus tour' first, just to wear you down."

"Bus tour?"

"The prison tour. 'Diesel therapy,' they call it. Except for solitary, it's almost the worst time you can do. They'll keep moving you from joint to joint until you don't know where you are, or even who you are. Sometimes every month, sometimes only after a few days or weeks, they pack you up and ship you off to any damn place they want, sometimes even to some county jail in the middle of nowhere. Every time you're moved, word travels on the prison grapevine that you're testifying against other inmates. You'll be kept in chains and shackles, and in protective custody—'P.C.' P.C. is supposed to protect inmates who are threatened, but it's also a dead giveaway to other inmates that you're cooperating, even if you're not. Everywhere you go, word will follow that you're a snitch. It's no way to do time, I can tell you that.

"To be real blunt about it," he went on, "I don't think you'll survive it. Not because you aren't smart enough, but because there are low-life scum in the places you'll be dragged through that will shank somebody for a carton of cigarettes. In the case of a snitch, they'll do it for *free*."

I thought long and hard about what he said. I could tell he was antsy and wanting to go, but I was desperate for a real friend I could trust—someone to talk to. My head was spinning in disbelief. I was ready to do my time, and even do it *their* way, but this was tough to handle under any conditions. Suddenly, what had been hard enough to accept in the first place was now terrifying. I was facing what really amounted to a possible death sentence, and Ron was confirming it.

"What should I do?" I pleaded.

"There's not much choice, I'd say. It's down to a simple matter of living or dying."

"You mean I should take off?"

"I didn't say that. You never heard that from me." The tone in his voice turned suddenly cold and hard. "You do what you have to do, but forget we ever had this conversation. This meeting never took place. Is that clear?"

"Yeah, sure, if that's the way it has to be. Why? Do you think you're in some sort of danger?"

"Look, let me put it to you this way. You have no idea of the forces you've stirred up. You've gotten yourself in too deep to play the game, no matter how smart you think you are. I was in a similar situation once, for different reasons. I pissed some people off so badly they would've made me look like a serial killer. I had to take off for Brazil, where I lived for three years before I worked my way back. But I had *years* of experience you don't have, and some powerful connections. You've got nothing."

"I've got the truth, I know that much."

"Well, the 'truth' is, you've been caught. You got into something you shouldn't have, and they've got you by the short hairs. In this business, you have to play hardball. You don't have the time or the means to learn how to do that now. It's too bad, but sometimes that's the luck of the draw in this game.

"You're smart," he continued. "And if you play your cards right, things might eventually work out. But right now, it's too dangerous for you. I strongly urge you to get yourself out of the water before you're eaten alive. That's all I have to say. I can't do anything to help you now, except to tell you what you're up against. I've enjoyed our friendship, and I hope like hell you make it through okay. It's tough but it's how some of us learn. I wish you well, my friend."

He started his car and waited for me to get out. I barely had the door shut behind me when he stepped on the gas and pulled out of the cluster of trees. I stood there stunned, watching his tail lights disappear in a cloud of dust.

The fragrance of the piñon trees permeated the air as the dust slowly settled. I looked up and marveled at the twinkling of a billion stars overhead. Leaning back on my van, I wondered how, in the midst of such incredible splendor and simple beauty, I could be facing such a horrendous fate. How could I possibly untangle it all? Surely, I thought, there must be a way to turn it off, or stop it some-how. Resigned to my fate, I got in my car and headed home. By the time I pulled into my driveway, my course of action was clear. There really was nothing else to do but disappear.

In the remaining days before I was to turn myself in, I went about my daily affairs as if my plans hadn't changed. Quietly and carefully, I arranged my get-away with the only two remaining friends I could still count on. With two days left before I was to turn myself in to the authorities, I made conspicuous arrangements for Taos to see my boys one last time.

With Joan and the travel trailer safely moved to the home of a friend of hers in Durango, Colorado, I left my van with the boys' mother and slipped away in the night, heading north. I felt like Richard Kimball, a fugitive from justice with what I was certain would become a nationwide manhunt.

Chapter Twenty

The sound of bustling traffic in downtown Denver amplified the loneliness and panic I felt when I arrived at the city's huge bus terminal. I cautiously made my way toward a place where I could hide while I figured out my next move. It was spring of 1981—only a little more than a year since my first trip to Miami with Bill. Now, as far as I was concerned, every cop in every patrol car was on the lookout for me, and every seedy-looking character on the street was a hit man looking to fill the contract I assumed was out on me. Anyone hesitating near me or even glancing in my direction could be a threat. I imagined that any television screen in a public place bore the prospect of my picture with my name being broadcast in hourly news bulletins as one the nation's latest 'most wanted' fugitives.

Unable to use my own name or I.D., I felt like a POW released behind enemy lines. Without papers or proof of innocence to produce to agents on the prowl for sinister characters, I felt desperate and in fear for my life. The smallest mistake or careless move was certain to land me in prison or, worse yet, dead in an alleyway from a silencer in the night. I made my way warily through a now hostile world that a mere few weeks before had been home to me.

Joan was waiting in Durango, but I had to establish a new identity before I could go anywhere or do anything. I needed to find a place to do the research and lay the groundwork without being recognized. Developing a 'hometown' background would be essential, so after a couple of terrifying days on the streets of Denver, I got on another bus and followed a vague notion of where to go. I headed for Greeley, the little town where I had spent my last year in high school, and proceeded to put my mind to work.

Nearly twenty years had passed since I had graduated, and since I had lived there less than a year, the chances of my being recognized would be slim. I knew enough about the town and some former residents to feel I'd be able to create a new history for myself. One such former resident was a young man who had befriended me when I was still struggling to cope with my father's death and our sudden relocation to this "cow town" in northeastern Colorado.

He was respected and admired by everyone in town. He and I became the best of friends, although our friendship was brief. The next year, he was killed in a car accident traveling home from college. But now, this could become my opportunity. I knew enough about him and his family to produce the information required to obtain a birth certificate, and sent it off with a request for urgent handling for a pending 'overseas' assignment."

While I waited for that all-important document to arrive in the mail, I felt moved to visit the cemetery where he was buried. It was a Sunday, so the visitors' center containing the directory was closed. To find his grave, I had to walk from headstone to headstone through the entire cemetery. It was a macabre search that conjured up images of the people who had once lived and died there, a few of whom I had actually known in my short stay there.

A morbid sense of the hopelessness and futility of my life's events welled up in me as I slowly made my way from one marker to the next. With my father's death the year before I graduated, and then my uncle's the following year, the death of this friend had hit me particularly hard. After that, I lost several close friends in Viet Nam, and later two more to cancer. Death seemed like a silent stalker through my life, and now as I searched for this particular headstone, death seemed my new companion.

Gary had been a decent, honest young man, loved by all. I, on the other hand, had squandered every decent break I ever got. I should have been the one to go...not him. By the time I finally found his grave, I was ready to crawl in with him.

Collapsing on the grave in a torrent of tears, I felt the loss of both of our lives. His had been snuffed out like a candle, while mine had raged like a bonfire. Two brilliant futures cut short—his by accident, and mine by self-delusion and arrogance.

I stayed at the grave for the rest of the afternoon until I felt as if I had buried a part of myself with him. When I was clear about my course of action, I pledged an oath to his memory that I would never bring shame or dishonor to his name. I would find a way to make everything turn out right someday.

I knew I needed more material to build my new history, so while I waited for the birth certificate, I collected more documentation. I mailed a couple of letters to my new address with Gary's name on the envelopes. I folded and carried them in my pocket to look well worn, and then used them to obtain a library card. I added a utility bill and membership cards to a local 4H club and a few social groups to my emerging new identity. By the time the birth certificate arrived, I had more than enough material to accomplish the most crucial task…securing a driver's license.

With my new license in hand, I found a clean, well-used pickup truck capable of towing the travel trailer. With great trepidation, I departed for Durango to pick up Joan to begin our journey. We headed north into Wyoming, and wandered toward the Great Northwest like a couple of nomads working at odd jobs wherever we could find them.

Later that summer, Barbara and the boys joined us for a weekend visit. It was decided that Channon, now six, would go with us. Eventually, when we found a place to settle, Jonathan could join us. It was tricky at first with my change of identity, but having Channon along actually made things a little easier. Adaptable and charming, he made us look like a normal young family, just getting by. To him, life with "Rad Dad" was one adventure after another anyway, so he had little trouble with the change.

Intending to leave a trail in the direction of Seattle and Canada, we sent a few postcards from a truck stop in Oregon to certain friends with a penchant for gossip. Then we turned south for the Bay Area of San Francisco. Appearing quite normal in every respect, we were hardly a suspicious target as we made our way down the coast of California, looking for work and a place to call home.

By August, we found an aging resort in southern Marin County, where we were able to trade landscaping labor for a temporary place to live. Later, I managed to land a job as a shift manager at an upscale restaurant in Sausalito. We stayed until October, when it was clear that the cost of living in that area was too high for us. We longed for the mountains, where we felt we could find a small community to settle in and eventually work things out. In November, we were back on the road again, this time headed across Nevada and Northern Arizona towards Colorado. With winter fast approaching, we decided to wait until the spring to take to the high country, so we turned south at Flagstaff and headed toward the red rock canyon country of Sedona and the Verde Valley.

I found a job waiting tables and cooking at a popular new restaurant in this tourist community I had visited a couple of years before. The scenic beauty of the red rock canyons there was breathtaking, and we found a perfect house in a garden community near the banks of Oak Creek. Neighbors were elderly and kind, and took us in like long-lost family. By now, Joan had become pregnant. Channon was in first grade at the local elementary school, and we joined one of the more active neighborhood churches.

A haven for a rapidly growing number of wealthy elite, Sedona's majestic red rock canyons and mystical allure drew people of every background. Steeped in ancient, Native American folklore and appealing to a growing number of spiritual seekers, it was rapidly becoming a melting pot of New Agers, fundamentalist Christians, retired people and business developers, all vying for a strong voice in the affairs of a town increasingly recognized as a premier destination resort. Over the next few years, the town doubled in size and became an incorporated city. It was a perfect time and place for us to blend in and grow with the flow of social, philosophical and economic change.

By spring of the next year, it seemed we knew everyone in town. In late May, Joan gave birth to our daughter, Amber, and by the time she was old enough to crawl, we had lost the urge to move on to the mountains. Gradually, the fear of suddenly being apprehended or snatched in the night diminished, and then disappeared altogether.

My contacts at the restaurant, together with a pie catering business Joan and I started, enabled us to raise money to invest in an oil and gas leasing partnership. I hoped that investment would do well enough for me to eventually go back and fight my case in New Mexico with a decent lawyer. By the end of 1983, my business status was nearly the same as it was just before my old business in Santa Fe had failed. In fact, I had made such an impression on other investors in the partnership that I was asked to take over and manage their investments. Among the group was the owner of the local air charter business, and I was given access to his five airplanes anytime I needed them for the business. By 1984, I was flying back and forth to our investment properties in Utah with an air of complete confidence, and near-ambivalence about my unresolved past.

With money and credibility generated from managing the investments, I started my own company, marketing startup business ventures. My ideas attracted the interest of several investors who perceived my efforts in both businesses as an indication of a bright young entrepreneur on the rise. It had been barely three years since my hurried departure from New Mexico, and I was well on my way to financial and professional success as a completely different person. The fact that I was still a fugitive did little to deter me. Now married to Joan and living in Sedona with two children, I kept moving doggedly—and blindly—ahead as if nothing else mattered.

Despite the relatively short time it took to create a fairly decent lifestyle under an alias, the underlying uneasiness began to unravel the fabric of our relationship. Feeling guilty and vulnerable, Joan became increasingly more frightened that my past would catch up with us. Voicing her fear that she would somehow be held morally, if not legally, accountable, she railed against the front we had to maintain, and became moody, distant and irritable. Despite what appeared to be a fairly solid standing in the community by then, she knew, and I knew, the pretense couldn't continue indefinitely. Somehow, in some way, it had to come undone.

Our relationship suffered a steady erosion in emotional strength, and with Jonathan's arrival in 1983, the pressure on her began to take an even more obvious toll. Finally, it became too much for either of us to maintain. We agreed to separate and go our own way.

Over the next couple of years, we maintained a good friendship and helped each other with the kids, personal problems and financial needs. With each succeeding month, however, I sensed a subtle but growing fear that my time might be running out. The oil business had fallen victim to plummeting world oil prices and, along with it went my hopes of going back to New Mexico with enough money to fight my case. With a decent lawyer, I felt I could get a better outcome, but the dwindling oil investment activity demanded my full attention just to keep the business alive. To add to the dilemma, my own new business required more attention to satisfy expectations of clients and investors.

I was a man with a past that could consume me, and a present that was consuming me. The harder I worked to prepare for what might come, the bigger it loomed in front of me. It was now the summer of 1985. My only consolation, apart from the five years' reprieve I had had with my boys and the birth of my daughter, was that the Old Man and his entire organization had long-since been arrested, tried and convicted. At least I wouldn't have to face the prospect of finding myself on the witness stand testifying against them.

Barbara informed me about this news when she brought Jonathan to live with the kids and me. She had moved away from Santa Fe, but heard about the Florida bust from a friend. No mention was made of my possible implication in the case, and I didn't care to dig any deeper to find out. Just that briefest of exposure to her, and thus to investigators who might be watching her, did little to help me sleep.

At least my decent standing in the community was a testament to my character, along with the fact I had been responsible for investors' money and airplanes. I had always acted with impeccable integrity and forthrightness, never taking a dime that wasn't earned. It was clear to anyone who knew me that I had made my best effort to build two businesses, and raise a family.

During this time, I had become friends with a woman who provided childcare for Amber. Debra had been an acquaintance for several years, but until my separation from Joan we had maintained only a casual relationship. We had dinner together one evening, and that began to change. By fall of 1985 my relationship with her had blossomed into something much more. Increasingly enamored by this woman of great depth, character and high ideals, I felt more and more pressured to come clean—not only with her, but with everyone I felt personally and professionally responsible towards. To do so would mean the end of everything I had fabricated in my attempt to rebuild my life. The consequences of telling the truth was a "Catch 22" situation for me, however. It would force them to turn me in, or be implicated for harboring a known fugitive.

Surrounded on all sides by people who were dependent on me to make both businesses work, the remnants of my family work, and now my new relationship with Debra work, I was a man on the verge of a breakdown. I was haggard and exhausted. Several close friends told me later that I looked like a man on his way to the grave.

By this point, I had reached a level of credibility with local banks that would allow me to take out unsecured, signature loans for as much as $25,000. My credit was excellent and my reputation in the community was superb. With access to airplanes and large amounts of money, the gnawing sense that I was on the brink of disaster made the possibility of a quick flight to Mexico grow more tempting every day. Something had to give, and come the next summer I knew what I would have to do. I couldn't run the game much longer. Come what may, I would turn myself in.

Thanksgiving that year brought an unexpected turn of events. In Barbara's misguided but innocent attempt to explain her respect and affection for me to a man she was dating, she inadvertently let it be known to him that I was a good provider for the boys, in spite of such "unusual circumstances." Unaware that he fancied himself a self-appointed "undercover agent," she invited him for her visit with the boys that year for the holidays. Highly intellectual and overbearing, he immediately made it known to me that he was aware of my situation, but reassured me that my "secret" was safe with him.

But he was shifty, insecure and an alcoholic, adding all the more to my fear that my time was up. He and Barbara went off together after dinner, leaving me to pace the floor and agonize over how to deal with this turn of events. My thoughts were interrupted by his sudden return a few hours later, intoxicated and badly injured. They had gotten into an argument that led to a vicious fight between him and another man. She had taken off, but because of his injuries he stayed with me for several days, until he was well enough to leave.

The next several weeks were perhaps the most difficult ones since I had left New Mexico. Every knock on the door and every new face on the streets of town bore the prospect of my arrest, and the end of everything I had built over the years. After several weeks, however, nothing seemed to come of the incident, I nonetheless took it as a significant warning. I stepped up business activities and began detailed planning for accumulating enough money to retain a lawyer and begin the process of turning myself in.

On my birthday, December 20, 1985, a surprise party was planned for me at the home of a good friend. A cake had been baked for the occasion, presents were laid out, and a small group of friends had gathered, waiting for me to arrive. I had been invited "to lunch," as far as I knew, and thought nothing more of it. It was nearly noon, and everyone had left the building but me.

As I was about to leave, the telephone rang. I almost let it ring, then thought better of it and went back into my office to answer the call. It was the most important client I had at the time, wanting to finalize the terms of an imminent contract we had arranged for him with a buyer in Los Angeles. The contract promised to be fairly lucrative for both of us, so the conversation continued longer than usual. While we were talking, I heard the front door open, followed by silence. I knew someone had come in, but I couldn't hear voices or sounds of movement in the outer office. A minute later, two men in suits and ties appeared at my office doorway.

I knew that look. Though I hadn't seen it for a long time, it was a look I could never forget. Long before I heard them say it, or saw any badges, I knew they were cops.

Instantly my blood ran cold. My heart seemed to stop. My mind went into a frenzy, trying to come up with an analysis and a solution while I continued to talk with my client as calmly as possible.

Who were they? Were they after me, or was it just a fluke? Flukes happen all the time. After all, hadn't I had survived some big ones? They might be looking for someone else. It could be…

I kept talking on the phone while my insides twisted. My client must have thought I was an idiot, prattling on about something not even related to the deal we had been talking about. The faces of the two men were cold and indifferent as they stood there waiting for me to hang up. I was certain it was me they were looking for, but I had to play it out and see if the forces of fate might swing in my direction one more time. I couldn't just cave in at the first sign of trouble.

I could tell by the way they stood there on each side of the door with their coats open that they were purposeful and fully intent on their mission. I squeezed every second out of my now-babbling telephone conversation while I tried to pull my thoughts together. I wondered if they could tell I was nervous. I attempted a smile and a nod, motioning for them to have a seat, but they just stood waiting.

This was it. This was the way it was going to come down, and all that kept it from happening was my pathetic, verbal meandering on the phone that had to be driving my client crazy. I was crazy...crazy with fear, frustration and heartache.

My heart pounded like a hammer against my chest. It took every ounce of nerve I had to keep myself standing steady and looking as if everything were perfectly normal. The temptation to bolt out the back door was overpowering. I quickly glanced at the parking lot through my office window to determine if I could make a run for it, but I had just locked the door. There was no way I could get it unlocked and open before they would seize me. My mind was racing furiously.

What the hell do they want? Is this it? Has my time run out now, of all times? Everything is just now finally starting to fall into place. I just need a couple more months...

On the other end of the line, my client was growing irritated with my distracted replies to his questions. He demanded I pay more attention. As desperately as I wanted to cling to the phone and prolong the inevitable, I finally told him I had to go. After taking a long, deep breath, I said goodbye to him in a tone that must have made him feel as if I was going to a funeral. Slowly, I put the receiver down as gently as if it might explode.

I looked at the two men, and my eyes locked on the badge one of them held in his hand as he stepped forward. Moving closer still, while the other one strategically blocked the doorway with his large frame, he spoke directly to me.

"Sir, my name is John Lopez. I'm a Deputy United States Marshal. I'm going to give you one chance to tell me who you are."

My mind raced wildly as I forced my face to show a look of disdain and puzzlement. My legs went weak, as a blur of images, faces, names, dates, places and circumstances raced through my head.

What the hell do I do now? Could I possibly bluff my way out of this? This could be something wildly coincidental. Things like that do happen sometimes. It's happened before. Why not now? I've talked my way out of some incredible shit before. If I admit my true identity, and it turns out they're looking for someone else, what a colossal blunder that would be.

No, I knew this was too powerful to be a coincidence. Besides, I was tired. More than tired. I was spent...totally exhausted. I had run this game for nearly five years. I had three kids who weren't even sure what their real names were, a broken marriage, a serious criminal record, investors everywhere looking for their payoffs, and a whole other life left behind on a grave back in Colorado.

For three and a half years, I had been running a million dollar investment fund, totally dependent on my ability to work miracles in a crumbling industry I knew little about, and still had barely enough money of my own to make it through Christmas.

Yes, I was tired. Tired of running. Tired of hiding. Tired of living a never-ending lie. Too damned tired of the insanity of it all. No matter how close I might come to making any sense of my charade, success would always elude me until the truth was out. It was time to bring it to a close.

I looked at the one who called himself Lopez, straightened myself, and uttered the name I hadn't used or even heard in nearly five years. With no further word, the cuffs were out and my arms were pulled behind my back. The room seemed to close in on me and their words were muffled as they hustled me out the door to their waiting sedan. Out on the main street of town, I was shocked to see two highway patrol cars blocking traffic as if they were expecting a shootout. From the back seat of the marshals' sedan, I watched several sheriffs' deputies converging from strategic places where they had been waiting. The whole thing had been well planned and arranged, probably weeks in advance.

I was taken to the local sheriff's station while the marshals prepared for the trip to Phoenix. I was allowed a phone call, which I used to get Debra to come to the station and pick up the cash and valuables I had in my possession. I had just enough money for what was to have been Christmas shopping with her that night. In an act of pure decency on their part, the marshals allowed me to give her the money for what would prove to be an otherwise miserable Christmas for my kids. It was some kind of birthday present for me, and one I would not likely ever forget. Within two hours, I was on my way into the darkest, bleakest period of my life.

Chapter Twenty-One

The sound of giant metal doors slamming shut in the night and solid steel bolts locking into place jolted me from a fitful sleep. Heavy leather bootsteps echoed in long, concrete corridors, and the jingling of brass keys triggered unbearable feelings of desperation in me as I listened to the guard making his way slowly toward our cellblock.

Electronic locks of the door to our cellblock unbolted and the sound of an electric motor whirred loudly as the massive door slid open. The bootsteps entered, then paused as the motor reversed and the big door slid closed. The slam of metal against metal reverberated through the walls, and through the thin, plastic mattress I was lying on. In slow, evenly measured steps, the guard moved down the row of cells toward mine. Anticipation welled up in me as the sound of the bootsteps moved closer.

He stopped at my cell. Unconsciously, I held my breath and waited. The jingle of his keys quickened my heartbeat and my hopes soared.

Maybe I'm getting out. Maybe someone out there pulled it off, and I'm being released...

A frantic, inner dialog started in my head. *We'll make good this time, we promise. Thank God in Heaven. Freedom from this madness.*

I felt myself tense up, ready to leap to my feet and roll up my gear. *Was this it? Could I be home yet tonight? It had happened before...*

A flashlight beam probed the darkness of my cell.

Yes, I'm here! It's me! I'm ready. Sweet Jesus, am I ever ready. Oh, God—let me hear that sweet sound of the key turning in the lock. What's he waiting for?

Suddenly, the beam disappeared and the cell went dark again. The bootsteps moved on down the row of cells. My hopes plummeted into despair as the motor whirred again, and the big cellblock door opened. I heard the bootsteps move through, and the door slam shut again. The shock wave once again pulsed through the walls and into my mattress, accentuating the empty stillness of the night. The echo of jingling keys and bootsteps faded away down another corridor.

Every night was the same during my stay at the Maricopa County Jail in Phoenix. Hour after hour, the same hollow sounds echoed in the night as I lay tossing and turning. A hundred miles to the north, my kids were lying in their own beds wondering what the hell had happened to me. All those people who thought they knew me were now finding out that they didn't even know who I really was.

I hadn't mustered the courage to tell even Debra until it was too late. What a shock it must be to her now. We had become so close the previous few months, we had begun to feel like we might have a future together. Even our kids were starting to act like brothers and sisters.

I desperately wanted to be back with them—anywhere but *here.* I could always hope for some twist of fate or act of God to get me out. This *would* take an act of God—that was certain. But then, twists had happened before. I recalled that credit card deal years ago back in Denver. That certainly twisted in my favor—big time. I had naively stumbled into someone else's scam, and nearly did some serious time over it. Spent three weeks in the county jail before it was determined that I wasn't who they were looking for. I had used the stolen card only once, but it tied me to a string of unsolved burglaries in the area.

The judge felt that three weeks locked up with the "big boys" was more than enough punishment for what I had actually done, and dismissed the charges. He was so moved by my comments at the pretrial hearing, he later even had the record expunged. The experience of those three weeks left a very deep imprint on me. *Obviously not deep enough,* I thought, as I tossed and turned on another jailhouse bunk nearly fifteen years later. How could I have forgotten *that* ordeal? I swore back then I would never, *ever* put myself through such an experience again.

The only good thing that had come of the incident was my initiation to confinement. While there, I met a master at doing time, "Big Jim" Valentine. Meeting Jim was worth the time there. God, what a zoo that place was.

No rural jail in a sleepy Nebraska town this time—this was a cold, hard look at *real* time, with hardcore inmates. These were convicted felons, all waiting for their court appearances or to be transferred to another facility. This was an exercise in survival among the baddest and toughest, compressed into an area the size of a high school gym.

With four men to a cell, sixteen cells per tier and three tiers per cellblock, it was more like a small prison than it was a jail. The noise and pandemonium were indescribable, with virtually all of the inmates milling about on each cellblock floor at any given time of the day or night. To break the monotony and work off the intense fear I felt, I would walk the main floor from one end to the other, then climb the metal stairs to the second tier, walk the length of it, then up to the third tier and back down again. I repeated this routine several times a day.

By the third day, I had noticed an older man on the upper tier who seemed unbothered by the noise and confinement. He seldom left his cell, except at meal-times. I was intrigued by his calmness, and even more so by the fact that he had a cell to himself. With three and four men jammed into each of the other cells, rage and tension would flare up with the least provocation.

Whenever I walked by his cell, I noticed it was clean—even immaculate. He would be sitting calmly on his bunk reading a book and looking like someone in a Norman Rockwell painting. One evening, I fell into place behind him in the chow line. While we were waiting for the main doors of the cellblock to open so we could file into the hallway and down to the mess hall, he looked at me long enough for me to attempt a contact.

"Hello," I said.

"Evenin'," he replied curtly, then looked away. I didn't get a sense of open-ness in his response, so I waited a few minutes before saying anything else. When he looked my way again, I spoke with some hesitation.

"You been here very long?" I asked.

"Nope," he replied curtly, then held his eyes on me as I felt a chill run up my spine. "Just passing through," he said, then looked away again.

I paused for a moment before saying anything more. He knew things I needed to know—like how to stay cool in the midst of chaos, and much more. Whatever he knew, I needed to learn it fast. I was fresh meat in a cage full of predators. Even though I noticed everyone gave him a wide berth, I sensed that he might be approachable. Very cautiously, I pressed him a bit further.

"What do you mean, 'passing through'?" There was a moment's hesitation, long enough to make me nervous that I had stepped over the line. He looked at me straight in the eyes with a look that eliminated any attempt at small-talk.

"Exactly what I said. I'm just passin' through. Going from one joint to another."

The big doors opened and we moved out into the hallway. Nothing more was said as we filed into the mess hall and took our seats on the benches at the stain-less steel tables. I took a seat opposite him and, as inconspicuously as possible, watched how he acted and what he did. I was intrigued that even in his silence it was apparent that he was like the dominant male in a pack of wolves. As long as he was quiet, everyone around him seemed fine. But most of the men, I noticed, kept a wary eye on him.

We ate in silence, but I could feel him sizing me up without appearing to look at me. There was a certain strength in his mere presence that was fascinating. As we finished our meals, he shifted ever so slightly, wiped his mouth and spoke to me. His tone was soft and quiet, but his manner was direct and commanding.

"You haven't been down long, have you?" It was more of a statement than it was a question.

"Down?" I asked.

"Yeah. Locked up."

"Oh, that." I said, "No, this is my first time. It shows that much?"

"Totally. I can usually tell. You might as well have college clothes on. These places are tough to take the first time or two. It takes a while before a guy's insides settle down. Yours might take a while."

"I've noticed that it doesn't seem to bother you too much."

"Been here before. And far worse. This is an *improvement* from where I've been."

Worse? It was hard to imagine anything worse, but I could tell he had been around. It showed in the way he moved, chose his words and pierced the space around him with his eyes. We moved out of the dining hall and back to the cell-block with nothing more said.

Right after breakfast the next morning, I started my routine of walking the tiers. When I reached his cell, he was inside as usual, with his cell door locked. He looked pensive.

"Good morning," I said, pausing long enough for a reply.

"Mornin'," he replied.

"You're not reading your book."

"Finished it last night. You want to read it?"

"Yeah, maybe. As soon as I get a little calmer."

"Let me know when you do. It's a good book."

"You read quite a bit, don't you?"

"Sure. Otherwise, it's too easy to get caught up in the games out there."

"Sounds like you know the routine pretty well. Is that why you stay in while everyone else comes out?"

"No. It's just that I've done enough time not to let it bother me."

"You mind my asking you how much time?"

"No. Not at all. Just finished my twentieth year down."

I was dumbfounded. I'm sure my jaw dropped, but I tried not to appear overwhelmed.

"Twenty *years?*" I exclaimed. "What for? Or is that too personal?"

"No. But it's a long story. I'm sure you don't want to hear all of it."

"On the contrary. This place is full of stories, but as far as I can tell most of them are bullshit. If you feel like telling it, I'd like to hear it. Looks to me like we've both got some time on our hands."

He sat down on his bunk and wiped his glasses as if he were about to read to me. I took his cue and squatted against the steel rail of the catwalk outside his cell.

"I was eighteen," he began. "We lived in a small town in the mountains of Colorado. I was pretty big for my age, and spent most of my earlier years hunting, fishing and living off the land. We lived in a cabin back in the woods, heated with firewood I cut myself. By the time I graduated from high school, I stood six-two, weighed a little over two hundred pounds, and was stronger than most guys my age. I didn't have a lot of friends because I was always doing chores or spending most of my time in the backcountry. But the few friends I did have, I felt pretty close to.

"One day, one of those friends got into a scuffle with some strange guy at the local drive-in. I happened to be nearby. The guy was older and bigger, and was treating my friend pretty rough. They got to shoving each other around, and before I knew it I jumped in the middle of it. The guy hit me pretty hard in the gut with his elbow, but I managed to get an arm around his neck."

"People used to say I was too strong for my own good and this was one of those times. I didn't realize what I did, but I must've snapped his neck. When I rolled off of him, he was dead. In the scuffle, we both hit the pavement pretty hard, so it could have been the fall that killed him. I never did know for sure, 'cause when I looked down at him, all lifeless like that, I panicked. Someone said 'run!' and I lit out of there for the high country. I don't know what got into me. I guess I was hoping he wasn't really dead. You know…maybe he'd come to and things would work out.

"But he didn't. To make matters even worse, it turned out he was an off-duty cop from another town. The media went crazy with the story, and a statewide manhunt was launched for a 'savage cop-killer.' It didn't take long for them to find out who I was, and where I might be hiding. I was just a *kid,* scared out of my wits. I holed up in one of my hunting blinds where I had enough ammunition and provisions to last for a few months, if I had to. But someone spotted me a few days later, and soon cops were everywhere. They didn't give a shit about what had really happened. They just wanted to get their 'cop-killer.' They were out for blood. Naturally, I tried to defend myself.

"They didn't even try to talk to me. They came at me with guns blazing and bullets flying. At first, I just shot high to back them off until I could figure things out. But that only made it worse. They were convinced I was a mad dog, and they wanted me dead or alive.

"I knew they'd kill me if they got close enough, so I finally had to shoot with more purpose. I did my best just to wound the ones closest to me so I could buy enough time until it got dark and I could get away. Let me tell you, I learned how it feels to be a cornered wild animal. The killer instinct takes over. It was everything I could do to keep myself from wasting a bunch of them. I could have taken out four or five of 'em if I'd wanted to, but finally they backed down and let me surrender. I think it was only because some reporters finally showed up, along with a photographer. Unfortunately for me, one of the cops I wounded died later in the hospital. Whatever chance I had of getting a break was gone after that. The local press now had a hot story that made the national news. *Two* cops killed by a crazed mad man.

"The hysteria generated by the news coverage was too much for anything reasonable to come out of it for me. I was tried and convicted on two counts of second-degree murder. I got two life sentences, running concurrent. They told me they were being 'lenient' on me, that I could get paroled in twenty years. What the hell does *that* mean to an eighteen-year-old kid? They shipped me off to the state pen in Canyon City—the worst joint in the state. I went in terrified and confused, still hoping to turn things around somehow.

"I laid awake night after night, month after month, year after year. It only got worse. I think my size and my growing resentment was all that kept me alive in that stink hole. I had to fight every day to keep my sanity and my physical safety. I was a two-time cop-killer, always ganged up on by the guards or challenged by some macho inmate who wanted to make a name for himself. The guards didn't give a shit, either. In fact they *provoked* fights, hoping someone would do me in.

"After a while, I lost all hope. I didn't care about anything, anymore. I started focusing on how to escape. Nothing else mattered. With each year, I grew more and more bitter toward everyone.

"After nine years, they finally lost interest in me. I spent my time planning and watching. One day, I had my chance. They forgot about me long enough for me to make an escape in the undercarriage of a delivery truck. It was the dead of winter, in the mountains of Colorado. I damn near froze to death, but managed to get my hands on some clothes and caught a ride with a trucker who took me clear to Kansas City.

"I stayed there for a few weeks, worked at some odd jobs and laid low as long as possible. I made the FBI's 'Most Wanted' list. My picture was on every news bulletin on every TV station in the country. I had to dodge questions and got so many suspicious looks, I'm still amazed I got as far as I did. I drifted from place to place, but kept to the hills and backcountry as much as possible."

He paused for a minute, wiped his glasses again, then went on.

"I changed my appearance as much as possible, and managed to steal some clothes and a gun from a farm somewhere in Iowa. I made it all the way to a small town in Ohio before I was discovered. I was hiding out in an abandoned farmhouse when a schoolteacher brought some kids to see the place. I guess it belonged to her family once, and she was giving them a tour. She was courageous—I'll give her that. I was a pretty ornery dude by that time, but she stood right up to me. I could've squashed her like a bug, but she was kind and respectful to me. She tried to get me to turn myself in, but I just couldn't do it. I couldn't waste her, either. She was doing what she thought was right in a hopeless situation. I couldn't bring myself to hurt her or those kids, so I had no choice but to light out of there as fast as I could go.

"But that blew my cover. I was plannin' to head out that night, but now I had to make a run for it in broad daylight. To make matters worse, it was cold and heavy snow was falling. I was out in the open and my tracks were easy to follow. Before long, the police cars and helicopters were comin' at me from everywhere. I made it to a vacant garage, where they opened up on me like a target at a shooting gallery.

"Well, I figured, what the hell. I might as well get it over with. So I shot back, figuring it would all be over soon, and I'd never have to see the inside of another cell. I really didn't want to kill anyone else, but then some macho cop came runnin' toward me with a .45 in each hand. He must have seen too many Rambo movies, 'cause he sure thought he was bulletproof. He found out he wasn't, though. It only took one well-placed shot, and he was down in the dirt and snow, screamin' like a stuck pig. I aimed for his leg, but they called it 'multiple' bullet wounds later. Mind you, I only took one shot at him.

"Finally, the shooting stopped. They needed to get macho-man out of there, so all of sudden they wanted to talk. As if they could really offer me a deal that would mean anything. It was the usual ration of crap they use, as if no one ever heard it before. You know, the come-out-now-and-we'll-see-that-you-get-a-fair-trial crock of shit. But it bought enough time for the press to get there with their 'live-action' camera crews. When I finally walked out with my hands in the air, I expected to be ripped apart with bullets before I got ten feet, but not a shot was fired.

"I guess they wanted the world to see that no prison escapee was too tough for Ohio cops, I don't know. But I got another life sentence for killing Rambo, and found myself in a joint far worse than Canyon City. The Ohio State Pen showed me the depth of human cruelty.

"Anyway, life in their joint at first was about as bad as Canyon City. Before long, I was fightin' off every badass in there. Now I was a *three*-time cop-killer, so the guards did nothing to stop the attacks. I didn't give a shit about anything. My life was over. As far as I was concerned, there was someone else occupying my body. Within a couple of years, I lost any sense of decency I might have had left. Even that schoolteacher wouldn't have gotten any mercy from me after that point. I was a tortured wild animal in a cage. After a few years, once the guards were convinced they had sufficiently beaten their rules into me, I was pretty much left alone.

"But one day, some guards jumped an inmate that hadn't done a damn thing. One of 'em was pissed off about something, and this dude just happened to be in the wrong place at the wrong time. It could have been any of us, but they jumped him because he had a bit of a smart mouth. He was a small guy, even a little frail. The way they were going at it, they would have killed him. I didn't really give a shit about the guy, but something in me snapped when I saw them beat him for no reason. It was the principle of the thing. He hadn't done shit to them, but they were about to end his life, just because he happened to be an inmate.

"One of the guards had a personal vendetta against inmates. His self-appointed duty was to make life as miserable as possible for us. He instigated the whole thing with this poor bastard. I saw him do it at least three different times before. I waited for the right opportunity, then jumped into it. I laid two of 'em out on the floor and then tore into that one asshole. He died of a broken neck, and for the first time I didn't regret it one bit. He was the only person I ever actually *wanted* to kill. He deserved to die more than anyone I ever knew.

"To this day, I don't know why they didn't waste me. Maybe it was a little 'Divine intervention,' I don't know. But there was a moratorium on capital punishment back then, so they couldn't give me the death penalty. My lawyer at the time was an over-achieving, young public defender, just out of law school. He argued that the death was really 'self-defense,' under the circumstances, and got the charge dropped to Murder Two. The judge agreed, and my sentence was to run concurrent with the other three. They must have thought they were giving me a break, but what happened next was far worse. When I got back to the joint, prison officials had their own way of imposing the sentence. They stripped me naked and threw me in the hole."

He stopped for a moment before going on. I could tell he was troubled with this part. His voice even seemed to tremble a bit as he cleared his throat and continued.

"Now, I'm not talking about 'the hole' as most inmates know solitary confinement. I mean literally this was a *hole*. Until you've seen one, you have no idea they could even *exist*. There were four walls and a floor, but that was about it. The door was solid iron that they *welded* shut once I was inside. Can you imagine the psychological impact of being in a cell with no visible light, and they *weld* the friggin' door shut?

"I had to crawl around on all fours in the dark to find a hole in the floor in the far corner; that was my toilet. It stunk worse than an outhouse, because I doubt they ever cleaned it out. I found a piece of mattress to sleep on, with nothing in the way of sheets or blankets to cover myself. I had no clothes, no bedding, no *nothing*. Stark naked in a hole in the ground beneath that stinking prison, with water dripping down on me every goddamn day. Every so often, a flap in the door would open. They'd stick a hose in to wash down the cell, and me with it. Once a day, I got something that felt like a soggy sandwich to eat, probably pissed on or spit on, just out of pure hatred for me.

"I couldn't tell day from night. It was either dead quiet, or they would come by with their clubs and beat on the door just to drive me nuts. I never got more than a few hours' sleep, 'cause they'd keep beating on the door with those damn clubs. I guess they figured if they couldn't kill me, they would ride me 'til I cracked.

"I had heard about such places, but I never really grasped the inhumanity of it until I was *in* one. I heard that nobody ever came back from a hole like this, but figured that was only because they shipped 'em off to another joint. In there, I learned the hard truth. If they couldn't legally kill us, they would just drive us over the edge, mentally. That was their own private revenge."

He sat back on his bunk and looked up at the ceiling. I sensed he hadn't told the story very often. Reliving the whole thing must have been painful to him. Finally he looked back at me, paused long enough to feel my anticipation, then continued the story.

"How long do you suppose a man could take living like that? Three months? Six months? You couldn't really call it 'living.' It was barely *existing*. I was in that cesspool every day for *eighteen months*. I thought I knew what it was like for a man to turn into an animal, but until then I had no idea. I lost all track of time in there. With no light, I lost twenty-five percent of my vision. Gradually, I became nothing but a grunting, raging creature—not *even* an animal. After a long time, they stopped beating on the door, except every once in a while just to get a rise out of me.

"Somewhere in all of that, something interesting began to happen. I was beyond any emotional or psychological help. All that was left of me was my mind, which started a sort of inner dialog. It kept saying to me that this was some kind of challenge to overcome, that it was a test of my will power, and that I should 'surrender' to something much bigger." He noticed my raised eyebrows.

"Now, I'm not going to tell you that it was some kind of 'born again,' Christian revelation. Although something like that did happen later, this began to make sense. Oh, I fought it off, believe me. For a long time, I wouldn't listen to the words in my head. But with all that time on my hands and nothing to distract me, it finally began to sink in. I *could* beat the bastards if I could just give up the struggle and the resistance. At first I thought it was just crazy mind talk, but the voice kept telling me to just let it all go and conserve my strength. Sooner or later, they would have to let me out. The calmer I became, the more crazy *they* got, just trying to figure out what was going on with me.

"Eventually, they would have to return me to the prison population, where I decided I would devote the rest of my time to learning everything I could. I would become an expert on matters of the mind. I'd beat them not with my hands, but with my *mind*. The more I thought about it, the more sense it made. Besides, what else did I have to do in there? It was apparent they weren't going to be able to kill me or drive me nuts, so I had my whole life ahead of me. Ironically, time was on my side.

"After a while, I became so quiet they never knew what happened. No more reactions to their beating on the doors, or their hosing me down. Nothing. I just kept quiet. Didn't make a sound for what must have been months. I started working out as much as possible, too. I got to where I could do five hundred pushups without stopping, and sit-ups until I lost count.

"Finally, they came with the torch and cut the door open. A doctor and a prison psychologist came with them, most likely to pronounce me dead or insane. When that door opened, I just stood up and looked 'em square in the eyes and never said a word. It was just enough to make them wonder if I was sane or not, but at least I wasn't flippin' out or babbling like a fool. They couldn't ship me out to an asylum unless I was clearly insane, so they didn't know what to do except put me back in the prison population.

"From that point, everybody gave me plenty of room. Not one word of disrespect was ever directed at me. Guards *or* inmates. No one had ever come back from so long in the hole, so no one knew what to think. After that, I spent all my time in the gym or in the prison library, reading everything I could get my hands on about the justice system, the prison system, criminology, psychology and so on. I took enough correspondence courses to get a degree, if I had wanted one.

"Then people I didn't even know started writing to me, and sending me magazines like 'Psychology Today' and 'Playboy'—not for the more common reasons, but because the magazine was hot on prison issues back then. Eventually, I began to talk again, but on a very limited basis. After what I'd been through, words seemed so useless. I didn't even *want* to talk to most people.

"One day I got word that the warden wanted to see me. After an hour or so with him, he decided that I would work on his personal staff as a clerk. Either he figured I could help him, or he was nervous enough that he wanted to keep an eye on me himself.

"Over the next ten years, I worked my way up to Chief Administrative Clerk. I practically ran the place. 'Playboy's' articles on prison life started catching on, and I became their expert on the inside. Once they found out I could write, they asked me to do an article on sex in prison. A few other magazines got into the act and asked me to write for them, too.

"Last year I came up for parole on the two life terms in Ohio, and it was granted. Now they're taking me back to the Colorado State Pen, where everyone says I'll most likely get paroled as soon as I get there. If I do, and I'm pretty sure I will, I've got a job offer as an associate editor for one of those magazines."

Silence hung in the air between us as I felt the full impact of his story. Shortly after, the loudspeakers announced lockdown for the night. As I stood up to leave, he said one more thing that only now, years later in the Maricopa County Jail, was beginning to sink in.

"Just remember," he said, "no matter how bad things might look, the real power is always in your own choice of attitude. It's only ego and emotional imbalance that get people in trouble."

With that, he handed me the book he had been reading. It was Victor Frankel's *Man's Search for Meaning.* That night after the noise in the cellblock had finally tapered off, I sat up and read it. The author wrote of his three and a half years in a Nazi concentration camp, where he discovered that his freedom wasn't in getting away from his tormentors but in how he chose to live each moment. "Our only real freedom," he wrote with a depth of passion that could only come from having experienced that horror, "is our choice of attitude."

As I sat in the corner of my cell that night so long ago reading that book in the little bit of light that filtered in, I tried to imagine Jim as a young man, and having his whole life twisted by the events he had described. And yet, because he had come to know the power of choosing his own attitude, he was about to step back into the world like just Victor Frankel had—with renewed hope and promise that he could, indeed, create what he really wanted. He was calmer, steadier, and clearer about who he was and what he wanted than most people in the 'real' world.

The long nights at the Maricopa County Jail gradually seemed easier to take as I recalled Big Jim's story from time to time. It had happened so long ago, and seemed so unreal to me now. But as I felt the steel bars of my tiny cell and remembered how calm and strong he was, the memory of his story played a critical part in my handling of the events yet to come.

Chapter Twenty-Two

Two weeks had passed since my arrest as a fugitive. Christmas had come and gone, along with New Year's Day, 1986. A friend managed to find a lawyer who convinced me and the shocked members of my community that he could get me out. Reassuring us that there were several precedents in recent state court cases to gain my release on the basis of proven "self-rehabilitation," he convinced us that several acquittals had been won in cases where fugitives had demonstrated strong, law-abiding lifestyle changes.

This was encouraging for everyone who knew, or thought they knew, me. Convinced that I would soon be released, loyal friends proceeded to organize a legal defense fund for me. The fact remained, however, that I was a convicted felon who had been a fugitive for five years. Given that fact alone, along with the prospect of other serious charges pending, there were more than sufficient grounds to seriously question any attempt to liberate me. But I had kids out there whose fate was uncertain, and I had managed to make a deep impression on a number of people who were determined to help. Understandably, I did little to dissuade them. After all, nobody wanted to believe I could be freed more than I did.

A month later, two hearings in federal court and over four thousand dollars in legal fees proved him wrong. The government clearly had other plans. Early one Sunday morning, I was taken to the Phoenix airport by two more U.S. Marshals. Not wishing to draw unwanted attention, they allowed me to accompany them without handcuffs. Firmly warned of the consequences of creating any "problems" for them, I walked between them as if we were on a business trip.

It was depressing to be escorted through the same airport terminal where only a few months earlier, I had come and gone so freely. To make matters worse, an old friend spotted us walking briskly toward the gates. She insisted on talking with me, despite the two imposing figures on either side of me. Much to her obvious dismay, they brushed her aside as rudely as if they were bodyguards, and forcefully moved me in the direction of our assigned gate.

When we arrived in Albuquerque, we were met by two more marshals who immediately slapped handcuffs on me and whisked me off to the Bernalillo County Detention Center. After five years and virtually another lifetime, I could hardly believe I was now back in the hellhole where I had spent those first two weeks after my arrest on the mesa.

Modern in appearance and technology, the Bernalillo County Detention Center (BCDC) was one of the newest of its kind in a burgeoning new American industry—building and maintaining of prisons and detention facilities. A departure from old-time jails with their steel bars and dungeon-like appearance, BCDC was a showcase of modern electronic security in the 1980's.

Originally built to house 650 prisoners awaiting court cases, transfers to other facilities, or serving time for less serious offenses, BCDC's population had soared to over 1,000. By sheer number of inmates, that made it the largest correctional facility in New Mexico at that time. It was even larger than the infamous State Penitentiary in Santa Fe that had only four years before experienced the most brutal riot in American penal history. The most serious problem with the over-crowding at BCDC was that as a facility designed to hold prisoners temporarily, it lacked the resources to deal with long-term mental, physical and emotional problems that arose from large numbers of inmates compressed within its walls. In the most basic sense of the term, it was "busting at the seams."

Even though I had spent two weeks there after my first arrest, I was ill prepared for what hit me when the huge steel door to my assigned cellblock slid open to let me in. It was mayhem. I stood in disbelief inside the inner cage of the cellblock while the huge outer door slammed shut behind me. When the inside door of the cage opened, it took every ounce of strength I could muster just to step into the huge cellblock with my bedroll and sack of toilet articles.

The din of a hundred men jammed into a space designed for forty-eight was deafening. In one corner, a group of twenty or so inmates milled around an overhead TV that even at full volume couldn't be heard over the yelling and the shouting going on throughout the cellblock. In another corner, a Nautilus weight set held the attention of a group of muscle-bound macho types that even in the first few minutes of my arrival made it clear by the show of biceps and pectorals who were the "big dogs" and who weren't. In the back of the room, the tatick-tatack of a ping-pong ball added a discordant rhythm to the noise echoing off the concrete walls.

In the middle of the huge room, eight stainless steel tables provided seating for forty-eight for meals, card-playing, chess and dominoes—the latter of which I camp to despise for the way each player slammed his pieces on the metal tables as if the slamming was more the object of the game than the game itself. Over the deafening clamor, a P.A. system continually blasted announcements that appeared to go unnoticed by the inmates. Those who weren't watching TV, lifting weights, playing chess or slamming dominoes would sit or stand in groups of similar interests or cultures talking among themselves about their legal cases, the women in their lives or their various criminal exploits.

Each group had a distinctive appearance and feeling. The bikers, with elaborate, full-body tattoos were so imposing they formed a group even if there were only two of them. Latinos, most often with tattoos of tear drops falling from their eyes, cobwebs on their elbows, or "The Lady of Guadalupe" covering their backs, congregated in groups of fours and fives, usually with a taunting or antagonistic manner…not just toward the whites and the blacks, but often with other groups of Latinos.

The blacks, too cool to appear as if they needed to hang out in groups, formed a loose-knit group distinguishable primarily by the raucous, ear-splitting manner in which they shouted at one another across the cellblock. For the most part, they kept an eye out for each other, and delighted in feeling that their slick jive kept them above the rest, and in control.

The Anglos, except for the bikers, had no real groups. They would stand around and talk with each other, primarily in pairs. With little cohesiveness or unity, they generally hung out on their own, read books or paced the floor. They called it "exercising," but it was really only pacing. Outwardly, they tried to appear calm and unbothered, but inwardly they were as skittish as horses in a corral with a pack of wolves lurking about.

Beyond three walls of the main floor, and separated from it by large sheets of thick Plexiglas, were smaller rooms with four cells upstairs and four cells downstairs. Originally designed for two occupants each, most of the cells had been converted to triples by use of an extra mat on the floor. For federal prisoners like me, double bunking in a county facility was not permitted—a policy which I found to be both a relief and a curse. Although it was good to have a cell to myself, it meant that someone else had to triple up in other cells. Being older, white and educated, I was already suspect as a possible "plant" by the government, so having a cell to myself only added all the more to their suspicions about me.

Other than the Anglo biker-types and a few black inmates, seventy percent of the population was Latino. I belonged to a minority of ten or so non-biker Anglos few of whom were considered worth being approached by the rest. As far as most of them were concerned, we were most likely snitches, cops or ex-lawyers.

Over a thousand inmates filled the BCDC complex at any one time, with dozens more entering or being released each day. If there was space anywhere another body could always be squeezed in, even if bare mattresses had to be laid out on the main cellblock floor. The old-timers prayed to get their cases over with I was later told, so that they could get transferred to prison and out of such insanity.

Across the hallway from our cellblock was an identical one, with four similar floors above ours. Below were several floors of administrative offices, with hallways and corridors leading in every direction. Office workers and clerks scurried busily from one office to another on a daily basis, with officials in suits and ties issuing instructions to supervisors too busy to be bothered. Harried guards, too low-ranking to avoid the more mundane duties, led small groups of manacled inmates to and from hearings, to sickbay, or to the Hole, at all hours of any given day. There were so many corridors and hallways, an escapee wouldn't have a prayer of getting out without a map, a schedule, and a two-hour head start.

It took me a full two weeks to even begin to settle in and adjust to the constant noise. The only peace I came to know was after lockdown each night when everyone was in their cells and closed off by solid steel doors. In the quiet hours after lockdown, I found time to get my nerves calmed down, my thoughts together and letters written. I also kept a journal, which I always wrote in before dropping off for a few fitful hours' sleep.

By the end of the second week, I noticed the comings and goings of a man in a wheelchair who was obviously a member of the staff. Inmates gathered around him whenever he was on the floor, and seemed to genuinely respect him despite his being both white and an authority figure. I was intrigued with the respect they showed him, and his ease of manner and style.

One day when he wasn't besieged by inmates pressing him for favors or requests, I approached him. He was a kind, decent sort of person, and greeted me with sincere interest.

"How are you doing," he asked me directly. "I'm the educational coordinator here. The name's Gordon. You must be getting settled in by now." He was aware that I was new to the cellblock, in spite of the hundreds of inmates on all floors that he had to deal with every day.

"Well, it hasn't been easy," I replied, "but I'm starting to get the hang of it. There's an educational program here?"

"Yes—such as it is," he said. "We're not really budgeted for such programs, nor is it mandated by the county or the state. We're technically not a 'long-term' facility. But it's such a waste for most of these inmates to be in here as long as they are, and not have a chance to better themselves. Most of them are illiterate."

"So what can you do about that?"

"We've started a G.E.D. program in one of the cellblocks that has been converted to a 'live-in' classroom. Men who qualify, and who stay out of trouble, get to move there and take classes taught by teachers from the outside. If they do well, it can be a factor in reducing their sentences. It's pitifully small, however. We can't accommodate even ten percent of the inmates who want to participate. We don't have the room or the budget. I come here to let inmates know that someone cares and to sometimes pass around educational material they can work on themselves."

"If they're illiterate," I asked, "how can they read it?"

"That's the biggest problem. A lot of them can't. Most of these guys are barely able to *speak* English, let alone read or write it."

Several inmates suddenly gathered around him with more requests, so we were unable to finish the conversation before chowtime was called. I thought about his comments the rest of the day as I watched everyone milling about in the cellblock. I thought about it more that night, and gradually felt inspired to do something. Friction with some of the younger Latinos, who had only contempt for educated white boys with private cells, would be a challenge to overcome. I spoke enough Spanish to help the ones who wanted to learn. If I got a few of them involved, perhaps they would get a bit of an education out of the effort, and I would have something that would keep my mind off of my own situation. I wouldn't mind the chance to improve my Spanish in the process.

The next day when Gordon returned, I approached him again.

"What if I were to offer to teach the men basic reading and writing? Could you get me the materials I need?"

"Of course, but what's your angle?" Correctional officials, I was rapidly learning, suspected any effort to do anything worthwhile to be both insincere and manipulative. But the idea had grown on me, and perhaps it could be something that would show the authorities that I had more useful things to offer than just sitting in prison. Besides, why not try to turn a bad situation into something at least a little better?

"No angle, really," I said. "Just thought I might be able to put my time in here to better use."

"Sounds pretty noble to me," he said. "But my supervisors will most likely be a little suspicious. As far as they're concerned, inmates are always up to something. I'll check into it, though, and see if I can get you something. If you manage to get a few inmates interested enough to stick with it, I might actually be able to get you moved to the educational unit. Federal inmates aren't permitted to participate in the program, but if you can show some progress I might be able to get you a bunk over there. The Feds don't care where we bunk you, just so long as we don't put you in with any of *our* 'rabble.' God knows we could use a good tutor right now."

"That would be great, but you may have a problem with that. Before I was apprehended, I was a fugitive for five years. I'm not an escape risk as far as I'm concerned, but their records will most likely show that I am."

"Yeah, you might be right." He paused and then continued, "That might be a problem, but I think I can get around it. This is a new program, and I have some influential supporters who want to see it work. If I see that you can get something going, I'll let them know about it. Besides, even though it's a bit more comfortable over there, it's no less secure."

"I'll give it my best, but so far not too many of the inmates trust me. I'm just another inmate to them. Worse than that, I'm a 'smart-ass white boy,' and probably a snitch at that."

"That's pretty common with new inmates, especially guys with any education. I'll talk to some of the older ones. If they take an interest, some of the younger ones might. It'll be good experience for you."

With that, the inner cage door to the cellblock suddenly opened—a signal for him to exit the cellblock. He wheeled himself inside, and it slammed shut with a force that was unnerving even when I was watching it happen. While he waited for the main, outer door to the corridor to open, he looked back at me and said, "You know, you could make a difference in here. Some of these guys never made it through elementary school, and consequently didn't learn even the basics of reading and writing. A lot of them are actually pretty bright. If you're serious, it could change their lives...and maybe yours, too."

"Well, I don't have much else to do around here," I said, looking at him through the bars. "If any of them are interested, and you can get me some basic materials, I'll give it a shot."

During the next few days, I made a little headway with a couple of older Latinos. After a few chats with them, and Gordon's support to encourage them to talk to the others, I seemed to get the point across that I could offer something of value. Still, they were hesitant. Pride and machismo are big factors in the Latino culture. No one wanted to admit to a lack of education. To allow me to tutor them would mean they'd have to admit to some "defectiveness" on their part, as well as to set aside their prejudices about educated white boys and trust that I wasn't a snitch. Given the peer pressure in the cellblock, particularly among Latinos, that might be a tall order.

Several days passed, but nothing positive came of my efforts. In fact, things actually seemed to get worse. Suddenly I was avoided even more than before. Any attempt I made to talk with Latino inmates was met with cold, blank stares or turned backs. I began to hear occasional snide remarks, and noticed sneers and glaring faces as I went back and forth from meals. The more I tried to show my sincerity, the more I was greeted with indifference and even insults. Finally, when it was apparent their general attitude might lead to physical confrontation, I determined it would be best for me to stay in my cell and just read. I was discouraged, and felt as if my intention to establish a good record by contributing to an obvious need was turning against me.

Chapter Twenty-Three

One day as I was reading in my cell, a man paused at my door. It was one of the older Mexican inmates I hadn't yet approached. He was a big man, and his face bore the scars of more than a few battles with life. He spoke very little English and usually stayed to himself, so I was surprised to see him standing there as if he wanted to say something.

His name, I learned later, was Simon Hernandez. Like me, he was a federal inmate waiting for his case to come up in district court. When I first arrived, I noticed that he was quiet and generally well respected by inmates and guards alike. As I looked into his eyes, I detected a kind and gentle man beneath his large frame and imposing appearance.

My Spanish was nearly as bad as his English, so it took us a while to understand each other, but eventually I was able to determine that he needed help with his case. He couldn't read or speak English, and consequently was unable to comprehend the legal proceedings and what his attorney was saying to him. He had heard that I was educated, and evidently it was more important to him to learn about his case than it was whether or not he would be viewed as "uneducated." In short, he wanted to know if I could help him. In as sincere a manner as possible, I told him that I had very little legal experience and to depend on me for anything of a legal nature could actually be dangerous for him. He thanked me and went on his way.

I guessed Simon's age to be in the mid-forties. Strong and fearsome in appearance, he was looked up to by many of the Latino inmates who saw him as a "big brother." Even the guards, most of whom were also Latino, respected him enough to let him out of his cell at night after lock-up to perform orderly work in the cellblock. That allowed him access to the "instant hot" water faucet to make tea and coffee, and to watch TV for as long as he wished while everyone else slept in their cells. Generally not permitted for federal inmates, being an orderly was a special privilege afforded to only the least troublesome inmates. There were only four such orderlies who had the run of the place during the quiet hours after lockdown, and he appeared to be the oldest among them.

Late one night while sitting on my bunk writing furiously, a quiet tapping on my cell door broke my concentration. It was Simon peering in at me through the little window in the door. With a hint of impishness in his eyes, he held up a styrofoam cup of steaming liquid, which I assumed to be coffee. He seemed to be offering it to me, but the door was locked for the night. At first I thought he was only having some fun with me, but then realized he was serious.

"Sure, why not?" I said to him in Spanish through the door, thinking maybe he would have one of the guards open it. With a pleased expression, he scurried off. He was back a few minutes later with a cup of steaming hot water and a sheet of plain paper folded lengthwise. He pushed the paper through the doorjamb until one end was on my side, then motioned for me to hold my cup under what was now a little chute for the hot water to flow into my cup. Delighted with this amazing technique, I reached into my personal effects for a packet of instant coffee. With great disappointment, I realized I had none. From the look on his face, I could tell that he was equally disappointed, but I tried to reassure him that a cup of hot water was as welcome as a cup of coffee would've been. He was unconvinced.

Hardly any time passed before I heard a shuffle of paper under my door. Several packets of instant coffee appeared, and another paper chute emerged in the doorjamb. Throughout the rest of the night, I was delighted to have a continuous supply of hot water and instant coffee.

The following week, several full sets of G.E.D. materials along with math and grammar books arrived with my name on them. Hour after hour, day after day, Simon and I went through those books. Gradually, he became more conversant in English, and as a result was better able to understand the specifics of his case. His attorney was amazed by Simon's newly acquired communication skills. Still, Simon's case was a tough one, and things weren't going well. He had allowed his sixteen-year-old son to get involved with him in a drug transaction that involved heroin. Penalties for any quantity of heroin, however small, were severe. A deal had been made to let the son off in return for a more severe sentence for Simon. Evidently, as his sentencing date approached, he hadn't realized how severe it could be, and he was worried. Neither did he realize that he was being 'worked.'

The small amount of heroin in this case, according to Simon, had been for his own personal use. Although admittedly more serious an offense than most other drugs, it wasn't for sale to anyone. A transaction for a relatively small amount of marijuana was Simon's actual conviction, but because there was heroin involved, a stiffer sentence was imminent. Since he wasn't caught in possession of the drugs, Simon could have gotten off, but with the threat of his son doing time, he chose to cooperate with the authorities. What he didn't realize was that he was being prosecuted as a "career criminal," the penalties for which could include anything from ten years to life.

Simon had the courage to believe things would eventually turn in his favor if he stayed strong. After each visit with his attorney, we would sit and try to understand what he was up against. Special days such as Valentine's Day, Easter and Mothers' Day came and went. For each one, he drew elaborate floral designs on folded sheets of paper, which he gave to inmates to send to their wives and sweethearts. They were like custom-made greeting cards.

His drawings and letters to his wife were works of art, poetically written in Spanish. Her letters to him were equally poetic and loving. He often used them to teach me to read Spanish. The bond he had with his wife gave me hope and encouragement. Every visiting day, he came back into the cellblock beaming from being with her. My eyes often filled with tears of both joy and sorrow, remembering my own loved ones at home.

Simon's sentencing day finally came, and we sent him off with as much bravado as we could muster. Waiting for his return was agonizing. Finally, late in the afternoon, the outer door to the cellblock opened and the inner cage filled with inmates returning from court. Last to enter the cage was Simon, spirit-broken and head hung low with obvious bad news. We knew better than to approach him just then, but word spread quickly around the cellblock that Simon had gotten fifteen years…with no chance of parole.

For the next few days, Simon wasn't seen except at mealtimes, and then only briefly. Within weeks, he was on his way to the federal prison system. As the inner door of the cage opened to let him out of the cellblock, he handed me a stack of papers and smiled in a way that let me know he would be okay. In spite of his troubled past, he was a good man who wanted the best for his wife and family. As the outer door slammed shut behind him, I looked at the papers he had handed me. It was his artwork, "Hernandez Originals," to do with as I pleased. In there, they would bring a lot in the way of trade goods, if I were inclined to use them that way.

During the next few weeks, my own case came before the court. I had two hearings; a plea appearance and sentencing on a new felony count for having failed to appear. Even though I had been released back then on my own personal recognizance, not showing up was the same as "bail jumping."

Once again I stood before the same federal district judge, this time in the orange jumpsuit and shackles worn by prisoners. It was clear from the start that he had no sympathy for anyone who ran from the law, regardless of the circumstances. Even with a carefully prepared affidavit attesting to the extreme duress arising from personal threats at the time, and my exemplary record while a fugitive, there would be no tolerance on his part for what amounted to "absconding." With other prisoners listening intently on their benches behind me, my attempt to explain my situation in any detail fell way short as the judge glared coldly down at me. With a slam of his gavel, he added two years to my original sentence—to be served *consecutively* to my prior two felonies. I was now suddenly a three-time felon serving *six* years, and with a five-year fugitive history.

Back in the cellblock at BCDC, I managed to add a few "students" to my G.E.D. classes, and was given Simon's job as the newest Bay Orderly. Now I could sit out in the main room and write during the quiet hours, and occasionally the guards even let one or two inmates out to study with me. My credibility among both inmates and guards began to grow to the point where even a guard or two would stand nearby and occasionally even participate.

During my interaction with the men I tutored, I noticed patterns of behavior that were highly consistent with much of what I had heard about so-called "criminal behavior." Of course…I was in prison. But what intrigued me most was the frequency, similarity and even near-identical nature of each one's life development. Most of the inmates had long histories of juvenile crime, and I was noticing what appeared to be a completely predictable pattern based upon their upbringing.

The longer I worked with the younger prisoners in the cellblock, the more I became inspired to study juvenile crime and methods to help prevent it. The core of their problem, which I discovered over and over, was lack of self-esteem often resulting from horrific childhoods and a lack of education. As I continued to work with the prisoners, I noticed slight but significant changes in their attitudes. Each night I would write up my notes and observations and send them off to Debra. She and other friends sent me magazine and newspaper articles on juvenile crime, which I studied in the light of first-hand experiences I had every day with the products of such criminal behavior. The BCDC librarian brought me books on the subject, and before long I had accumulated enough information to practically write a graduate thesis on the subject.

Meanwhile, Debra compiled all of my writings and ideas into a proposal I wrote for a juvenile diversion project I felt could lead to lasting, effective changes in their behavior. The finished proposal, entitled "A Return to Honor," was sent to U.S. Senator Barry Goldwater, who forwarded it to the U.S. Office of Juvenile Justice. They evaluated it and sent it back to him with recommendations for possible funding. Senator Goldwater then contacted the U.S. Pardons Attorney, and took the initial steps to apply for an executive clemency on my behalf. That effort was joined in the form of letters of support from U.S. Congressman John McCain and several other notable government officials in both Arizona and California.

Meanwhile, I was moved to the "classroom" cellblock, where I continued my tutoring and counseling in a more structured setting. Despite the two years added to my sentence, things were beginning to look promising. My adaptability in turning the experience into something worthwhile amazed everyone who knew me.

The wheels of justice grind slowly, however, and my case was no exception. The weeks passed until late June of that year, when Gordon wheeled over to me and asked to speak with me privately.

"You're being shipped out soon," he said in a low voice. "I don't know exactly when, or where you're going, but I've been told to have you start wrapping things up in here."

"Well, I'm not sure exactly how to do that," I said.

"Just be aware, and make sure everything is in order. It could happen tomorrow, for all I know. They just want us to be sure you're ready when they come for you."

"Okay," I sighed. "Well, it's been an inspiration being here."

"Yes, it has. You've done a lot of good here, although you may not ever see the long-term benefit of it. I thought perhaps it might be of some help for you to have this." He handed me a letter on official BCDC letterhead.

"I have to get to a meeting," he said, "and I'll be gone for the next few days. I wanted to make sure to see you before you left, and to wish you good luck. I think you'll do well if you keep up this kind of work."

"Thanks," I said. "Maybe I'll be able to get back here someday, and say hello from a different perspective. Maybe we could even have lunch. Now, wouldn't that be an enjoyable twist?"

"Yes, it would. I'll look forward to it." With that, he wheeled himself around and headed for the exit. I waved goodbye to him, and went back to my cell to think about what might lie ahead. Sitting on my bunk, I opened the letter and read it.

The purpose of this letter is to express my appreciation for the assistance that you have been rendering the residents at the Bernalillo County Detention Center during the period of your incarceration (January 7, 1986 until present). During this period you have served as a tutor/counselor for numerous other residents in a sincere effort to help them prepare for better education and to improve themselves. You have also assisted several residents in their preparation for G.E.D. examinations.

I also want to commend you for your outstanding performance of duty as a Bay Orderly on your housing level, and on your outstanding conduct.

Once again, thank you for your assistance.

It was signed by none other than the "iron-fisted" director of the facility himself, an ex-military commander who prided himself in running the place as tightly as any warden of a maximum-security prison. I was told later that he never wrote such letters, and had forbidden any of his staff from writing letters on behalf of inmates.

With no apparent new developments regarding the action for clemency, I felt a growing disappointment as the weeks, then months, had passed. Finally something positive had come from my time and work. Holding the letter as if it were a historic document, I marveled at how some things actually work out.

The very next morning, I was notified to roll up my things. After breakfast, a guard with whom I had had many pleasant talks came to escort me to the change-out room. Under the impression that I was being released, he waited while I changed into the same street clothes I had worn six months earlier, and then led me to a processing room for prisoners being *released*. With cheerful wishes for good days ahead, he walked off down the corridor and left me ten feet from an *unlocked* door that opened directly onto the streets of downtown Albuquerque. Along the wall to the left of the room was a large, Plexiglas window, behind which sat a clerk who monitored activity in the small room.

I stood paralyzed with the realization that just beyond that door was freedom, short-lived though it might be. A mistake like that wouldn't go unnoticed for long. U.S. Marshals would be fast on my trail. Even though I knew I wouldn't make it three blocks, I was nevertheless gripped with panic that I might actually attempt an exit.

Just then, a former inmate I had seen in another cellblock, now dressed in his street clothes, stepped into the room. He casually signed a form at the window, took his things from the clerk, and stepped out the door. As it opened, I caught a glimpse of the outside world, a world of cars and trucks and scurrying pedestrians, and blue skies, fresh air and sweet, precious freedom.

Lying on the desk next to the clerk was a large envelope with my name on it in big, bold letters. It was all of my personal effects, where the guard had placed them for my release. All I had to do was step up to the window and sign the release form. The clerk looked up at me, waiting for me to step forward. In that moment, my life hung in a precarious balance. Should I sign the form and step out into a world I would never be able to live in again as a truly free person? Or refuse to sign and signal the entire facility that a mistake had been made? I felt dizzy. My head was spinning, and my heart was pounding.

Suddenly, the inside door flew open and a panicked sergeant lunged for me, grabbing me like I was just about to run for the door. He yelled behind him that he had "caught" me as two marshals burst in behind him. All three roughly escorted me to the release area for prisoners being transferred.

As far as the marshals were concerned, they had just prevented an escape by a convicted felon with an already established "fugitive" history. Chained and shackled, I was pushed into the back seat of their sedan, along with two other prisoners bound for some unknown destination in the federal prison system. The possibility of freedom had played in my consciousness for a fleeting moment. My reality was now met with the stale stink of the clothes I had on that I'd worn when I was first arrested. Obviously not cleaned during that six months in storage, they still carried the smell of sweat from that day of my first arrest, along with that of the trip from Arizona to Albuquerque. Now, having been on the brink of escape, even more sweat was added to the already foul mix of everything else, which made for the most unpleasant of circumstances for my companions in the backseat of the marshal's sedan.

Where I was headed remained a mystery. Only when I heard the marshals talking as we made our way across the city to the southbound lanes of Interstate 25, was I able to determine that it was to begin at La Tuna.

It was the dreariest, smelliest four-hour ride of my life.

Chapter Twenty-Four

Sounds of voices and activity out in the corridor brought me wide-awake, and suddenly it all came back to me. I was in prison. La Tuna. I had just fallen into a deep sleep from months of stress, anxiety and mental exhaustion. It was my first official day in the "Fed," and even through the solid door of my cell, the smell of hot food was drifting in. Suddenly it seemed as if it had been a long time since I had last eaten. It had only been the evening before, in the holding cage just after the three of us had arrived from BCDC, but I was so exhausted that I lost track of where I was or how much time had passed since then. I couldn't tell for certain, but it seemed to me to be mid-morning of the next day...a Saturday.

I strained to look down the corridor through the little window in my door, but could only see the doors of the cells across from me. Again I was struck with the size of the padlocks on each of the flaps, and wondered what useful purpose they could possibly serve. Not only were the flaps already bolted shut, but the openings they covered were hardly bigger than a mail slot. What could they possibly need padlocks for?

I could hear the muffled sounds of prisoners stirring in the other cells as the smell of food began to permeate the whole corridor. As I listened to them, I sensed how animals in zoos must feel at feeding time. I could feel their anticipation growing more intense as the food cart worked its way along the corridor.

Suddenly I noticed movement behind the window of the door directly across from me. Startled, I realized there was someone in there looking back at me. Framed by the tiny window of his door, and partially obscured by the wiremesh covering, the white in his eyes accentuated the blackness of his face. Just then, a white-shirted guard momentarily blocked our view as he unlocked the padlocks on both of our flaps and dropped them open. Jutting out horizontally from the doors, each flap then formed a flat surface large enough to hold a food tray. The guard moved on down the corridor, and the man across from me motioned for me to drop down to talk through the slot in our doors.

"Duhs y'all eat pohk?" he shouted through his slot. I thought about it for a minute, hesitant to say anything more or less than necessary on my first contact. I had been forewarned that in prison, first impressions were everything.

"No," I replied. "I don't eat much meat. If I do, it's rarely pork."

"Tha's cool," he smiled back at me. "T'day be Sa'day, an' on weekends dey ahways gib us meat. If it be *pohk,* ah' cain't eat it 'cause ahm Muslim. Ah don' eat no swine, man. Thought mabbee ah'd give ya ma' pohk, and we could trade fo' sumpthin' latah on. But if y'all don' eat no meat, den das' a whole 'nutha thing..."

"Well, I do eat meat sometimes, but not much. Especially in places like this. I'm sure they use the cheapest stuff they can get."

"What 'chu mean, 'places like 'dis'? You be travlin' 'roun, checkin' 'em out, o' what?"

"I don't know. I might be staying here, or I might be on my way somewhere else. I don't know where I'm going to end up."

"Ah hear that, man. Las' guy who was in theah, he been on da' bus fo' t'ree muhnz. Din' know wheah he was headin', neithuh."

"Well, I hope that doesn't happen to me. They don't tell you much in here, do they?"

"Shit, no. Dey don' gib a shit 'bout 'chu. Dey think dey might catch sumpthin' talkin' ta us. Dey likes ta ack real tough, y' know..."

"Yeah, well it's probably because they're outnumbered, and because they think we're wild animals who'll attack them if they show any weakness."

"Dey right, man. Ah'd take one a' dem assholes down in a minute if ah had a chance. Dey scum, man. Dey spit in ya face, if dey could. Mos' of 'em be da' kind a' dude dat kicks ya when ya down."

"Not all of them. I've seen some that care. I don't think they're all that way."

"Mos' of 'em ah. Sides, y'all ain't black. In dis joint, da' Man be mosly Ch'cano. Dey th' *wuhs* kind. Dey be eben hardah on dey *own* kine in heah. Dey hates ev'body. Dey 'speshly don' like no smaht-ass white boys, neitha', so ah'd keep ta' yo' 'sef, if ya know whad ah mean."

"Yeah, I get the picture. Last place I was in was like that. Up in Albuquerque. It was almost all Latino. I'll keep to myself. Anyway, most of my meat you can have. If there's any pork, maybe you can trade it with someone else. I just have to figure out how to get it over to you."

"No sweat, man. Jes' wrap it up and gib it ta' da' ohdahly. He come by latah befo' da' Man lock us up agin. He pass it ovah ta' me."

I thought about it for a minute or two, and wondered what else the orderly could do, and what it would cost me. I had heard that very little passes between inmates that doesn't get paid for in some way. Thank God for the time I'd had with guys like Simon and Big Jim. Still, there were traps a man could get caught in, not knowing the rules. There were written rules of the "Man," and unwritten rules of the inmates. Both had to be learned by experience, which could prove costly. I thought about that for a minute, then spoke to him again.

"This orderly, can he do anything more than pass food between us?"

"Sho', man. What chu' wahnt?"

"Something to write with. A pen, maybe. And some paper. Even a pencil would be okay, but at least one that's sharp. A pen would be great."

"A PEN? Ah you crazy? Weah you think you is, anyway, da' Hilton? Dey don' let us have no goddamn *pens* in heah. Dis' is *SEG,* man. In hcah, y'all be lucky ta' get a *pencil*—and not *even* shahp. What chu wahnt wif' a *shahp* pencil, enny-ways? You gonna shank sumbuddy?"

"No, I want to write some letters, maybe keep some notes in a journal. I just got here last night. What's 'SEG'?"

"What chu mean, 'Wa's SEG?' Ain't *nobody* don' know what 'SEG' is. It's da' *HOLE,* man. Dey calls it 'segragashun', but ta' us it jes' be da' 'hole'—an' you *in* it."

The food cart and two orderlies came into view, followed by a guard wearing the same white shirt and gray slacks as the ones who processed us in the night before. On his hip was the ever-present two-way radio, constantly crackling with important-sounding but pointless chatter of men consumed with self-importance. On his belt were those damned jingling keys, some of which I doubted even fit anything.

A tray of food was placed on the flap in my door. Once again there were ample portions—even more so than my first one the night before. I hadn't seen real, honest-to-God, fried eggs in so long, I just stared at them like they were some kind of rare jewels. Next to them, on another part of the tray was a pile of fried potatoes, smothered with gravy. Then there was TOAST—*real* toast—still with a hint of warmth, and a couple of pats of butter half melted into the bread.

A big slab of ham lay next to the eggs. For a moment I fought back an urge to stuff the whole thing into my mouth before I could think about it, but discipline won out and I wrapped the ham in a napkin for the orderly to pass to my new friend to trade with someone other than Muslims. There was enough other food on the tray to satisfy my hunger, and I intended to savor every bite.

A few minutes later, the orderly came by and nonchalantly tossed the ham I had left on the flap into a certain corner of the cart as if it were trash. He hesitated, then looked at me through the tiny window.

"I need a couple of things," I asked him through the flap.

"Yeah? What?" he asked.

"Could you get me some paper and pencils?" I asked.

He half-grunted, and moved on down the corridor. A wasted effort, I thought, but a while later a few sheets of lined notepaper and two stubby pencils appeared on the still-open flap of the door.

I leaped from the bunk and grabbed the paper like a kid at Christmas. Even the little pencil stubs were a joy to have, for now I could keep a journal again and perhaps even write a letter or two. If meat were a regular thing here, I would have plenty of writing material.

I sat back down on my bunk with the still warm tray on my lap, and dug into that breakfast like someone who hadn't eaten in days. It was the best meal I had eaten since my arrest seven months before. If they fed us like that every day, I might actually enjoy the place for a while. My moment of whimsy was interrupted by the voice from across the hall.

"Psssst!" I heard the voice through the slot in my door. "Hey, *New Guy...*," the voice was more insistent.

I got up and went to the door, crouching down to look over at him through the open slot.

"Yeah. What's up?"

"Did ya eat yo' shit, man?"

"I'm eating it right now, except the ham. Is that what you mean?"

"Yeah, man. Whad' ja' do wi' da' meat?"

"The orderly picked it up. Why?"

"Which one?"

"I don't know. The big guy with the mustache, I think."

"Oh, *man*...he da' wrong dude. Dat bitch don' do shit roun' heah. He nevah do nuthin' fo' nobody, 'cept fo' da' Man."

"He brought me some paper and some pencils... "

"He *spose'* ta' do that. Bet he din' eben gib' ya much, neithuh. How much he gib' ya?"

"About ten pages," I lied.

"Sheeeit, man. Ya' cuhda' got a bunch more 'n 'nat. He don' gib' a shit 'bout nothin' or nobuhdy but hissef. When I get outta' heah, ah'm gonna dance on his haid...dah's fo' sho'. Dat creehp has aw' kinda' chances ta' help us pass da' time in heah, an' aw he do is kiss up ta' da' Man. Don' gib that bitch *nothin'.*"

"I thought you said he'd pass meat over to you."

"Thas' right...but not that dude. Ah don' know how he got on 'dis block. He spose' ta' be in tha othuh one."

"Okay. How can I get some stamps?"

"Stamps? You mean lahk *pose' offise* stamps?"

"Yeah...to write letters."

'No sweat, man. I can get chu' all kinda' stamps. Ain't nobody in heah dat wants ta' write ta nobody ennyhow. But don' let nobody know you think dey be wuhth nuthin', leastwhys you'll be gibin' up mo' n' you need to."

"Okay. You can have all my meat, if you'll get me stamps. And if you can arrange it, I need more paper and some better pencils, too. Deal?"

"Sho, man. Weah y'all fruhm, ennyway?"

"Arizona."

"No shit? You mean like cactuses and snakes an' shit?"

"Yeah, but it's not all like that. Where *you* from?"

"Ah'm from DEE CEE," he accented the letters proudly. "Mos' of us bruhthas in da' Fed ah frum DEE CEE. Y'all be runnin' inta' us all ovah da'place. We be evryweah in da' Fed, 'cause ennythin' you do in D.C. be a Fedral *AH*fense."

From somewhere down the corridor, I heard voices of authority again. Sounds of metal flaps closing and padlocks slamming into place echoed down the corridor. I felt a quickening as the tiny bit of freedom I had had in talking with the man across from me was about to be snatched away. The metal flap on my door slammed shut, and I felt like the lid of a cheap metal coffin had just been closed on me.

The sounds of keys jingling and radios crackling faded away down the corridor, and I was alone again with my thoughts. The cell suddenly seemed even smaller than when I had first stepped into it.

Sleep during those first days at La Tuna came a little easier than it had when I was back at BCDC and Maricopa County. Maybe this was one of the "blessings" others had told me about being in prison. There certainly wasn't much to do, that was clear. At least I was away from the madness of detention centers. It was hardly restful, but I was stressed to the max. Physically I was okay, but mentally and emotionally, I was exhausted.

Prison was a strange new twist for me. The quiet of the cell compelled me to think about how isolation might affect me, and how I would handle it. How long would I be in there? Why wouldn't anyone tell me anything? I could accept that I was being punished, but what was so harmful in telling me what to expect?

Ever so subtly, the physical and emotional tension that I had felt during seven long months in detention centers began to be replaced by another kind of tension—a deep, psychological sense of gnawing uneasiness that comes with being isolated for long periods of time. Left alone long enough, one is forced to come to grips with a lifetime of choices and actions that ultimately have proven fruitless and self-destructive.

I had no idea of the dragon that was only just beginning to awaken in the darkest reaches of my mind. As I lay on my bunk, a picture of him began to form, lying quietly in a darkened cave. I had seen him before, but only briefly in earlier times when moments of impulsiveness or weakness had forced me into a corner of some sort. But always I had managed to escape his wrath by creating diversions or distractions of many different kinds. Now I felt a deep sense of foreboding as I realized that I was trapped in far worse than a "corner." I was in the cave with him, with no place to run and no way to create a diversion.

A wave of terror swept over me as I pictured one of his eyes open slowly and look in my direction. There was no place to hide this time. It was just me and the dragon in a tiny little prison cell, locked away and sealed off from the rest of the world. The dragon was awake, and I was its prey.

Chapter Twenty-Five

Suddenly I was awake. It was dark outside. Dim light filtering in through the tiny window in the door told me the nightmare was still underway. I had been dreaming again. Something about dragons. Voices and bootsteps in the night. Giant cell doors slamming shut behind me and all around me, over and over and over again. Niagara Falls. I was in a dinghy, my wrists cuffed behind my back, kicking frantically to keep from being swept over the edge. Then it wasn't a dinghy, but a floating cage being pulled closer and closer to the edge of a giant, swirling, heaving maelstrom. The roaring of the water, the screams of the crowd watching, then...I was in a darkened room. The dragon was in there with me somewhere. I had to get my bearings...find his menacing green eyes peering back at me. If I could just see his eyes, I could inch my way out of his reach, or somehow divert his attention. I could hear him breathing. I could feel movement, an almost imperceptible sound.

A noise came from outside the room, and suddenly I was awake...again? Had it been a dream...again? Or a dream within a dream? I reached up and felt the upper bunk, and the walls on each side of me. I was really awake this time. Or was I?

I reached back and felt the window behind me, then the little desk beside me. Yes, I was awake. I was in my little rat hole of a cell in La Tuna. I lay still for a while and allowed the realization to sweep over me that every day might be the same, waking up from one nightmare to find myself in yet another one. A feeling of intense despair welled up in me at the prospect that the time might come when I wouldn't be able to tell which one I was in. It was already happening, and I had only been in the cell two days. Or was it three, now? No watch. No clock. Nothing but the night and day to mark the passage of time.

Muffled voices from inmates in the other cells down the hallway, giving me the eerie feeling of being locked in a medieval dungeon. With each passing hour the voices grew louder and more pervasive as insults, racial slurs and jeers were shouted at inmates in other cells the taunters couldn't even see. Hour after hour, they taunted and jeered each other from one end of the hallway to the other with a rage that was unabated and senseless.

I tried to picture the faces behind the tormented voices. Who were they? Were they anything like their voices? What were they like outside the cages? Had they been like that as kids? Did they have kids of their own?

Finally, the sounds of padlocks unlocking and door flaps dropping open indicated it was mealtime again. Anticipation surged in me, even though I wasn't really hungry. Was it lunchtime or dinnertime? I couldn't tell if three hours had passed, or six. Maybe the beasts in the other cells would quiet down once they had eaten again. The Feds had it down: Feed the animals well and keep them subdued. That was the only positive thing I had heard about the federal system. I hoped like hell it was true, for other reasons now than just hunger.

A guard appeared in my tiny window, and I heard the sound of the padlock unlocking. The flap dropped opened, and I got up to see if my friend across the hall was at his door. I squatted down to look through the slot and saw him looking back at me through his.

"Waz up, man?" he shouted at me over all the clamor.

"Nothin' much," I replied. "How was your day?"

"How was ma day? Lemmee see. Aftah I took masef on a long ol' walk out dere ta' the highway, ah got me a ride ta' town. Took in a movie and picked up on a couple a' classy babes. What chu' *think* ah did? Ah sat on mah ass and stared at the goddamn walls all day."

"How long you been in here?" I ignored the comment.

"T'ree weeks...mabbee foh', now."

"Are you on your way somewhere?"

"Ah might be, now. Ah been heah two yeahs. Had me a crib ovah in the main dohmatory. Ah got into it wid' some dude been gibbin' me some shit fo' a wyuhl. Ah bus' him up pretty good, tho. He won' be talkin' shit 'bout nobody 'roun heah agin'. Ah belieb he still in da' hospital."

"So what did they do to you?"

"Dey put me in heah 'til th' 'ef-bee-eye' interrogates me. Den ah s'pose dey'll hang some new rap on me. Prob'ly gib me anotha yeah o' two, tha's all."

"How long do you have to stay in here?"

"Don' know. Prob'ly 'til it be ovah wid. Could be foah, mabbee fi' mo' munz. Too bad, too. Had me a good job down at the prison fac'try. Ah waz makin' ahmose a hunert dollah a month. Wuhn't fo' dat asshole, ah'd be sendin' home some change fo' Chris'mahs. Took me ahmose a yeah ta git dat job."

"What were you doing there?"

"Glubs. Dat's da'factry dat make glubs fo' da' whole prison system. Used ta make shuhts an' pants too, but now we only make glubs. We waz makin' some purty good change fo' a wyuhl, 'til some dudes on th' outside said we waz takin' *bizniss* away fruhm dem. Can you belieb dat? I waz makin' ahmose thuhty-two cent a ahwa til den. Aftah dat, da' bes' we could do waz sebenteen cent a ahwa. Now ah ain't makin' shit."

My view was suddenly blocked by the arrival of the food cart, and a tray was shoved into my slot. The cart moved on and my friend was gone. I took my tray to my bunk like I was out for dinner. Balancing the tray on my folded-over pillow, I sat cross-legged on the bunk and surveyed its still-warm contents. Once again, the portions were ample. A decent, even somewhat fresh, tossed salad was a delightful surprise. A hamburger steak smothered in gravy, potatoes and something that looked like a fruit cobbler reassured me that meals in this place might make up at least somewhat for the lack of other basic necessities. I didn't want to get my hopes up too high, so I considered that it was a Saturday and perhaps this was just a weekend meal. The bologna and cheese sandwiches and cold cereal were bound to come, sooner or later.

As I sat on my bunk and ate, I thought about my friend's predicament. I was amazed that he so readily put himself at such risk, just to make a point. I wondered how it was with the rest of the inmates in the system. Was he typical, or was he one of the extremes? He was proud of his actions, and didn't seem to care that it would bring added hardship and even more time to do.

Maybe the other guy deserved it, but could it really have been worth all that extra time and misery? What about all the macho types yelling and shouting down the corridor? What were they in segregation for? Some of them were on the "bus tour," I supposed, but others were probably in for the same reason as this guy— blind and senseless lashing out at anything and everything in their way, just to find a place in the pecking order of a world that for most of them never made sense anyway. No doubt some of them were hard-core "incorrigibles," but I wondered how many just had never had an even break.

I tried to imagine the conditions in the main part of the prison, and how many other inmates were like this guy. How would I handle confrontation with blind rage like his, once I got to my own destination?

I had been told I would most likely be sent to Safford, Arizona, a minimum-security facility northeast of Tucson. Both of the other prisoners with me in the sedan were designated there, so it seemed reasonable to assume that's where we were headed. But the marshals had driven right past the turnoff for Arizona, so we didn't have a clue where we were going or even if we actually were going to Safford. It was just the way things were in the federal prison system, and I would just have to get used to it. As far as they were concerned, a dingy cell in La Tuna was as good a place as anywhere else in the system to get started.

La Tuna. What a miserable hole it was. The building I was in reminded me of Alcatraz, from the movies I had seen. It was filthy and squalid. From my point of view at that time, La Tuna was a testament to society's inability to use reason and compassion in place of blind retribution. There was nothing "correctional" about the place at all. It was "penal," pure and simple.

The shouts and jeers began to echo along the corridor again as the gladiators finished their meals. I could feel anger rising in me, and the more it did, the more I understood why my wall locker was caved in. The poor bastard before me probably couldn't take it anymore, and lashed out in the only way he could against the only thing in the room that was breakable.

I put my tray back in the slot in the door, then looked through the small window and tried to make out faces in the little windows of the doors across from me. Another black face appeared in the window of the door next to the one across from me. I could barely make it out, but as he dropped down to yell out of his open flap, I recognized him as one of the taunters. While his voice carried the strength of someone much bigger, I was startled to see how small he was. Black or white, they all reminded me of apes in the wild...yelling and screaming and flailing of arms to show their strength and intimidate others not to challenge them. The whole process of confinement had reduced them to their most primitive beginnings.

I sat back down on my bunk and remembered an old con's comment to me once. "Everyone should do some time," he said. It was hard to imagine what he meant back then, when my whole focus was on getting out. But as I let the thought linger in my mind, it began to sink in. Maybe everyone *should* do a little time in one of these places. It would certainly make a lasting impression, that was for certain. It would give everyone a whole new perspective on life, and on human nature on both sides of the walls.

"Pssst! Hey, *New* Guy!" My thoughts were interrupted by the insistent voice from across the hall. I moved to the door, took my tray out of the slot and answered him.

"Yeah?"

"You still want 'dem stamps?"

"Yeah, sure. You got some?"

"Nah, but ah kin get 'em. You got enny smokes?"

"No, I don't smoke."

"Well, yah ahttah be thinkin' 'bout gettin' you a coupla' packs. Dudes in heah be tradn' *ennything* fo' some smokes. You got enny money in yo' com'sary?"

"I don't know. I had some money when they brought me in here."

"Well, den it be on yo' books, less dem assholes kep' it. What do it say on yo' papah?"

I looked at the property receipt still lying on the top bunk. The only things indicated were a few books, my clothes, and whatever I had in my pockets when I was first arrested back in December.

"Nothing about any money," I replied.

"Well, den, you don' hab shit. Dem misruble fuckheads took yo' bread. Kin you belieb dat shit? How much wuz it?"

"There was nine dollars and some change."

"Well, dat' be 'nuff fo' some tradin'. Dem bastahds. Dey know you can't do shit 'bout it, so dey jus' ripped you off. As if it ain't misruble 'nuff 'roun' heah, dey go an' do that kine a shit ta us."

I noticed his emphasis on "us," and wondered how much his attitude would change now that he knew I had no money.

"Ne'mine," he said. "Don' wohry 'bout da' stamps. Dey gib 'em ta us, enny-way. Ah can git 'chu 'nuff stamps ta' keep you wrahtin' fo' a coupla' munz. We still got a deal on yo' meat?"

"Sure. But tell me something."

"Okay, talk ta' me."

"That fight you got into. Was it really worth all this, and the extra time you might have to do?"

"You betch yo' ass. Dey be some dudes jes' love ta aggravate a guy. Dey live ta' make trouble. Mos' of 'em be doin' a whole lotta tahm, an' if dey kin make yo' life as misruble as dey own, den dat makes 'em happy. If you let 'em get ovah on you, dey make life eben wuhse dan' it is awreddy. Dey be in yo' face ev'ry day. You got to stop 'em in dey tracks, man. If you don', den evahbody else be jumpin on you, too—less you get yo'sef a ol' man."

"Old man? What do you mean?"

"You get yo' sef a bad-ass dude to proteck you. If you ain't in a gang, o' don'
know how t' take care a' yosef, den you bettah hook up wid a ol' man to take care
a you...else someone will jes' take you fo' his own. Den you got to fight him, too
—o' else gib him what he wants. You be his 'ol lady, make his bed, do his laundry; shit like dat. Don' chu know 'bout dat?"

"Yeah, I've heard about it. So even though you might get another year or two
plus a bunch of time in the hole, you still think it was worth it? Even losing you
job?"

"Sheeyit yeah, man. Dey got ta lemmee outta heah soonah o' latah. An' when
ah get back in da'yahd, dey won' nobody gib me shit 'bout nothin'. *Dat* be wuhth
it. An' bein' somebody's ol' lady ain't no way ta do tahm...not fo' me."

"So you either fight and rack up more time in here, or you give in to someone who makes your life more miserable?"

"Das' da' way it is. Unless you fine yosef da' raht ol' man. Some dudes car
be real good ta ya'. Won' let nobody mess wit' chu, an' mabbee dey be easy or
you. Ah jes' can't stomach doin' anotha' dude, tha's all."

"I hear you. Me, neither."

"Well, you best be gettin' yo'sef ready fo' some fightn' den, 'cause dey
ahways be *somebody* wants what you got. An' you nevah know who it gonna be
You cain't trust nobody. One day you got a friend; next day he be stabbin' you ir
da' back."

Down the hallway, the unmistakable sounds of metal flaps slamming shut
quickened my heartbeat again. I was enjoying having someone to talk to, and
there was so much more I wanted to ask him. Now I would have to wait until
morning. A minute later, the orderly took my tray, followed by the guard who
slammed the flap shut with a coldness that seemed like he *wanted* to irritate me.
As I stepped back to my bunk and sat down, a wave of loneliness swept over me.

After a while, I began to notice the stench of the toilet, and the filth of the cell.
Using one of my pencil stubs to plug the drainhole in the sink, I held the "hot"
button down and let a trickle of lukewarm water slowly fill it. With another pencil carefully positioned to hold the button down, I opened the locker and rum-
maged through the items that had been left there until I found an old T-shirt.
Tearing it into pieces the size of washcloths, I reached for my bar of soap, sprin-
kled some tooth powder in the toilet, and went to work.

Several hours and many disgusting sinksful of putrid, brown water later, I dropped onto my bunk exhausted. The walls were clean, the floor was clean, and the toilet hadn't looked that good probably since it was new. My arms ached and I smelled like a used mop, but at least I could breathe a little easier.

The next morning, I washed my T-shirt and socks in the tiny sink. While they dried, I tried some exercising. Even deep knee bends were a challenge in such a tiny space, but with some practice I managed fairly well. Push-ups were somewhat contorted, but over the next several days I could do multiple sets of each exercise. I ran in place by holding one hand against a corner of the bunk bed to keep my balance. Counting out each step, I marked groups of ten steps with a knot in a string I held in my other hand. Counting each stride as three feet, I was able to approximate a mile's distance. With my window open and birds chirping outside, I "ran" a mile and a half that morning, then cleaned myself with a washcloth torn from an old towel I found in the locker.

Lying back on my bunk, I let my thoughts drift for a while. Memories and impressions of a lifetime of adventure, romance and personal challenges came and went through my mind like clouds passing. I wondered how my children were holding up through it all. The boys had been shipped off to maternal relatives they didn't even know in the remote northland of Minnesota, and Amber had gone with her Mom to the congestion and pollution of Los Angeles. It was as if I had suddenly died and disappeared from their lives.

The boys were nearing adolescence, and they adored their little sister. Now they were apart from each other, as well as from me. The pain and anguish of the memory of Amber's little arms wrapped tightly around my neck, and the snowball fights and bicycle rides all four us went on together burned deeply in my heart and mind.

The walls closed in on me as I tried to find enough room to pace while I tried to fight back the tears. I did some more push-ups and deep-knee bends to work off the rage and frustration running through every part of my body. Finally, I lay back down on the bunk and let the anger surface.

How could I have been so blind...so stupid? I had always been so smart, so quick to get into and out of trouble. I had become too clever for my own good. Even the several times I had gotten myself into real trouble before, the message hadn't sunk in. I had outsmarted them all, but in the process I had only buried myself in the delusion that somehow I was invincible. Now I was alone in a dingy cell in Texas, with my kids ripped apart from each other and from me. What a stupid, arrogant asshole I had been. How could I have ever justified such idiocy? How could I ever explain all this to them?

Demons of my own making had led me to believe I was clever enough and "innocent" enough to play the games and never lose. I felt such outrage at the thought of it I wanted to scream. This couldn't be happening to me. Hadn't I done well during all that time at the detention center? I had worked hard to make it clear that I didn't need "correcting." I had spent every day and night helping others deal with their problems, and felt I had learned more about criminal behavior than some graduate students in criminology.

That didn't matter, now. It didn't matter to the authorities, and it didn't matter to all those people I had left at home, wondering how they had been so duped by my slickness and smooth talk. It didn't matter to the guards outside, and it damn sure didn't matter to the gladiators down the corridor or to my friend across the way. I was just another inmate in their system. Another face with a number on a file folder in a pile of hundreds, even thousands, just like it being processed through a vast and slow-moving bureaucratic mill out there beyond the walls and the gun towers and the fences.

Suddenly, someone was at my cell door. Keys jingled as the door unlocked. I sprang to my feet, ready to go anywhere they wanted to take me. Maybe I was being moved somewhere more sensible. Maybe this had just been a horribly dramatic way to scare the hell out of me.

The door swung open and a guard stood there looking at me. A middle-aged man of Mexican descent, he was paunchy and out of shape. A hint of a mustache lined his upper lip, and I guessed from the sweat on his brow he wasn't used to the heat outside or much physical exertion.

"You want some exercise?" he asked flatly.

"What do you mean, 'exercise'?" I asked.

"*Exercise,* dim-wit. What the hell could I mean? Out in the yard. Something wrong with you or what?" I was taken aback, surprised both by his manner and by the nature of his question. "You wanna go outside or not?"

"Yeah, I suppose so. Sure. Hold on a second. Let me get my shoes."

"Well, hurry it up. I got six more of you to exercise, and a lot more important things to do than stand around waiting for you deadbeats to get ready."

"Okay, okay. Just give me a minute. I didn't know I was supposed to be ready the second you open the door." I wondered what "more important" things this man could possibly have to do at the moment. This was part of his *job*.

The shoes were a joke. Oversized and brightly two-toned, they had to be that way for recognizability and blisters in case of an escape. I couldn't believe anyone would actually *buy* a pair of shoes like that, I thought, as I laced each one up with a six-inch piece of string…unless they were clowns in a circus or a rodeo. I stood up and saw handcuffs dangling from the guard's hand.

"What are those for?" I asked. "I'm already locked up."

"Yep, you damn sure are. But I ain't takin' any chances with you holdovers. Bad enough with the regular scum around here, but I don't know nothin' 'bout you. You wanna go outside, you wear these until we get out there. I'll take 'em off when you're in the yard. You should know the routine by now."

"I just got here. How am I supposed to know 'the routine'? Besides, I'm not in here for a violent crime."

"*I* don't know that. And I don't much care, neither. I'm not takin' any chances. Now, you want outside or not? Don' much matter to me, one way or the other. You can wait 'til next *year,* for all I care."

"Okay. Do what you have to do."

I turned around and held my arms behind me while he put the cuffs on and led me out the door.

Halfway down the hallway, a flight of stairs led to the main floor where there was a heavy steel gate blocking the entrance to a side hallway. A few yards down that hallway was a huge, solid steel door. As we stepped into the space between the two, the guard locked the gate behind us, then turned and unlocked the big door, swinging it open. Half-blinded by the bright afternoon sun, I walked haltingly with him down a long, concrete walkway to a tall, chainlink gate. In the middle of the gate, at about waist level, was a small, square opening. The guard unlocked the gate, motioned for me to step into the courtyard, then closed and locked the gate.

"Turn around and put your hands through there, so I can take the cuffs off," he said, pointing to the opening in the gate.

In order to do that, I had to back up to the gate, bend slightly forward, and half-squat with my arms extended back and through the opening. While I stood there in a half-crouch, he fumbled with his keys then dropped them on the ground. Cussing to himself, he picked them up, then tried again. For what seemed like minutes, he tried to turn the key in the cuffs while I attempted to maintain my balance and, at the same time, adjust my eyes to the bright sunlight. The heat was intense. As he continued to fumble with his keys, twisting my arms as if I was a mannequin, I surveyed the tiny, dirt courtyard.

It was an open area, completely enclosed by four brick buildings, each at least three stories high. Lining the tops of the buildings and angled inwardly was a chainlink fence with several rows of razor wire lining both sides. *Another bit of overkill,* I thought. *As if an inmate with oversized shoes or bare feet could actually scale these walls...*

The courtyard itself was little more than a square of dirt no bigger than a tennis court. Lying along one side were a couple of tired, worn-out basketballs. Patches of crabgrass and a few weeds growing at the base of one of the buildings was the extent of the landscaping, while countless cigarette butts marked the circular trail left by others who had "exercised" before me.

With the intense heat of a Texas sun beating down on my back, I took my first few steps toward the clump of crabgrass and bent over to touch it. It felt good just to touch something alive, even if it was just crabgrass.

Just then, a couple of pigeons flew to their perch just above me, and I watched them billing and cooing and ruffling their feathers. Waves of loneliness swept over me at the sight of such a simple, natural act. *They're just pigeons,* I thought to myself. *Get a grip.* But watching the two of them only amplified my yearning for something as simple as a gentle stroke, and the soft touch of a loved one. Then I noticed sparrows and wrens also fluttering about their nests on the window ledges high above me, and my heart ached for the freedom to fly again. Walking in circles below them, I envied their freedom to come and go at will like that. It had been just like that for me not very long ago. Now it seemed an impossibility.

Suddenly, a movement in one of the upper windows startled the pigeons, and they fluttered off to another ledge. As they did, a feather fell from their nest and spiraled gently downward and landed softly in the dirt in front of me. I bent over and picked it up. It was only a pigeon feather, but so beautiful and intricately formed. My heart warmed with the thought that this was a good sign. I slipped the feather into one of my shirt pockets and started looking for more.

I was amazed that such a simple thing could have such a positive effect on me. As I walked on, I spotted a few more, and put them in my other shirt pocket. I could send them off in letters to my kids, and to close friends, as a symbol of my freedom of spirit. They would understand, I thought, and it would make my letters a bit more interesting.

The heat was getting intense, and I could tell from the guard's increasing restlessness that my hour was about up. I walked over to the gate and waited for him to go through the routine of getting out the cuffs and making me back my arms into that tiny hole again.

Just before we stepped back into the building, the guard ran his hands over my pockets and, feeling the lump of feathers inside one of them, stuck his fat, brown fingers in and pulled them out. He looked at them and made a face like he'd just put his fingers in a toilet.

"What's this shit?" he demanded.

"Just some pigeon feathers," I replied. "I figured I could send them to my kids."

"Well, you figured wrong. Whatza' matter...there aren't pigeons where they live?" he sneered, crumpling the feathers in his fist and tossing them into a near-by trash can. "I swear, you inmates do some of the dumbest things I ever saw."

I was heartbroken. How simple and harmless yet so foreign and offensive to him. It would have felt so good to me just to stick a little feather in with some of my letters home.

Back in my cell, I took off my shirt in the sweltering heat and laid it over the railing at the foot of my bunk. As I did, a feather fell onto the bed. It was the first one I had picked up, and had put in the other pocket. Happily, I sat down at the little desk and began a letter to my daughter.

My Precious Little Angel; I began. *I'm sending you a gift from two feathered friends I met today, who wanted me to tell you hello....*

Chapter Twenty-Six

Day passed into night and night into day. Time ground monotonously on through another 24 hours, and another, and yet another. Alone day after day, night after night, I began to feel I was separate from my trying ordeal. I was merely an observer of my own mind digging endlessly into every nook and cranny of my memory. My psyche pressed into an obsessive need to figure everything out, to rationalize circumstances of the past, and to remember events and impressions the way my ego-self preferred to see them. Often I would feel myself drifting away in thought that carried painful insights while my mind busily tried to distract me with nonsensical things.

"This is all so perfect, really," my inner dialog reflected. "It's a perfect way to prepare for all those great and noble things you've wanted to do." I couldn't change my circumstances, but I *could* affect my attitude. I could choose my perspective on this journey. I was determined to make something worthwhile come of the experience, but my mind wasn't at all certain how I was going to do that. It was scared. *Real* scared. I had faced challenging situations before, but my mind was always quick to think of a way out. Or around. Or under.

This time there was no way out of my grim situation. No matter how impossible things had gotten before, something would always break in my favor. But this was beyond any of that. This was *real* trouble. There would be no way out of it, except going *through* it. The hard way.

No fast-talking this time. No posturing. No "lucky" breaks. There was a death process going on, and my mind sensed *it* was the target. In a way, this was just like back in 'Nam, flying into a hot LZ with muzzle flashes from everywhere in the bushes. I knew I was the target then, and the unmistakable thud of bullets hitting the metal skin of the chopper confirmed it. But I had to go in. Our guys were in there, waving desperately for us to pull them out. We couldn't turn away and leave them there.

I had that same feeling just then in this damnable prison cell. I felt my heart tart pounding. Somewhere in a darkened cave, a dragon's eyes opened again. Someone was in there with him, waving desperately for me to save him. I felt myself plunging, diving into the clearing, knowing I couldn't pull out even if I had the strength. My mind was at the controls, fully committed to the battle, no matter the damage sustained. The thud of bullets was replaced now by thuds of a different kind. These thuds hit me right in the heart, and killed something inside each time they hit.

The news of my children's fate haunted me. The thought of my little girl's arms wrapped tightly around my neck, and her Shirley Temple smiles now turned to crying in the night a thousand miles away—*that* was a major thud. My boys enduring winters in the frozen northland of Minnesota with people they didn't even know, each having had a birthday now without me, and no more B'rer Rabbit stories read to them at bedtime—*several* piercing thuds.

I re-ran the series of events that brought me to this point: my college days—the Army scholarship I had walked away from, my best friend's death the year after we graduated high school and later taking his identity in my futile attempt to do things *my* way. Those thuds damaged the ship beyond repair. But never mind the damage. We could fix it later, if we just kept going. It would all make sense later. Everyone would see that I could make it come out right, if I could just keep moving toward the goal. But what was the goal, anyway? It got lost somewhere in all the juggling and dancing around.

My mind knew it was in trouble all right, and it was squirming like never before. I had always taken great pride in the workings of my mind, and had often been praised for how quick and clever it was. That mind of mine could maneuver me into and out of trouble, and had a compulsion to flirt with danger. It seemed to relish the opportunity for challenge, even if the price was occasional "collateral damage."

Well, we were going in again just like the plane we bellied in on that mesa. We were going down and this time there would be no coming out. No amount of scheming or strategizing could pull us out of this one. This time, nobody but me cared enough to notice.

There, right in front of me every damn day and night was the cold, hard reminder; a dirty, graffiti-stained, stinking, nasty, rotten, green metal door with its wiremesh-covered, Plexiglas window, and that damn slot with its metal flap slamming open and closed three times a day. That door marked the end of the line. We'd gone down in flames, and it just wasn't the way we thought it would be.

That damage back there…we should have taken a closer look, set 'er down mad
some repairs and adjusted our thinking.

"Yeah, but it was all pretty harmless," my mind justified itself. "We neve
took anything from anyone, and no one got hurt."

"Oh, yeah?" I retorted. "You and your 'yeah, buts.' I've been hearing thos
'yeah, buts' for too damn long. We took something from *us,* man. *We're* the one
who got hurt. And what about the kids scattered across the country, and all th
people back home in shock? What about Mom and the family, who haven't hear
a word from me in five years? What about *them?* Just shut up with your 'yeah
buts' and keep looking at that locked door over there. And when you've ha
enough of that, slide over here and look out this window with the bars and thi
damned wiremesh, and then look at that blue sky and those clouds we used to fl
in, and then give me all those 'yeah, buts', you asshole."

The dragon was wide awake now, and piercing the darkness with angry eye
and blazing breath. This time I had to face him head on. The only way I stood
chance was to watch him closely and find his weak spots. It was a mental battle
I knew, but it was nonetheless terrifying. With no place else to run or hide, it coul
still do me in. That much was clear.

There was something to be gained from this, I knew, but the constant pain tor
at my heart too much to calm down and listen. Inside me a battle was ragin
between heart and mind. I could do nothing but lie on my bunk and let it rage.
tried to control my thoughts, direct my mind toward something useful and con
structive, but with all that empty time on my hands, it would eventually go bac
to the broken, scattered pieces of the mirror of my life, and the taunting dragon.

I had no choice but to look at what it dredged up. It was a strange feeling
being detached enough from the process to observe, and yet feel such anguish.
could see everything so clearly at times. I was amazed how simple it was, an
wondered how I'd missed all the warning signs along the way. Surely, enoug
good-hearted people had alerted me to the hazards and folly of playing by my ow
rules. I had been to a dozen self-awareness workshops and seminars. I *knew* bette

"Yeah, but that was *after* all the craziness started," the voice in my hea
protested.

"Yeah, but…? There you go again. We could have cleared all this up long ago
and it would've been far better than *this.* Face it…you've been a coward all along
Couldn't face up to your own crap. Well, take a good look: There it i
now…scrambling around, looking for some easy way out again. Anything t

weasel out of yet another 'misadventure', as you like to call these messes you keep getting us into. Well, it isn't just a mess, this time, brother. This is the god-damn end of the line for us."

Days passed. On and on the battle raged. "Yeah, but's" and "should'ves" and "could'ves" until I wore myself into a mental frazzle. In between it all, I ran in place and did hundreds of push-ups, sit-ups and deep-knee bends. No one came to "exercise" me for days. Three times a day, the food trays came and went, and not once did I see my friend from across the hall. Apparently he was gone, but he did arrange for the orderly to give me a few stamps. Meanwhile, the gladiators continued yelling and screaming every day. But after a while, it became just so much noise I learned to block out. Sometimes it was actually entertaining.

One particularly hot day during a lull in the noise, a familiar sound came in through my open window, and brought me to my feet. There was no mistaking that sound. It was the heavy whop-whop of the rotor blades of a UH-1 helicop-ter—a "Huey," like the ones I flew in Viet Nam.

It was easy to imagine it working its way over the brown cotton fields out-side, most likely in a gradual descent for nearby Ft. Bliss. I could almost hear the pilots talking on the intercom.

"There's the prison right over there," the Aircraft Commander called out as he pointed over the nose. "It's one of the landmarks we use as a reporting point for the approach to the field. Take 'er on over there, and I'll call for clearance for the final approach."

I was wild with excitement. I hadn't seen a Huey up close in years. Kneeling on my pillow, I pressed my face against the window and strained to focus my eyes through the bars and wiremesh to find it. I could hear it, but I couldn't see it. The sound of the huge rotor blades slapping the air filled my head with memories of the times I sat in the cockpits of those wondrous machines, and pulled more than a few battle-weary soldiers out of the pits of hell. Now *I* was in hell, and out there somewhere was the sound of freedom, growing louder and louder as it approached. It had to be nearly on top of us.

"Bank 'er hard when you go over the biggest building," the Commander spoke into his mike. "You can start your approach from there. Might as well shake those boys up a bit, just for the hell of it."

From the change in turbine RPM and the much louder slap of the blades, I could tell they had rolled hard into a descending left turn. The noise nearly knocked me off the bunk. I knew what they were doing. In Viet Nam, we delighted in doing the same thing over the temporary quarters set up for new arrivals.

Finally, it came into sight. Just for a second, it appeared as they passed directly overhead. They were so close I could make out one of the pilots and a crewman with their bulbous flight helmets. The crewman's legs were dangling from the open door, just like back in 'Nam. The high-pitched whine of the turbine was deafening.

God, what a sight to see! I leaned back on my bunk and felt another thud. Why couldn't *I* be up there flying? Why did *I* have to be such a goddamn wise guy and think I could take all those shortcuts and still get back on the right track?

I closed my eyes and listened as the sound of the Huey faded away. Memories rushed into my head of the many times I had climbed into one, started it up and hovered out for takeoff as easily as some people drive their cars. I remembered how exciting it was in flight school to see one of them fly by while we were bare-ly able to bring a little trainer to a hover. It was hard to believe all that was so far behind me now—only faded memories buried in the depths of my always calcu-lating, slippery mind. The flights into Cambodia, the multi-ship sorties, the single-ship missions I preferred to fly, and the trips to Saigon. How I loved those free-flights to Saigon.

As I lay there half-dozing, half-thinking, my mind moved in and out of mem-ories of Viet Nam and the succeeding years. I could tell it was still busily search-ing for something to distract me from thinking about the present, and where I was. I thought back over the years that had passed since that fateful day I flew to Miami with Bill. I thought about where things had gone wrong, and what changes could have been made. It wasn't that hard, really. Of course, the simplest solution was not to have gotten involved in the first place. But given the choices I did make, what would have been a better course of action?

Should I have given in to the investigators and taken my chances with their system? Let them use me as a stool pigeon and trust that they would take care of me? No, I still didn't believe they would have come through. They didn't care, no matter what they said. By the nature of their job, they had to be duplicitous. Some cops worked both sides of the street, and some of them were pretty high up in rank.

I reasoned that though I had harder time to do, at least I was alive. And I had five important extra years with my boys. That was worth the added hardship. Amber would never have been born, either. *That* certainly was worth it. But I had-n't done much to prepare them for what happened. At least they knew I loved them. I could only hope their memory of my love was strong enough to carry them through.

My thoughts were interrupted by the sound of the guard at my door. Keys jingled, then turned in the lock. It had been a week and a half since my last "exercise" period. I was beginning to think they had forgotten about me. The door swung open, and a different guard stood there with cuffs in hand.

"You want some exercise?"

Out in the courtyard, I quickly grew tired of bouncing a basketball against the wall. I walked around the courtyard a few times, but felt hot and a little dizzy. Stopping at the gate, I bent over as if to tie my shoe, straightened, then leaned against the fence. Just inside the covered walkway, the guard was sitting in the shade watching me. This one was younger, and appeared just as bored as the previous one had been.

"Where's the other officer?" I asked.

"He's working in a different area," he replied tersely, then looked off in the other direction as if not wanting to be bothered.

"You been working here long?"

"Long enough."

"You like this kind of work?"

"What's it to you? You writin' a book?"

"Just thought I'd ask. No harm asking, is there?"

"Some think there is. We don't tell inmates personal things."

"Well, I didn't ask what shifts you work, or where you live. I just asked if you've been here long, and if you like the work. Just conversation, that's all."

He peered at me in the glare of the sun behind me. I sensed an opportunity for conversation, however slim. Nonetheless, this guy could be a powder keg so I would have to choose my words carefully. He feigned a yawn, and stretched as if he was bored with the whole thing, then spoke to me.

"I've been here a little over two years, and no—I don't like it much. It's a boring, stinking job."

"I can imagine," I replied. "You planning to stick with it and retire, or waiting for something better? Or is that too personal?"

"If something better comes along, I'll take it in a heartbeat. But I've got ten years with the military that counts toward retirement, and a couple years with the El Paso PD. With these two years, I've only got six more to go."

Except for the difference in our circumstances, he sounded just like an inmate. I lobbed the basketball against the building a couple of more times, and thought about the irony of his words.

"Army?" I asked.

"Yep. Drove tanks right over there at Ft. Bliss for a couple of years. Before that, I was in Germany three years. Almost went to OCS—'Officer Candidate School'—but didn't want to do the extra time."

"Yeah, I know about OCS. I was raised in the Army. Did a couple of years myself. OCS is for lifers who don't know or care about anything but the *Army* way." Knowing the 80% attrition rate for officer candidates, I had a feeling that was probably more the case with him. A little sympathizing couldn't hurt.

"That's right. I wasn't sure I wanted to make a career of military bullshit. I did make sergeant, though—E-6, even. That was enough for me."

"Why'd you get out?"

"Wasn't enough money in it for me, for one reason. With Viet Nam over with, there were too many asshole punk officers around with nothing better to do than push people around, for another."

His responses were classic irony, considering his present job. It was fascinating to hear him lamenting the same kind of treatment he and his cohorts were dishing out on us. We couldn't quit or move on, like he could. I felt his frustration, and wanted to know more.

"Didn't like police work?" I pressed him a bit further. "Or was it just El Paso PD you didn't like?"

"Nah. Shit, you're a walking target for any yay-hoo that has a grudge against authority, or a scheme to get over on the system. Down here on the border, it just got too nasty and unpredictable. Got shot at three times. After the third time, my marriage began to suffer. Never did get it back on the right track, even after I left the force. I was good, too. Got to where I could tell who was clean and who wasn't. I was up for promotion to sergeant in just two years."

"That's no small feat," I responded. I could feel the lack of recognition pent up inside of him. I knew better than to ask about his wife, although it seemed to me he was forgetting that he was talking to an inmate. "Why not just transfer to a different city?"

"No difference," he muttered as he shuffled his feet in the dirt. "It'd still be the same. My wife couldn't take the hours and the tension, and I couldn't take her constant nagging and paranoia." I could tell he was growing uncomfortable.

"Does she like you doing this kind of work any better?"

"No, she doesn't. But then she doesn't have to, 'cause she ain't around anymore. Why you asking all these questions, anyway?" He was beginning to get defensive.

"Sorry. It's just like I said before. Just curious, that's all. Just making a little conversation. On the outside, I used to ask people questions all the time. It helped me understand more about human nature, and about my own nature. It was always fascinating."

"Yeah, well you got a lot of 'fascination' in store for you now, don't you? You better be careful how you go about asking questions around here. Some people don't take it too kindly, *especially* correctional officers." His emphasis on "officers" was apparent.

"I understand. I found out about that while I was in the detention center in Albuquerque. You know they've got over a *thousand* inmates in there? It's bigger than this place."

"Not by much. And not for much longer." His tone was almost prideful, as if "bigger" was automatically "better."

"So, do you ever talk with other inmates in here?" I asked, as if we were sitting outside the walls, comparing notes on life.

"Not too much. You can get yourself in a real bind doin' that. Most of 'em are shiftless no-accounts, anyway. You can't trust 'em as far as you can throw 'em. What good you could get out of most of this scum wouldn't buy you a cup of coffee. Even when you try to be decent, they spit in your face or insult you."

Evidently, he *had* forgotten who he was talking to. I hoped we would be able to keep talking for a while. This was giving me some insights on what made them tick, and why. He was pissed off, felt like a failure, and had lost his wife. Working as a guard in a prison was the perfect place for him to lick his wounds and assert his authority over others. The only trouble was, he was working out his grudges and frustrations on men who couldn't fight back.

"Really?" I asked. "*Most* of them?"

"Yeah, most of them. A few might be decent, depending on the mood they're in."

"Isn't that the same with most anybody?"

"I suppose so. But then 'most anybody' didn't break the law. *You* did, and now you're paying your dues. Frankly, I wouldn't give most inmates the time of day."

"I don't blame you," I replied as respectfully as possible. "I'd probably feel the same way myself, if I were in your position. Have you ever met any that are any better?"

"Every once in a while one comes along that seems decent enough, but not many. Not enough to change my attitude toward them. Just look at 'em. All they do is lie around on their bunks all damn day and give us shit when we walk by."

"Well, not to defend them, but what would *you* do if you were in one of those cells? There's no room to do anything else *but* lie on the bunk and think. Meanwhile, they know they're wasting the prime of their lives."

"That's their problem. They broke the law and got caught. Besides, I think I could find *something* of interest to do."

"Maybe. But in a cell like mine, there's hardly enough room to exercise…and nothing to do."

"Well, that ain't my fault. I didn't rob a bank, or shoot somebody, or smuggle drugs. Most of these guys always take the short cuts. They can't work for a living. They don't care who or what they step on to get what they want."

There was a long pause. Getting noticeably more uncomfortable…probably from realizing that he was talking to an inmate about other inmates…he looked at his watch and jumped to his feet.

"Time's up. Turn around and put your hands through that hole."

In minutes, we were back in the hallway and on our way back to my cell. Along the way, I noticed the faces of other inmates in the little windows of their cells, all glaring out at us as we walked by. I wondered which ones had been screaming and shouting at each other every day and night, and how much longer I was going to have to put up with this place, and with the isolation.

Just to kill some time, I cleaned my floor again, and the toilet. It was sweltering inside. To cope with the heat, I soaked my T-shirt in the sink, wrung it out and wore it until it dried. Several times a day, I did that until the shirt began to smell of stale sweat and mildew.

Several more days went by. I began to lose track of time. The Fourth of July had come and gone, and one day was just the same as the next. Time was becoming just a series of endless days and nights, with three meal trays each day to mark its passage. At least my mind had calmed down somewhat, and I had developed a relationship of my own with the various orderlies that came and went. I had enough paper to keep a journal, and enough stamps to send letters every day. I spent my time reading, whenever the orderlies brought me books, exercising and writing. After a while, I got so immersed in such simple things that when the lights went out, I had no idea where the day had gone.

Chapter Twenty-Seven

Every day was a scorcher. Staying cool in my cell was impossible, but at least the monsoon season had finally begun. Every once in a while when the rains came, I would work my hand and forearm around the old window as it angled inward toward me from the top, and press my palm against the wiremesh just outside the bars. If I got lucky, enough cool, fresh rain would moisten my hands enough to rub into my face and feel the momentary relief of a man in the desert after a fleeting Summer rain.

Another day was just beginning, and black clouds were already forming on the horizon. I hoped that would mean some cooling later in the afternoon. I was miserable. My damp, mildewed T-shirt clung to my skin, accentuating the stifling heat building in the cell. I wanted to pound on the door in protest, but I remembered Big Jim and how he had endured far worse conditions. If he could handle the insanity of his experience, I could deal with this relatively minor discomfort a little longer.

The day passed without any rain on the wiremesh. Soon it would be time for the dinner tray to arrive. Voices in the hallway indicated that several men were moving in my direction, stopping at each cell along the way. Finally, they stopped at my door. I heard the sound of keys turning my lock. I sat up on my bunk as the guard pushed the door open. A lieutenant, dressed in an official Bureau of Prisons blue blazer and tie, stepped into my cell. Preoccupied with papers on a clipboard, he spoke without looking at me.

"You're shipping out tomorrow," he said. "Have all your stuff together for us to pack up tonight, and be ready to roll up the rest of your gear before breakfast. Any questions?" He finally looked up from his clipboard.

"Sure. For starters, where am I going?"

"Can't tell you that."

"You can't tell me where I'm going?"

"No. Security reasons. Besides, we're not required to tell you anything. You go where we take you; you do what you're told. This isn't a school field trip. Also, no phone calls or talking to anyone tonight."

"Phone calls? How am I supposed to make a phone call? Except for an occasional walk in that dirt courtyard you call an exercise yard, I haven't been out of this cell in six weeks."

"That's just as well. Be sure you're ready as soon as the guards wake you up." With that, he turned and left. I could hear him repeat the process several more times down the corridor. It looked like this was going to be a big move.

The next morning, the lights came on well before dawn, and I could hear activity up and down the corridor. Loud voices and banging on cell doors amplified the apprehension I felt at being suddenly taken away from my now-familiar surroundings. I was shocked to realize that I had become so accustomed to my little cell, and now felt fear of what might come. Even though I hated the confinement of my cell, at least I had come to have some measure of control in it. I could sleep when I wanted to, read when I wanted to, and exercise when I wanted to. Now, everything was subject to change.

Finally, the officers reached my door, unlocked it and swung it open. They stood by while I got my stuff and stepped out into the corridor. When everyone was out of their cells, the officers herded us along the corridor and down a flight of stairs to the same room where I had been processed after my arrival. We were instructed to discard our clothes and wait while each of us was strip-searched, and then handed flimsy khaki pants and a shirt to put on. Then it was back through the large metal doorway I had first entered after meeting "Johnson," and down another corridor into the large cage where I was first introduced to prison life. I took a seat on one of the long, wooden benches, looked over at the smaller cage across from us where Johnson had stood that day, and wondered what had become of him.

The large cage began to fill with sleepy-eyed inmates. Complete strangers to one another, we all sat or stood around the cage, acting as if this was a perfectly normal way to begin a day. Gradually, a few words were exchanged, cigarettes were lit, and eyes probed for signs of mutual strength and familiarity. Within minutes, men of like color and/or similar background began to gravitate to one another in groups of twos and threes.

As the chatter began to increase, I recalled warnings about trusting anyone at first meeting them. "Never trust anyone," was the most common advice, yet the need to bond and form alliances was so ingrained that often one's first comments formed instant presumed bonds of friendship. In less than an hour, a pecking order was well established. When the last of us was in the cage, the guards came with cuffs, waist chains and leg shackles to prepare us for the trip.

Hours seemed to pass while we waited. Wrists were cuffed in front, and then secured to waist chains with just enough length to allow the minimum movement needed for walking, eating and scratching. Once all the chains and shackles were properly secured, the guards left us to ourselves. I looked up at the tiny window at the top of the wall outside the cage, and couldn't believe that it still wasn't even daylight yet.

The chatter in the cage resumed, and gradually everyone wanted to know where we were being taken. Those more experienced with the process seized the opportunity to capture the attention of the rest, and soon stories of improbable proportions were bantered about that had little bearing on what actually might be happening.

As the first rays of morning light began to filter in through the window, the guards returned. We were then ordered to stand and file out the doorway as each of our names and numbers were called. One by one, we stepped out of the cage and through the doorway into the open air. Guards armed with shotguns stood in strategic positions while we shuffled in our chains and shackles down a long walkway to a waiting bus. Chains jingled as we stepped awkwardly onto the bus and settled in for the long ride to an unknown destination.

"El Reno," one of the older prisoners finally spoke up. "That's the only place in the federal system this heap could make it to from here." All eyes turned to look at him. "It's about an hour west of Oklahoma City. It's a Level Four joint, and one of the worst in the system. It's an old place, with live gun towers. They must've built the sucker back in the forties. It looks like the one in that James Cagney movie."

"'The Big House'?" someone called out from the back of the bus

"Yeah, just like that. They got a regular joint for the permanent inmates, and another place for holdovers like us."

"What's a 'holdover'?" someone asked.

"A holdover is an inmate being transferred somewhere. It's a bitch, doing time as a holdover, because nobody gives a shit about you. Not that they do anyway, but it's even worse as a holdover because they don't know anything about you. So you just sit and wait, like we've been doing here. They don't have to do anything but feed you and give you some 'exercise' once a week."

He had everyone's full attention. We could be going to Alcatraz, for all he knew. But he had enough experience to hold everyone's imagination…and it was clear that he was enjoying every minute of it.

"It's the main joint in the federal system," he went on, "for processing inmates in the eastern states. Some stay there, and the rest get shipped to other joints, or to a court somewhere. It's a real zoo. They've got a big rec yard, a decent weight pile, and some prison industries. That's about it. But that's only for the permanent inmates. Holdovers have to stay in the holdover unit until they check you out. Some they let out into the main yard, and some they don't."

"They've got live gun towers?" someone asked from the front of the bus.

"Yeah," the first guy went on. "It's a trip to look up there and see those dudes with their rifles lookin' down on you." He let that thought hang in the air as the guards loaded boxes of our files, personal effects and box lunches onto the bus. When the guards left, he continued.

"For those who don't get out of the holdover unit, it's a bitch. It ain't nothin' but a big-ass building with four tiers of cells smaller than the ones we were in here. And they stick two dudes in each one of 'em. That's why they let some guys out during the day, I think, just to keep inmates from killin' each other.

"I bet there's as many as three, four hundred swinging dicks in that hot house at any one time. In the winter, it's even worse. It's a goddamn icehouse. No ventilation, no heat, no *nothin'*. Just a big ol' brick building, with cages full of assholes yelling and screaming all damn day and night. And goddamn Okies for guards. A bunch of cowboys out to show us we made a 'big mistake' gettin' caught and havin' them as guards. There are damn few dudes in the federal system as stupid and ignorant as Okie guards. You'll see what I mean."

Outside, the guards finished their final inspection of the bus, which was similar to the Greyhound and Trailways coaches of the late Fifties. The bus had been stripped down to bare essentials, and then fitted with wiremesh grillwork that formed a fully enclosed cage inside that separated us from the guards in front and back. The cage had seats for as many as thirty prisoners, with access to the on-board toilet. In front of the cage were the driver, an armed guard, and the officer in charge—in this case, the same Bureau of Prisons' lieutenant that had checked us out the day before. At the rear sat another armed guard with his own door to the outside.

After final preparations were complete, the guards secured themselves in their seats, the driver closed the door, and the lieutenant stood up to announce what he expected from us. He was tough sounding, but respectful. He picked one of the prisoners to be the orderly, and then uncuffed him so he could serve us coffee and meals from the containers stacked in the back of the bus.

Once we were out on the highway, our new orderly served our "breakfast," which consisted of untoasted English muffins and cold scrambled eggs, with barely-cooked hash browns. Eating the meal and holding a cup of coffee with my wrists chained to my waist proved to be a challenge, but I was hungry enough to manage. The hot coffee made the meal almost palatable.

Before long, the cotton fields gave way to suburbs and shopping malls as we neared El Paso. Fast-food restaurants, shopping centers and strip malls appeared, reminding me of similar cities and towns I had long since left behind. Now I was seeing it all again from the inside of a prison bus. All I could do was shake my head and drink my coffee as if it was just another bad dream.

After the first hour, my bare ankles began to hurt from the heavy steel leg irons. Squirming and shifting constantly to ease the discomfort, I took some consolation from the fact that at least I was going somewhere—even if it *was* El Reno. Despite that grim description, it couldn't be much worse than La Tuna had been.

Soon we were on the freeway, rolling eastward. For a while, we paralleled the border of Mexico and the irony was killing me. Out there across the river, just beyond the high fences, was the very airspace I had flown the Bonanza with Iron Mike that fateful day now so long ago.

Cars, trucks and buses routinely passed us as our driver made his way slowly along the open road. It was late July, and it seemed as if everyone was on vacation. As they passed us, eyes gazed back, first out of idle curiosity, then in gaping astonishment as they realized what we were. A few of my more brazen comrades in chains leered in perversion at the women and made ghoulish faces at the kids. The shocked reactions of their audience moving past the windows elicited mockery and laughter from the prisoners. Fingers pointed and open-jawed faces stared back at us as each vehicle sped up in sudden urgency to put as much distance between them and the bus as possible.

My hands gripped the chains tightly as I recalled some of my earlier travels in years gone by. How I relished the privilege of pulling off at a roadside cafe for a cup of coffee and a piece of pie. For three summers and two winters in college, I drove 18-wheelers over the Rockies, and later in the dairy country of the Midwest. I cherished the sense of freedom it gave me to come and go from truck stops as I traveled along.

The bus passed town after town in the heart of west Texas, then turned north and gradually made its way toward Oklahoma. Old men sat on park benches prattling about the economy, the weather, women or politics, while kids played softball in grass-covered parks. I stared silently through the wiremesh and felt tears work their way down my cheeks. I ached to get off the bus and take a simple little walk around one of those parks, or sit quietly and listen to those old men.

But that was impossible for me now. They were fleeting memories replaced by steel bars, shackles, and shotguns reflected back at me in the windows covered with that damned wiremesh. I wanted to scream for it all to stop. I would do it all differently, if I could. I'd play with those kids, and I'd stop and chat with those old men. I would listen more intently and not waste another day chasing rainbows and wild "misadventures."

Yes, sir, I would make my life count for something next time—if I could only stop for a minute, get off the bus and go in and have a simple cup of coffee and a wedge of pie. God, how blessed I would feel. If only I could go back to that truck stop in Florida where it all started, and then just keep driving.

My coffee had grown cold as the miles rolled by. Box lunches were served next. I slowly ate dry bologna sandwiches while we passed over the plains and through the now-dormant oil fields of west Texas. Several hours later the skyline of Midland came into view, and the lieutenant stood up to inform us we would be staying for the night.

We pulled up to an ancient brick building in the center of town, and waited while the lieutenant went inside. I wondered what kind of accommodations they could possibly have for us in such a dilapidated building. A few minutes later, a couple of old men and some kids walked by. They caught an eyeful of something to talk about at their dinner tables that night as we filed off the bus and hobbled in chains into the decrepit old jailhouse that must have dated back to the turn of the last century. Before bedding down, we once again went through the tedious process of being strip-searched, and issued clothing and toilet gear. Done with their duties for the day, the lieutenant and his guards left us for the night, lying on ancient steel bunks made for midgets, in a building that groaned and creaked most of the night.

The next morning we were back on the road again after another strip-search and security routine. The hills of Oklahoma seemed a bit greener as we slowly made our way northward toward our presumed destination. Like kids on a long trip, we craned our necks to catch sight of landmarks our self-appointed "guide" had described earlier.

Finally, late in the afternoon, El Reno came into view. About fifteen minutes beyond the town, we could see the prison through the front window. It was, indeed, a forlorn and ominous-looking place—far more depressing to look at than La Tuna. With huge oak and Dutch elm trees lining the long entranceway to the buildings, it obviously had more history. The grounds were immaculate, but the gun towers positioned in every corner gave me the chills. The main buildings were massive, and beyond them were double rows of very high, chainlink fences lined with razor wire, just like La Tuna.

Our bus pulled up behind a row of other buses that were unloading prisoners. We watched in silence as manacled prisoners made their way one by one through gates in the outer, then inner fences, then through the inner yard to a small, unmarked doorway leading into the main building. Hours passed while we sat on the bus, waiting for all three buses ahead of us to unload. Finally, a team of officers came out of the building and escorted us roughly into the receiving room. We were the fourth contingent of new arrivals that they had to process that afternoon, and their brusque attitudes showed it.

This was no small operation like La Tuna. These guys handled our entire busload of prisoners as if we were just another shipment of goods for their warehouse. Even so, it was three hours after our arrival before I finally eased my tired body into the upper bunk of the tiniest, dirtiest cell I could imagine. It was midway down the third of four tiers in the north half of what was indeed "a big, old brick building full of assholes," all screaming and shouting at anyone and everything. Officially designated a "Level Three/Four" facility, FCI El Reno was home to over 1,200 prisoners, most of whom were serving ten to twenty-five years for crimes of a more violent or serious nature. It was also a processing center for prisoners being transferred between institutions and criminal courts across the United States. At any one time, 350 to 400 transient prisoners were being held in the holdover unit—the largest of the buildings in the complex. Inside there were sixteen tiers of small cells, four tiers on each side of the north end of the building and four tiers on each side of the south end.

Access to each cell was by means of a narrow catwalk running outside. At the end, a series of levers enabled the guards to open and close all or any combination of cells at will. Whenever those levers were pulled, multiple cell doors opened or closed with a resounding slam that echoed throughout the steel-reinforced, tired brick building. A bunk bed and toilet virtually eliminated movement in the cell by either inmate, other than to use the toilet. Along the inside of the outer walls of the building, well beyond reach of the inner catwalk, was another catwalk for use by guards in the event of hostilities or emergencies.

It was late in the summer of 1986, and the heat from the scorching Oklahoma sun built up each day inside the cavernous building like a brick oven. Large electric fans at the end of each catwalk droned night and day in a begrudging, futile effort to provide ventilation to those sixteen tiers. Only by rigging pieces of cardboard as deflectors between the bars could inmates hope to coax even a hint of a breeze into their cells to relieve the stifling heat.

For someone locked down as a holdover, obtaining a piece of cardboard and some tape or string with which to make such a device was next to impossible, which made release into the general population all the more urgent. Even then, using such a device was often an exercise in futility since it bore the likelihood that it would be torn down by night guards who were prone to write up the occupants for "contraband." Yet without one, each cell was a nonstop, unrelenting sweat bath, and an insufferable ordeal.

One careless move inside the cell, or anything said that could be taken the least bit offensively, could incite the wrath of a cellmate whose background and temperament were unknown. The angry cacophony of several hundred men clamoring for attention and vocal superiority reverberated off the brick walls, adding to the constant metallic noises of an archaic prison built in the 1940s by minds still preoccupied with the need to punish someone…anyone…for the atrocities of a world war raging around the globe.

On each tier, white-shirted officers with two-way radios and jingling keys reinforced their heavy-handed authority as if they held the power of life and death over men in cages smaller than an average, modern-day walk-in closet. A visit by a clipboard-toting caseworker brought the hope of a possible release from the din, sweat and oppression of the holdover unit. Only those who were least likely to cause trouble would be given that chance. As the caseworkers made their way from cell to cell, hearts pounded and unspoken promises formed in the minds of inmates up and down each tier. *Anything*, just to get out of the sweat-box and into the relatively fresh air outside and mingle among a thousand-plus other prisoners waiting for nothing.

After enduring six days of torturous heat and the accompanying stench in that tiny cell with a succession of unshowered, unshaven and generally irritable cellmates arriving and departing each day, fortune finally smiled on me. I was released into the main population with a stern warning not to mingle with regular inmates other than at meals and in the exercise yard. As long as I was in my designated place for the six head counts each day, and in my cell at night for lockdown, I was free to roam the grounds at will.

After six weeks in isolation at La Tuna, and seven months in two detention centers, suddenly I could walk among other inmates in the relative freedom of the exercise yard, the track and in the dining hall. I was free of restraint, free to enjoy the illusion that in some uncertain way, I was on my way out of the system. I had hit the bottom, I thought, and now, perhaps, I was on my way out of the pit.

How long would it take? I had six years to serve, but I was told that federal statutes allowed prisoners to be released after serving only a third of their sentence. The Parole Board determined when a prisoner could be released, based upon good behavior and work in the prison. As a holdover with no work and no way to earn good time, I was adrift in the system. No one knew me or my history, or gave a damn about me. To them I was just another warm body waiting for shipment to an unknown destination.

Days passed, always with the same routine. Out of the cell at 6:30 in the morning for breakfast, then to the exercise yard. Back and forth all day from the yard to the cell to make the six head counts each day. From the cell to the dining room, out to the yard again, and then back to the cell for the final count and lockdown. Lockdown always came too early, leaving me wide-awake to toss and turn most of the night in sweat-soaked, worn-out sheets. Each morning, the whole routine started all over again.

One day, a break in the monotony came with the appearance of a familiar face. Standing among a small group of his friends near the dining room and laughing loudly was Simon Hernandez. Just as I took my place in the chow line, he looked in my direction and recognized me. His face lit up, and with the exuberance of a long-lost friend, he started for me without thinking. Spooked like nervous horses, the men around me parted quickly, fearing the big man was on the attack. Grinning and shaking hands excitedly, we exchanged boisterous pleasantries as he pulled me from the chow line and towards his buddies, who were watching with skeptical restraint.

It was good to see him again, and to share his excitement about reconnecting. We swapped exaggerated stories about our time at BCDC, and how he had kept me in coffee all those weeks while I helped him with his case. For the next two weeks, Simon and I deepened our friendship as we walked together and talked about how our lives were progressing. His wife had moved to the nearby town, where she had made friends with wives and girlfriends of other inmates. He insisted that I let him arrange for one of her friends to visit me at the same time she visited him so that we could sit together and meet each other. Once again I was pressed into service reading legal documents for him and now for his friends, all of whom were unconvinced—no matter what I said to the contrary—that I was not an attorney. Suddenly there was no shortage of postage stamps, fresh fruit, candy and packs of cigarettes for trading. There were always two or three Latino inmates nearby to keep a watchful eye for any sign of trouble from other inmates. Through Simon, I met the prison chaplain, who gave me a temporary position as an "assistant" to his clerk. I sorted files and wrote letters for the chaplain, and spent many hours in the chapel reading legal cases and teaching an occasional lesson in English grammar. Working for the chaplain permitted me more freedom from the holdover unit, and longer hours out on the grounds. Now I only had to be in the holdover unit for the main head count at four o'clock, and for lockdown at night.

After the four o'clock headcount each day, those who had clearance to come out of their cells milled about on the main floor, waiting to be released for dinner. The next day's ship-outs were posted on a bulletin board by the main doors. Days came and went, then a week, and still another week without my name or number appearing on the list. After four weeks, I still had no word on my status or my destination. Although I was growing somewhat comfortable with my daily routine, I was also feeling displaced and anxious about the lack of official record of my activities.

On any given day, as many as 150 holdovers would ship out, and an equal number, or more, would arrive. Prisoners would be taken by bus to the airport in Oklahoma City, then loaded onto aging airliners stripped of everything non-functional. These were operated by agents and pilots of the U.S. Marshal Service. Referred to by inmates as "Con-Air," there were three such airliners, all Boeing 727's. These were used exclusively for the purpose of moving groups of federal prisoners across the United States. While one flew from the west coast to various facilities on the east coast, another did the reverse. When your name and number appeared on the ship-out roster, the day indicated which direction you were headed. Most inmates knew where they were going, but I could only hope I would be heading west.

By that time, I was one of the most "senior" holdovers in the building. Very few inmates had been in the holdover unit longer than me. Feathers were plentiful in the courtyard, and after a while I was able to be selective in collecting and arranging them in artistic ways to send home. Access to the row of telephones on the grounds enabled me to talk frequently with Debra, giving us the opportunity to deepen the bond of trust and affection we were feeling.

Finally one evening, my name appeared on the list. It was the westbound flight which, I was told by inmates, landed in Phoenix before continuing to the west coast. It appeared from some of the other names on the list that I was at long last being taken to FCI Safford. Consistent with their policy, I wasn't given any information by officials, but guessed at that for myself. Anyone on the ship-out list was immediately confined to the holdover unit and prohibited from making phone calls, lest the potential for escape be enhanced by friends on the outside. I could only hope that once I got to Phoenix, I would have a chance to call Debra and hopefully arrange a visit.

Very early the next morning, I said a silent good-bye to Simon and his friends as I was led once again in chains and shackles to a bus waiting in the pre-dawn darkness. Back in my cell were notebooks of information and research material on the legal cases of several of Simon's friends, entrusted to a new cellmate I barely knew to give to Simon. Hopefully, my stash of candy bars, fruit and cigarettes would prove to be sufficient inducement for him to do so. I also gave a note to one of the officers to pass along to the chaplain, letting Simon know what had happened to me.

Such was the nature of prison life. One has to be prepared for instant changes of direction, sudden displacements, loss of personal property, or the disappearance of a friend. Detachment became one of my greatest lessons as the months came and went, and friends were lost without warning.

Chapter Twenty-Eight

The Boeing 727 began a slow descent high over northern Arizona, banking gradually in the direction of Phoenix. I shifted uneasily, my legs shackled and my wrists cuffed to a waist chain as I strained to see the landscape far below. From 35,000 feet, I could barely make out the red rock canyons of my former home far below, where life continued normally for the people I had lived and worked with for five years.

I looked around the plane—150 prisoners clad in khaki, each one chained and shackled just like me. A mental picture of the slave galleys of wooden ships depicted in movies like "Ben-Hur" played in my mind as I looked around at rows of three men chained on each side of the entire length of the plane—all "menaces to society" as far as the marshals were concerned. In the front rows sat a dozen or so women prisoners—"females," as authorities referred to them—each, I was sure, with her own mournful tale of deprivation and hardship to tell.

A trip to the lavatory presented formidable obstacles. Under the circumstances, it was preferable to endure waiting the entire trip rather than submit to the ordeal of getting up and shuffling to the back of the plane in chains and shackles, only to learn that the marshals would not remove the chains for any reason. Using the lavatory under such conditions required the skills of a contortionist.

"Con-Air" planes were reportedly foreign airliners confiscated by the federal government that had been used to import drugs into the United States. It was rumored that the planes were part of a Colombian airline, a notion that did little to reassure me of the mechanical condition of the plane we were on. Based upon stories I heard, and a vivid imagination of my own, I presumed I knew the kind of pilots who flew for the government—not men necessarily dressed in crisp, sharp uniforms, but rather sporting leather jackets and beards, with bottles of Tequila in their flight bags. Having known pilots who flew for the CIA's infamous "Air America," it was difficult for me to imagine that I could distinguish pilots on one side of the drug business from pilots of the other side. But such was my state of mind as we made our way southward toward Phoenix and the "Valley of the Sun."

According to inmates who seemed knowledgeable, moving large numbers of prisoners around from one facility to another was part of a strategy. It was rumored to be part of the Bureau of Prisons' agenda to generate more revenue by creating an appearance of overcrowded conditions. Whether or not that rumor was true, it was common knowledge that just before an inspection at a facility, a sudden influx of prisoners arrived, thereby reinforcing the belief that prisons were filling up as fast as they were being built. Not surprisingly, publicity gained in the process often resulted in increased funding to deal with the "problem."

There *was* a problem of overcrowding, of course. But I came to believe that it wasn't necessarily from lack of space. Bureau of Prisons officials, increasingly consumed with the notion that painting the most extreme picture possible would increase its significance in the eyes of the American public, were creating a monster to feed. In the process of dealing with what they increasingly perceived was a mounting problem, the Bureau maintained a severe, even brutal attitude toward inmates in general. Such an attitude was maintained and even promoted aggressively in all training programs and indoctrination of correctional officers and staff, which only served to heighten and amplify contempt and distrust on both sides.

Over time, even the most docile and nonviolent prisoner could be, and often was, driven to deep resentment and hatred of the system. Every prisoner was automatically assumed to be dangerous and an escape risk, which in turn justified the need for harsh treatment. Any act of kindness or compassion between inmates and officials was most likely met with resistance and distrust on both sides. Subject to unwritten codes of behavior among themselves, and severe consequences for violating them, inmates seldom spoke openly with officials. When they did, it was done in the most contemptuous manner possible. To speak respectfully toward anyone on either side raised immediate suspicion from both factions. Eyes and ears were ever vigilant for any deviation. If any did occur—perceived or actual—retribution of some form was certain to follow, sooner or later.

Rays of the late afternoon sun streamed in through the plane's tiny windows. The whine of the engines dropped off sharply, indicating the beginning of our descent into the Phoenix area. I half-expected to hear a pleasant voice announcing our approach, and instructing us to make sure our seat backs and tray tables were in the full upright position.

The plane landed at Luke Air Force Base, northwest of Phoenix, and taxied to a remote ramp at the far end of an inactive runway where four buses from the U.S. Bureau of Prisons sat with engines running. A contingent of corrections officers, U.S. marshals and Air Police waited with shotguns, side arms and clipboards to transport us to the prison, ten miles north of the city. We were instructed to stay in our seats and wait for our number to be called. Waist chains jingled as restless men squirmed in their seats in nervous expectation of facing more stern officials intent on insuring a safe and uneventful transfer.

Unloading took hours. No chances were taken, no details missed. Procedures were handled with extreme care—not for the prisoner's sake, but for that of the officers. The least detail overlooked could result in serious injury or a possible escape, which would cause embarrassment to the Bureau of Prisons and a probable loss of someone's career.

By the time we were processed in at FCI Phoenix, complete with the usual strip search, fingerprinting and mug shots, we had been awake and in chains for sixteen hours, sitting on benches, buses and the plane. Some prisoners were processed in as regular inmates, while others were held in a holdover unit for shipment to their eventual destinations. Like FCI El Reno, FCI Phoenix was the central processing facility for transferees coming from or going to the western region. Also a Level Three/Four, "medium security" facility, FCI Phoenix was the showplace of the Bureau of Prisons. Built only five years earlier, its presence came as yet another irony for me, for during my fugitive years when I was on business trips back and forth from my home in Sedona, I had watched the place being built. Intrigued with the massive construction project north of Phoenix, I often slowed down, or whenever flying a light plane near it, circled it a few times to get a better look. I couldn't imagine who would be building something so immense in the desert that far from the city. By the time I learned it was a prison, I was so entrenched in my new persona, I never dreamed I might someday be one of its residents.

The latest in modern prison architecture, FCI Phoenix was the pride and joy of then Director of the U.S. Bureau of Prisons, Norman Carlson. It boasted more humane conditions and escape-proof security than any other federal prison. Inside it was, in fact, more pleasant to look at than La Tuna or El Reno, and the attitude of the staff was surprisingly civil. There was even a hint of respect toward inmates, but there was no doubt about unwavering discipline and their intent to keep their "escape-free" record intact. Surrounded by double 12-foot chainlink fences and multiple coils of razor wire, microwave sensors and motion detectors, the facility was an immense fortress of concrete and steel. Several dozen high-intensity lights towering high above the place cast an eerie glow in the desert sky that could be seen for miles. Each building within the complex was secured by a double set of doors, neither of which could be opened without the other being closed and locked. Guards on the inside had keys only to the inside doors, while guards on the outside had keys only to the outside doors. Consequently, since no one guard was able to open both doors, an attempted escape by an inmate who might seize a guard and grab their keys was eliminated. Around the brightly lit perimeter, two armed vehicles patrolled twenty-four hours a day in three eight-hour shifts.

By my second day there, I was able to reinforce my expectation from other inmates waiting to get to Safford that I was probably headed there also. But I learned that no one could get into Safford until others were shipped out. That notion seemed to be borne out by the fact that as soon as inmates arrived *from* Safford, other ones waiting ahead of us shipped out the next day. There were five waiting ahead of me, so it looked like it might be several weeks before I would get there.

Formerly a Level One, minimum-security prison near Tucson, FCI Safford had the distinction of housing such notables as John Erlichman, Nixon's Chief of Staff during Watergate. His presence at FCI Safford reinforced the notion that it was one of the "country clubs" for which the federal prison system was famous. According to the inmates who had come from there, it did, in fact, have two tennis courts, but it was hardly a country club.

According to them, Safford had become a facility for foreign nationals convicted of federal crimes, but who were not considered particularly dangerous. Because of their foreign citizenship, however, they were considered escape risks, so Safford's status was upgraded to Level Two, with added security precautions such as a chainlink fence, microwave sensors and 24-hour patrols. As a former fugitive, I was technically considered an "escape risk" but like the foreign inmates, not necessarily dangerous. According to the outgoing inmates, living at Safford was less desirable than some other facilities because of the pettiness and personality quirks of staff members and guards who constantly held the threat of transfer over the heads of the inmates.

At least the delay in Phoenix would allow for some visits with Debra, and perhaps with other friends and family. Soon after my arrival, I was able to call her and tell her the good news. Excited, she agreed to visit the following Saturday.

During the three days before her visit, I reflected over what a strong influence she had been to help me through the hardest part of the journey. With the exception of two half-hour visits while I was at BCDC in Albuquerque, I hadn't seen her in almost nine months. I smiled warmly at the thought of her willingness to drive six hours each way *twice,* just for those brief visits.

We had written to each other almost daily during that time, and she allowed me to call her as often as I could get to a phone. Telephone calls from institutions were always collect, so her willingness to accept the calls added all the more to my rapidly growing affection for her. Many times, being able to talk with her and feel her loving presence made the difference in my ability to deal with the periodic insanity of my changing living conditions. Our respect and appreciation for one another had grown tremendously over the months. Impressed with my insights and plans regarding the juvenile diversion program, she had worked tirelessly to put it into a formal proposal. We felt a deep love growing between us, and had even discussed the prospect of marriage when I got out.

That Saturday morning, I sat staring through my window at the visitor's parking lot, and at the huge flagpole between it and the main entrance to the prison. I was taken with the size of the flag as it waved gently in the desert breeze. My thoughts wandered back to the time I had served in the military under that flag, and the years that I had grown up in its protective shadow. I felt such pain not to be able to walk out and stand under it a free man. Although a scant fifty yards away, it might as well have been on the moon for all the chainlink and razor wire between it and me.

For the first hour or so, visitors pulled into the parking lot and made their way to the front entrance, all dressed in their Sunday best. With each group of arrivals, I grew increasingly nervous that she might not make it. Another half-hour passed, and soon we would be called out for breakfast. If she arrived after that point, they would make her wait at least another hour, or they could turn her away altogether. Finally, I saw her car speeding down the long road leading to the prison. I watched every detail of her arrival as she got out of the car, crossed the parking lot and entered the huge outside gate that led to the visitor's center.

A short while later, my name was called. My heart raced as I walked to the inside door of the holdover unit to wait for the outside guard to arrive. Would she still feel the same, now that I was really *in* prison? All that time I was at BCDC, there was the persistent hope that I would be out soon. Now I was in much deeper, and had no idea when I would be out. Was she only humoring me? Feeling sympathy for me? Was she growing weary of the ordeal with nothing to comfort or reassure her? Were we deluding ourselves? Such questions raced through my mind as the outside guard arrived and escorted me to the visitors' area.

At the main building, the escort guard unlocked the door and motioned for me to step inside. Another guard opened the inside door and led me to a small receiving room where I was strip-searched. The anticipation was almost too much to contain. Finally, the guard signaled the control room, and a loud buzz indicated the moment had finally arrived. The door opened, and I stepped inside.

The look in Debra's eyes told me all I needed to know. Her smile lit up the room. Her expression clearly showed she cared as much as ever. There was no doubt about what we were both feeling. It didn't matter that I was in prison. None of that mattered. We were just glad to be alive and in each other's arms again, even if only briefly. I was ecstatic. She was radiantly beautiful, with that engaging, heartwarming smile and laugh that had captured my heart so many years before. Everything and everyone else faded away as we sat together the rest of the day, talking, laughing and holding hands like a couple of love-smitten teenagers. It was glorious yet bizarre to sit next to her like that, unable to do anything more than talk and hold hands.

The day passed far too quickly. We were the last to finally stand, embrace each other and say goodbye. We were so happy that now we could see each other on weekends and begin planning to build a future together. Our visit was reassuring to both of us, and restored our hopes that we could overcome any adversity and make the best of a bad situation. In fact, the very nature of the circumstances made us stronger and more purposeful. I could hold on indefinitely with Debra out there waiting. She was worth it, and what we could accomplish together was certainly worth it.

Several days passed. Even though Phoenix was closer to Debra, and would make visits easier for her, I wanted to get to my final destination and get started on a work program that would establish a good prison record for me. Debra and I talked excitedly on the phone that week about her plans to visit the next weekend. She even arranged to stay in Phoenix overnight so she could visit both days. At the slow rate men were coming in from Safford, it looked like I might have several weeks to wait, but at least a few more visits with Debra was pleasant consolation.

Early the next morning, however, fate moved against me. I was awakened by loud voices outside my cell, and keys turning in my lock. I sat up to face a guard

I hadn't seen before who told me to get up and roll up my things. I was shipping out in one hour. I looked out my small window. Still pitch black outside, there wasn't even a hint of dawn breaking anywhere. There was a sense of urgency in the air, and I felt very apprehensive.

Why so early? There were only six of us waiting to go to Safford, and it was supposed to be only a few hours away. *How much time could it take to get six of us ready to go?*

The guard came for me a short while later, and I fell in with the other prisoners shuffling to the main room. I gaped in disbelief as I watched not six but ten, then fifteen, then *thirty* more sleepy-eyed inmates filing into the main room to be processed out. Through one of the larger windows of the room I counted three buses waiting outside the fences.

Why three buses? That meant ninety or more prisoners were being moved. They couldn't be going to Safford. They didn't have room enough for six of us, let alone ninety. Maybe they were going somewhere beyond Safford, and were just going to drop us off on the way. That had to be it.

I looked around the room that was filling rapidly. Not one of the other five I knew were waiting to go to Safford was there.

Where were they?

As casually as possible, I began questioning the other inmates. A deep fear began to build in me as each one indicated a destination on the east coast…including several going to Florida.

"Florida?!" The thought of it sent chills up my spine. *Why in hell would I be part of a group going to the east coast?* Nervously, I questioned more arrivals. Not one said anything about Safford or anywhere *near* Arizona. Every one was headed *east.*

There must be some mistake, I agonized. I was supposed to go to *Safford,* goddamit—not the friggin' east coast. That's what the judge had ordered, and by God I had spent enough time trying to get there. I had friends and family nearby, all waiting to see me. And Debra was now eagerly planning visits, and expecting my early release. Everyone I knew was already planning to visit me at Safford, and some were even planning their vacations around it. How the hell was I ever going to get my early release if they kept moving me from one place to another?

My heart pounded even more as we lined up for the usual strip-search, change of clothes, and shackling. It was no use asking the guards where we were going. Even if they knew, they wouldn't tell me. Once again in chains, I shuffled over to a corner bench and sat down. I was devastated. What the hell was going on? This couldn't be happening. I was certain I had already been through the worst of it. *They couldn't be taking me all the way to the damned east coast. Why?*

A warm summer breeze blew lightly across the Arizona desert as we lined up to board the buses in the gathering light of dawn. I looked at the nearly full moon now low in the western sky and wondered. Perhaps my number had been mixed up with someone else's who was supposed to be going to Florida. It could be months before they would get it straightened out. I had heard stories that were hard to believe, and this was beginning to look like it might one of them. I looked at the silhouettes of the surrounding mountains. They reminded me of nights like that spent with Debra under star-filled desert skies. I remembered how beautiful she looked in the moonlight, and how good it felt to hold her in the quiet calm of balmy desert nights.

The harsh, commanding voices of the guards, and the clinking of chains against leg irons filled the air as the line of prisoners shuffled toward the buses. My eyes filled with tears as I said a silent goodbye to Debra, not knowing when I would be able to reach a phone to let her know we wouldn't be seeing each other for a while.

At least we had one chance to meet. It was her birthday the day we visited, so I was thankful that fate had granted us that much. It was a small sign but a good one, nevertheless, in the face of this latest twist of fate. Her face, her fragrance and her touch were sharp reminders of the promise of the future in a quagmire of improbabilities that seemed to worsen every day. Memory of our parting kiss, the feel of her hair against my face, and the soft touch of her hand in mine was etched in my memory. It became my only remaining link to sanity in a world that for me was going steadily mad. As long as she was willing to wait, I would somehow be okay.

Chapter Twenty-Nine

The bus ride back to Luke Air Force Base was particularly hard for me. I was within a few hours of Safford and a chance to establish a good prison record, and now I was being yanked away again on Con-Air—this time bound for some unknown destination on the east coast. Ghostly images of the DC-6 came uncomfortably to mind, but I quickly pushed them away and focused on the unfairness of my present situation. The psychological impact of being helpless once again, after having come so close to seeing some light at the end of my tunnel was excruciating. I had to quietly let them take me wherever they chose, whenever they chose, and for whatever reason they chose.

My journey now ran in reverse. I boarded the jet at Luke AFB, flew back to Oklahoma City and boarded one of three buses headed back to El Reno. Barely three weeks had passed since I left the place. Waking up the next morning in a dingy cell in the holdover unit was like the dreams I had of being in prison, then waking up and discovering I *was* in prison. There was no mistaking this, however. This was no dream. I could smell it, feel it and hear it. It really *was* El Reno, and I was back again.

As the hours passed, the shouting and yelling of the prisoners intensified. I felt sick. The smell of four hundred men confined in a brick and metal sweatbox permeated the air without letup. To me it was as if I had never left the place. To the processing officers it was as if I had never been there in the first place. To them I was just another face in the endless stream of prisoners they processed every day. It didn't matter that I was there only a few weeks before, and had been approved for release into the general population. I would have to wait my turn and go through the entire evaluation process all over again. No shortcuts, no special privileges and no release into the general population until I was cleared by the caseworkers *again*.

The heat in the building was already noticeable as the guards collected the food trays from breakfast. I could feel it radiating off the brick and steel outer walls as the sun climbed over the red dirt of the Oklahoma landscape. The huge fans at the ends of the catwalks still brought pathetically little relief from the stifling heat and stagnant air. My only consolation was that it wasn't winter. If this place was so miserable in the summer, then winter must be unbearable. Since it was now September, perhaps the worst of the summer heat was over.

At least I had a cell to myself this time. I could choose which bunk I wanted to lie on, and I could use the toilet without looking into my cellmate's face. This was certain to change, since every day it seemed like more prisoners were brought in than were shipped out. I had sharp contrasts in cellmates during my previous stay at El Reno. The first one was actually enjoyable. He was from Puerto Rico, spoke very little English, and was very good-natured. We spent most of our time learning each other's language. Once we were able to converse a little, we even exchanged addresses as if we actually thought we might stay in touch.

The next one, on the other hand, was just the opposite. He was a very angry young man from New Hampshire who was technically a state inmate. According to him, the authorities there couldn't handle him. By special arrangement that he seemed proud of, he had been turned over to federal authorities. He boasted that he had been convicted of murder, and later killed two inmates and seriously injured a guard. When he showed up in my cell, he was on his way to the maximum-security federal penitentiary at Marion, Ohio, where the worst, most violent prisoners were locked down twenty-three hours a day. With nothing to look forward to, he was ready and willing to go off on anyone at any moment.

I didn't know how much of his story was true, but if even part of it was, I was locked in a tiny cell with a convicted murderer that proudly claimed his right to take anything he wanted, whenever he wanted, from anyone he wanted. But Big Jim came sharply to mind, and for most of the night as I kept him talking, I took on as much of Big Jim's persona as I could muster. By the next morning, I felt we had connected at a deep enough level that I would be okay for a while. He needed someone to talk to, and I was willing to listen. He even had the impression that I was a "long-time" inmate, which I did nothing to convince him otherwise. Fortunately, he shipped out two days later, and I finally got some much-needed rest.

Some cellmates were easy to get along with no matter how small the cells were, while others would be obnoxious and belligerent if the space was as big as a football field. As far as the guards and staff were concerned, none of that mattered. As long as there was room for two bodies, two beds, the toilet flushed and the inmates didn't kill each other, all was in order. What inmates went through in order to survive each day wasn't their concern.

Relieved to be free of cellmate issues for the moment, I focused on how to speed up the process of getting approved for release into the general population. It would be good to see Simon and his buddies again, and to get back into my exercise routine. As grim as El Reno was, the track and the exercise yard made up for it somewhat. With actual green grass, and a half-mile track to use, I often lost myself in thought as I walked and ran mile after mile after mile during my previous stay. This time, I noticed that whether or not I had a cellmate didn't matter much. Gradually, I was getting hardened to the system, and El Reno was accelerating the process. Increasingly, I felt Big Jim in the cell with me…and cleaned it accordingly.

Because I arrived on a Friday evening, along with close to ninety other prisoners, my file wouldn't be processed until Monday. My file would show that I had already been approved for release into the general population, but with all those files to review, mine might not be looked at for days. I could be stuck in that cell for a *week* before they even got to my file.

Then I remembered that on Sundays the Chaplain always visited the holdover unit. I put in a request to see him for an "emergency" need, and just before lunch that Sunday he came to my cell. He was surprised but delighted to see me. His regular clerk had suddenly been shipped off to a court hearing, and now he needed an actual replacement for his clerk. Within hours he had me out of the cell and into his carpeted, air-conditioned office, where I spent the rest of my stay, other than during lockdown. I had actually gotten a regular prison job…as a holdover! Permanent inmates at El Reno waited months for jobs like that. During the evenings, when I wasn't at my clerking duties, I would be out on the track or with Simon and his buddies. Once again, there was no shortage of trade goods to make my time pass a little easier.

With a little help from the Chaplain, I was able to find out that I was indeed being shipped east. No destination was revealed, but mention of a court appearance was involved. Even in his official capacity, he was unable to determine what it was, or why I was being sent east. I also learned from him that I was under "Central Inmate Monitoring" status, which meant that I was being closely watched by someone at a higher level. Ordinarily, such status is intended to keep co-defendants in a given case separated from one another, or in cases where one inmate is a possible witness against another inmate in the prison system. Consequently, an inmate under CIM status was usually considered a "snitch."

CIM status was a red flag to any inmate clerk who might see the file and choose to spread the word. The inmate on CIM status might not even be aware of his status, or may not actually be supplying information, but the designation could easily be misconstrued and quickly blown out of proportion by other inmates already highly prone to jumping to conclusions. Under such circumstances, CIM status could actually be even more dangerous than to be officially held under protective custody, or "PC," since the inmate mingles with the general population. Either I was being set up to appear as an informant, just as my CIA friend in Santa Fe had warned me would happen, or someone higher up had a particularly strong interest in my case.

This time, only a week passed before my name came up on the ship-out roster, so it appeared that I was being given some degree of priority. It was the eastbound flight, which I heard went to Miami, then to FCI Taladega, near Birmingham, Alabama. From there, it went all over the east coast and up to New England. The federal marshals, it seemed, had themselves a damn *airline* with regularly scheduled routes.

The thought of doing time in Miami, or worse yet, in Alabama was hardly encouraging, particularly if it was anywhere near Birmingham. When I drove through that area years ago, it had an oppressiveness to it that I could feel just driving through it. Perhaps it was all the civil rights issues that had taken place there, but whatever it was, I didn't like it. FCI Taladega, I was told, was definitely not a good place to do time. The guards, most of whom were black, were known to be extremely harsh on white inmates. I was told the female guards had a bad "score-to-settle" attitude toward *all* male inmates—not just whites.

By the end of the next day, after eleven hours in holding cells, on the plane, and riding buses, I found myself in solitary at FCI Taladega. Something about the place gave me the creeps, and it wasn't just the confinement. Maybe it was the hot, muggy air, or the spooky movies filmed in the Deep South that I had seen as a kid. Whatever it was, everything about the place was spooky. It seemed like the kind of place where a guy could disappear without a trace. The flat countryside was blanketed with thick stands of Southern Yellow Pine, with Spanish moss hanging from every tree limb. It gave me the uneasy feeling that I was gradually being drawn back to a place I had hoped I would never see again. I shuddered at the thought that I might actually be on my way back to Florida.

The Old Man and his entire operation had been caught and successfully prosecuted three years before, so the DC-6 case should have long since been closed.

As far as I knew, my name was never even brought up. A law clerk at BCDC in Albuquerque let me read the actual details of the trial in one of his case law books. At that time, it was one of the largest drug busts prosecuted in the northern district of Florida. The Old Man got *sixty* years, his brother, Michael, *forty,* and everyone else close to them a mandatory minimum of twenty-five years—including the "outlaw," Vinnie. Prosecuted under the RICO act, their crimes (classified as "racketeering") made each of them ineligible for parole. It was extremely disturbing to read the disposition of a major criminal case like that, and see the names of men I had known personally. Although my name wasn't mentioned, that had hit too close to home for me at the time I read it, and now it was returning to haunt me.

What, I wondered, *could the authorities want with* me, *three years after the case had been closed?* I couldn't be of any use to them now…unless the case *wasn't* closed. I was such a little fish in that operation, and was already so deep into my own legal mess that it couldn't be about making sure I "paid my dues." *Why clutter court dockets with such trivial matters at this point?*

This had to be a mistake…unless they simply wanted to interrogate me to tie up some loose ends. Whatever this was about, it was a bitch to have to go through. Every day that I sat in a holdover cell, or rode their buses or airplanes from one place to another, was one less day I had to establish a good prison record and get before the parole board at my presumed destination of FCI Safford.

Trying to stay somewhat hopeful, I thought perhaps this was one of those things that only appeared to get worse, but would turn out to be a blessing in disguise. If I was patient, and maintained a good attitude, eventually things might break in my favor. Again I recalled Big Jim and the book he gave me. In it, the author's main point was to find something to be grateful for in times of adversity. Doing so, he wrote, would inevitably change one's circumstances in a positive, often dramatic way. I had little else going for me at that point, so I began to notice anything and everything for which I could be appreciative. I lingered on thoughts of Debra, and on how the Bureau of Prisons had gotten me all the way to Phoenix in time to celebrate her birthday. That was an interesting way to frame it.

Then there was the reconnection with Simon and his friends, and the sunsets or sunrises I watched from any window I could get close to, wherever I found myself. That always gave me hope for another day, and the reassurance that out there in the Universe, all still seemed to be in good working order. I was grateful that I didn't have a ten or fifteen year prison sentence, like many of the inmates around me, or a death sentence or a "contract" out on me. When I looked at my situation from that perspective, there were many things for which I could be grateful, and the more I thought about them the better I began to feel.

Several days after my arrival at Taladega, I was allowed into the main room with the rest of the holdovers. I had mixed feelings, because although I was relieved to be able to stretch a bit and move around, I wasn't in the mood to commiserate with other inmates or be part of the constant noise and milling about. It reminded me too much of BCDC. Nonetheless, I could walk around a little, play an occasional card game or actually have an intelligent conversation with someone. There were two TV rooms, but they were always jammed with inmates watching inane sitcoms, professional wrestling or B-rated Kung Fu movies. Exercise periods came only a few times a week, and always en masse. We had to go with the group, or be locked in our cells while everyone else went. We would file out the door and walk in a line to the athletic field like a bunch of elementary school kids on a field day. Unlike El Reno, holdovers at Taladega were kept in one building only, and not allowed outside except for exercise periods and meals. No contact whatsoever was permitted with the regular population.

Two weeks passed, and occasionally female guards came through the unit. I had little opportunity to find out what they were like, but from the stern looks on their faces I had little doubt that at least a part of what I had heard might be true. I had no intention of finding out first-hand. My time at La Tuna and El Reno had helped condition me, for as much as I disliked Taladega, the time seemed to pass more quickly. Gradually I found myself less and less bothered by things that previously would have me pacing furiously and fretting unceasingly.

One morning I was awakened by a surly guard, instructing me to roll up my things and get ready to ship out. As usual, it was pitch black outside. Where this time? Florida? It was getting to the point where I hardly cared anymore. My mind had begun to wander so far away, it was as if only my body was in the cell. It took considerable effort to focus on the simple details of preparation to step out into the outside world again. I rolled up my mattress and sat in the dark, wondering what the next part of the journey would be like.

The sound of bootsteps and keys jingling outside my door ended my quiet reflecting, and I was ordered into the main room for a rerun of the same scene I had experienced at now five previous facilities. A team of officers called out numbers and checked them off as each of several dozen sleepy-eyed inmates dragged themselves into a smaller room for the standard strip search and out-processing.

Going through it was humiliating enough, but standing there buck-naked and watching it being done to one another was demoralizing and degrading. But finally I was growing indifferent to the whole process. After the searches, we were handed thin khaki shirts and pants, then led to another room to wait while each inmate was cuffed, chained and shackled.

For an hour we shivered in the air-conditioned room while the transport team assembled their things and casually finished their coffee and small-talk. Finally they called our numbers and one by one we hobbled outside and boarded the one waiting bus.

Expecting a trip to the Birmingham airport for another flight on Con-Air, I was surprised to see the bus turn south toward Montgomery and work its way through the heart of the city to the open highway. For several hours it continued southward, stopping at various jails along the way and at a U.S. Air Force base to drop someone off, or to pick someone up. Except for the differences in on-board amenities and the type of passengers, it could just as well have been a Greyhound bus on a regular scheduled run.

Further and further south we drove, gradually heading toward the panhandle of Florida. The terrain, and even some of the towns and buildings we passed began to look uncomfortably familiar.

Finally, we rounded a turn in the road and entered the eastbound ramp of a freeway I knew all too well. I knew then where I was headed. It was Interstate 10 and the first mileage sign that came into view had me squirming in my seat.

"Pensacola—44 Miles."

Chapter Thirty

The Escambia County Jail was cold and hard—cold from the air conditioning set for the comfort of staff people who came and went from the stifling heat outside every day, and hard from the solid steel bunks with thin, plastic mattresses to sleep on. Everything was steel, concrete or Plexiglas. Even the "pillows" were hard, made of impermeable plastic to prevent abuse or misuse by inmates.

Modern and efficient, the jail had even more electronic gadgetry and high-tech security than BCDC in Albuquerque. Located in the heart of downtown Pensacola, it was one more giant fortress built to accommodate the rapidly increasing population of prisoners being held for arraignment, trial or sentencing. It was also a place to hold drunk drivers and prisoners serving short sentences for minor crimes. It was frustrating for me to listen to men complain bitterly of the "hardship" of having to do thirty or sixty days for misdemeanors, knowing I had a six *year* sentence barely underway. I watched in disbelief to see some of them do their brief sentences, get released, then return within weeks to begin another stint after getting themselves in trouble again.

My initial impression of the conditions there was a mixture of relief and shock. Operated by the County Sheriff's Department, the jail was more lenient in terms of what inmates could have in their possession and how they spent their time. But it was more limited in space than BCDC. In such a confined environment, tempers often flared and attitudes were as hard and cold as the steel surfaces that surrounded us. The cellblock I occupied was one of four that faced a round observation post in the center referred to as a "tower." Each cellblock was triangular in shape, so that the guard in the tower could monitor the activities of every inmate without having to leave his or her post. Each cellblock slept sixteen inmates in four rows. Two toilets with sinks on top were situated to one side, with two open showers on the other, all in full view of the guard, whether male or female. The tower's Plexiglas windows were smoke-tinted to prevent inmates from seeing which direction the guard was facing. Only when an inside reading light was on could we see the ghostly image of the guard's face through the darkened glass.

Access to each cellblock was through a large, Plexiglas door that slid open and closed electronically into an inner cage constructed of heavy steel bars. Just like the ones at BCDC, the cage had an inner door of steel bars that opened and closed with a loud, metallic slam that reverberated through the cellblock. Two steel picnic-style tables were bolted to the floor at the front of the cellblock. Each table was hardly big enough for six men to sit together at the same time. Above one of the tables was a small black-and-white TV. The noise of the blaring TV, loud voices, the slamming of dominoes and card-playing was almost unbearable as it echoed off the cinder block walls and steel surfaces of a room one-fourth the size of the cellblocks at BCDC. A video arcade was quieter by comparison.

Adding to the insanity, personal transistor radios owned by various inmates who could afford them played a continuous, mind-numbing and chaotic combination of rap, country/western, rock & roll, and soul music, all at the same time. Even "lights-out" brought no relief from the cacophony of disjointed sounds and disharmonic rhythms as the walls echoed with each inmate's choice of distraction from their respective demons of the night. Much to my dismay, many of them left their radios on all night while they slept.

Three days into this latest nightmare, and I was ready for a straitjacket. Once again, my identity as an educated, white male represented everything the predominantly black inmates hated. I wore the face of every teacher, landlord, lawyer, prosecutor, probation officer, judge and cop they had learned to hate, so any opportunity to challenge or bring added torment to this "smart-ass white boy" caught on their side of the walls was not to be missed. Any effort on my part to reduce the volume of the TV, the radios, or the general noise level in the small cellblock was met with instantaneous resistance and a corresponding increase in noise level in direct proportion to the amount of protest they felt from me.

This quickly taught me to keep my protests to myself, no matter how offensive or irritating the racket became, and to simply numb my senses and jangled nerves. Witnessing the constant adversity and taunting between inmates reduced us to a form of primal self-preservation. The process for me became not as much one of survival of the fittest, but of the most tolerant and stubborn.

Sleeping became a nightly routine of caving into the mental and emotional exhaustion from the constant, unrelenting noise of the cellblock, and to somehow flow with it. To discover that some inmates actually found comfort from the mayhem made me wonder what kind of internal strife they had grown up with. Determined to find a way to turn things around, I was forced to look for ways to join them rather than fight them.

One day a small group began exercising in the shower area, which was the only space open enough to move around. It was more a show of muscle than it was "exercising," so their attempt to goad me into something they thought would make me look bad backfired. Well-conditioned from my time in solitary at La Tuna and later at Taladega, I joined in and matched the strongest of them push-up for push-up, and sit-up for sit-up. Having bet that I couldn't keep up with them, their "loss" was to run in place with me until they...or I...dropped. They were impressed with my fitness, and soon joined me in regular workouts and running sessions every day.

To the amazement of guards who later began to make a point of stopping by our cellblock to watch, half the cellblock eventually got into the act and started running in place with me. We even held "marathon runs" and created a variety of fitness contests. Gradually the noise level in the cellblock began to diminish whenever we weren't exercising. A few holdouts still tried to rattle me by turning up the volume on their wrestling matches and action movies, and the yelling across the cellblock and the slamming of dominoes continued. I remained quiet and acted unbothered.

After a while, my silence began to bother them, particularly when I appeared to be absorbed in reading, or asleep. Pulling that off required tolerance and self-discipline I never dreamed I had. Showing the slightest weakness, or even a hint of faking it, would give them an opening to ride me until I broke, and would end any chance of peace for me in the cellblock. At one point well into the third week, I began to write ideas for short stories on a tablet and clipboard that one of the counselors gave me. Gradually, I was able to divert my attention from the noise to my writing. That clipboard was worth its weight in gold. Hour after hour, and well into each night, I continued to write until gradually I became impervious to the noise.

One day, a young man sitting on the bunk opposite me interrupted my writing with a question aimed at my clipboard.

"What chu' wratin', ennyway?" he queried, his face twisted inquisitively. He had been one of the worst to challenge me when I first arrived and had been so hostile that the sincere, almost boyish tone of his question surprised me. This could either be an opportunity for a breakthrough, or it could blow up in my face.

I looked into his eyes for a moment before answering, and through all the hate and meanness I saw instead a little boy—hurting and just as scared as I was. I felt a softness come over me as I answered him.

"A story."

"A *story?* Wha kine a' stohry?" he scrunched up his face in feigned disgust.

"Just a story," I replied. "I'm just passing the time by writing about my experiences."

"Yeah?" he puzzled. "Who gonna' read 'em?"

"Anybody," I said. "My kids, I hope. But by the time I get out of here, maybe I'll have enough to write a book."

"You got kids? How many?"

"I've got two boys, fourteen and eleven, and a daughter, four. I've been collecting stories to send to them, some of them mine and some I've read in books and magazines."

"Yeah? Does dey lahk 'em?"

"I suppose so. At least some of them. I think maybe later on they'll like them better; maybe when they have kids."

"So what 'chu doin' in heah? You don' seem lahk a bad dude."

"Smuggling."

"Dat so? Heroin? Coke?"

"No. Pot."

"Dat's no big deal."

"That's what *I* thought, too. But the cops think differently."

"Dey ahways do. You be gettin' outta heah soon, mos' lahkly, if it wuz only weed."

"No, I won't. I have six years to do."

"Six *yeahs??* Sheeyit. Musta' been a shitload o' pot. So what 'chu doin' in *dis* place?"

"I don't know. My conviction was in New Mexico, and it was a federal rap. I guess they think I was involved in something down here."

"Yeah? Bin a lotta that goin' on roun' heah. People from down Miama way bin bringin' they shit up here. Things bin gettin' pretty hot roun' heah lately. You get mixed up wid some o' dem?"

"I knew some people out here a while back, but haven't seen them in a long time. I don't know what I'm here for, yet. I'm just trying to get to my joint and do my time." I was beginning to sound like one of the old-timers I had met earlier.

"I hear that. So what chu' gon' do wid yo' stories? Dey got enny sex in 'em? Drug runnin'? Killin'?"

"No, they're mostly kids' stories."

"Yeah? Dey enny good? Ah wanna read one."

"Okay, I'll see if I've got something." I pulled out a thick folder of papers and looked through them for a story I thought he might like.

"Here," I said as I handed it to him. "See what you think of this one."

As he grabbed the papers like a kid with a newfound toy, I was amazed at his muscular build, yet how boyish and youthful he also was. I guessed him to be about twenty, but I could feel a ten year old reaching for the story. There was an innocence in his face as he read. I could hardly believe he had been one of the guys who had strutted around menacingly in the first few days I was there. The change I noticed in him as he read the story was fascinating.

I returned to my writing and lost myself in it until I heard my name called over the P.A. Looking up, I saw a man in a suit and tie standing outside the cell-block. In his hand was a well-worn briefcase. A lawyer, I thought to myself, as I gathered my papers and shoved them under my bunk. Now, perhaps, I would get to see what I was up against. As I walked to the cage, the big electric motor whirred and the inner cage door slid open. I stepped inside. As soon as it slammed shut behind me, the outer door opened. I noticed a uniformed guard standing a few yards beyond the man in the hallway.

"I'm Nathan Rogers," he said casually. "I've been appointed by the U.S. Magistrate to represent you. Are you aware of the charges against you?"

"No, I'm not. What charges? I've already been convicted and sentenced in New Mexico." I felt uncertain and confused.

"Different case. This one's here in the Northern District of Florida, Judge Roger Vinson presiding. In case you don't know about him, he's considered a 'hanging judge.' So far, he's put everyone else in the case away for a long time. I don't know much about you yet, but unless you've got some kind of miracle up your sleeve, this is going to be a tough case. You'd better read these over," he said, handing me a bound set of legal documents. "We'll talk about the particulars before court in the morning. You'll be brought before a magistrate for arraignment. Here's my card."

He motioned to the guard in the tower. Without further comment, he turned and walked away down the long corridor. I felt my blood run cold as I walked towards the outer door to the cellblock. It slid open, and I stepped into the cage.

As it closed behind me, I looked at the documents.

"THE PEOPLE OF THE UNITED STATES OF AMERICA," the words stood out across the top of the page, followed by the innocuous little word, *"Versus..."*

My eyes scanned the list of names below the "Versus," and a chill worked its way up my spine as I recognized them one by one. My heart started pounding, and a deep foreboding gripped me as each name I read brought me closer to the realization that I was about to be implicated in something horrible. As I got to the last name on the list, I felt dizzy. My knees went weak as I read it. There, as big as all the rest, was *my* name.

My face flushed. Suddenly I felt hot. My palms turned wet with sweat. A wave of diarrhea nearly overpowered my bowels as I felt the unmistakable threat of death. *This* was death for me. This made me out to be far more culpable, far more criminal in nature than anything I had really done. This identified me as a major figure in a "continuing criminal enterprise" in direct concert with men who had built entire criminal careers with their lives.

It was true that for one relatively brief part of it, I had been there with them. The prosecution wouldn't have any trouble proving that. On top of that, I was already convicted as a smuggler. If that could possibly leave a trace of doubt in the minds of any judge and jury, there was also the fact that I had been a fugitive for five years. That alone would likely seal my fate.

My future looked very bleak. In fact, from what I was reading, there would be no future for me. The inner cage door opened and I stepped haltingly back into the cellblock, still reading. My heart sank deeper with each page. My name appeared in four of the six counts, each having to do with major drug smuggling, conspiracy, possession with intent to distribute extremely large quantities of controlled substances, and racketeering. The papers described operations covering a period of more than *seven* years, and implicated me during the entire period. Each count carried a maximum of five years in prison, which would likely run consecutively, given my new lawyer's assessment of the judge's disposition and my growing criminal record.

The racketeering part bore the grim prospect that if convicted on any of the counts, I would have no chance of parole, just like the others in the case. Whatever my sentence, I would have to serve it *all*. A chill came over me as I read the bottom of the indictment. An official notation drove home the stark reality of what I was facing. Bond in the original case had been set at ten *million* dollars, a testament in itself of the value placed on the Old Man's operation by the authorities. I just happened to be a name on the list. Already convicted and sentenced in New Mexico, I couldn't have posted bond if it were ten dollars.

My boyish innocence screamed out that this just wasn't possible. I hadn't been involved with them that long. I knew them, yes. I had traveled with the Old Man a few times. But my total involvement had only been a few *months,* not *seven years.* I had been with them at the landing strip, yes. I had been involved in some of the planning, yes. But I really wasn't "one of them."

It was only marijuana, I had rationalized back then. We were all so certain that it would soon be legalized. Besides, we were the "good guys"...or so we thought. We had dreams and visions for the future good we could do. But the prosecutor didn't give a damn about our plans or visions. And we damn sure weren't "good guys" as far as he was concerned. None of that mattered. He was out to put everyone involved away for a long time. The fact that I was *already* behind bars didn't matter. As an already convicted smuggler, that made for an easy conviction to add to his long list of successes.

I sat down on my bunk and let the full impact bear down on me. After nearly a year of forging my way through a mental and emotional labyrinth, I began to realize that this entire ordeal might well be hopeless. I couldn't give up, I knew. But the weight of it all hung heavily like a cross to which I was about to be nailed. I was only the residue of a big case that was near its finish, but I had defied the court and the authorities by running, and had unwittingly given them reason to believe the worst about me. Now I was caught in an uncaring, unfeeling system of retribution and even revenge. The wheels of justice were only beginning to turn, grinding to dust what little threads of hope to which I had been clinging.

I lay back on my bunk and felt the pain of a man wrongly accused. And yet, I knew I wasn't entirely innocent. I *had* been there. I *had* been responsible, in large part, for making the operation successful. Even if I had only been involved with them for "a few months," I couldn't justify indignation or innocence no matter how much the little boy inside me pleaded, nor how much my conniving self tried to convince me it could get me through the maze.

Another wave of nausea and diarrhea swept over me as I fought to hold back a torrent of tears filling my eyes.

As far as I was concerned, I was doomed.

Chapter Thirty-One

The next morning was dismal, with dark clouds outside and drops of rain on the windows of our cellblock. Just back from breakfast, I was still reeling in disbelief over yesterday's shock and what I knew now loomed in front of me. There it was in black and white, lying on my bunk—a stack of legal documents that spelled the end for me. My entire future was in those papers…a future that looked so bleak now that I could not possibly imagine how I could salvage it. Hopelessness had never been a factor in any of the lamebrain, stupid stunts I had survived in my life, but this was beyond my ability to fathom. This was, in fact, a hopeless situation. There simply was no way out.

I picked up the documents, read them again, then laid them down and thought about the situation some more. Desperate, my mind frantically searched for something, *anything,* to find some escape from this mess. But this wasn't even in the *realm* of "mess." This was more in the category of an abyss…a bottomless pit of darkness. With a deep sense of resignation, I pushed the papers aside and leaned back on the bunk.

It was now daylight, and the inmates who hadn't gone off to breakfast in the chow room were stirring. The young black man across the aisle opened his eyes, sat up and looked around. Stretching, he rubbed his eyes like a little kid and looked over at me.

"Waz up wid chu', man? You look lahk sumbuddy jest died or sumpthin'."

"No," I sighed. "Nobody died. I got served papers last night, and right now things don't look so good for me."

"Yeah? Well da's da' way it be wid da' law, you know. If dey got sumpthin' on you, dey hit chu wid ev'thing 'til sumpthin' sticks...o' you squeal lahk a pig."

"Yeah, I know. But in this case, there's nothing to squeal about. Everybody else in the case is already busted and doing time. It looks like I'm the one who got fingered."

"Wayhl, things don' ahways tuhn out da' way dey look at fuhst. You run wid it, and don' say nuthin' to nobuddy, an' you'll be okay. Thas' what we all say roun' heah, an' it ahways seem to wuhk out dat way." I appreciated his sincere attempt to console me.

"Well, I sure hope so."

"Hey, ah lahked dat stohry o' yours. You got enny more?"

"Sure. I'll get a couple more for you in a little while. Right now, I need to think a little bit. Got an arraignment to go to this morning."

"Okay. Whenevah. You wraht pretty guhd."

"Thanks. I'll talk to you in a little while."

With that, he was off to the showers while I read the documents again, and agonized over a possible solution. An hour later, my name was called and a guard appeared outside the cellblock door to escort me to the holding cell for court.

The arraignment came and went so quickly, it seemed as if it was over before it began. It had taken nearly two months to get me from FCI Phoenix to this federal magistrate's courtroom, and four hours of processing and waiting in the courthouse holding cell just to stand before him and hear the charges against me. It took less than fifteen minutes for him to read the charges, and for me to enter a plea of "not guilty."

Nathan, my new lawyer, was as nonchalant as if we were appearing for a traffic ticket. Once again he let me know that as far as he was concerned, this was a hopeless case with very little evidence to support a claim of innocence. To be exact, he intimated, there was none. There was one ray of hope, I discovered, in the fact that he had once been an Assistant U.S. Attorney. At least he knew how their side worked. What I didn't know until later, but began to surmise as the case developed, was that there was a significant reason why a man of such legal stature would now be a defense attorney taking court-appointed cases. He had a drinking problem...or so I heard from other inmates who had heard about him. He had been on a steady decline for several years. Had I known that earlier, it would have deepened the mistrust I already felt for court-appointed lawyers.

Different from public defenders who are salaried employees of the government, and whose principle responsibility is to represent indigent defendants, court-appointed attorneys are regular defense attorneys in private practice who are assigned a case by a presiding judge. Since the public defender's office can only represent one defendant in the case, no matter how much time may have passed between their cases, any co-defendant who is unable to hire his own attorney must have an attorney appointed by the court. If that attorney happens to be a good one, and fully commits to the case, the arrangement can work very much in the defendant's favor. Most often, however, it doesn't work at all well for the inmate, since the attorney is paid a nominal fee to handle the case.

Having a private practice to support, many defense attorneys resent spending more time on such cases than is absolutely necessary to satisfy the court that the defendant is receiving "due representation." With few exceptions, inmates are painfully aware that court-appointed lawyers often work sympathetically with the prosecutor's office. Financially unable to support a strong defense, an indigent defendant is often pressured and manipulated by both sides to plead guilty, which is often accomplished by charging the defendant with every conceivable violation and then making an offer to settle out of court on "reduced charges." If the defendant fights the charges, he or she faces the prospect of receiving the maximum sentence allowed if even one count sticks. Lacking the money it takes to mount a proper defense, the case is frequently settled before it ever reaches trial.

The court-appointed lawyer is often too busy with paying clients, or is new in practice. An easy conviction of a hapless defendant provides an ideal way to gain favor with the opposition, while the government pays for services *not* necessarily rendered. Sacrificial lambs on the altar of the great American judicial system, indigent defendants are at the mercy of legal forces they little comprehend, let alone can cope with. No small wonder that lawyers who go to prison are only slightly better off than ex-cops, snitches and child molesters.

Pretrial hearings in my case began a few weeks later, and I began to see what actually lay before me. The witness list was formidable, the evidence overwhelming, and the prosecutor was highly skilled at his job. As I watched him lay the case before the judge and interrogate witnesses, I realized why he had such a good record. He was thorough, fully committed to his cause, believed in what he was doing and devoted himself completely to the effort.

He was convinced I was a manager in the DC-6 operation, and had been involved with the organization all along. He was out to put me away for a long time, yet in a strange way I actually admired him. A part of me even cheered him on as he laid out his case, even though *I* was the one sitting at the defendant's table. It was true that I had been involved with smugglers, even had *become* one, but in him I saw a staunch defender of everything I had learned to respect and honor in my youth and as a military officer and pilot.

I had strayed from my earlier goal in college of being on his side of the law. I had allowed myself to believe that because corruption was pervasive in our social structure, and laws had become so "unfair" and poorly enforced, that it was okay to live according to my own rules. In the process, I developed a sense of invincibility. I came to believe that my good intentions would prevail in the end, no matter what shortcuts I took or laws I broke.

Over the next three weeks, the prosecutor pressed on with his case. He brought up my prior conviction, all the pertinent evidence, and called in the law enforcement officers from New Mexico who had testified in my earlier case. Taking the stand with a distinct air of self-righteousness was the former lieutenant—now captain—from the New Mexico State Police who had tried to convince me that I should help them. Referring to me in the same demeaning manner as the "scum" he said I was involved with, he portrayed me as a liar and a manipulating "con-man" who would stop at nothing to get my way. My insides twisted to hear a respected, credible authority describe me in such degrading, hateful terms.

The prosecutor drove home my fugitive status, and convincingly portrayed me as someone who obviously had much to hide. He produced pictures, names, dates, motel and car rental receipts with thoroughness and proficiency. Step-by-step, he moved me closer and closer to a totally predictable fate. The deck was hopelessly stacked against me.

As my lawyer kept reminding me, this was an unsympathetic judge when it came to sentencing drug offenders. If I maintained my plea of innocence and was found guilty on even one count, he would give me the maximum penalty allowed. If found guilty on more than one count, he would likely stack the sentences by making them consecutive. If I forced the time and expense of a trial, the judge would most likely add the overall sentence to the six years I already had. If, on the other hand, I copped a plea to reduced charges, I might get only half the time I was facing. In that case, the judge might be inclined to make the sentences run concurrently.

The "best-case scenario," Nathan told me, would be "a few more years" added to my present sentence. He made it sound like I was in the military again, and would only be extending my tour of duty a few years. What would it matter to him if I rotted in prison for "a few more years?" In any case, there was no guarantee the judge would go along with the deal…especially this one.

I was in a terrible fix. They had enough witnesses and evidence to convict me on every count, even though I was really only guilty of one. I had never "possessed" or imported the marijuana, nor had I ever sold or *intended* to sell it. But I *had* conspired to import it, and that was enough to hang me. A jury in that part of the country wouldn't hesitate to find me guilty on that one count, but most likely on all of the others as well. I had nothing to prove otherwise. The judge, jury, prosecutor and eventually the parole board would all assume that I had been with the organization for the entire seven years. Since racketeering was a factor in this case, there was no way I was going to come out of a trial with less than twenty years of *mandatory* imprisonment, added to the six I already had.

After seeing the evidence against me, and the prosecutor's intention clearly enough, I searched desperately in my mind for something…anything…that could mitigate the situation somewhat. Then I remembered a magazine article a friend of mine had sent me. It praised five of the "most honest" attorneys in the country, and described in detail how each of them had taken up a banner for a worthy cause and had won against tremendous odds. Given the worsening condition of my case, I decided it couldn't hurt to send a plea for help to one of them. I picked one described as having handled drug cases, who lived in Baltimore. I sent him the most sincere letter I could possibly write. A few days before the next hearing, I received his reply.

He regretted that he could not take my case without a retainer, but he felt moved by the circumstances and recommended a plausible solution. His advice to me was to enter a defense of "Post-Traumatic Stress Disorder," more commonly known among Viet Nam veterans as "Viet Nam Syndrome." He said it had proven effective in a number of state courts, gaining several actual acquittals. Even though there was nothing in federal records to indicate any precedent, it certainly couldn't hurt to try. Nothing else seemed at all promising, he wrote.

My lawyer wasn't exactly wild about the idea. He said it hadn't been established in federal cases, and was unproven as a legal precedent. Little did I realize at the time that his resistance was more a factor of the work and time involved than because it was "unprecedented." After all, such a motion to the court would require the development of an actual legal defense which he wasn't prepared to mount. Given the lack of an acceptable alternative, I pressed him to enter the motion. To do so meant that I would be taking direct responsibility for the outcome of the case, for it was clear that he did not like the approach and would be of little or no assistance to me.

The next pretrial hearing convened two weeks later. Given the weight of the evidence against me, it was all but a foregone conclusion that I would go to trial if I didn't cop a plea. With great reluctance and obvious distaste for my decision, my lawyer stood up and addressed the court.

"May it please the Court, Your Honor," he said with disdain, "my *client* wishes to enter a motion of defense as a victim of 'Post-Traumatic Stress Syndrome.'"

I could tell right away the judge was not pleased with what he saw as an attempt to skirt the real issue. Looking at me like a decorated war hero at a draft dodger, he replied:

"Is your client aware that no such defense has yet been upheld in a federal court?"

"Yes, Your Honor, I have so advised him."

"And is he aware that he is asking this court to consider what amounts to an insanity plea?"

"Yes, Your Honor, he is so advised." He had never said a word about that to me. The judge glared directly at me.

"You're certain you wish to enter this motion?"

I swallowed hard, and my head started spinning. Was I hanging myself? I looked back at the judge meekly, barely able to breathe, let alone think. I forced myself to take a deep breath and replied as confidently as was possible for a man facing his own gallows.

"Yes, Your Honor, I do. I believe it could be a factor in my case."

He straightened in his chair and leafed through some papers in my file. "All right, then let the record show that the defendant wishes to enter a motion of 'Post-hypnotic'...make that 'Post-*Traumatic* Stress Syndrome' as his defense. Counsel for the defense will draw up the necessary documents and submit them to the Court. The defendant is hereby ordered to the Federal Prison Hospital in Springfield, Missouri for complete psychiatric evaluation and observation. Any further questions?"

The prosecutor and my lawyer exchanged knowing glances. No one replied. My body was quaking with apprehension, and my mind was a blur of frantic thoughts. With the greatest effort, I fought back the urge to jump up and change my motion. Was I being a complete *idiot,* on top of everything else I had done so far? Yes, of *course* I had questions, but I couldn't possibly formulate them quickly enough. Besides, who would answer them fairly and accurately at this point? The judge glared down at me, as if daring me to ask anything.

"Court's dismissed," he announced flatly, and rose from his lofty position and strode into his chambers.

As a convicted federal prisoner already serving time, I was federal property and therefore not entitled to an evaluation by a local psychiatrist as I had anticipated. This was a whole new twist. The judge was not going to allow me to run up the cost of this case any more than was absolutely necessary. Besides, this would take me off his docket for at least another month or so.

Meanwhile, back in the detention center, things had taken an interesting turn. My young friend across the way, who by now had told me his name was Michael, had taken a personal interest in my well-being. Enchanted with the stories I had given him to read, he kept pushing me for more. He let it be known around the cellblock that I was to be left alone and not disturbed with a lot of noise. If I even looked disdainfully at the TV, he would walk over and turn it off, no matter who was watching it. I started writing a new story, and couldn't write fast enough to keep him satisfied. Gradually, other inmates took an interest and created a comical scene of practically standing in line to read the pages as fast as I could write them.

Soon, a few inmates who had particular difficulty with writing asked me to write letters for them. To their mothers, they had the most respectful things to say. To their girlfriends, I might as well have been a writer for a porn magazine as they dictated graphic details of what they intended to do with them when they got out. The days passed quickly, and for the time being I let myself forget about my plight. It was almost as if nothing else mattered except being a scribe for a bunch of scared little boys in fearsome, scarred and tattooed grown-up bodies.

Two weeks later, I was once again in the back seat of a U.S. Marshal's sedan on my way back to FCI Taladega. For whatever reason, I hated the place. It made my blood run cold. But at least there would be room to move around and talk with other inmates. There was also access to a telephone, which I might be able to use to generate financial help and bolster moral support. By that point, Debra was understandably alarmed and needed better information than I had been able to give her since Phoenix.

The Baltimore lawyer had written that "cases had been acquitted with PTS Syndrome as a defense." If there really was a chance to win this case, and he would confirm the fact, I might be able to marshal the forces needed to get him his retainer and take the case. Teetering on the brink of legal as well as personal disaster, I needed help now more than ever, and this lawyer offered a ray of hope. Just as importantly, I needed emotional support. I needed to talk with Debra.

But the authorities had other plans for me this time. Brought in by U.S. Marshals rather than with a busload of other inmates, and with the destination "Federal Prison Hospital; Psych Unit" boldly written on my transfer papers, I was hustled off to solitary confinement. Placed in a cell by myself at the end of a long corridor leading away from the main room, I was a "nut case," as far as the guards were concerned —someone to be left strictly alone.

I was completely avoided, except for the required meal trays in my slot. Humiliated and dejected, labeled as a mental case, I was more alone now than ever. In that state of mind, I was live bait for the dragon now stirring in the murky depths of my mind.

Chapter Thirty-Two

Day after day, night after night, I waited alone in that cell with nothing to do but think, pace and wonder what the hell would happen next. A vertical, 6" wide strip of thick Plexiglas in one wall allowed me a bleak view of the world beyond the heavily fenced and razor-wired perimeter of the prison. In the distance, a dark forest of tall pine trees with that damn Spanish moss hanging drearily from every branch gave me a foreboding sense of death beyond the shadows. A tiny window in yet another solid steel door allowed me a shadowy glimpse of occasional movement in the corridor.

More days went by. I paced the floor like a caged animal. I couldn't talk to anyone, take a walk or even read a book. Like my first days at La Tuna, my only contact with anyone was an occasional guard peering through the window in the door. Even the orderlies avoided me, other than to leave a few sheets of paper and occasional pencil stubs on the flap in the door when they took my food trays.

The urge to call home was more intense than ever. Weeks had gone by since I had last spoken with Debra, and I felt something was wrong. We had grown so close that we could sense each other's thoughts and feelings, and would often confirm our intuitive impressions in our letters to each other.

Something wasn't right. I tried to convince myself that it was just fear from my deteriorating situation, but there was something more festering in my mind. I had been feeling it for more than a week, and with each passing day my concern seemed to grow. I needed to talk with her. I needed to hear the sweet sound of her voice, and feel her loving reassurance that she was still with me.

It took two days just to get an official request form *to get on the list* for the telephone. Two more days passed. I was beside myself. *Four goddamn days,* and I couldn't even get a few minutes on the phone. *What the hell was the matter with them?* I wasn't asking for a weekend furlough. I put in a third request, and then a fourth. Two more days came and went as I paced hour after hour. Every few minutes I would stop and peer through the tiny window in the door, or try to get someone's attention through the slot whenever it was open.

When the hell would they come for me? It was only a request for a phone call. It didn't take a damn act of Congress, or permission from the warden. Six days, now. I was going wild with panic. Something was wrong at home, I knew it. It wasn't just me and my legal problems. I could *feel* it.

At long last, I heard the welcome sound of keys jingling outside my door. Normally I hated those keys, but now that sound was music to my ears. If they would just please open the door and let me make a simple phone call, I could ease the pain in my heart.

The sound of a key turning in the lock brought me to my feet. *Finally.* The heavy door swung open, and a burly guard stood in the doorway glaring at me. In his hands dangled a pair of open handcuffs.

"You've got fifteen minutes on the phone," he said flatly. "And your time starts *now.* Turn around and put your hands behind you."

My heart was pounding so hard, I could barely stand it. My hands trembled as he squeezed the cuffs tightly on my wrists and pulled me into the corridor by the shoulder. As we walked down the corridor and into the main room, two other guards cleared the way for us through inmates milling about. For a moment, idle chatter subsided as they gawked at me as if I were some serial killer.

At the phone, the two guards took up positions on each side of me while my escort uncuffed one wrist, then re-cuffed it to a bar in the wall by the phone. I was beyond caring what they did at that point, as long as I could dial her number and hear her voice again. My heart was still pounding, and cold sweat dripped from my armpits as the noise around me faded from my consciousness. I dialed her number and the operator came on the line to make the collect call. An eternity passed as I heard the familiar sounds of lines connecting.

Busy.

The operator tried again.

Still busy.

I hung up the phone and looked at the guard. He looked at his watch and stared at the wall.

I dialed again. Another operator came on the line. Again, a busy signal.

God, what agony! Half my allotted time was gone. The guard shifted his weight and looked at the other two guards. They had better things to do than stand around a damn phone waiting for an inmate to make a stupid phone call. Inmates were scum, and shouldn't have any privileges in the first place. And this one was a nut case at that.

Frantically, I dialed again. The line clicked and I could hear the connection on the other end. *Please, God...*

Then, finally, I heard the sweet sound of her phone ringing! I heard a click, then Debra's soft, unmistakable voice.

"Yes," I heard her hesitant reply to the operator when asked if she would accept the charges. *Why the hesitation?* A call this long overdue would ordinarily be greeted with instantaneous excitement and delight. Something *was* wrong. When the operator left the line, there was uncharacteristic silence on the other end.

"Hi," I said, anxiously into the silence. "Are you there?"

"Yes, I'm here," came the halting reply. It was her voice, but it was definitely not her normal tone. Seldom did we have the chance to talk very long, so we had learned to communicate our feelings quickly in the short periods of time we had. This call was already near its end, and I couldn't feel her at all.

"Is something wrong?" I asked, trying to feel her out.

"No, I'm fine," she said. "Well, sort of..."

"What do you mean, 'sort of'?"

"Well, it's hard to say right now. There's so much we need to talk about, and there's no time. Right?"

"Right. I'm sorry. My time's almost up already. I'm back in Taladega, on my way to Springfield for an evaluation. For some reason, they're keeping me segregated. I only have fifteen minutes, and it took ten to get through to you. It took almost a week just to get to the phone. Anyway, you should have gotten a letter from me by now."

"Yes, I just got it today. I've been gone a few days."

It wasn't like her to be gone at all, let alone "for a few days." Our phone calls, sporadic and infrequent as they were, were too important to miss, especially when I was being moved. When she did go anywhere, it was only to work or grocery shopping. Going away for a few days at this point just wasn't like her. Something was going on.

"Really?" I answered. "Where to?"

"Phoenix."

"How come? Something important come up?"

"Just a seminar, and a chance to get away for a while with a friend. The kids were gone with their dad, and I needed a break. So what's happening with you?

Why all the moving around now?"

"Well, like I wrote you, it's a bigger case than I realized. They're trying to pin some stuff on me that I didn't do, so I'm fighting it. They're sending me for an evaluation because I may use 'Viet Nam Syndrome' as a defense. I wrote to you about it, and about that lawyer in Baltimore who says that approach has been successful in several cases. You know how prosecutors always throw as much at you as they can, then try to get you to plea bargain. If they know I'm going to fight it, they'll finally get real. Don't worry; this will turn out to be a minor thing, I'm sure. I should be back in Arizona within a month or two." She didn't respond. Awkwardly, I continued.

"I don't know when I'll get to Springfield, or how long I'll be here. As long as I'm in isolation, I won't be able to call you. It might be another week or two."

I could feel her holding something back. She was too quiet. I knew that quietness in her, and it spelled trouble. Anyway, who was this "friend" of hers?

"Please tell me what's wrong," I implored.

I sensed what it was before she said anything. She didn't really have to say much at that point. She tried to tiptoe around the issue, but I knew what she couldn't bring herself to tell me. There was somebody new in her life.

"I'm seeing someone," she finally said. "It's just a friendship, but I feel good about it. And I feel bad about hurting you. I don't know how else to tell you."

Suddenly I was lost—cut adrift from the tether that had kept me connected to her. I felt like a space walker with his lifeline to the ship severed. Helpless to do anything to stop it, I watched it pull away and disappear into the darkness. Clinging desperately to the phone, I tried to form the words to bring her back, but my mind was too frantic. I had to fix this before it got worse. I needed to contain the damage, make her feel excited and positive again. I felt myself grasping at threads to hold it together, but I couldn't think of what to say as the seconds ticked away that would close the door to my connection with her. The magic between us disintegrated like a lucid dream shattered by a sudden awakening. My fairytale romance was crumbling into dust, scattered by the winds of fate.

"Time's up," the guard announced flatly as he motioned for me to hang up the phone. My whole world was crumbling, and the son-of-a-bitch couldn't wait to yank away my only hope for saving it. Maybe she had just gotten scared, and now that she had heard my voice again she would come to her senses. There was always a chance. If I could just talk to her a little more, the magic could still work...

"Hang it up, shithead. I've got other things to do."

With all the strength I could muster in those final, fleeting seconds I had left, I had to say goodbye, perhaps for a long while. But how? I couldn't get a sense of her feelings enough to know how to hold onto her. What could I say to reassure her?

It was as if she had just died in my arms and I felt her spirit leave her body. I grasped and I clutched, but there just wasn't anything there. There was nothing I could do. I needed to catch my breath, steady myself. My head was spinning. Suddenly my arms were twisted roughly behind my back as the guard cuffed my wrists and pulled me from the phone. Everything went gray and surreal as I felt my legs move just enough to accommodate the guard's forceful pull toward the corridor and back to my cell.

I was a basket case. When the cell door slammed shut and the key turned, something in me snapped. A garage door appeared in my mind, and I could smell death in the air. In the haze of exhaust fumes, an Altar Boy and Boy Scout stood paralyzed in fear and disbelief. Someone else was needed now—someone tough and strong who knew how to take charge. Death was stalking me, and only one part of me knew how to deal with it.

From the foggy reaches of my consciousness, an entirely different person emerged. I knew him. He terrified me. He was that part of my interior self that was capable of anything. Stepping forcefully into the forefront of my mind, he glared back at me like my usual self was just a clod of dirt on his spit-shined boot. Suddenly I didn't care about anything. It wasn't the emotional upheaval of the moment either, but something cold and ruthless stirring in me. With this one in charge, I knew I could kill without remorse. As I observed this feeling, it strangely intrigued me. Fascinated me. It took my mind off the pain spreading throughout my body.

Yes, I *could* kill—with cold indifference, even. My eyes, I was sure, had grown cold and gray like the steel bars that had become an integral part of my life. I felt the predator within me. If I could look at myself now through someone else's eyes, I would have been terrified. My life in the outside world was over. The Altar Boy and Boy Scout no longer served a useful purpose. They were totally ineffective now, nothing more than useless impediments to the emergence of a destructive force to be reckoned with. God*damn* her and her weakness. *Goddamn them all.*

They were nothing but a bunch of stinking, worthless, mindless sheep. *All* of them. Like in *Jonathon Livingston Seagull*...a goddamn flock of scavenging seagulls—groveling and squawking and pecking at each other for scraps of garbage, every one of them out for themselves. And they had the audacity to lock *me* up? For what? For a bunch of *weeds?* I could have made a difference in their world, but not now. I couldn't care less. *They* certainly didn't. They hadn't even noticed the good I had done, even in *prison.*

Hadn't I towed the line? Hadn't I made the best of every situation in this godforsaken journey? Hadn't I been a model prisoner? Hadn't I shown that I cared about everyone else's problems? Hadn't I proven I was worthy of her love? Hadn't I been a good father to my kids? Why this? Why now? Where the hell was God...witness to it all?

I felt myself plummeting over the edge of an abyss I couldn't describe. I was falling into a darkness I only thought I knew. This was some real shit. I had convinced myself I had become an expert on confinement, but suddenly I was coming to grips with the fact that I had only been dancing around the edge of it. Yes sir, this was some kind of shit. There was no reason to fight it anymore. There was no one to hold back for, or run back to, or convince of anything. I was alone in a thick, soupy fog and I sensed real danger in it. There was no one left now to go to for consolation, or for confirmation that I was okay. Not anymore.

What the hell was going on? What was she doing? Who was she doing it with? We were going to be *married.* That was real, I thought. She even wore an engagement ring, and had sent me a picture of her with it on to show me she meant it. How could she pull out now? Hadn't she said she could wait five years if need be? It hadn't even been *one* year, yet.

Who was she with? Who was pulling her away from me? Was it a sexual thing? A new lover? God, what an agonizing thought to sit with alone in that hellhole. A mental picture began to form in my mind of her with another lover, and deep inside of me the dragon opened its eyes and lifted its head. The picture of her and a lover formed in more graphic detail, and the dragon rose angrily to peer sharply back at me through the thickening fog. The more I looked at the picture, the more the dragon squirmed and twisted in the darkened cave in my mind.

I pictured her pulling multiple lovers lustfully to her. The dragon raged in fury—fire and smoke belching from his nostrils as he was searched through the darkness to find me. Then I felt him slash the veil of innocence I hid under like a child in the night. Suddenly my blanket was gone. The monster was out of the closet, and I was exposed.

Like a jungle cat fixed hypnotically on its hapless prey, he pierced the fog with menacing green eyes that held me transfixed in time. A figment of my imagination, he was nonetheless a formidable foe. I knew I was in for a fight to the death. It was just the two of us, alone in that concrete cell. A terrified young boy suddenly yanked from a dark garage of the buried past was now cringing in the shadow of a killer I had called forth to face the monster I myself had awakened.

On a mythic battlefield in my mind, I stood among the bloodied bodies of others who had tried and failed to face the dragons of their own making. Now mine stood in full fury to consume me. But I had no sword or spear, no weapon to use against him—save for the killer now emerging from inside me.

What I did have were my words. Words and how I had used them had created the whole mess in the first place, but words now formed the mental pictures that were hurting this green-eyed monster. Maybe that was the key. Maybe words could do what weapons could not.

Yes. I could taunt him and wound him with words and mental pictures. I would drive the hurt deep into his ravenous heart until he was too weak to fight. Then I would push them in his face until he was too weak to live. That's how I could do it. I always claimed in romantic moments that I could "slay the dragons" for love. Now I was alone to face the dragon I had eluded for most of my life. But it wouldn't be for love that I would slay this one.

Chapter Thirty-Three

It was dark by the time I'd gotten myself somewhat under control. Only a few hours had passed since I talked with Debra, but every minute had seemed like an hour. It felt like the middle of the night, but the dinner tray hadn't even come yet. It looked like a long time before lights out, and then things would only get worse. I felt hot and flushed.

Damn! I had to *do* something. If I were home right now, I'd be in the car and headed to her place. Of course, if I hadn't left, none of this would have happened in the first place. In futile desperation, I grabbed the doorknob, tried to turn it, and shook it furiously.

What a fool. Jesus! What the hell was the matter with me? Did I really think it would OPEN??

I starting pacing to relieve the anxiety, but the more I paced the more anxious I became. In the dark cave of my mind, the dragon stirred restlessly.

I laid down and tried to close my eyes. *I had to talk to Debra...get her to listen to reason.* I covered my face with my pillow. If I could force myself to sleep, maybe the tension would ease a bit. I could make more sense of things in the morning. But my body was shaking and my mind was running wild. I jumped up and started pacing again.

Three steps to the wall, turn, three steps to the door. Three steps back to the wall, turn, and three steps back to the door. With each three steps, my pace quickened until I became dizzy and nauseous. At least dizziness would get my mind off the anxiety. *Anything* was better than the anxiety and torment I was feeling. It was eating me alive.

Furiously I paced. The more I paced, the more frantic I became. I broke into a run, standing in place. *Maybe I could run this shit out of my system.* I moved my legs at a mind-numbing pace as I visualized a steam locomotive at full speed coming down a mountain grade. That seemed to work for a while. Holding on to the bunk to steady myself, I shifted into a dead sprint as fast as my legs could move.

For what seemed like an hour, I was a marathon runner. The crowd was ecstatic, on their feet, cheering and waving in adulation. I made it across the finish line, and beat all challengers. No one could touch me. My heart was pounding. My body felt like it would explode. I was invincible. Finally I collapsed on the bunk, dripping with sweat and gasping for breath. My gut hurt like a knife was sticking into it, but for the moment I was alive and powerful.

Then it came back. She was home and I was in fucking *jail*. Not jail. *Prison*. How long had I duped myself into thinking I would be home soon? The whole goddamned *year* I had carried on like I was some kind of visitor. "I'll be home any day now," I kept telling everyone. Oh, *sure*... I had convinced myself that this whole ordeal was just another "exercise" to work my way through, just like I had all the other times. I was in *prison*, goddamnit…and still I had myself deluded enough to think it would simply go away soon.

Okay, so I screwed up. But after all, I was still one of the good guys. Guys like me didn't deserve to be locked up. Certainly not in prison, and not like this. What a fool. What a *stupid,* egotistical, pathetic *fool* I had been.

Yeah, she was home right now, probably talking to him on the phone. Maybe he was even there with her right *now. God,* how could I have been so naive? So what if she had stuck it out with me so far? She convinced me she would wait. But then again, I had convinced her I would be out soon.

'Convinced.' I wondered if that was where the term "con" had come from. *Con*vince. I had spent most of my life *con*vincing people I was such a decent person. Teachers. Cops. Women. Priests. Nuns. Even that judge back in Denver. Total *con*…

Jesus! How many goddamned warnings did I have? Three? Four? I had actually been in jail *four times.* You would think that would be enough to wake anybody up. In two cases, the charges were serious enough to put me away for some time. But there was always an element of doubt that I could work to my advantage. I could pour on the charm until they felt they were locking up their own son, or grandson. To some I was Audie Murphie, the war hero. To others, Little Timmy from "Lassie." I could play any role I wanted to from TV shows I'd seen as a kid. I knew them all—from Johnny Yuma to Ricky Nelson to Dr. Kildare. Sooner or later, it always got me off.

Well, how about con*nive*? Yeah, that was closer to it. Conniving bastard…I had even connived my*self.* I was above it all. I had it in my head that I was immune from the shit everyone else had to go through. I hated myself each time

I ran my games, and I swore I would never do it again. "It" was my own brand of addiction. *Now* look at me. How much worse could it get?

"Racketeering," the indictment had said. *Racketeering?* No way. Those guys were *Mafia*—clearly the bad guys. I wasn't any "racketeer." What the hell was the matter with them? I had organized prison self-help programs and juvenile programs, had letters from senators and judges and dozens of respectable citizens. Before I left Pensacola, my lawyer told me 62 letters had been received by the Court from people who praised my hard work and "upstanding nature." Clearly, I was someone who could do something *useful*. Prison was a place to sit and *rot*. It wasn't my nature to sit and rot.

The words came rushing into my head in a torrent of realization of the wake I had left behind me. All words having something to do with the term "con"—not the least of which was to gain someone's *con*fidence.

Convince. Connive. Concoct. Conjure. Condemn. Consort. Conspire. Confine. Convict. *Con*vict. No wonder they called us "cons."

My breathing was almost back to normal, but I could still feel my pulse throbbing in my temples and the sweat running down into my ears. Goddamn, conniving son-of-a-bitch. Yeah, I had "conned" myself. Did I really believe she would stick it out with me?

Yes! Yes, I did. And if I did, then why wouldn't she? Now she was with someone else. We had planned a future together. We were going to do meaningful work as a team. This was going to be the time for me to prove my value. How was I supposed to do that if she was with someone else? Who the hell was this guy, anyway? I wondered if they had made love, yet. Maybe. If not, they would be soon. I felt a rush of pain and anger at the mere thought of it.

The dragon was fully awake now, and peering through the darkness. I curled up on the bunk like a little kid, and hoped he wouldn't notice me. There was a strange silence...not a sound anywhere...out in the hallway or even in the big room where the inmates communed for their daily routines with each other.

I tried to put it all out of my head...tried to think about other things until the danger had passed. I thought about the mountains where I camped, the oceans I swam, the planes I'd flown. I thought about Viet Nam, and every detail of my time there. I remembered the tension I felt on that airliner flying across the Pacific, thinking I would have to run for the nearest bunker as soon as we landed.

But as we made our approach to that war-torn, embattled country, much to my surprise I saw water-skiers on the rivers below, golf courses and well-constructed barracks. But I knew military procedures, and before long I was right there among them. I didn't water ski or play golf, but I knew how to fill out their official forms, and I knew how to connive. I piloted waxed and polished command helicopters for colonels and generals who fought wars on maps and charts in air-conditioned headquarters, whose greatest daily threat to life and limb was crossing the crowded streets of Saigon. I watched more money change hands in the backs of helicopters than bank tellers see in their entire careers.

Yeah, it was a war to save the world for democracy, all right...so politicians and generals and corporate fat cats could play their own brand of games...like so many grown up boys playing war and empire-building with other people's lives.

Explain *that* to the poor bastards I pulled out of hot landing zones...bodies shot up, legs blown off—all of them screaming for their mothers. But in Saigon, a different war was going on. It was a war for money and power and prestige that didn't give a damn about other people's lives. It was all a bunch of patriotic, flag-waving, sentimental crap that enabled them to keep playing their devastating, soul-slaying games all over the world.

But why the hell did that matter to me *now?* I was deep in a war of my own, and I was losing on all fronts. I was under attack...heavy attack...and I was out of ammunition. Call it sincerity, enthusiasm, charm or resilience...I was out of it. I couldn't charm my way to a goddamn *telephone*, let alone out the door or onto the streets. Why couldn't I have *listened* to all of those warnings? How many goddamned warnings did a guy need, anyway? Now I was a prisoner. I was losing her. I was losing my life...my future...and there wasn't a damn thing I could do about it. My kids were scattered all over the country like orphans, my friends and partners were still in shock, and my family wouldn't speak to me. Hope was an unreasonable delusion that I could no longer keep alive.

She was with somebody else now. Yeah, they were damn sure making love. She was beautiful, and she had her needs, too. He would have to be a real simpleton not to come on to her. She was sharp enough to pick someone attractive. She liked strong, masculine men, and she had been in a prison of her own making over me long enough.

The dragon was on his feet now, and glaring through the darkness. His green-yellow eyes were looking right at me. I could feel his rage building.

I imagined her pulling the guy toward her in that sultry style of hers, and unbutton his shirt, quickening her breath in that erotic way that drove me wild. I saw them kiss deeply, both of them working their tongues lustfully into each other's mouths. Then I saw her tugging hungrily at the zipper of his pants.

The dragon roared ferociously, rearing up with wings outstretched and shooting a stream of fire in my direction. But I knew it wasn't only his anger that was driving him. It was pain—mortal pain. I felt it, too. The thought of her in bed with some other guy was killing me.

I got up and paced again. Then I noticed the food tray sitting on the slot in my door. How could I miss that? That wasn't something a guy in solitary would normally miss. The mere unlocking of the flap was usually enough to bring me out of the heaviest sleep. Three meals a day and an occasional peek-in by someone carrying a clipboard, a flashlight or a Bible were the only signs of life in that dismal place –the only highlights of otherwise mindless, endlessly boring, monotonous days. Activity anywhere near my door was never missed. But this time I did miss it. That was scary. Where the hell had I *been?*

I looked at the tray. Normally, I would have been glad to have it. I usually made a big deal of setting it up on the little desk by my bunk as if it were a hospital tray. I would imagine I was recovering from a serious illness, or in a monastery. Being in solitary was more tolerable that way.

But this time I could hardly look at it. I put it on the desk and started pacing again. I tried to work up a hunger that might take my mind off things for a while. But hunger wouldn't come. I kept seeing her with him, and I couldn't keep the pictures from my mind. I couldn't eat, but if I left the food untouched they might start watching me more closely. I didn't feel like dealing with that, so I flushed the food down the toilet and put the tray back into the slot. Then the thought occurred to me that I could do that with every tray until I just wasted away. I had no motivation now to maintain a good attitude. I was ready. I would simply shut all systems down and die.

Yes…I would just stop eating. It wouldn't matter to them if I were lying in bed sleeping, cold and dead. It wouldn't matter to her either, now. My death wouldn't even rate a mention in my hometown newspaper. Who would want to write about a second-rate con-man that had never amounted to anything? Most of the people where I used to live didn't even know my real name, anyway. Who the hell was I to them?

Despair now was turning to terror. This kind of thinking had occurred to me before, but had never gone very far. In all the tight spots I'd gotten myself into over the years, I never felt like I could just give up and quit living. A few times over a lost love affair, the thought had come up and lingered for a day or two, but

I always got through it. This time, there was nothing there to hope for. Nothing but emptiness and hopelessness accompanied this feeling. I knew in that moment I was capable of just checking out. This must be how my father felt when he got into his car that day and took his ride out on carbon monoxide.

I knew now what jealousy was all about. If I were on the outside, I could kill someone over this. In my prison cell, I could only kill myself. This was a pain that had to get out, one way or the other. It was a pain borne of anger and hatred and jealousy all mixed together. I felt them all. I hated her, hated him, hated the system that kept me trapped so I couldn't do anything to fix it.

I had worked damn hard to make a difference…a positive, constructive, *meaningful* difference. Everywhere I went I had kept a good attitude. I spent long hours helping other inmates turn their lives around, improve their outlook and hold their heads up. I had tutored them in grammar and math, and counseled them about family matters and personal growth. I'd put up with more shit from other inmates, and from guards and staff members, than *anyone* deserved. Yet through it all, I kept my attitude open and respectful toward all of them. I stood in waist chains and leg irons in public, and watched children looking at me like I was a murderer. I was dragged through one institution after another, and always kept my head up and my heart open. I never blamed anyone else. So why *this?*

It wasn't fair. She *knew* me. She knew my heart, my hopes, and my dreams. She had been a part of it. The past year, even with imprisonment, had been so uplifting for me. If you told the truth, I was learning, and stood your ground with courage, people would believe in you. Now everything was the *opposite.*

I might actually have to do 25 years. That was unthinkable. Unimaginable. Even the six years I was given was too much to think about. I'd managed to bury that prospect in the back of my mind, and keep my sights on the two years I knew I could work with. That could be considered reasonable for what I had actually done. Now, my last hope for recognition and reassurance had just pulled away from me.

Twenty-five *years.* How could that be possible? Couldn't they see that I hadn't done what they were accusing me of? Where the hell was *justice* in all of this? So I'd screwed up. So what? I wasn't one of the organizers. I didn't kill anyone, or even hurt anyone. Why should I have to do twenty-five years just for hanging out with those guys for a few months? The authorities *had* to know I wasn't one of them. They must be trying to coerce me into doing something for them. They *must* be. But there wasn't anyone left to prosecute, except me. There were two others, but one guy had taken off for Italy about the same time I had gone underground, and they didn't even know about Bill. There was nothing to gain by putting the screws to me now. Maybe it was just their way. Maybe they were so pissed that I ran away that they wanted to bury me, hoping to make an example of me to scare anybody who might even think about trying to split.

No, it was more of a predator thing—going after the weak and injured. In this business, there were predators on *both* sides. Either way, I was fresh meat. Now it looked like I was about to be devoured by the good guys at a time when I was losing the woman I loved. How much weaker could I be now? How much more injured could I be than sitting helpless in solitary confinement while she entertained another man?

Entertained. Nice word for what I knew must be going on. My stomach churned at the thought of it. A few deep knee bends and a bunch of sit-ups took my mind off of it for a while, but still the erotic projections kept flashing back. *God, I was going crazy.* Inside I could feel the dragon thrashing about in fury. Yeah, that was the way to get the bastard. Keep showing him the pictures. The son-of-a-bitch had ruined my life. Whoever he was, and whatever he represented, his time with me was over. He had undermined every good and decent thing I ever tried to do in my life.

He had to go. His destructive nature had influenced my life too long. Family relationships. Business deals. Romantic relationships. School. Jobs. Everything. This twisted part of myself had to have his own damn way, even if it meant destroying everything. Because of him, I had blown every decent opportunity that ever came my way.

What about West Point? That opportunity was an unwitting gift from my father, left behind in his hasty exit. "Sole-surviving son of a military officer" gave me the edge for the nomination. But I let some hard-talking Army lifer scare me away from it. I was too busy living life and playing with fires I little understood.

What about the Merchant Marine Academy? That was an *appointment*—not just a nomination. That would have suited my personality just fine, but I was too good for that. *Merchant marines? What the hell were they, anyway? Didn't sound very military...or ego-enhancing to me.*

And what about that Army scholarship? I won *that* one on my own, and it was sweet. Snatched it right out from under all those ROTC candy-asses with their make-believe medals and spit-shined boots. They learned how to march and how to look good, but I knew how to *be* good—how to salute, how to snap-to and talk to the brass on the review committee. *"Yes, SIR; I know the answer to that question. Would you like it in local or regional terms? No, SIR; I do NOT smoke marijuana...never have, never will. "*

That would have paid all my college expenses for the final two years, made me the Cadet Commander, and given me a Regular Army commission upon graduation. Preferential duty assignments on top of that. Could have gone through flight school as a *lieutenant,* not as a damn warrant officer *candidate.* Would've been damn near as good as West Point, without all the hype and harassment that lifer had warned us about. But no...not *me.* I walked away from something a hundred fifty other cadets would have fought over.

Goddammit! How could I have screwed up so badly? I could have had all the benefits and even more military prestige than my father had. Now, I was on the verge of becoming a career inmate, with my whole life about to go down the drain. *Who the hell was in charge of my life, anyway?*

The dragon was pacing and glaring, but quieter. He seemed pacified as long as I directed my attention to my own misdeeds. Who the hell was he, anyway? What was he all about? What did he want, and how was I going to deal with him? After all, he was just a figment of my imagination. What did I need *him* for?

He stopped his pacing and turned toward me. I saw him in my mind, just as real as if I could reach out and touch him. I *knew* it was just my imagination, but I couldn't shake the terrible feeling that this was real. It was something ancient and mythological—a mystery that I could no longer play with, or avoid. Whatever it was, I knew it could kill me. I was on the edge of something big and powerful, and if I couldn't come to grips with it now, it would be the end of me.

Chapter Thirty-Four

A flashlight beam playing on the wall through the tiny window of my cell door let me know the night watch was on. I felt like a kid alone in a graveyard in the dark of night. My rational self knew there really wasn't anything in there to be afraid of, but the kid in me knew differently. He was terrified. Death was stalking him.

Once, when I was twelve, I really was alone in a graveyard at night. Walking home from a movie, I decided to take a short cut through a nearby cemetery. Among the gravestones, I began to imagine something creeping up on me. At first I was able to convince myself it was only my imagination, but as I continued to walk I couldn't suppress the fear building in my gut. By the time I got to the middle of the graveyard, a wave of terror swept over me. I lost all sense of reason and broke into a run, which only amplified my fear. The faster I ran, the greater the fear. The more the fear grew, the faster I ran. By the time I got home, I was white as a sheet, according to my sisters, and gasping for breath. My heart was pounding so hard that years later I could still remember it as vividly as if it were yesterday.

It was like that now, alone in that dark cell. I was fighting with my imagination over something I knew logically didn't exist, but the fear was just as gripping. Behind it I could feel that same terror building, only this time I had no place to run or hide. I could see the dragon in my mind. The more I did, the more real he became. His presence was amplified by my increasing anger at my dilemma. The more I imagined him, the more I felt he was responsible for the horrendous mess I was in. Twenty-five years…without chance of parole. That was more time than Big Jim had to do for killing four cops.

The dragon was quiet now, lying down in his cave. He even seemed docile, like a dog curled up for a nap. But he wasn't docile, and he certainly was no friend of mine. He had played a big part in this mess, and I wanted to rid my life of him. I sat back on my bunk in the darkness of the cell, closed my eyes and watched him breathing peacefully. I imagined myself creeping up on him to get a closer look.

The thought of Debra and what she might be doing came flooding back. It had to be around ten o'clock where she was, so she might even be in bed with the guy. I knew it wasn't just my imagination, or a jealous streak. I could *feel* it. I knew her too well. Although she had been loyal, I knew she was lonely.

The dragon's eyes opened. He sensed the coming of a new attack.

I pictured her with the guy. I saw them in a passionate embrace, just the way I used to hold her. She would always surrender to me, and let me move her however I wanted. She responded to strong men, and I was certain she had picked one who even at this moment held her in his arms.

The dragon was on his feet, ready for battle. The mental pictures continued.

I saw them in bed, caressing each other just the way she had written she was eager to do with me as soon as I got home. I could smell the oils she liked to use. I could feel the warmth of the tiny room she kept for herself—her "sacred space" where she and I had spent so many nights together. *He* was with her now. *He* was smelling the oils and feeling the warmth of her soft skin. *He* was filling her need, her hunger, her craving to be held and touched and caressed.

The dragon was infuriated. He roared and thrashed about, but not quite as ferociously as before. I thought I detected a hint of a bluff in his tirade, and began to feel a sense of pity for him, mixed with anger. As my anger grew, my fear of him began to diminish. He was hurt by the pictures. As much as I hated to look at them myself, I sensed a chance that they could beat him.

I went back to the pictures again. Daggers pierced the dragon's heart. Anger and outrage over my lifetime of disappointments and heartache surfaced as the dragon thrashed about. Desperate to tear me apart, he charged for me again and again.

We went on and on like that throughout the night and into the next day. Food trays came and went, but I couldn't touch them. I dumped the food down the toilet and continued with the battle. I didn't want to see anyone or talk with anyone. Sleep wouldn't come, except for fitful moments when the dragon and I both dropped from exhaustion.

By the third day, there was still no progress. I was wasted from very little sleep and no food, but much more from fighting this mental battle. Each time I brought up the pictures, the dragon reared up and we would go at it again. I stood in front of him with full-length pictures as if they were a sword and shield. We fought one battle after another until we both collapsed again, exhausted. An hour or two of rest, and we were at it again, always with the same agonizing, monotonous results. Throughout that night and into the fourth day we kept at it, with neither of us able to gain anything.

Near sundown on the fourth day, I awoke from a fitful doze to the sound of activity in the hall. I started to lift my head, but fell back too tired to even care. It didn't matter anymore what they did or what they thought. I looked around the cell. It seemed more than ever like a dungeon. I closed my eyes and tried to imagine where the dragon might be. I pictured him lying apparently lifeless in his cave. His eyes were closed and his wings were folded along his bulbous, sagging, green body. I watched him for a while and wondered if this might be it. Could he finally be dead?

The instant that thought crossed my mind, his eyes opened and he raised his head with a malevolent glare that searched the darkness between us. Lifting his giant body up on his feet, he spread his giant wings and started toward me.

I took a deep breath, then pictured the lovers again, locked in a passionate, naked embrace. Flames and smoke engulfed me as he lunged again. Then I thought of other pictures. I showed him women I had been with in the past––women I had loved and lost over the years. My boys living in northern Minnesota with people they hardly knew, and my little girl crying herself to sleep at night over the disappearance of her daddy and her brothers.

I picked up my pencil and paper, and wrote down every decent thing I had ever tried to do in my life, and pictured it all in a heap of smoldering rubble. A crippling pain shot through both of us. Then I wrote every indecent, stupid, arrogant thing I had ever done in my life. Page after page I wrote as the dragon writhed in agony. Tears streamed down my face. The more I wrote, the more they flowed. My pencil was a sword and each word, each detailed illusion, delusion and misdeed stabbed deeper into his heart. In mortal pain, he withdrew again to a dark part of his cave.

I wrote about the many times I had been warned, the times I found myself on the wrong side of the law, or was caught in a lie. Each time my anguish had been real, but never enough to stop me. The damage I did ran deep, but I had always managed to cover it up with a song and dance, or an innocent face to mask the wrongs I refused to own.

I continued this process until he was spent and could no longer fight. My victory seemed at hand. The dinner tray sat cold and dry in the slot again. I didn't have enough strength to look at it. I was on the brink of total collapse, but somehow I knew he still wasn't dead. I could feel a flicker of life in him, but for now it seemed I might at least get some sleep.

I nodded off. When I awoke, the lights were still on, so I knew it wasn't later than ten o'clock. I couldn't have slept more than an hour or two. The dinner tray was gone and the flap was closed. They didn't notice I hadn't eaten, nor did it seem to matter. I wondered how many uneaten meals it would take before they would finally check on me. Footsteps in the hall meant the ten o'clock head count was underway. The night shift was taking over, and soon the lights would go out. I tried pacing the floor, but barely made it to the toilet and back before the lights did go out. Once again, I was alone in the darkness.

Another long night loomed ahead. I was weak from the lack of nourishment, but weaker still from fighting a battle that wouldn't end. In my mind I saw the dragon lying in his cave, no longer full of fury and rage, but a lifeless mass of reptilian scales and limp, webbed wings. I imagined myself prodding him for signs of life.

Maybe he was finally gone. Was I free of him at last? I imagined moving closer, until I could almost touch him. Up close, he didn't seem so ferocious. One touch, and I would know if he was dead. At that thought, one of his eyes half opened and fixed on me. In that instant I knew that if he'd been real, I would have been vaporized by the fury of his hatred and malice.

Then it dawned on me. It wasn't hatred but fear that drove him. He feared me as much as I feared him. The more I tried to hurt him, the more he tried to hurt me back. He was a mirror of my own suppressed rage and fury. He was *me,* and he was as intent on his defense as I was on his destruction. I backed away as I suddenly realized that we were locked in a battle of mutual destruction. But it was too late. My imagination seized the moment, and fanned the flames of hatred and vengeance once again. His head lifted and both eyes locked on me. He rolled his immense body onto his massive, clawed feet and started for me. Weak and exhausted, but unwilling to give up the fight, I raised an imaginary sword and shield and stood my ground. He towered above me, ready to finish me with one fiery blast.

In a sudden flash of insight, a deeper realization came to me. If he was only my reflection, then "mutual destruction" could also be its opposite. Fear and resistance suddenly left me. A new voice I hadn't heard before told me to abandon the fight and surrender—not to the dragon, but to something vastly more powerful than either of us. Suddenly, I saw myself kneeling by a cool stream of water. The sword and shield lay next to me and I was bathed in bright light.

A calm voice from deep within began to speak to me with profound clarity and kindness. I knew immediately the source of it was very wise. The voice was as distinct and direct as if another person were sitting beside me, talking.

"Have you had enough?" the voice asked.

"What do you mean?" I thought in reply.

"Do you feel you've had enough drama in your life?"

"Yes, of course. But I always feel that way when I'm in the middle of it."

"Yes, but consider where you are now, and what the future holds for you. Do you suppose you could have made it any more dramatic?"

"I suppose I could, but I doubt that I would."

"I wouldn't doubt anything at this point, if I were you. The way things are going, you may be shocked to know what you're capable of. You are certain to find yourself in situations that lead to violence. And that always brings more violence, destruction and outrage. Your present course seems to be eliminating other options, don't you think?"

"Maybe. But I don't think I could actually kill anyone."

"You didn't think you'd be in prison, either…let alone facing 25 years."

"True."

"Most violent people never thought they could kill. You have a good heart and great intentions, but look where you've gotten yourself. If you do 25 years, how long do you think you'll be able to maintain your good intentions? You've seen what others do here to survive."

"Yes, that's true, I have. But I could never compromise my values and stoop as low as I've seen some people go."

"You've already done that, haven't you? Far more than you ever thought you would. And what do you mean, 'these people'? Do you think you're really that much different from them?"

"In appearance, maybe, and in lifestyle, perhaps. But I'll have to admit that I've been surprised at the similarities when I look deeply enough. And yes, I have compromised my values. Is that what the dragon was all about?"

"What do *you* think?"

"Like I just said, I did things I wasn't proud of, and let my ego control my actions. The dragon was just an exaggerated, graphic result of my own self out of control."

"That's close. But what's more important is the situation you've created so you could get in touch with how out of control you were. Few people delve this deep into delusion and can still fathom the causes and effects that put them there. By this point, they're either dead or psychotic."

"You don't think this is psychotic? Fighting for four days and four nights with an imaginary dragon in a prison cell? It's no wonder they're sending me to Springfield."

"No, you're not psychotic. It may feel like that because many people would view it that way. If you were psychotic, you would have killed yourself by now, or someone else would have done it for you. This kind of energy demands an outlet, and it's usually something violent. Wars have been waged with this kind of energy. You know in your heart what this is all about. You created this entire ordeal to work this all out."

"No kidding. So this is *all* my creation?"

"Yes, of course. You've said that yourself, in different ways."

"Yes, I do realize that no one else 'did this to me.' I'm not a victim. But don't you think things are just a bit out of hand on this one?"

"Things are exactly as you want them to be. This is what you needed in order to experience the power of your own mind. It's as *de*structive as it is *con*structive. You needed to see for yourself that this is totally your own creation."

"What do you mean by that?"

"I mean, it's your script, and your stage. You wrote it, you directed it, and you produced it."

"Does that mean I can rewrite it?"

"Good! Yes, you can. But, using that same analogy, you may not be able to get all the actors to go along with you."

"How do I change that?"

"That you'll have to figure out yourself. You certainly can't fire them. That's why you're here, to learn to do things more effectively and *con*sciously, to give you another spin on your "con" word game. You haven't learned that yet because you've always managed to get someone else to do it for you. Now you have no choice but to find your own way out."

"Thanks a lot."

"Don't mention it."

"Is this a joke to you? I'm looking at 25 *years* of hard time to 'find my way out,' as you put it."

"It's not as bad as it seems. Once you figure it out, you'll laugh at yourself. Certainly it's no joke right now, because you're in the worst of it. But you chose this to force yourself to look deep into your own psyche to discover the full range of choices you have. It's nothing you can't clean up and put in order with relative ease."

"Relative *ease?* I'm on my way to the federal *nuthouse,* as a convicted criminal, facing my own execution. And you say I can change all *that* with 'relative ease'?"

"Well 'execution' seems a bit extreme."

"It feels like that right now."

"Good. Maybe it will finally get your attention."

"It did. But the government takes this stuff pretty seriously. *This* is extreme to me."

"Who created it, the government?"

"No, of course not. They created the justice system, but I created the circumstances that sucked me into it."

"Right. And you can create the circumstances to work your way out of it. You just need to do it more consciously, and not by manipulating the circumstances. How long that takes is up to you."

"Really? And I suppose next you're going to say that it could just as well take 25 minutes as 25 years, right?"

"Well, 25 minutes may be a bit unrealistic. It *is* possible, of course, but you might have a difficult time getting the authorities to go along with it. After all, you've entered into something they're rather attached to. The solution is to get them to detach from *you.* That might actually take more like 25 months, in your time."

"Interesting. That seems worth 25 months to learn."

"25 months, 25 years. It's all relative, don't you think? Haven't you been learning that?"

"I suppose so. Sometimes I've felt that minutes dragged like they were hours. But sometimes months have shot by like they were weeks. And some days go by like a few hours."

"You're catching on. The same thing applies to most anything, although you may have a hard time persuading people who have rigid points of view. People get attached to their conditioned beliefs. Once you discover that you made the choices that got you into a situation, you must then take responsibility for your attitude and what may ultimately come from those choices. If you do, you'll learn that *you* are the one that determines what happens in your life."

"I see what you mean. I don't suppose I could speed up the process a little, could I?"

"You just did. But it wouldn't be wise to push it much more. How do you suppose you ended up here?"

"Being in a hurry?"

"To say the least. As you've said so often, you've taken 'Herculean steps' in your life. You missed out on a lot of details along the way. Try taking small steps for a while. Soon enough, you'll be able to take bigger ones."

"Good point. That's certainly enough to work with for a while. What about the dragon? Is he still around?"

"You'll find out soon enough. Just a word of caution, though..."

"What's that?"

"Be careful about using mental or emotional forces to get others to do your bidding. Do what you do because it's right to do it—not because you're able to make it happen. That's what creates dragons."

"I see. Well, seems I have some work to do."

"Couldn't think of a better place to do it, can you?"

"Well..."

"Hey, it beats a dungeon."

"Okay. I get the point."

"Good. You'll do well. Just don't get caught up in the images. This could be exciting."

"*Exciting?* I don't think I can handle much more 'excitement'. I'm ready for something dull."

"Well, how about 25 years of this? Is that enough 'dullness' for you?"

"No, thanks. Let's just settle for a little quiet time for now."

"Good. That's the stuff. Just pay attention. Stay in the present. You've got everything you need inside yourself. Think of this place, and the next ones, as exactly what you need to begin anew to create a life you really want. Who knows? You might actually enjoy it."

With that, the voice was gone. A wave of peace and calmness came over me unlike anything I had ever known. Literally, I felt a rush of cool air move through my body like a breeze. I laid down on my bunk and curled up with my pillow like a little boy in the safety of his own room with the door closed. I couldn't have felt more secure if my mother had just tucked me in and sung me to sleep.

Chapter Thirty-Five

Two more days passed before the buses finally came. Mechanical problems with Con-Air had delayed the plane long enough for me to have had my battles with the dragon under the most "perfect" conditions. Another long day of being processed, riding on buses and Con-Air came as a welcome relief from the "war" I had just fought. I had become so accustomed to the routine, I didn't need to be told what to do or how to do it. Like Big Jim, I kept silent and watched everything and everyone around me through cold, indifferent eyes. No one bothered me. In fact, it was almost as if they wanted to stay out of my way.

My arrival at the United States Federal Prison Hospital in Springfield, Missouri, was surprisingly different. Apart from the usual strip-searches and the tedium of in-processing, there was a much lighter attitude among the guards and staff. It was, after all, a hospital, and according to their own terminology, we were patients...not just inmates. I was there for "observation and evaluation," but as far as I was concerned, I was recovering from major battle wounds. It would take time and a lot of rest to heal. Despite my new revelations and spirited inner dialog, I was still depressed and mourning the loss of a loved one.

Once the in-processing was complete, things actually seemed somewhat mellow. Steel gates dividing the wards and white-shirted officers patrolling the corridors with their two-way radios drove home the point that we were still in prison. But there was a very different feeling in the air.

At first, I wondered if medication was the reason, and panicked at the thought of tie-down straps and forced sedatives. But as I settled in, I realized it was just the relaxed hospital atmosphere. As I was escorted to my assigned ward, I did notice some rooms that had bunks with tie-down straps. I knew those doors weren't left open by accident. The mere glimpse of those bunks left an indelible imprint in our minds of what awaited troublemakers.

It worked for me. I reminded myself that this was still prison, no matter how laid-back it appeared. I was still their property, and they could do with me whatever they chose, at any time. Nevertheless, the guards were unusually respectful. Their firm manner left little doubt that they could be tough, if necessary, but I felt a certain degree of compassion in most of them. I learned later that many were well-seasoned correctional officers who had been selected on the basis of psychological and medical aptitude, rather than their brawn or ability to be authoritative.

The staff and guards at Springfield worked under a different set of priorities. Assigned the task of administering medical as well as correctional attention to hundreds of federal prisoners with maladies from ulcers to AIDS to chronic psychosis, their attitudes were tempered with sensitivity and caring. The result, I noticed, was less need for disciplinary action. As a patient, rather than just another inmate, I felt like a human being instead of a menace to be caged. Most of the inmates bore the same scars and tattoos they did in other institutions, but at Springfield there was no provocation or consequent aggressive behavior. Despite their menacing appearance, most of the prisoners behaved like normal, decent people.

The grounds consisted of an open courtyard less than a quarter-mile around, enclosed by buildings and high, brick walls with gun towers typical of older prisons. As a facility for medical treatment of all federal prisoners, FPH Springfield had to be as secure as the highest security facility in the system. The prevailing attitude of the staff, however, was more like at a minimum-security prison. In my ward, the cells were like rooms, with *real* beds—not just steel bunks with sagging wires and springs. Not only that, I had a room to myself. Except for periods of clinical study or evaluation by the staff, I was free to roam the grounds at will.

My days consisted of long walks through the basement level corridors that connected all the buildings, and on circular paths in the grass-covered courtyard inside the walls. Towering oak, maple and Dutch elm trees dropped the last of their crimson, gold and chocolate-colored autumn leaves onto the grass of the courtyard. In place of feathers, I collected leaves and took great delight in sending them off in homemade envelopes to friends and family. The cool, crispness of the air made my heart ache to be with my family before the onset of another winter.

As the days passed, and the air grew colder, I felt myself more and more withdrawn. I made no attempt to be friendly, and kept largely to myself. According to rumor, Springfield was supposed to be a horror. I wanted to remain as calm and quiet as possible, and not draw attention to myself. This was a place where men were supposedly strapped down on their bunks, and where frontal lobotomies were as commonplace as hemorrhoid removals. But for me, Springfield was restful and quiet…even a bit monastic in nature.

After a while, my inner dialog began again, but this time the messages were more like intuitional impressions. I began to notice that I could feel what someone was going to say or do before it actually happened. Gradually, I came to realize that I wasn't at Springfield simply because the authorities had sent me there. I was there because I needed the time and the right conditions for deep reflection, and to work on a change of attitude that would alter my behavior in a lasting way. I needed a new way of thinking. It was a time to retrain myself to listen and be more responsive to intuitive feelings instead of reacting impulsively to random thoughts and fleeting emotions.

In holdover units and county jails, I couldn't listen to that inner dialog, distracted as I was by my intense fears and influences by other prisoners and the games they played. Mind games, board games and card games—they were all just ways to avoid facing personal issues and the debris left behind from living coercive, manipulative lives. Most inmates were experts at finding excuses for their behavior, and at blaming other people and circumstances for their troubles. There was something inside each of them that few wanted to face. Most kept themselves distracted from dealing with the aftermath of entire lives spent in self-delusion and in the pursuit of instant gratification.

Relationship breakups, I learned first-hand, were good—albeit painful—opportunities to go inside and see who you really are. If it was a particularly close relationship, such as a marriage, the opportunity for self-examination was unwittingly enhanced by the authorities and their way of dealing with the issue. Keenly aware of the potential for erratic or violent behavior resulting from emotional and psychological stress, inmate mail and telephone conversations are carefully monitored for just such reasons. As soon as an inmate's relationship troubles become evident, they isolate the inmate.

The same is true in the event of a death in an inmate's family. Either situation results in automatic solitary confinement for a period long enough to insure minimal potential trouble. Although the immediate threat of violent reaction is avoided this way, the long-term result is usually deep-seated and generally irreversible embitterment that is eventually acted out in unpredictable ways. Unfortunately, people in the outside world end up at the brunt of that seething, long-suppressed rage that often comes within months of an inmate's release.

Springfield had its isolation cells and bunks with tie-down straps, but I still had enough sense to avoid that fate. Had my break-up with Debra happened before Taladega, things might have been very different. In that vulnerable state, I might have gone off on someone...with drastic consequences. But I had finally come to terms with myself. My dragon was no longer a vicious monster I had to slay, but rather had become a friend and ally. In the lonely days of Springfield, as I stayed quiet and "healed," I began to realize that he was my protector—more a guardian than an adversary. If I needed to protect myself, he could be called upon instantly.

The days and weeks passed quickly. The food was good, and my stay at Springfield became a welcome reprieve from the insanity of the rest of the prison system. At least I was rested, well fed and more aware of the cause of my behavior patterns and how to change them. I entered the prison system scared, naive and running on impulse. Now I was calmer, more clear-headed and accepting of my situation. Time spent with the staff psychologists went well, and often resulted in considerable one-on-one time with the chief of the psychiatric wing. Often my "evaluations" turned into deep conversations that went late into the evenings.

Christmas was only two months away. Unlikely that I would get to my designated facility in time to arrange to send anything home, the good doctor arranged for me to have access to the arts and crafts section of the ward, which was normally restricted to inmates requiring intensive mental therapy. Before long, handmade leather items, elaborately beaded bracelets, autumn leaves, feathers and latch-hook wall hangings began arriving in mailboxes of friends and family around the country, postmarked "Springfield, MO."

As I worked on different crafts, I began to open up again to other inmates, and soon found myself actually enjoying the experience. I started attending Sunday services and stayed afterwards to talk with inmates and the Chaplain. Before long, I had access to the chapel and its piano, where I spent countless hours playing the few chords and scales I knew until I could play with my eyes closed.

Before long, I was on my way back to Pensacola. It was late November, and once again—much to my dismay—the plane landed at Oklahoma City. On the way to El Reno, I felt my insides wrenching at the prospect of spending even one more night in its miserable holdover unit. Upon our arrival, however, I was pulled from the mass of prisoners awaiting processing, and taken to their medical unit on one of the upper floors of the main prison building. There, as a "medical transfer" from FPH Springfield, I was put in a large, hospital room to myself, with a real bed and its own private bathroom.

Normally reserved for prisoners recuperating from surgery and serious illnesses, the room was not necessary in my case. I didn't really belong there, but having endured two previous, insufferable stays in the holdover unit that I was now looking down on through the window of a huge room of my own, I wasn't about to bring it to anyone's attention. Except, perhaps, for the Chaplain.

He was delighted to see me again, and chatted openly with me about the ironies and inequities of the prison system. Checking my transfer records, he told me that I had been assigned to the medical unit because the psychiatrist at Springfield had indicated personally on my records that I was to have "privacy and rest." I smiled and told him of the psychiatrist's fascination with my story, and how intrigued he had been with the "battle" I had waged at Taledega. As a doctor, and as the chief psychiatrist at Springfield, his signature carried a lot of weight. That designation stayed with me all the way back to Pensacola, and made things much more comfortable along the way. I was grateful that finally someone in authority understood what I was going through.

As I talked with the chaplain, I noticed that I was sounding more and more like the old-timers that used to tell me stories I found hard to believe. Now, it seemed, I had become just like them. My total time in confinement since my original arrest was just under a year, but it felt more like five. I couldn't believe it had only been five months since I arrived at El Reno the first time. A lifetime had passed in those months. I felt like a battle-scarred veteran, just returning from a foreign war. I wondered what had become of Big Jim in all the years since I met him, and even mused over how we might talk again someday and "compare notes" on our respective experiences. He would be fascinated with all that had taken place with me in such a short time.

I lay back in my bed and wondered if, in fact, I was beginning to "rewrite my script." For many more nights than I cared to count, I had lain awake tossing and turning on hard prison bunks and plastic jail mattresses, wondering how, when, or even if my break would finally come. I thought long and hard about what I would do to make up for the time lost. Then instantly, I heard myself thinking that no time had been "lost" at all. Rather, much inner growth and development had come about because of the journey. I was much stronger now, and more ready to endure the coming challenges. It *was* just a game they were playing, as I had been told in the beginning, and I was just a pawn in it. If I stayed objective, and focused on learning what I could from the process, I might indeed fall from their attention, and could begin finding my way out.

"The solution," I heard myself thinking, "is to stop focusing on *my* problems and to focus on helping others with theirs."

I had thought that was what I had been doing all along, but I realized it wasn't that at all. It was much more because I wanted to impress the authorities so I could earn—or, more accurately—squirm my way out of the system. Now I was much clearer on how to get out. No matter what course my legal action took, I would use my skills and knowledge to assist others in improving their outlook. Whether I did 25 years or 25 months, I would stop thinking about getting *out*, and focus on getting *through*.

When I arrived back at Pensacola in early December, I was a very different person.

Chapter Thirty-Six

The Escambia County Jail didn't feel the same. Neither did FCI Taladega, as I came through it for the third time. I was looking through very different eyes. I stood a little taller, felt more confident and moved more calmly through the routines than when I had left. Lacking only the physical scars and tattoos typical of long-term inmates, I was now a seasoned veteran of the concrete jungle of the correctional world. Adding to my air of confidence was a letter from Debra that caught up with me just before I left El Reno for the third time. She wrote warmly of her recollection of our more tender moments together, and that she missed her contact with me. She concluded her letter with a request that I call her as soon as I could.

As luck would have it, the marshals brought me in just as the prisoners were being fed, so the jail staff was too shorthanded to process me in right away. One of the guards in charge of processing recognized me from my previous stay, so he was somewhat casual as he led me to a small holding cell. When I asked to use the phone, he handed me one on a long cord, locked the cell and walked away. I called Debra, and we talked for nearly an hour before he came back to process me in.

She was happy to hear from me again, and I could tell it was more than casual interest. She had genuinely missed me. She was sorry she had "put me through" so much agony, but felt at the time that it was important for her to break away for her own sanity. In her own way, she had been doing time along with me, and had felt trapped in her own home. When someone with good character came along that showed a strong interest, she was only too willing to be cared for and comforted. The man who entered her life was highly sensitive, caring, and respectful. So respectful, in fact, that he had even written to *me* while I was at Springfield. He had heard about me from mutual friends, and from her, and felt moved to let me know what was going on. Saying that he respected what I was going through, he added a personal request to correspond with him, and to look him up when I got out. We exchanged several letters after that, and have remained best of friends ever since.

At any rate, it was over between them, and she had come to realize that she'd gotten herself too emotionally attached to what was happening with me. We talked as if nothing had changed, and felt that our love had grown stronger because of the experience. My heart was soaring again. It didn't matter at that moment that I was locked in a tiny cage in a county jail two thousand miles from her. It didn't matter that I was facing the prospect of a long prison sentence, or that I couldn't even begin to promise her anything but my deepest love. For the moment, that was enough for her. When I was finally led to my new cellblock, I couldn't have been happier if I had the whole place to myself. I was in love again.

Two weeks passed. My new cellblock was just as chaotic as the previous one, but this time I had very little trouble with cellmates. There was something about being perceived as a "seasoned" inmate that made an impact. I began to understand why so many inmates wore fearsome tattoos. Now it was as if I wore invisible tattoos of my own that could be felt rather than seen. There was little opportunity to speak with Debra on the phone again, but her letters began to catch up with me. It seemed as if everything was back on track.

Time passed slowly. The cellblock was identical to the last one I was in, and the routine was exactly the same. Even some of the guards were the same. Except for different cellmates, and the fact that I *knew* I had been to Springfield, it was as if I'd never left.

One day, a correctional counselor I had talked with on my previous stay came to the cellblock. Just like Gordon back at BCDC, he was responsible for educational services there. I told him of my experience in Albuquerque, and that I would like to try the same thing there. He was skeptical, so I gave him the information he would need to verify what I had done. A few days later, I was taken to his office. After he had the cuffs removed, he talked openly about the problems they were having with their program. My references were good, he said. So good, in fact, that it was startling. He said he had been told about my juvenile diversion program, and about Senator Goldwater's interest. He had called the Senator's office and confirmed that the Senator had indeed taken a "keen interest" in the program, but because of his wife's serious illness that summer, the Senator had just retired from office.

The counselor wanted to know what I had done in Albuquerque that was so effective in changing prisoner attitudes and gaining such political attention. I explained what I had personally experienced in my own incarceration, and how that had given me a better understanding of the causes of criminal behavior. Once I understood that, it was easier to understand the nature of the inmates I was dealing with. I had learned to look beyond the outward images, no matter how tough or challenging they appeared.

He was intrigued. We talked for most of the afternoon, and almost lost track of the fact that I was still an inmate. For a moment, I almost felt as if I could have just stood up and walked out of his office into the outside world. The next day, he had several G.E.D. manuals and basic books on math and grammar brought to the cellblock. Within a couple of days, I had three inmates studying with me, and several others curiously hovering around but acting like they weren't interested.

My lawyer finally came to discuss my case with me. The next pretrial hearing was only a few days away. Still reluctant to mount an aggressive defense on the "PTS Syndrome" motion, he pushed me to make a deal. The only way the motion could work would be to prove that other cases had been successfully overturned using that tactic, and then be able to establish a strong parallel in my case. He would have to convince the judge that it was a reasonable and viable defense. My intuitive sense of his reluctance, however, was that he wasn't in the judge's good graces, and didn't want to rock the boat. For that reason, and the possibility that he had made some kind of arrangement with the prosecutor's office, he felt my best course of action was to cop a plea to reduced charges and run the "minimal risk," he said, of increasing my total sentence by five years. Evidently, he had had a lot of hard-case clients in the past, because he didn't seem to feel that five years was all that much. He didn't think too much of my suggestion that we trade places for a year so he could develop a better feel for what he was pushing me to accept.

Back in my cell, I contemplated what I was up against. I still didn't have much going for me. Nothing compared with what the prosecutor had. But there were a few things. The most significant was my attitude, and the powerful effect it had on others. Despite extreme challenges, gross ignorance and abusive behavior on the part of guards and inmates alike, I had managed to avoid conflicts. In every possible case, I chose to see something behind the anger and hostility displayed. The results were often astonishing.

One day, I was waiting to use the telephone on the outside of the tower, the only one available for use by all 48 inmates on that floor. To gain access to the phone required a two-to-three day wait on a list kept by the guards in the tower.

Calls were limited to ten minutes, no matter who you were calling. It didn't matter if it was an attorney, a spouse or the President. Ten minutes was the limit. Some guards enforced the time limit, others didn't. If the guard on duty happened to be in a good mood, or favored a particular inmate, the caller would be allowed to stay on longer. When that happened, which was frequently, it caused tension among other inmates waiting to make their calls.

Two days had passed since I submitted my request, and it was late in the third afternoon. I was going crazy with anticipation. I hadn't spoken to Debra in two weeks. I was anxious to find out if anything had developed to get the Baltimore attorney involved in my case.

Finally, the first name from our cellblock was called. The guard apparently favored some of the inmates, or perhaps thought he was doing us a favor by allowing us talk at length. The afternoon dragged on, and the tension climbed to a boiling point. Dinner came and went, and with it, a change of guard.

The night guard was an older man, a particularly serious, no-nonsense type. He always had a tight, hard expression on his face, and never deviated from his routine. That night he sat in the tower reading intently, never even looking up until nearly 7:30. Tension in our cellblock was extreme. Inmates began to pound on the window, which only made the guard angry. My attempt to convince the inmates we had to remain calm was met with hostility and contempt. Still the guard kept reading, as if we weren't even there. Tempers were at a flash point.

Two *hours* had passed since dinner, and still the phone went unused. Clearly, he was tormenting us, or getting even for the pounding on the cellblock window. We'd all been on the list for three days waiting while all three of the other cellblocks made their calls.

Finally, the guard grudgingly called out the next name on the list. One by one, each inmate took his turn on the phone. After five names had been called, I was in a tizzy. It was already 8:30, and the phones were turned off at 9:00. I had to be getting close. With the tone set by the previous guard's laxness, inmates pushed beyond their ten-minute limit. With each infraction the new guard dealt with, he became noticeably more irritable. I watched his facial expressions as each inmate finally hung up the phone and returned to the cellblock. I could tell he was angry.

I looked at the clock. It was five minutes before nine. My name was finally called. As strict as he was, I had a feeling he wouldn't allow me the full ten minutes, but if I refused to take my turn, I ran the risk of my name being dropped from the list and I'd have to start all over again. Five minutes with Debra would be worth it, just to connect with her. I could sense that she was anxious to hear from me.

I hustled to the exit cage of the cellblock, and stood at the inner door until the guard pushed the button to open it. The massive cage door slammed open. I stepped inside. The electric motor whirred again, and the door closed slowly behind me. Another motor whirred, and the outer Plexiglas door to the hallway opened. With precious seconds ticking away, everything seemed to be in slow-motion.

Three steps, and I was at the phone. I dialed the number. The operator came on the line, took my name, and tried to put the call through. It was busy. I waited a few seconds, then dialed again. Another operator came on the line. Still busy. The big clock in the hallway said 9:00, straight up.

I tried again, my heart pounding wildly. I was certain my name was scratched off the phone list by then. I wouldn't have another chance for days.

Finally her phone rang, followed by Debra's sweet voice. The operator told her it was a collect call. Would she accept? I was going crazy.

"Yes, absolutely!" came Debra's gleeful reply. I was delighted to feel her ecstatic response, yet flustered and angry at being forced to cram everything I wanted to say into a scant few minutes...maybe even seconds, now. Sure enough, we were only a few sentences into our conversation when the guard rapped on the window of his little tower and signaled for me to hang up. It was 9:02. He wasn't going to allow me the full ten minutes. *Son-of-a-bitch!* I didn't even get *five* minutes, let alone ten. I was torn apart. I couldn't just hang up cold, so I took an extra minute to explain what was happening and say goodbye. She couldn't believe I had to hang up. Again the guard rapped on his window, this time more forcefully. I reluctantly said goodbye and hung up the phone.

In disbelief, I walked angrily to the door of the cellblock. Behind me I could hear the guard rapping on his window again. I turned and looked at him, feeling such bitterness that I had to fight back the urge to show my contempt for his unfairness. Sternly, he motioned for me to come around to the door of the tower. As I did, he opened it slightly and handed me a yellow form that looked like a traffic ticket. At the top, in bold print appeared the words "**Disciplinary Report**."

"What's this?" I asked, puzzled.

"It's a 'D.R.'," he shot back at me tersely. "A Disciplinary Report. You abused your phone time."

"But I didn't even get ten minutes!" I protested. "It's only five minutes after nine right now," I said as I pointed to the large clock.

"I don't care," he said flatly. "You know the rules. Phone's off at nine o' clock. Besides, I signaled you to hang up. That was an order."

"I DID hang up. It took me a minute to say goodbye. I couldn't just hang up in the middle of her words. Besides, you didn't even call me out until five minutes before nine. Then it took a couple of minutes to get through. Give me a break, will you?" Somewhere deep inside of me, an angry dragon raised its head.

"I'll give you a break, all right. I'm adding "Insubordination" to that D.R."

"What?!? What's the matter with you? I haven't done anything but try to talk to my fiancé. Why do you want to give me such a hard time? A D.R. will ruin my record in here." The dragon rose, ready to do battle with this insolent, insensitive bastard.

"I don't give a shit about your 'record'. Neither do you, or you wouldn't be in here in the first place. I'm sick of you inmates always violating phone privileges and acting like a bunch of animals."

"Well, if you wouldn't TREAT us like animals, maybe we wouldn't need to act like animals," I raised my voice at him.

"You get back in your cellblock or I'm throwing you in the hole. How do ya' think that'll look on your precious record?"

His face reddened, and his fist clenched the door handle. I stepped back a bit. I could see that I had pushed him too far. My dragon was ready for a fight, and I was ready to let him loose. But I could see I was heading for trouble fast. Behind the Plexiglas windows of the cellblocks, inmates had gathered and were watching intently.

I backed away a little further, straining with all my might to keep from saying anything more. The cellblock door slid open, and I retreated into the cage. The outside door closed, and the inner cage door slid open. I stepped into the cellblock greeted by the gaping stares of a few of the inmates, and the snide grins of some who loved to see other people miserable.

I was stunned. This was an outrage. He couldn't possibly be taking such harsh action over something so trivial. This would ruin any chance I had of proving to federal authorities that I was a "model prisoner." I had worked damn hard on that, and it wasn't just for the image. It was real.

The next night, I was visited by a sergeant and another officer, who presented me with two more citations, one for "disrupting the safety and security of the cellblock," and another for "threatening an officer." The latter was one of the worst offenses an inmate could be cited for, and carried the most severe penalties. I was instructed to appear at a hearing the following week.

I was devastated. I felt such anger toward that guard, I knew now why some inmates had violent outbursts. In that moment standing outside his tower, I could have wasted him if I had had the chance. I had long ago accepted the circumstances of my confinement, including the prison guards. I understood the nature of their personalities and their beliefs. I had reached a point of accepting the most illogical and prejudiced attitudes, but this had gone too far.

Fortunately for both of us, he was off for the next two days. By the time he reappeared in the tower, I had managed to gain some control over my emotions—enough to consider why he did what he did, and what his life might be like on the outside. He was miserable, I decided, and had to have something terrible eating inside of him to have so much hatred and contempt for us. By the time I saw him again, I had actually begun to feel sorry for him, and much of my own anger had begun to dissipate.

During the next few days, I watched him and tried to feel what he might be feeling. Even from a distance, and through the two Plexiglas barriers that separated us, I could see the tightness in his face. I could feel the anger pent up in his body. The way he spoke to everyone was an indication of some deep pain he was carrying inside. I tried to see him as a little boy, and imagined being his father trying to comfort him.

Several times when we lined up in the hallway outside the tower to be escorted to the dining hall, I looked at him with compassion and a sense of interest in how he was doing. Although I couldn't voice my feelings, nor give the impression I was playing up to him, I could at least send him a nonverbal message that I cared. A couple of times he looked at me as I was looking at him. Once I thought I could make out just a hint of softening in his eyes.

The time for the hearing came, and I appeared before a "courtroom" of uniformed jail deputies. It was presided over by a sergeant, who sat like a judge high above everyone. This was the closest I had ever come to witnessing a "kangaroo court." On either side of the sergeant sat two corporals, one a woman. I had heard about these hearings—the outcome, of course, always being in favor of the guards. Inmates could count on a severe penalty. Considering what was at stake, and their need to maintain their dominance over greatly outnumbered odds, the outcome was totally predictable.

A very stern-faced male corporal read the citations. It could have been a TV sitcom, except that the punishments were no joke. Like a bunch of grown-up kids playing judge and jury in a mock courtroom, they sat in pious judgment of a situation that none of them had any inclination to understand. I couldn't believe they were taking themselves so seriously, or that *anyone* would.

When the corporal finished reading, the sergeant looked down at me, and asked how I wished to plea—as if it really made any difference. I purposefully hesitated long enough to make sure I had their full attention.

"Guilty," I replied. They were taken aback by the ready admission. Inmates *never* admit to anything. I let my statement hang there for a minute, then continued.

"But I'd like to make a comment, if you don't mind." I looked directly at the sergeant, who suddenly appeared uncertain. He looked nervously at the papers in front of him, then at the two corporals on either side of him. I directed my gaze at the woman corporal, who looked back at me, then at the sergeant. She shrugged her shoulders.

"Go ahead, but keep it short. We've got other cases to handle yet."

"I *am* guilty of having abused my telephone privilege," I said, "in that I took two extra minutes to hang up. And I'm guilty of having talked back to the officer. He was under a great deal of stress, and I took his actions personally. I didn't get my full ten minutes on the phone, and I tried to protest that. Whatever the penalty is for having done so, I accept the consequences and I won't let it happen again. But as for the other charges, I must tell you that they are not true."

I could see them tighten up and glance at each other. I knew I was pushing it, but before the sergeant could stop me, I went on.

"But I will also say that I don't blame the officer for feeling as if things might have escalated quickly. Inmates were watching, and he was stressed and angry. I'm sure he felt on the spot and that he needed to set an example. In that sense, I can understand what you all must feel at times. But I think it's important to point out that not every inmate in here is ready to go off on you at any moment. In fact, very few will. What you feel is what we feel…tension, amplified by everyone's attitude toward each other. It's hard enough to be in here for *all* of us, even you, too. But when everybody anticipates the worst from each other, it makes it doubly hard on everyone."

I waited for a moment to see what effect it was having on them, then continued.

"The truth is, that officer may have *felt* threatened by the circumstances, but it didn't come from me. It was the aggravation he felt from everybody going over their time limit, compounded by his anticipation of trouble. He's normally a decent person, and treats us respectfully."

That was stretching the truth a bit, but I didn't think it could hurt under the circumstances.

"That's actually a greater deterrent for trouble," I continued, "than being hard on us. So I meant him no harm or ill will. I was just the 'last straw' in a long, hard day for him."

Everyone was silent for a moment, not knowing what to say. Finally, the sergeant asked me to step outside and wait. The inmates waiting outside quizzed me, eagerly wanting to know how it went. No one ever came out of one of these hearings without at least some time in the hole. After a few minutes, the door opened and I was told to retake my seat.

"The court finds you guilty on all counts," the sergeant announced. My heart sank. Visions of weeks in the hole flashed in my mind. My record was ruined.

"However," he continued, "we find you to be clear of any *intention* of wrong-doing, and therefore suspend any penalties. If you remain free of further incidents during your time here, we will drop it from your record. If there are any further infractions, we will impose the maximum penalty on all counts."

I was escorted back to the cellblock, where I was met with mixed feelings by other inmates. I was relieved not have to go to the hole, but I could tell that a few of the inmates were suspicious when I wasn't punished. I didn't see that guard again for a while. Evidently, they had moved him to another floor to avoid any further problems, or signs of weakness on their part.

My next pretrial hearing was set for early the following week, but was post-poned by the prosecution. No date was rescheduled, so I was brought back to the jail with no indication of what would happen next. I had waited for four hours in the courthouse holding cell for nothing. I was not in a good mood. As my escort and I waited at the elevator to return to the cellblock, we heard a yell from the other end of the corridor. It was the guard I'd had my altercation with. I tensed slightly as he walked briskly up to us and instructed my escort to let him take me back to the cellblock. He acted tough and appeared as though he had a personal reason to take me back. My escort smiled wryly and turned me over to him.

Once in the elevator, the guard turned to me and asked, "How was court?" I was surprised at his pleasant, even sincere tone.

"It was postponed," I answered cautiously. "It'll be at least two more weeks before I'll even know if there will be a trial. Maybe longer."

"Yeah, it's a bitch, I'm sure," he said. "I'm sorry I made it any harder for you."

I was stunned. They *never* admit that they've done anything wrong, much less *apologize* for it.

"That's okay," I reassured him. "It was a good lesson for all of us, I think. All that's really important is that we at least try to understand each other's problems. A little compassion never hurt anyone."

"Yeah, I know," he sighed. "In my case, I've been having some health problems, and some trouble at home that's been festering for a long time. I guess I've been taking it out on inmates here. I've made it pretty rough for a bunch of them."

"Well, at least you're aware of that now. Maybe you can find a way to do your job without feeling like you have to be so hard on them. It might even help at home. It's amazing how that works."

"You might be right about that. I may give it a try," he sighed.

"I think you just did."

A trace of a smile flashed across his face as the elevator door opened. We walked out onto the main floor and down the hallway to the tower and the cellblocks. He removed my cuffs and stepped up to the tower.

"This inmate is returning from federal court," he announced authoritatively to the guard in the tower. "He's allowed to use the phone for as long as he needs it." To emphasize the significance of his apology, he reached over, lifted the receiver from the cradle, and handed it to me.

"Have a nice talk with your fiancé," he said, and walked away.

Debra was home, and we talked for most of the afternoon.

That experience gave me great hope, and showed me that there were prisoners on both sides of the wall.

Chapter Thirty-Seven

Two weeks later, the third pretrial hearing was held and with it another chance to watch the prosecutor move me ever closer to becoming a career prisoner. The judge called the hearing to order, announced the docket number, and stated once again that it was me against the entire United States of America. I stiffened at the sound of his steely voice, and a pain shot through my heart to hear those words once again. Cold and stern-faced, he flipped through the pages of the psychiatric report while we all sat quietly waiting for him to continue. Certainly he had read the damn thing by now, but judges seem to love to hold their courtrooms in suspense.

Finally, he looked across the room at my lawyer and spoke as if no time had passed since the previous hearing four months ago.

"It says here, Counselor, that your client is just fine. In fact, their Chief Psychiatrist writes personally that he was an 'exemplary' case. What do you make of that?"

"No surprise to us, Your Honor," Nathan replied smartly. "He is a very capable young man. *Now.* But it's not his *present* state of mind that's at issue. It's a question of what his state of mind was at the time of his involvement with the organization." At last it appeared my attorney was beginning to work on *my* side.

"We don't have the means to determine what his state of mind was at that time, nor does the Court deem that to be of concern in this matter. He's competent to stand trial *now*, and I've had enough delay in this case. Counsel for the People, are you ready to proceed?"

"Yes, Your Honor, we are."

"Then let's get on with it. Call your next witness."

"The People wish to call Leonard Wilcox."

A thin, balding man rose in the back of the courtroom and came forward. He wore khaki pants and a dark, plaid shirt, and reminded me of a man likely to be found sitting on a stool at a roadside cafe drinking coffee and chain-smoking cigarettes. A deputy held the gate open for Wilcox to take the witness stand. As he passed the defendant's table he looked at me and smiled as if he knew me. It was a well-rehearsed smile. Although he looked slightly familiar, I didn't recognize him. He was so ordinary looking, he could have been any one of dozens of men I had seen in my travels.

After a few questions from the prosecutor, I began to recall seeing someone briefly who resembled Wilcox on the strip during the DC-6 landing. I didn't know his name nor had I ever spoken with him. Carefully and methodically, the prosecutor asked him all the right questions, extracting from him the answers that placed me squarely in the middle of everything. Wilcox testified that he had seen me issuing instructions to his "bosses," and that I had been referred to by all the others as "the boss from Miami."

Again, it was clear to me that his responses were scripted and rehearsed. Most of his testimony would be thrown out at a trial as hearsay, but it would be certain to come up if this went to trial. Even if my attorney's objection was sustained, the implication would remain in the minds of the jurors as one more incriminating factor.

One by one, the prosecutor called more witnesses to the stand. Every one of them identified me as "one of the bosses." Of course, each of them had received probation or short prison sentences in exchange for testifying in the exact manner laid out by the prosecution. They were local people, with local ties, who had done their time by then. They had "paid their dues," and had long since been back at work in the community. Even the Old Man's high-powered lawyers had been unable to discredit them at the original trial. The jury would be comprised of local people, some of whom might even know the witnesses personally.

Despite my dilemma, I had to admit I still admired the prosecutor. The fact that I was on the run after my sentencing had him convinced I was one of the core group. I could have been the perfect witness for him against the rest, but I had disappeared. That was the fatal step, as far as his side was concerned. In his world, there was no in-between. You were either for the government or against it. It hurt me deeply to sit at the defendant's table and watch him convincingly portray me as an *enemy* of the people when I had risked my life numerous times fighting for those "people." When he looked in my direction, I tried to look beyond the uncaring, mechanical demeanor he displayed in the courtroom. I tried to sense what he was really like. What kind of father was he? Did he have kids like I did? Did he give them kind and loving attention? Or was he constantly at his law books, fighting the criminals of the world? It was difficult to experience him building a case against me so devastatingly, and at the same time imagine him as a father at home, bouncing children on his knee.

Finally, he was through. One witness probably would have been sufficient, but he had six. And those were just the local ones. Their testimonies added to those of the New Mexico authorities, and the local merchants who had testified earlier of my presence in their town before and during the event. This was overkill, as far as I was concerned. It was also Friday afternoon, and the judge was tired.

"If you have no further witnesses," he directed his statement to the prosecutor, "then Court will recess until Monday at 10 a.m. I will render my decision at that time. Court's adjourned."

After dinner, I laid back on my bunk amid the usual noise in the cellblock and tried to focus on next Monday. The judge was certain to bind the case over for trial. The prosecutor clearly had sufficient evidence to put me away, and showed not a hint of letting up on me. How would I convince any jury I wasn't guilty? My actions during and before the DC-6 event had resulted in success for the operation. But I could honestly say I hadn't done all that the prosecutor was charging me with. I damn sure hadn't been involved for the seven-year period he was alleging. Of course, he believed that I had. Government officials always assume offenders have been involved in much more than the evidence shows. I couldn't blame the prosecutor for assuming the worst.

Even though I wasn't guilty of all that I was charged with, I was ultimately responsible for pulling it off. And I had to admit there were a string of "misdeeds" in my life that I never had come to terms with. Although I hadn't actually cultivated a criminal career, the fact was I had danced around it most of my life. I had deluded myself into believing I wasn't really a "criminal," yet down deep inside I knew I couldn't call myself innocent.

The way I had lived my life was worse than being one or the other. Each side had reason to distrust me. For that I was about to pay a very heavy price—spending the next 25 years of my life in prison. Other prisoners would know, just as I knew, that I didn't really fit. I would not be trusted unless I acted like them, talked like them and even looked like them. I was being forced by circumstances to *become* more of a criminal just to survive. I could no longer play on the fringes. I had to face it—I *was* a criminal. Even though I had maintained a front of decency and innocence in my "normal" life, I had a criminal element active within me.

It was to that part of me I defaulted for quick money, adventure, or intrigue with the darker side of life. I could not deny that punishment was in order, and the time had come to pay the price. But twenty-five *years* was more than I felt was fair.

All these thoughts were going through my head when two guards appeared outside the cellblock door. One of them had a clipboard, which indicated something official was happening. They spoke with the tower guard for a few minutes, then turned and stepped up to the main door of our cellblock. Then the door of the inner cage opened, indicating someone was being taken out. A few seconds later I was startled to hear my name called.

"Dispensary call," the tower guard announced. Everyone looked at the two guards standing outside the main door, then back at me. It was just before 9:00 PM—a little late at night for a dispensary call.

I had no idea what this could be about. I looked around the cellblock, and saw that everyone was staring at me. Again, the tower guard called my name.

"Dispensary call," The guard repeated more sternly. "You've got an appointment to see the Doc. Let's go."

I knew of no such appointment. I wasn't the least bit sick, nor had I requested any medical attention. What the hell was this about? I shoved my things under my bunk, put on my jail slippers and stepped into the cage. The inner door slammed shut, and the outer door opened. In the hallway, the two guards placed the cuffs on my wrists and led me to the elevator. From there we went to the ground floor, then down a corridor that led to the front entrance. We weren't going to the dispensary at all, but to the change-out room. At nine o'clock on a Friday night, this was highly unusual.

We turned the corner by the holding cells and came face to face with two U.S. Marshals holding leg shackles and handcuffs. My escorts turned me over to them and walked away. It appeared that we weren't going to the change-out room, either.

"Let's go," one of the marshals said sharply. I looked at them in bewilderment, then down at my jail clothes.

"You're not going far," he said. "You won't need to change clothes." I was perplexed and apprehensive. I had come to accept just about any sudden change of direction, but this was not like the others. Was I being set up for some bizarre "attempt to escape" routine? That seemed unlikely, but what else could they want with me at that hour?

With no further comment, they each grabbed one of my arms and pulled me toward the door and out to their waiting sedan. Obviously, there would be no discussion about this. Driving out of the detention center, they turned and headed downtown. It was so interesting to see downtown Pensacola bustling with people. Nightlife was in full swing, with music blaring from bars, sailors walking on both sides of the streets, and cars full of teenagers everywhere. I slumped down in the back seat, unable to comprehend this bizarre development.

The sedan turned down one of the busiest streets in the central district of town, and there ahead of us was the U.S. Courthouse. It was dark and closed, but high in one of the upper-story windows, a light burned in one of the offices. The marshals drove around to the back entrance, parked and then opened the back door for me to get out. Using their keys, they opened the back door of the courthouse and rather forcefully pulled me inside. I knew their offices were in the building, so for them to be there wasn't so unusual. But what the hell did they want with *me* at that hour of the night?

Down the corridor we went, past the darkened courtroom where earlier that day my case had gone from bad to worse. It was an eerie feeling, shuffling by it in chains and shackles at night. Except for the chains and the marshals, I felt like a burglar. At the elevator, one of the marshals pushed the "up" button, and we waited as casually as if this were something they did every night. The door opened and we stepped inside. One of them pushed the button for the third floor, and up we went. When the elevator stopped, we stepped out into the corridor and made our way to the office with the light on.

On the translucent window of the door, in aging but distinctive, gold leaf letters appeared the words "**United States Attorney**." The marshal pushed the button on the intercom and waited. A man's voice answered, and the marshal identified himself. A buzzer sounded, and he pushed the door open. Beyond several rows of desks was a corner office with the door slightly ajar.

"Come on in," called the voice from inside, as warmly as if he were expecting an old friend. The voice was disturbingly familiar.

The marshal pushed the door open and motioned for me to enter. Sitting at his desk with his feet propped up on a stack of files was my prosecutor. Well-worn shoes with small holes beginning to form in the soles accentuated his down-home attitude as he instructed the marshals to take my chains off and wait outside. His lanky body was stretched back in an old leather chair that creaked as he leaned back to wait while the marshals removed the chains. After they left and closed the door behind them, he spoke to me.

"Would you like a cup of coffee?" he asked cordially as he swung his long legs down from the desktop without disturbing a single piece of paper, rose and moved toward the coffee maker.

"Sure." I hadn't had a cup of real brewed coffee since Springfield.

"Please sit down," he invited warmly, as he motioned me toward a heavy leather chair in front of his desk. He placed the coffee on the corner of his desk for me to reach, then stood back for a moment and looked down at me. His sleeves were rolled up, his tie was undone, and he looked for the moment more like an overworked bookkeeper than my courtroom adversary.

"Would you like to talk?" he asked me as casually as if he had asked me if I wanted cream with my coffee. His question had a much deeper significance to him than simply to pry information out of me. All the major figures in this case were already locked up. He had a 7-0 record so far, and my case was certain to make it 8-0.

I sensed something more than that. There was a strong hint in his voice that he wanted more than just extra ammunition with which to bury me. For an instant, I felt a hundred voices inside of me screaming, "YES! FOR GOD'S SAKE, YES!!" But I took a deep breath, and exhaled ever so slowly while I listened inwardly for the one voice I needed to speak for me. When I was satisfied that the prosecutor's intention was clear, and that the right voice in me would do the talking, I answered.

"Yes, I would...of course. In fact, I've waited for a long time to be able to tell someone with real authority the story. But why, exactly, do you want to know?"

He looked at me for a long time, weighing carefully what he wanted to say. Seldom ever does a prosecutor have a chance to speak directly with a defendant in a case without attorneys being present, or a tape recorder running. I glanced up at the overhead lamp and around the desk, not wanting to show undue alarm or nervousness.

"It's not being recorded," he addressed my apparent show of concern. I knew he was telling the truth, even though alarms were flashing wildly in every part of my psyche. A year of conditioned fear and suspicion had me intensely apprehensive of anyone's motives.

"You're in a lot of trouble," he said flatly. As if I didn't know that by now. His tone was sincere, however, so I sat back and listened quietly as he went on.

"I've been reading over your file. In fact, I've read your file quite a bit over the years. I probably know you better right now than your own mother, judging from what I've read. You did yourself a lot of harm by taking off like you did. It didn't have to come out like this, you know. From what I've read, you had a pretty decent record until this. You're even something of a war hero, according to your military record."

He paused to see how I would react to his warming up to me. He was very smooth, and clever. He knew how to ease into your mind and disarm you, even though he carried the power to destroy you. I took another deep breath, and then answered very cautiously.

"I wanted it to come out differently, of *course,* " I said. "But you guys don't seem to know what each other is doing. One agent wants this, another wants that. In between, personal egos get in the way and each guy wants what *he* thinks is best. What that really means is 'what's best for *him.*' Lives get snuffed out like that. My children came damn close to it, and others as well...myself included. I may have crossed the line, but ultimately people like us are just pawns in a much bigger game you people play that even you can't control. In the long run, no one seems to know who is on which side."

He thought about that for a while. "Yes, that may be true. But I think we could have taken care of you. You didn't have to spend any time inside, you know."

"Maybe *now* I know that, but not back then. That was hinted a couple of times, but never in a way that I could trust. There were some off-handed comments, obscure hints of '*maybe we can talk to the judge*' and '*we might be able to get you a reduced sentence,*' but that's all. I had four years coming—that's all I knew for sure, which I was fully prepared to do once the shock of the sentence itself wore off. Nobody told me about only having to do a third of it. I learned that after I was picked up and had a chance to do some reading in a law library at one of the many nice places you guys provided me.

"When I did meet with investigators, all they wanted to know was information I didn't have. Local stuff I didn't know anything about—to cover their own backyard. They didn't care about me or my family. Once they found out about the Miami connection, they tried to make it look like *they* had done all the work—like they were dragging the information out of me. They didn't care about you, either...or about how their self-serving interests might adversely affect this case."

"I suspected that. That often happens when different agencies get involved in overlapping cases. A lot falls through the cracks."

"Well, my kids and I just about fell through those 'cracks.' That's why I had to run. I hadn't even told them anything substantial yet, and they leaked information all over town. They were either plain stupid, or they thought it might intimidate me into giving information I didn't have. If that was true, that was a hell of a way to treat a potential witness. I had bricks thrown through my window, threatening phone calls, and my boys had been harassed coming home from school. That was idiotic, if you ask me."

"Maybe so. But you could have gotten in touch with someone in all that time you were on the run."

"Like *who?* Who do you trust when you're a convicted felon and a fugitive to boot? How was I to know who was on whose side, anyway? It was one of *your* guys who leaked the information about me. A *federal* parole officer. He told two of his parolees and the word was out that I was an informant. That's *bullshit.*"

"I understand. That was most unfortunate, but that's what comes with playing this game. It comes with the territory. You just didn't learn it fast enough to know who you were dealing with."

"Yes, and I'm paying a damn high price for that education. Besides, it looks to me like you never learn enough to be safe. Look what happened to Barry Seals. He knew more about this business than all of us put together. He stuck his neck *way* out to help you guys. And it wasn't just to reduce his prison time, from what I've heard. He really wanted to straighten out some bad choices and a wrong lifestyle. He was willing to pay his 'dues,' but some judge got his feathers ruffled, and Barry got wasted. The very people he was helping hung him out like a target at a shooting gallery. You have any idea how many potential 'witnesses' and cooperative defendants your side lost because of that? They even made a movie out of it."

The conversation continued for two hours. We talked about my experience with the Old Man's operation from beginning to end. He gave me information about the case from his point of view that astounded me, based on evidence his office had compiled. I gave him missing pieces to a puzzle he had not yet been able to put together completely.

Telling the prosecutor anything would have been hard to justify if I had done what he thought I had done. It would have been even harder to turn on someone else just to save my own skin. But in this case, there was a unique opportunity for two adversaries to sit together and talk as equals without compromising each other's side.

Finally, when all was said that needed to be said, and the coffee pot was empty, he stood up and shook my hand. He thanked me for my willingness to be open and honest with him, and then called for the marshals waiting outside.

"It's too bad," he said as they entered the office, his voice suddenly as stern and cold as it had been in the courtroom. "Not cooperating any more than you have isn't going to set well with the judge. What you've told me isn't going to help much."

As the marshals went about replacing the chains and shackles, the briefest hint of a smile flashed across his face. I had no clue what would happen next. When I returned to the detention center, everyone was asleep. For the first time in over a year, I laid back on my bunk and felt as if something sensible might yet come of an unending nightmare. Finally, it seemed as if I had an ally on the other side. A prosecutor for an ally? That made about as much sense as getting a pardon.

It was an interesting possibility, however. As close as I was to the bottom of the pit, *anything* at this point was an improvement.

Chapter Thirty-Eight

The weekend dragged more monotonously than usual as I endured the normal routines in the cellblock. Each hour brought me closer to the moment when everything would finally come to a conclusion. On Monday the judge would render his decision whether to bind the case over for trial. Either way, the prosecutor would have his way with me.

To continue to maintain innocence on the thread of hope that a jury would believe I had been "mentally incapacitated" by the Viet Nam War was foolish and dangerous. Even the lowest-level defendants in the case had been sentenced to five years each, and they had all cooperated with the government. Hour after hour, and late into each night, I struggled with the realization that the very *least* I could come out of this with would be another five years added to my six. A total of *eleven years*. And that was only the minimum.

Putting up with inmates' petty antics and obsessive need to have me write porno letters to their girlfriends was too much for me to deal with as I agonized over all possibilities all weekend long. Inmates running their trips on each other were wearing my patience thin. I was looking at a hopeless situation, and these guys had nothing better to do than play their stupid games. I stared out of one of the tiny windows in the cellblock and wondered what the impact might be from meeting with the prosecutor. Was he only setting me up? He was the *prosecutor,* after all. It was his *job* to put guys like me away for as long as he could.

What had I done? Was talking with him part of a carefully planned strategy on his part? Was it part of a clever plot to get me to show my hand and insure my defeat? Had I just put the last nail in my own coffin by talking with him? Any well-seasoned inmate would think me a moron for even meeting with him.

I was out of options, and almost out of time. It would all be decided in a few short moments on Monday. I didn't have the strength *or* the means to go through a trial that in actuality was only a bluff. They knew, and I knew, I couldn't get through it without a determined legal defense team.

All these thoughts played havoc in my head while inane sitcoms, wrestling matches and B-rated karate movies played on TV all weekend long. I couldn't read. I couldn't write. All I could do was sit, or pace, or exercise…and hope that I hadn't been a complete idiot.

My one ray of hope was that the prosecutor's intentions might be good, and that my intuition about him was accurate. I felt that he just wanted to know if there was something decent in me, and maybe…just maybe…he'd throw me a lifeline. Something inside me wanted so much to believe that. Based upon that hope, I had put everything on the table without asking for anything in return.

There were other forces to deal with, however…forces that went beyond him and his position. Once those forces were in motion, even the prosecutor might be powerless to stop them—even if he wanted to. Did I really think he might risk his position or look like he was going soft? People in his position just don't take risks like that. It gains them nothing, and makes them look bad if they're wrong.

Finally I calmed my nerves enough to reflect back to my time in solitary. I thought of Big Jim again, and the many times that guards and inmates alike had shifted from belligerence to openness with me. I had to trust in that for now. There was nothing else left for me to do. I had to accept that what was done was done. If it came down against me, I had to be ready and willing to accept it, no matter what.

Monday morning finally arrived. I had been awake long before dawn, and inside I was completely surrendered to my future fate. From here on, all I could do was swim with the current. I would save my strength for other battles that might come later. I would not fight this one any longer. I let go of the need to have it turn out my way, and opened myself to all possibilities. I felt at peace, ready to do the time if I had to.

After breakfast, two guards came to escort those of us going to court to the processing area to be transported to our hearings and court appearances around town. My ride to the federal courthouse was a slow and quiet one. In the front, the two marshals chatted about their weekend, and the outcome of Sunday's football games. The back door of the federal courthouse looked much the same as it did on Friday night, but the memory of seeing it in the dark gave me an eerie sense of only having dreamt the scene. The marshals opened the door, and I shuffled in.

Only a few people were waiting for the morning's session to begin. I was thankful that no other prisoners were in the courtroom to report the details of my case back to the cellblock for that day's jailhouse banter. It also meant that my case would be handled quickly.

As a few officials took their places in the courtroom, I took in a long, deep breath, and exhaled slowly. The prosecutor entered the courtroom and strode casually but purposefully to the table on his side of the room. He was well dressed, but he still had the same shoes on. I smiled to myself, knowing there was almost a hole in the bottom of one of them. He didn't even glance in my direction.

The clerk, bailiff and court reporter came in and took their seats. The proceedings were about to begin. My heartbeat quickened and my breathing tightened in spite of my effort to remain calm. Once again, I felt cold drops of sweat under my arms.

"All rise," the Court Clerk announced loudly as the chamber door opened and the judge entered. He sat down in the overstuffed, black leather chair, then opened the files in front of him and read aloud the all-too-familiar file number and name of the case. I sat up straight, but inside I wanted to crawl into a hole and hide.

The judge cleared his throat and got that stern, no-nonsense look on his face.

"Before I render my decision in this case, are there any further comments from either side?"

There was dead silence. This was it. The time had come. If no one said anything, the judge would announce his decision and seal my fate. Just then, the prosecutor pushed his chair back and stood up.

"Yes, Your Honor," he stated. "The People wish to amend their position in this case."

The judge was noticeably taken aback. This was an unexpected move on the part the prosecution. Last-minute motions and a sudden change of position were expected from *defense* attorneys, but not from prosecutors. This was a surprising shift for him to make, especially in light of the obviously solid case he had. Whatever the prosecutor's intention to "amend his position" in this case, it was apparent the judge hadn't been informed about it.

"You may proceed," the judge stated warily and leaned back in his chair.

"Your Honor, we have new evidence that causes us to believe that the defendant was not a manager in this operation, but rather was only a 'courier of information.' The People wish to amend the charges, and move to dismiss the counts of 'Possession with Intent' and 'Importation of a Controlled Substance.'"

The courtroom was silent, and so was the judge. My attorney's face went blank, and his eyes showed disbelief. Some murmuring could be heard in a back corner of the large, ornate room. The judge was quiet for a moment, then looked through some more pages in my file.

"Very well," the judge said flatly, then looked at Nathan. "I assume counsel for the defense has no objection?"

"No, Your Honor," Nathan replied, obviously thrown off by the new development. "Of course not."

"Assuming that the defendant consents to enter into a plea agreement, I'll expect to see everyone back here two weeks hence." Looking at the prosecutor, he added "And I'll see *you* in my chambers. Court is adjourned."

Nathan looked at me in total bewilderment.

"What was all that about?" he quizzed me.

I told him what had happened Friday night. He shook his head in amazement.

"I've never heard of such a thing," he said as he shoved papers into his briefcase. "They'll have some documents for you to sign. No telling how *this* is going to go, but it's a damn-sight better than what I thought was going to happen. I'll see you at the jail to talk about the plea agreement." He picked up his briefcase and walked away as the deputies approached to place the shackles on me again.

I had no idea what would come of this new development, but it seemed the clouds had finally parted. As I waited in the courthouse holding cell, the U.S. Probation Officer assigned to my case came in.

"Well," he said. "That was certainly an unexpected break for you. I'll see you at the jail to start my pre-sentence report. Since you've already had one done on you in the New Mexico case, it shouldn't take very long." He shook his head. "I can't understand why he would take such a dramatic turn when there was so much evidence to support his case. Amazing."

"Well, you never know how the truth will come out," I said, as the marshals came to take me back to the detention center.

I knew the prosecutor's statement was significant, but not *how* significant. "Courier of information," he had said. Those three simple words changed my status immediately to one of far less culpability. It removed me from the category of "racketeering," thereby opening the door to parole.

The prospect of 25 years in prison had suddenly melted to a maximum allowable ten. Being officially less culpable, I had a much better chance of being sentenced concurrently, rather than consecutively.

Two weeks later, we were back in the courtroom. A plea agreement had been reached, which stipulated that if there were further need for my testimony regarding the case, I would so testify. No names were given, and no deals were made, other than for me to continue my work on prisoner self-education programs. The probation officer had completed his report, my lawyer seemed on good terms with the prosecutor, and the judge was clearly in a more receptive mood. He even seemed a bit jovial after the courtroom came to order. Once again I listened to him announce the docket number of my case, and its official title.

"We are here in the matter of sentencing of the defendant, who has agreed to plead guilty to Counts Three and Four. Prosecution has moved to dismiss Counts One and Two, and has removed all counts from consideration under the RICO Act, to wit: Involvement in a Continuing Criminal Enterprise."

Even though this was a very positive development, I was still overwhelmed by the implications of being sentenced again, this time for a substantially larger quantity of marijuana than in my case in New Mexico five years earlier. Both offenses had taken place within a few months of each other, and involved essentially the same people, but it could appear that I had committed two different offenses five years apart. Having "absconded" for five years made me look like a multiple offender, and an escape risk as well. Not a good thing for the parole board to consider.

It was difficult to stand before the judge as he read the charges and questioned me. Once again, my heart was pounding hard and my T-shirt was wet with sweat. I was trapped in their system with no choice over what to do or where to go. I would be forced to accept whatever the judge decided.

"Do you understand the charges against you?" the judge queried.

"Yes, Your Honor, I do."

"You understand that Counts One and Two will be dismissed, Counts Three and Four will stand, and that the possible sentence for each count is five years?"

"Yes, Your Honor."

"Very well, then. How do you plead to Counts Three and Four?"

I could hardly breathe. My heart pounded so hard I could feel it pulsing in my ears. I felt dizzy. My knees went weak. I couldn't bring myself to speak. Even with this seemingly positive new development, I might still be doing the wrong thing. Maybe the whole thing was just an elaborate scheme to manipulate me into pleading guilty to the two counts, and now I *could* end up getting the full ten years. Ten *years...* And those might be *added* to the six I already had. Given the maximum benefit possible for good time, at *best* that would still mean a minimum of five years before possible parole. My mouth went dry, and I felt feverish.

"Well?" The judge prodded. "How do you wish to plead?"

A thousand voices inside me jabbered frantically. "Do this!" "Don't do that!" "Don't be a fool!" "You're crazy!" "You're gonna DIE in prison!" I couldn't hear myself think.

Then another voice I had learned to trust finally spoke to me. "You are your own creator," it said to me. "You've set all this up for your own personal growth. Look how magnificently you've staged the whole thing, and look at all of these actors on your stage. Isn't it amazing? They're all playing their parts so well. It's time to do your part. Remember: *Trust the Process*." Finally, I felt my own voice come through.

"Guilty, Your Honor."

"Thank you," he replied. "I thought we'd lost you there for a minute."

"No Sir," I said. "I just had some apprehension."

"That's understandable. From what I've read in your PSI, and from the Prosecutor's report, I can see why you might feel that way. Nevertheless, I must be certain you understand the implications involved, and that you make this choice free of any promises, assertions or expectations. Do you so enter this plea?"

"Difficult as it is to plead guilty to *anything* at this point, under the circumstances, I feel it's the right thing to do. Yes, Your Honor."

"Good. Then let the record show that the defendant enters his plea of 'Guilty' on Counts Three and Four. Counts One and Two are hereby dismissed." He looked up from the papers before him, sighed and leaned back in his chair for a moment before he continued. He looked at me like a stern father in a moment of contemplation of a difficult situation.

"I believe from what I've read, and from what I have observed in the past several months of this case, that you have a lot of potential. In spite of having complicated your case by becoming a fugitive, you apparently conducted yourself honorably during that period of time.

"This court has received numerous letters from people in your community expressing their confidence in you and acknowledging your honesty in business dealings. They indicate that you handled large sums of money for them, and had access to their airplanes, yet you evidently didn't misuse the money or the planes. Your attention and devotion to your children was highly emphasized in nearly every letter. Even though you operated under an assumed name, they all request that I be lenient with you.

"Nevertheless, you have broken the law...and in no small way. Not once, but several times. Then you took matters into your own hands and defied the judicial system by running away. Neither this court, nor any court, can or will condone such behavior, no matter how much a defendant may appear to have been rehabilitated.

"I find myself intrigued, however, with what you have undertaken while incarcerated—the educating of other inmates and the formation of prisoner self-help programs. I have read your proposal for a juvenile diversion program, and find it to have substance and promise. If you manage to maintain such noble character through the challenges ahead of you, and not just to gain sympathy to reduce your punishment, I would like to offer my own personal support.

"Whichever the case may be, crimes have been committed that cannot be excused, and justice must be done in this case. Mainly because even with your limited experience in the smuggling business, it is doubtful that they would have succeeded if you weren't involved. You may be officially designated a 'courier of information', but you know, and I know, that you played a vital part in the operation, albeit a brief one.

"It is therefore the decision of this court that you be sentenced to four years on Count Three, and four years on Count Four; both sentences to run consecutively."

I felt like someone had just kicked me in the stomach. A wave of nausea swept over me, and my bowels nearly exploded. I felt faint. *Eight years?! Is that what he said??! EIGHT YEARS!!? CONSECUTIVELY??!*

I struggled desperately to keep standing. He continued.

"In light of the overwhelming mitigating circumstances in this case, I will make the combined sentences concurrent with the underlying sentence in the New Mexico case, and I will pass this sentence under subparagraph (B)(2) of the federal statutes. You are hereby remanded to the custody of the United States Attorney General. Court is dismissed."

I fell back into my chair, overcome with dizziness and my insides in upheaval. My head was swimming. I had just picked up another eight years. My attorney was talking to me, but I couldn't hear what he was saying. Behind me, someone was talking to me, but I couldn't make out what was being said. Everything was muffled and distant. I was hot and feverish. I felt the urge to vomit. Finally, the man behind me put his hand on my shoulder and jostled me. I turned and looked. It was my probation officer.

"What a break!" he exclaimed. "I've *never* seen this judge render a decision like this in a drug case. Do you realize what he's done?"

I swallowed hard to clear my throat, took a deep breath to ease the pressure in my chest, and answered him.

"Apart from the eight *years* he added to my sentence?"

"No. There's much more to it than that. First of all, he made the whole sentence *concurrent* with your present sentence, so the whole thing only adds a couple of years to your present sentence. With good behavior, that adds only about eight months to your time. But the (B)(2) provision of the statutes makes the entire sentence subject to the discretion of the Parole Commission. So when you get to your designated facility, and have your parole hearing, they have the authority to release you whenever they choose."

"So what does that really mean?"

"Essentially, that you could be out in less than a *year.* I don't want to build up your hopes, but you could conceivably be out as early as your first appearance in front of the parole board."

"Really?"

"Yes, really. That doesn't mean it will happen that way, but it *is* possible. It will depend entirely on how well you do from here, and on how closely the parole board looks into your record. When the judge said he was impressed with your potential, he was saying a lot more than 'you're a nice guy.' By saying *"for the record"* that he wanted to assist you, he was in essence telling the Parole Commission he believes that you deserve an early release."

The sheriff's deputies came up to the table with their cuffs and shackles. I looked over at Nathan, who was still somewhat in shock. He shrugged his shoulders.

"He's right," Nathan agreed. "It could go well for you now, unless you let up or blow any of this off. I think the judge will be watching you. He'll have the prosecutor's office and the probation office keep track of your progress. If he reviews your case and sees you're doing well, he may intervene and talk with the Parole Commission himself. Or, he may just stay out of it. Either way, your behavior will be a determining factor. This is a damn lucky break for you. It's about the best thing he could have done under the circumstances. An eight-year sentence satisfies the public mandate for deterrence and harsh punishment, but doing it under the (B)(2) provision allows a window for you through the Parole Commission."

My head was swimming with the realization of what this all meant. The two men continued talking as the deputies fastened the leg chains, cuffed my wrists to my waist chain, and nudged me toward the back door of the courthouse. I wondered how much longer the pain of chains and shackles would be a part of my life, now that I was officially declared a "courier of information." Shouldn't it be clear that I wasn't an escape risk? The case was now closed, and I would be at the mercy of the U.S. Bureau of Prisons and its even less caring, even vengeful component, the U.S. Parole Commission.

On the ride back, even though I fought against the angst of being delivered back to the Bureau of Prisons, I contemplated my "good fortune." It wasn't 25 years or even 8 more years that I had to tolerate. I was still dealing with an unknown number. At least it wasn't hopeless now. What had transpired in the mind of that prosecutor to cause this turn of events? I carefully reflected on our private meeting and combed through the details of our conversation, looking for clues.

It was, essentially, about trust and honesty...even between adversaries. More importantly, it was about mutual respect—that even in opposing positions, people can have respect for one another regardless of personalities or cultural differences. I had respected Big Jim, and he felt compelled to help me. I had respected that guard over the telephone issue, and he later felt compelled to help me. I respected the Chief Psychiatrist at Springfield, and the Chaplain at El Reno, and they both felt compelled to help me. I respected the many inmates I had met, and they let go of their preconceived notions about "smart-ass white boys." Everyone helped me, each in their own way, all because of mutual respect.

Now it was the same with the prosecutor. I respected him from the first hearing, and didn't stop respecting him even when it appeared likely that he would put me away for so long. That compelled him to look more deeply and find out more about me. He was the first authority to do so, and what he found was consistency in my attitude of respect for others. It didn't excuse my mistakes or my wrongful deeds, but it did make him want to offer a way out without coercing me to cooperate.

Back at the Escambia County Jail, it was difficult to get back into leading a study group and being a scribe for the other inmates. After a few days of moping around the cellblock, I began to notice the behavior of a new inmate. He was another young, black man with a bad attitude who immediately saw me as a typical "whitey," just as the others had when I first came in. He strutted around the cellblock just like young Michael had, as if he owned the place. The TV became his personal property, and he kept the volume up just to test everyone's temperament.

One day soon after his arrival, we sat across from each other at breakfast. Several times I noticed him glaring at me, but I just sipped my coffee quietly.

"Waz wid chu, anyway?" he finally snorted. "My bruthahs heah tell me you smaht 'nuff to hep dem out wid dey readin' and shit. Waz yo' angle? What chu want fruhm dem?"

"Nothing," I said. "No angle. I'm just doing my time. They asked me for help, and I helped them."

"Mah homeboys tell me you don't like the TV too loud."

"Doesn't matter to me. I never told them anything. They turn it down out of respect, and because several of them are studying for their G.E.D. exams. If you need it loud, turn it up. I'm out of here any day now, so I don't much care."

"That so? You some kine a lawyer or sumthin'?"

"Nope. Don't have much use for lawyers. Haven't had a decent one in six years."

"Six *yeahs?* What chu in heah fo'?"

"Drugs."

"Drugs? What drugs? Cocaine? You piss off some rich-boy lawyer or judge, mabbee?"

"No. It was just smoke. I just picked up my third sentence and I'm on my way back to finish my first two."

"*Damn.* Musta' been sum shit. How much time you lookin' at?"

"Eight years, all federal. What about you?"

"Parole violation, tha's all. Ah'll be outta here in two, three months. Mah bruthahs say you been hepin' 'em wraht lettahs home, too. You do that?"

"Sometimes. You want some help?"

"Maybee. Ah'll think on it a whyul."

"What's your name?"

"Darryl," he said, just as the guards signaled it was time to file back into the corridor to return to the cellblock. Darryl got up to leave, then looked back at me. "Ah'll catch you laytah."

We filed out the door to return to our cellblock. He never turned up the TV after that, and within a few days I was writing some of the steamiest letters ever for not one but two of his girlfriends. For the next two weeks I was back at work with the group to improve their basic academic and communication skills. Darryl became one of my best "students," and soon learned enough basics to write his own letters.

It was fascinating to observe the change in behavior of men who, normally prone to punching each other out over the simplest things, were now talking respectfully with each other. It was amusing to hear them slip into old speech patterns, then openly correct each other.

Very early one morning three weeks after my final hearing, the cellblock door opened for a guard to enter. He approached my bunk and told me to roll up my things. I was "shipping out." I squinted at the clock on the wall by the guard tower. It was 3:30 A.M.

As I packed up my few personal belongings, dressed and rolled up my mattress, Darryl got up and came over to shake hands and say goodbye. Two other inmates sat up in their bunks, then came over and did the same. These had once been the meanest, hardest antagonists I had encountered. The sight of them all standing there waiting to shake my hand and wish me well instilled in my heart such a deep feeling of gratitude and hope that the steel restraints I wore on my way back through the prison system didn't even faze me. This made it clear to me that there was, indeed, a whole new script being written, and I was writing it.

Chapter Thirty-Nine

The marshal's sedan pulled away from the detention center and headed north to the Interstate. Wherever we were going, it looked like it might be a long trip. Taladega again? Wherever it was, at least I was making some progress. Now it seemed that there was finally a destination. Even if it took eight years or, as the probation officer said, "only eight more months," at least I was on my way out of the system.

The aroma of fresh coffee from the marshal's thermos filled my nostrils as I leaned back on the seat and looked out through the back window. Suddenly, I was overwhelmed with a most breathtaking sight. Not since my departure from Phoenix nearly eight months before, had I seen stars. There above us, spread out across the celestial expanse of the early morning sky, the Big Dipper sparkled before my astonished eyes, and beyond it a dazzling array of stars and constellations everywhere. What a sight to see!

Nearly a year and a half had passed since my arrest, and this was the first time I had a chance to see something so dazzling. Something so commonplace that I had once taken for granted now filled my senses with awe and wonderment. It must have been as Victor Frankel had written about his time in Nazi concentration camps. He found delight in watching sunrises and sunsets, despite his dire circumstances. I felt like I had been on an odyssey that had spanned a decade, and felt certain I had aged at least that much.

Out on the freeway, the lights of cars and trucks moving against the backdrop of night painted red and white streaks on the windows of the sedan as we moved eastward toward Tallahassee. The traffic seemed unusually heavy for that hour of the morning, and I wondered where everyone could be going. Just as the first trace of morning light appeared on the horizon, the marshals exited the freeway and turned north onto a county highway that wound through some of the thickest forests and swampland I had seen since the DC-6 incident. Before long, we turned into a large clearing in the middle of which was an aging, concrete structure with high, chainlink fences. Above the door were the faded words, "Okaloosa County Jail."

At first I thought we might be picking someone up, so I was startled to see the marshals open the back door of the sedan and motioned for me to get out. They opened the front door of the building and led me into a dark, moldy-smelling receiving room. A sheriff's deputy appeared, and took the files the marshals offered.

"This one's going on to Tallahassee when the federal prison bus comes through today," one of the marshals said crisply. "Hopefully we made it in time."

"Seems to me you did," the deputy responded. "They're supposed to be comin' through sometime this mohnin'.We still got a few Fedrels waitin' to go. Cupla' them been here three, four weeks now."

"That figures," the marshal replied. "Doesn't really matter where they wait, does it?"

"Nah. Don' matter t' me one bit. One place seems just as good as anothah, really. Only heah they got it a little easier, I think. Nobody gets in their shit, unless they step outta line."

"Well, I'm supposed to tell you to make sure this one gets on that bus. They had us up at three o'clock this morning just to get him here on time. Evidently, they think it's important."

"No problem. When that bus gets here, I'll take 'im out and put 'im on it myself. That good enough?"

"We'd appreciate it."

The marshals left without even a nod or a glance in my direction, and the deputy led me to a holding cell. For the next several hours I sat alone and listened to the echo of voices up and down the hallways, and the cellblocks beyond.

The morning passed uneventfully. Breakfast was a bowl of cereal, a lukewarm piece of toast and a fairly decent cup of coffee. For lunch, collard greens, okra, a hot dog and a square of Jell-O. More time passed, and I couldn't understand why it had been so important to get me there this early. Finally, the deputy came and unlocked the cell.

"Let's go," he said. "Your bus is here."

Outside, the afternoon sun shone down on us so brightly I had to squint to see where I was going. Along with six others, I was escorted to the bus. The gray slacks and white shirts of federal correctional officers gave me an eerie sense of familiarity that startled me. It was strange feeling like I "belonged" with them, yet recalling the cold indifference of the Federal Bureau of Prisons. This time, at least, I was hopefully on my way to Safford.

The bus worked its way back down the same road we came in on that morning. Soon we were on the freeway, headed eastward toward Tallahassee. I could only guess that I was going to be held until another bus or, perhaps Con-Air, would take me back to Arizona. It would be nice not to have to see Taladega again, but with no urgency to get me to any particular destination I could spend months anywhere they wanted to leave me until my time eventually ran out. In a strange sense, I was okay with whatever happened.

As we moved along, I began to notice familiar landmarks. Ghosts of Vinnie, Charlie and the others drifted into my mind. As I kept pushing them aside, everything became sharply familiar. To my amazement, the very truck stop where we had staged the DC-6 landing came into view. I felt my insides crawl as the officers signaled for the driver to pull in. It seemed surreal as we pulled into the very place where so many lives had changed dramatically during those two fateful nights so long ago. The irony of sitting shackled on a prison bus while the officers refilled their coffee cups was almost amusing, yet torturous. Except for the seriousness of my present situation, I could feel a laugh somewhere deep inside of me.

We arrived at FCI Tallahassee late that afternoon. It was much the same as the older facilities I had been in. Its architecture resembled FCI El Reno, but it seemed a little newer and cleaner. After the usual intake routine, I was led to the transient unit while the rest of the inmates were taken to their designated living areas. Tallahassee was the final destination for the bus, which simply turned around the next day and started the run back to FCI Taladega.

The transient unit consisted of a row of cells on the lower floor of one wing. At the entrance to the wing, two officers sat at a small, wooden desk, its approximate age revealed by the dark, well-worn inkwell in its upper right corner. Behind the officers, a divider of steel bars similar to the ones back at La Tuna closed off the transient cells. Access to the wing was by a gate of steel bars reminiscent of old-time jail cell doors. The officer escorting me approached the two sitting at the desk.

"Got one more for you guys to squeeze in," he said. "Did they call it in to you?"

"Yeah, sure," the older one replied. "But I don't know where we're gonna put 'im. All these cells are full, 'cept the first one. You know who's in there..."

"Yeah. Murray, isn't it?"

"Yeah."

"So what's the problem? He's getting out in a few days. He can't be too bothered by anything at this point."

"Tell that to *him*. Last time he was out on parole, he put two guys in the hospital. I don't know if one of 'em ever came out."

"Yeah, but that was years ago. How long now? Seven? Eight?"

"Don' matter t' us. All we know is we're not supposed t' put anybody in with him."

I started getting real nervous. I knew the direction this dialog was going. I wasn't anxious to meet this guy, let alone spend any time in a tiny holding cell with him.

"It ain't gonna matter much," the escort went on. "It's only for one night. This one's going back to Taladega in the morning. What the hell could one night matter to Murray?"

"Why don't you ask him?"

"He's a fuckin' *inmate*, goddamit. I don't ask an *inmate* if he minds if I do something."

"Well, it'll matter to the warden if there's an incident."

"Gimme the keys. I'll just have me a little talk with Murray."

The guard got up from the desk, handed the officer a set of keys, and unlocked the divider gate.

"Be my guest," he said, and stepped back.

The escort officer opened the gate, stepped through and strutted down the corridor.

"Murray!" he shouted. "Get your ass up!"

He stopped at the first cell and leaned against the bars while he talked with whoever "Murray" was.

A few minutes later the officer yelled back at one of the unit guards.

"Al! Bring that one down here."

The older guard took me by the arm and walked me to the escort officer who was holding the door to Murray's cell open for me.

"Go on, get in there. You'll be fine 'til morning. I have Murray's word on it...right?" He looked in the direction of a man standing inside, leaning against the bunk bed.

"Not a problem," the man said calmly. The cell door slammed shut behind me, and the two officers walked off chuckling to each other.

Standing just inside the cell door with my issued bedding and toiletries in my arms, I looked up at a man who stood every bit of six-foot-six, which gave me a dwarfed feeling against my 5'10" very thin frame. His long gray hair was tied in a ponytail that reached the small of his back, and his face was scarred from what I suspected were many skirmishes in prison. A particularly prominent scar ran from his left ear across his left cheek and down under his chin. That was no skirmish.

My first thought was that he could be dangerous, particularly in the light of comments made by the guards. I held my position and looked into his eyes. As I did, I felt him smile, even though his outward expression didn't change. I felt no immediate threat, so I relaxed somewhat and moved toward the bunk. As I did, he stepped forward, extended his hand and introduced himself.

"Hi. I'm Nick Murray," he announced. His handshake was firm, genuine, and welcoming. "So, you're only in here for the night?"

"Yeah, looks like it," I replied politely. "Every place else in town is full," I quipped, glad to have a bit of humor to break the ice.

"You don't say," he smiled. "Must be some kind of convention going on." I was thankful his response was receptive.

"I guess. Good thing I'm only passing through."

"Yeah? Where to?"

"Taladega, I suppose. Then El Reno and, hopefully, Phoenix. If I make it there, I might actually get to Safford some day."

"Sounds like you've been doing the 'tour'."

"Yep. Several times around. By now I know the guards in four federal joints and three county jails. I feel like I oughta know the names of their wives and kids, too."

"Damn. How long you been down?"

"A year and three months…and I have yet to see my designated facility. I was in 'seg' at La Tuna, and so far I've been to FCI Phoenix once, three times at El Reno and three times at Taladega—each time as a holdover. Throw in three detention centers and two county jails for good measure, and I feel like I've been down for ten years."

"Jesus. That's a lot of time to be dragged around. You're headed for Safford, you say?"

"Yeah, that was my original designation. I'm not sure if it still is, now."

"I'm headed that way myself."

"Really? Safford?"

"No. Tucson."

"Tucson? I heard it's a fairly new joint. Might be halfway decent."

"No, no—not the joint. I'll be a free man. I'm getting out day after tomorrow."

"Out?!? *Really* out??"

"Yeah. I mean really out. I'm done. With this joint, with the system...everything."

"Wow! That's fantastic! How long have you been down?"

"Twenty-four years."

I almost fell over. I stared at him in disbelief, yet I knew what I had heard.

"Damn," I barely got the word out of my mouth.

"S'matter? You surprised?"

"Well, yes...and no. I'm surprised anytime I hear that. It's only been a couple of times I've talked with anyone who's done that kind of time, and still can talk civilly. You did say '24', didn't you?"

"Yes, I did. Every bit of it. Had a total of 30 to do, but I max out this week. They can't keep me in, no matter how much they want to."

The way he said that wasn't in the typically belligerent and defiant way I had heard so many "tough" guys boast. There was a kind, yet tough and determined quality in his voice, not unlike what I had experienced with Big Jim. I felt no threatening or menacing attitude, but rather a sense of his having survived his own particular hell. I was intrigued.

"What did you do to get that kind of sentence? That is, if you don't mind me asking."

"No, I don't mind. It wasn't just one sentence, though. It was a series of them, built up over time. It actually started out pretty short. But it's a long story."

"I don't mind. Looks like we've got all night. Besides, I like a good story...as long as you don't charge too much."

"Nah," he chuckled. "This one's on the house."

He sat down on the bed and wiped his glasses as if to pause for the effect. He would have made a good judge, from the way he let the tension build. I dropped my bedding on the floor opposite him and sat down on it. He continued.

"I was born in Alabama, in a big family. We didn't have any great love for blacks, so I grew up with a bad attitude toward them. As I got older, I fell in with a bad crowd. We were always into some kind of shit—joy-riding, shoplifting, you name it. And we were always gettin' into fights with the blacks. Long before you heard about gangs like nowadays, we had 'em. They could get real violent, too. A lot of guys got hurt in those fights, but usually that's as far as it went. Then things started to escalate. A black guy got killed, then a couple of our guys got ambushed. Before long, it was open warfare between sides. It was worse than drive-by shootings nowadays.

"Over several years, I started gettin' a record. Mostly juvenile shit, until I was eighteen. Then I picked up a bunch of jail time and some felony raps that I got probation for. When I was about twenty…no twenty-one, I think…I got popped for a simple burglary. No big deal, really, but I got a judge who thought prison time would change me. Or maybe he just didn't care, I don't know. Anyway, I got a six-year sentence, which should have worked out to a year and half or so down.

"But instead of sending me to a low-security joint, they sent me to the state pen—home of the 'baddest of the bad.' I guess they figured they'd scare the shit out of me and maybe I'd change. Or maybe they just blew it, and it was the luck of the draw. Whatever it was, my life went into the toilet from that point on.

"Because of my size, and because I was known to hate blacks, I was snapped right up by the 'White Brotherhood'—'skin-heads' as you know them now. A few of the members back then actually shaved their heads, but that stuff only caught on out in the world recently. It's some bad shit, let me tell you. It cost me most of my adult life, not to mention a lot of time in the infirmary. And in the hole.

"Anyway, I was always drawn into the fights. I was their gladiator. Once I was into it, I had to keep on going just to protect myself and survive. It got to where it was the personal vendetta of every black dude in the joint to nail me. They had guys actually work their way through the state prison system just to have a shot at me. My head would be a trophy that would show how tough they were if they rid the world of me.

"They nearly did me in several times. I've had over three hundred stitches, a broken jaw twice, got blinded for over a month from a chemical thrown in my face, both arms broken, a leg so badly beaten I can hardly walk right anymore, and migraine headaches you wouldn't believe.

"But I took more'n a few of 'em out along the way. And I fucked up at least a dozen of 'em so bad I'm sure they never got back to normal. It was some pretty bloody times, and I couldn't find my way out. All we ever did was plan for the next fight, or spend time in the hole or in the infirmary, planning our revenge.

"With each incident, my prison time increased. I got three murder raps with life sentences on each one, and a bunch of assault and manslaughter convictions. Some lawyer for the White Brotherhood got the sentences combined, and some reduced, but my overall time kept increasing with each new rap. I got paroled twice, but I had so much hate in me that I'd go off on the first black dude I ran into on the outside. Or I'd purposely rip off a store in a black neighborhood. Every time, I'd be back in the slammer again, facing off with another black dude with a grudge or an ego to stroke. I was in and out of the joint so much it became a joke among the prison guards. They had betting pools on how many months it would be before I'd be back in again.

"Finally I began to see it for what it was. I mean, I really began to see how it wasn't the system, or the blacks, or even the gangs. It wasn't anything on the outside, either…not my family or my financial problems, or drug problems or alcohol problems. Those were all things that affected me, but that's not where the source of the problem was. It was inside of *me*. It was the choices *I* made that kept getting me in trouble. It was the chip I had on my own shoulder that kept bringing me down. Nobody else, and nothing else. Just my own stupidity and hatred. It took me *fifteen years* to even get a clue about what was really causing my problems.

"Can you believe it? *Fifteen years!* And then it took another *nine* years just to make the changes. Both times I was out on parole were *after* I'd made that discovery. Even though I was aware of the cause of the problem, I couldn't change the behavior. It's only been in the last five years or so that I've been able to walk away from trouble and leave things be.

"About three years ago, a Baptist minister I'd been seeing brought his older daughter in to help him minister to the inmates. She wasn't any spring chicken, or "Playboy" foldout, but then I wasn't exactly Sean Connery, either. She was smart and kind, and even pretty in her own way…especially when she smiled. Anyway, we started to feel an attraction, and felt that we might be good for each other when my time was up. So, after I get out and we spend a few months gettin' to know each other on the outside, we plan to get married.

"I've been studying refrigeration and heating by correspondence. Her dad has a job lined up for me on the outside, and after we're really sure we're on the right track, I think we'll pack up and head out to Tucson where jobs for refrigeration technicians are plentiful. I've always wanted to live out west. There's so damn much *room* out there."

It took several hours for him to tell me the whole story in detail, and another several hours for me to ask questions and to explore the depths of what had taken him so long to master. It was awesome to feel the depth of his discovery, and to feel his joy in being able to start again with such new and powerful insights. Even though he appeared to be well into his fifties by then, he seemed ready to re-enter society as a useful, decent human being with hopes and dreams not unlike a younger person just starting out.

When the guards came for me early the next morning, I was still sitting on my bedroll, talking with Nick as if we were in some all-night diner, swapping stories. I had only gotten partway into my own story when it was time for me to leave. I never forgot the images Nick had burned into my mind that night…images of a twisted young man fighting demons of physical violence, lost on a hopeless tread-mill of survival of the fittest and the toughest…if not the sickest.

Those impressions, together with the one of a tall, tattooed and scarred older man with a kind face, rode with me all the way back through Taladega, El Reno, Phoenix and, at long last, to FCI Safford.

Chapter Forty

I arrived at FCI Phoenix three weeks later, and the next day was sent to Safford. Evidently, a high priority had been placed on my transfer since a number of other inmates were waiting ahead of me.

The long awaited, final leg of my journey to Safford was in the back of a 15-passenger van operated by the Bureau of Prisons. Two armed correctional officers in the front seats, and another officer and a BOP lieutenant in a sedan behind us insured that there would be no problem on the six-hour trip. A securely locked, wiremesh cage lining the passenger section of the van made that a certainty.

Twelve other prisoners—sweaty, unshaven, all chained and shackled in their seats—filled the van to the limit of my personal tolerance. Adding to my discomfort was the van's radio tuned to a hard rock station and turned up loud enough to drown out the conversation of the guards up front.

Four deafening, miserable hours later, we pulled into FCI Tucson—another large, modern facility similar to FCI Phoenix. To my immense gratitude, nine prisoners were unloaded. From there we traveled northeast along a winding, two-lane highway toward Safford. As I dined on two dry bologna sandwiches provided by FCI Tucson, I watched the arid, desert terrain of southeastern Arizona pass by through the wiremesh inside the windows. As far as I could see, giant Saguaro cactus punctuated the harsh landscape like cartoon figures in suspended animation. Spread out among them, vast expanses of prickly pear and cholla cactus, creosote bush, mesquite and chaparral defied the glaring desert sun. If they could live in such an inhospitable place, I thought, then I could, too. At least where I was going, there would have to be some water.

My first glimpse of FCI Safford was startling. Accustomed to seeing high walls, gun towers and other images typical of prisons, I was surprised to find none of these. Except for one row of high, chainlink fence, and the all-too-familiar coils of razor wire, Safford looked more like a military compound than a prison. Large Quonset huts, which comprised most of the buildings, reminded me of my childhood and my father's military career.

As one of the smallest facilities in the federal system, FCI Safford housed less than four hundred prisoners. Located at the base of Mt. Graham, a 10,000-foot mountain still splotched with the residue of the last winter's snow, it was rumored to have been an internment camp for Japanese/Americans during World War II. FCI Safford was not a pretty place, by any means. Not that any of the other facilities I had been to were, but because of the old, military "outpost" look and feel, and because of its remote location in the rugged desert mountains of southeastern Arizona, it was particularly bleak. There were only a few trees to provide any shade, most of which were outside the fences. The elevation—a little over 4,000'—provided the only hint of coolness in the evenings after the sun went down in summer. In winter, temperatures could drop into the thirties at night, with occasional light snow dusting the peaks.

Inmates slept dormitory-style in the six largest Quonset huts—sixty men jammed into spaces originally designed for 30 soldiers. I was assigned to an upper bunk midway down the right side of building number four, where I often sat watching the endless soap operas around me. From my vantage point, I could watch the comings and goings of all of the inmates and the various ways they chose to pass their time.

The bunks were so close to each other I could reach across and almost touch the beds on either side. The space was barely enough to squeeze our bodies between the bunk and the two half-size lockers in which we kept our personal belongings. Staying in the tiny cubicles for any length of time was virtually impossible for two men, except for napping, reading, head counts and waiting for chow or mail call.

Nighttime between dinner and "lights out," could be brutal. Those who weren't in the TV room in the main building, or waiting in long lines near the row of telephones by the administration building, were in the dormitories. Each added their own brand of noise to a decibel level that often approached that of some of the jails I had been in. During the day, when everyone was gone to their assigned work places, or to the library, the shop, the recreation area or to the "weight pile," the dormitory was blissfully quiet.

My job in the prison bakery was ideal for a while. I was up at three a.m. each day and finished by eight a.m., which gave me the rest of the day to relax in the relative quiet of my cubicle. My exposure to noise in the jails and detention centers enabled me to fall asleep in the midst of the clamor of the dormitory at night, a feat that amazed fellow inmates. My routine soon became one of going to sleep before lights out, then waking up in the middle of the night to read or write in the quiet of the dimly lit latrine. Only the sounds of men snoring broke the stillness. It was as if I was in a dormitory at a boarding school for wayward boys…except that these were no "boys" at all. These were full-grown men, with lifetimes of pent-up anger, hatred, fears and obsessive/compulsive ills that could give a battery of psychologists enough material to fill volumes of journals on human behavior.

My arrival came in the spring of 1986, which was too late to make the parole hearings already scheduled for the following month. Too new to make that schedule, I had to wait until the fall hearings. After working in the bakery for four months, I took a job as a clerk in the recreation department—a position that I felt might reflect more positively on my record. I also joined the prison chapter of Toastmasters' International, which was very active there. Weekly meetings were held inside the main administration building, away from the pettiness of the guards and the scoffing attitude of less educated inmates.

Toastmasters at Safford included a Spanish journalist and matador, several accomplished South African and German international businessmen, political and business professionals from all over South and Central America, and lawyers, doctors and scholars from all over the world. Numerous plaques and awards adorned the meeting room walls from rhetorical victories won over the often futile efforts of other Toastmasters' groups that pitted their skills against well-educated inmates with little else to do but orate their lives' missed pursuits in passionate detail during speech contests.

Talk among members of Toastmasters led to an idea to organize discussion groups as a part of the institution's educational program, and to get the warden to authorize regular meeting times during the day. Before long, rumors began to surface among the general population that some inmates were acting like they were "too good for other inmates," and that they might have to "be put in their place." Such talk spilled over to the easily rattled correctional staff, whose captain then let it be known that any gathering of more than four inmates at a time would be considered a "meeting," and that such gatherings would not be permitted.

One day not long after that, the new prison psychologist called me to her office. She was a rather large black woman with a no-nonsense manner, but she immediately put me at ease with a jovial laugh and a forthright approach to what she wanted.

"I understand from your files that you've had some experience teaching inmates basic grammar and G.E.D. preparedness," she said. "You have some fairly impressive letters in your files."

"I don't know what the letters say," I answered, "but yes, I've found ways to put my time to better use. It wasn't easy, though."

"I wouldn't think so. I've had a mountain to climb myself in that regard, and I have some fairly respectable credentials. I signed on with the Bureau of Prisons to make some 'innovative inroads' for self-help programs for prisoners, but so far I haven't been able to get anywhere. I spent two very frustrating years at the federal penitentiary at Lompoc, and just as I was gaining some ground, I was sent here."

"I can understand your frustration," I replied. "You should try it from my vantage point."

"No, thanks." She chuckled. "I've seen enough on both sides. I'll stick with mine for now, thank you." She clearly wanted something from me, but I couldn't figure out where she was going, yet.

"I'm not used to prison officials revealing their personal concerns," I said. "I assume there's a reason you're telling me all this."

"Yes, of course. I started out with the hope of developing programs to promote better self-esteem among inmates. All I got was scorn and derision for my efforts, and what now amounts to a demotion. I can either cave in to their macho, paramilitary pressure and simply rubber stamp whatever they want me to do, or I can keep pushing for reform based upon good psychology and compassion."

"Compassion? In the federal prison system? No wonder they booted you out of Lompoc. That's not in their vocabulary. Neither is 'rehabilitation'."

"Exactly," she retorted. "Now, don't get me wrong. I don't hold much confidence for the majority of inmates, but in the two years I was at Lompoc, I began to see significant behavior changes in inmates who had been incarcerated most of their lives. Some amazing breakthroughs were starting to happen."

"I'm sure there were, if your own motives were clear. It probably helped being a woman. And black. No doubt, that combination opened a few minds...at least among prisoners."

"It did. But that was also two handicaps against me with the predominantly white, male prison hierarchy." She paused and looked at me as if to size me up, then went on. "I may be stretching my neck way out even discussing this with you, but I think you can help me."

"Oh? How so?"

"First, I have to trust that this conversation goes no further than this room. If it does, and I hear about it, you won't think I'm such a nice person. So, I mean *no further.* Do I have your word on that?"

"Yes, of course. I can understand. If you've reviewed my records, I think you should have a sense of what I've had to endure just to get here, let alone accomplish anything along the way."

"Yes, I have. And I've made a few phone calls, too. Let's see, a Chief Deputy U.S. Attorney and a Federal District Judge in northern Florida, the Chief Psychiatrist at FPH Springfield, a correctional counselor at the Escambia County Jail, the chaplain at FCI El Reno, and the Director of Educational Services at the Bernalillo County Detention Center. They all praise your efforts highly. The last one said that the director of the detention center who commended you for your efforts even overrode his own directive stating he would not write letters on behalf of inmates. What the hell did you do, anyway? With maybe the exception of the Chaplain, people like that don't generally stick their necks out for an inmate."

"Well, to be honest, I don't think they were doing it just for me. They might have thought so at the time, but I think they were simply "induced," shall we say, by someone's willingness to find ways to produce something positive from a generally negative experience."

"Well, you've managed to "induce" some pretty important officials. I'm looking here at letters from Congressman John McCain and Senator Barry Goldwater. You do know Goldwater initiated an effort to get you an executive clemency, don't you?"

"Yes, of course. But I think that was dropped when he left office."

"Not according to what I'm reading here. It's still pending. But just so you know what you're up against with that, I'll tell you that such things are not well received in prisons. Prison authorities view them as manipulation, and they resent anyone who makes them work more than they have to. I already checked with the case manager's office, and they told me they don't intend to do anything more than they absolutely have to. Anything that comes up, they'll delay as long as they can."

"How nice of them, seeing how many 'more important' things they have to do. God forbid that anyone with any compunction to do something worthwhile might actually try to accomplish anything."

"I understand completely. Believe me, I'm not enjoying this job myself right now. It feels more like a tour of duty. But maybe we can help each other." Her military reference was amusing.

"How?"

"I want to start a class on self-improvement, and I would like you to run it."

"Me? How am I supposed to do that?"

"I'll clear the way. You'll have to initiate the process by making all the applications and developing a course syllabus. The BOP doesn't permit an inmate to 'run' anything. But I believe I can prove to my superiors that you have a substantial track record and have only the best of motives. As far as they're concerned, I'll be in charge—but you'll be running the class. I can use this as an example to develop a model for reform that might not alarm them so much. I'll characterize it as a 'bridge' concept to assist adult offenders on their way back into society. But you will have to write the syllabus and develop it as if it's your idea."

"It *is* my idea. It's an essential part of the juvenile diversion proposal I wrote that got the attention of Goldwater and McCain in the first place. 'Bridge' is exactly the term I used."

"I know. I've read your proposal. I think it's great. But it was written for juveniles. Even though most of your subjects are juveniles emotionally, they're still adults as far as the BOP is concerned. We have to direct our efforts at them first. Besides, that's supposed to be my job. Anyway, our mandate *is* 'correction.' That comes from the U.S. Congress, and is supposedly Director Carlson's prime directive."

"I agree. Punishment is necessary, but there must be a way for them to get reoriented. My use of the term 'bridge' was to create an image for a way back for those who can accept the concept of 'belonging' somewhere. Most of these guys have no connection with anyone in their community outside of their old contacts."

"Exactly. So, will you do it?"

"Do what?"

"Teach the class, of course."

"I think the appropriate response at this point would be to say 'I'll think about it'."

"I'll take that to mean 'yes.' But once again, I'll caution you. Do not discuss this with anyone, or it will never get approved. If certain staff members know I'm even discussing this with you, it'll die before I can even draft the proposal. I could even get another reprimand on my record."

"*Another* reprimand?"

"Yes, another one. At Lompoc they said I took 'too personal an interest' in the inmates. It was bullshit, but that was enough to justify sending me here. It went into my records as an official reprimand. Anyway, it will take me some time to get materials together, and talk with the warden. He's new here, but he's not new to the system. We've talked about such things before, and I think he'll let me do it. But I'll need to show him that you are capable of holding the interest of the inmates without posturing or manipulating the circumstances. This will be your show, but I'll assist and monitor. What comes of it may help me get similar programs up and running in the rest of the system. Your example could be a hell of a catalyst, I think."

"Well, good. I hope it at least gets me a decent cup of coffee on occasion."

"I'm sure. Well, nice talking with you. I'd like to see your syllabus within the next week or so."

"Well, I'll see if I can work it into my very demanding schedule."

"As soon as you do," she smiled, "I'll see if I can work it into the warden's demanding schedule."

By late that afternoon I was already at work, writing everything that could be useful in structuring a prisoner's course of education on self-esteem. A lot of my work had to be from memory, since most of my writing was lost in the vast expanse of the federal prison system. Supposedly, they were "on the way" to me from the various facilities I had been moved in and out of. With the help of a couple of inmates who had once been teachers—to whom I divulged only enough details to pique their interest—I soon had a syllabus for a ten-week course ready to submit to the psychologist.

Two months later, after planning, writing, submitting, re-writing and resubmitting all of the outlines, curricula and proposed schedules, the class was finally approved, and notices were posted on the bulletin boards of all the dormitories. This was a major breakthrough in the normal routines of the BOP, and one that the psychologist and I felt would be met with great enthusiasm by many inmates.

The night of the first scheduled class arrived, and we sat with eager expectation for inmates to fill the room. After nearly an hour of waiting, only three men showed up. Disappointed but undeterred, I started the class and began talking about what they could do to derive some form of benefit from imprisonment. From the looks on their faces, you would have thought I suggested that we all sign up for another two years at Safford. By the end of the session, however, the psychologist had managed to convince them that it really was safe to talk openly. If the course was successful, she told them, it might eventually have an impact on prison officials that could make a difference in how we were treated.

Three weeks and two classes later, the attendance grew to eight men. Recalling Margaret Mead's famous quote that the greatest accomplishments are made by the smallest of determined groups, I pressed on. By then, we began to see that there were ways to make a difference on our own, without official programs or authorization. We discovered that we could learn from living purposefully and consciously in a harsh and hostile environment.

In one experiment, for example, each student was to choose an inmate they disliked the most, or who was particularly threatening or intimidating. Then, they were to perform certain acts of kindness toward that person without them knowing who did it or why. One week into the experiment, each of us began to observe positive changes in behavior in those selected inmates. In several cases, we were astonished to discover that the attitude of the subject inmate changed noticeably toward the inmate who, unbeknownst to them, had performed the kind acts.

Techniques of meditation, visualization and dream interpretation were explored and discussed with amazing results—all under the watchful eye of the prison psychologist, who gradually joined us as one of the participants instead of as an authority. A few correctional officers began to look in on the meetings and gradually began to participate. Their presence resulted in a drop in attendance at first, but after a while it grew back again. For a brief period once each week, uniforms and tattoos disappeared from our consciousness, and people of extremely diverse cultures and personal backgrounds sat together in at least a *spirit* of cooperation and mutual respect.

My relationship with Debra had stabilized through our writing and phone calls, and a visit from her later that summer confirmed it. The parole hearings were coming up in October, and everything looked very good for an early release. My total time served at that point was just over eighteen months. A release in January, just six months away, was conceivable, even if only to a halfway house in Phoenix.

But there were other factors to be considered by the parole board. In the wake of what was being perceived as a "rising tide" of crime and drug abuse, the two main purposes of incarceration had become "deterrence" and "retribution", both of which had to be evident in each case being considered by the Board.

Incarceration, according to the emerging new correctional philosophy, should not be solely about "correction," but about exacting a measure of retribution for crimes committed. Rehabilitation, not surprisingly, was considered an impractical and unrealistic expectation—a joke, even—and not to be considered as a factor in the correctional process. Even though I could understand a part of their reasoning, it perplexed me to see how much at odds they were with their own basic purpose by calling themselves a 'correctional system.'

In my case, the parole board would have to be willing to consider what had actually happened, and then what I had done throughout my incarceration to demonstrate consistent "good behavior." That would require an evaluation by the local facility staff, who are not typically inclined to do so until they've had opportunity to observe the inmate's behavior over a period of time. Generally, there is very little reason for them to "expedite" an inmate's evaluation, or to go beyond what is actually required—particularly in violence or drug-related cases.

In order to get the facts before the parole board, someone on their side would have to study my case thoroughly, evaluate the merits of what I had gone through and make a recommendation to the Board for release. That was the sentencing judge's intention by making his comments "for the record," but getting someone in the bureaucratic sea of the Federal Parole Commission to take the time to even read the case for my first appearance was highly unlikely.

I hadn't been at Safford long enough to establish a history of good behavior in the eyes of the prison authorities. Even with my work with inmates, which to them could simply be an elaborate scheme to "get over" on the system, I was too new for them to risk such a recommendation without a minimum of a year's observation.

It was yet another twist of irony that the harder I worked with my class, and in my regular prison job, the more I alerted the authorities at Safford to a possible attempt to manipulate them. "No one goes to such lengths," I was told, "for no apparent reason. It could only be to impress the parole board." I was merely reinforcing their own preconceived notion about convicts as "con" men. Apprehensive but determined, I continued my work, and Debra and I made plans as if my release were imminent. Marriage was discussed as a probability rather than a possibility.

October finally came, and with it, the day of the parole hearing. Debra was there, along with an older friend of mine who was a well-respected member of my community. Both spoke highly of my character as an honest, productive man, and as a loving, dedicated father. The questions to me were routine, but I answered them with a sincerity borne of a long journey—not just through the hardships of prison, but of my years as a fugitive and the loss of so much time and opportunity. Never in my entire life had I felt such a deep conviction and genuine sense of desire to belong somewhere.

Two weeks went by. Then another, and another. Debra and I spoke on the telephone every day, always with the expectation that all would go well, and that the delay was a good sign. Someone evidently was taking the time to review the details of my case, and surely they couldn't hold me once they knew what had last taken place in court.

It was now early November, and the evening air signaled the coming of winter. I was growing increasingly anxious not knowing whether I would be out in time for Christmas. Finally, I was called to the case manager's office. The letter had come from the parole board. I couldn't tell from the look on his face whether it was good news or bad news.

"You've been denied," he stated flatly. "I'm not surprised at all," he went on, as if he were talking about a lost football game while I reeled in disbelief. "These guys never approve on the first hearing. They don't even look at the record. All they want to know is how long you've been in, and what the extent of your crime was.

"Let's see," he went on as he flipped through the pages. "Your case is a drug case. Two separate convictions, both drugs. One's a pretty big one, plus you were a fugitive. What was it, five years? Not good. Not good at all. I doubt they went any further than that. You know, you've only been here six months now. Can't make much of a determination from that."

I was in shock. I took a breath and tried to reply to this insanity.

"But what about the judge's ruling—the 'B-2' sentence, and his comments about my worthiness and cooperation? That should count for something..."

"Doesn't say anything about that in here. But then we don't keep all the files here. It would take way too much room to keep all the records on every inmate. They're supposed to review all that stuff on each inmate. You're still too new here. You're doing good work here, and you've got some positive things going for you, but you have to give this thing a little more time."

"This *thing*? This *thing* is my *life*. It's my *future*. I've paid my dues. More than you could possibly know. More than anyone on the Parole Commission has bothered to consider. I've gone way above and beyond what's expected of any prisoner. I could have just given up and caved in to the meaningless bullshit that goes on in this system. I was dragged four times through twelve different facilities, and even when I was cooped up in shit-house detention centers and county jails, I busted my ass to help other inmates—even *staff* members, more than a few times. And this is all the consideration I get? This system is supposed to be about correcting men who have made mistakes. Well, I've admitted mine, and I've paid dearly for it. And I *have* been "corrected"—no thanks to your system. You guys think 'a little more time' solves everything, but it doesn't. It just prolongs the agony and festering. It's no wonder guys come out of here ready and even *eager* to break the law again."

Inside of me, a slumbering dragon raised his head. I could feel a very deep anger rising fast. The case manager pushed himself back in his chair and glowered back at me. His eyes went steely gray, and his neck muscles tightened. I was losing him, and that could set me back an entire year. I had to temper my words...and fast.

"I'm sorry," I said. I forced the words out of my mouth, even though I wanted to rage. He couldn't do anything more at this point than what he was doing. He would keep track of my behavior and make entries in their precious records. That was all he was required to do. Maybe this was part of the routine—deny an inmate's release and watch how he handles it. Yeah, maybe that was it. His face was cold and stern. I had seen that look before, and it meant I was on thin ice with him. I forced myself to keep backtracking.

"You're right. You don't know me. You've got four hundred guys to keep track of, and I've hardly been here long enough to show consistent patterns. I know that. To you, it makes sense. To me, it's a killer. I've got kids out there that are desperate for my time and attention. They're good kids who don't need to suffer any more for my stupidity. But I know this must be an administrative screw-up. My own *prosecutor* wrote a letter of support. Two U.S. Senators, including Goldwater himself wants me out—and it's not because I'm some rich kid whose family has some pull." He seemed to soften a bit, and even leaned back in his seat a little. This guy stood between me and freedom because it would be his recommendation upon which the Parole Board would rely at the next hearing.

" You'd be wise to back off for a while," he said sternly. "There are other men in here who have done a lot more time than you have, and their records aren't much worse than yours, as we see it."

"I don't think I deserve more than other inmates," I softened my tone further.

"I *earned* the right to be considered more fairly. If you knew what I've been through, and what I've been consistently willing to stand for in the face of hopeless odds, you'd know what I mean."

"I think I know what you mean," he answered. "Maybe that's so. But it's not going to do you any good to get upset about it. Nothing's going to happen now until next spring. You keep working on your projects and stay straight, and I'll recommend your release myself. You may be the slickest con man that's ever come through here—and believe me, I've seen the best of 'em—or you just might be a real asset. I've talked to the Doc. She says you're on the level, and you've already done some good with a few of the inmates. That'll go into your record, but it'll carry a lot more weight if they see that you continue to prove that it isn't just a routine to get out of here. So go on with it, and keep your head up. If you're for real, we'll see it."

I left his office in disbelief. I could understand his point, but I found it difficult to comprehend that my records were not reviewed in depth, or that a simple, goddamn phone call wasn't made. If they had really listened to me at the hearing, they would at least have done that.

My wait to use the telephone that night seemed a particularly long one. How could I tell Debra it would be another six months before we could plan anything? Or that it could even be another *year* before I would get out?

Finally, my turn at the phone came. Normally making a call was the highlight of my day, hearing the fresh, sweet voice of a woman who had been through hell with me, and who was still out there waiting for my return. Tonight, my heart was heavy as I dialed her number. The operator put the call through with the usual routine, and Debra's voice came on the line.

"Hi," I began. "I'm afraid I have some bad news."

Chapter Forty-One

The next few weeks passed painfully slow. Debra took the bad news in typically good form, quickly affirming her love for me and her willingness to deal with the added delay. The reality of the situation, however, was lost on her at that moment. At the minimum, we most likely were looking at another year before I would be home. And in truth, I couldn't assure her even of that.

Over the next several weeks, I began to sense something unsettling in her voice that had me increasingly nervous. There was something slightly heavier in her manner that seemed to be more than simple discouragement. Something like resignation hung in the air after the last several times we talked with each other. Had it simply been a momentary reaction to a setback, I could understand it. Despite her efforts to reassure me that everything was okay and that she could wait, I knew something was different.

With all of her good intentions, she was having a hard time waiting with no certainty about what lay ahead for us. It had already been nearly two years since our last free time together. We had seen each other just four times since then, and those were only in jail or prison visiting rooms. She had two kids of her own to take care of, and a meager income from a private school she had set up in her home. My collect phone calls were running several hundred dollars a month, on top of which she was sending me money for commissary purchases. We had been through the hell of Taladega, El Reno, Springfield and Pensacola together, as well as La Tuna and Phoenix. Safford was a six hundred-mile round trip for her each time she wanted to visit, and now we were looking at another six months to a year of that.

It was too much to ask of her. Too much to expect her to keep going through. She needed her life back, and even though she wouldn't admit it, her personal circumstances were beginning to change again.

Finally, it began to happen. Gradually at first, then more frequently, she wouldn't be there when I called. At first, I forced myself to accept that she needed to get out, spend some time with her friends, enjoy life a little more. But as the pattern continued to build, I began to realize that she was seeing someone else again. When we did manage to talk on the phone, I could tell she was holding back because he was there in the room with her. I could feel her hesitation, as well as her dilemma. She was torn between what she felt she had to do with me, and what she wanted to do with him. She was miserable, lonely and aching for tender loving care, but she couldn't stand the thought of hurting me....again.

Then it finally came—the request not to call for a while. She said she needed some time to work things through her mind and heart. It was a reasonable request under the circumstances, but to me it was a deathblow. Suddenly her letters stopped coming. I would call and she wouldn't be there. One time she was actually there, but said flat out that she couldn't talk just then. My birthday came and went, then Christmas. No card. No letter. Five weeks passed without a word from her, when before her letters came as often as three or four times a week. After a while, I stopped showing up for mail call. Finally one evening, I heard my name called. A letter was passed back to me. It was addressed in her distinctive handwriting. My heart quickened, but at the same time I felt apprehensive. I sat on my bunk and held it for a few minutes, trying to feel where she was coming from. Then I tore it open and read it.

"I'm sorry I haven't written to you in so long, but so much has been going on for me that I just couldn't bring myself to write before now. I've been so confused and feeling so guilty, yet I know in my heart this is what's best for both of us. You know about Leonard; I've told you about him since he first started hanging around me last summer. He's been such a big help to me, and even though I've never been all that attracted to him, his kindness and willingness to support me has helped me get through all the pain and misery I've been feeling. I feel like I've been in prison, too. I'm sure you can understand. You've been so good about that, so caring and so understanding.

Anyway, Leonard and I have decided to marry. I know that will be hard for you to deal with, but there's no other way for me to say it. It's taken me a month to even get up the nerve to tell you, and I can't put it off any longer. Now that I've said it, there isn't much more I can say. Except that I do love you and I wish for you all the happiness you so richly deserve. This isn't about you being in prison, either. It's just the way things have worked out. You'll be out before you know it, and you will achieve your dreams. You have courage and love, and more determination than anyone I know. I will always love you.

Debra

I had a feeling it was coming, but the shock of it hit me like a freight train. I was blown apart, even though I had already been through six weeks of agonizing over why, how, and who. But down deep, I knew my time had run out with her. It wasn't reasonable to expect her to hold out all that time. Even married couples who had been together many years had a difficult time staying together under these circumstances.

I started going crazy again. I knew what had to have been going on. I even accepted the fact that she deserved something better...some*one* better. But accepting in principle and accepting in actuality were two different things. I quit my job as a recreation clerk and took one in the dish room.. Four hundred meal trays, three times a day. Cleaning up garbage left by men whose lives and attitudes were generally garbage. Every day I stood at the sinks full of putrid dishwater, feeling empty inside and scraping leftover food off trays piled up by hundreds of men I wanted to despise but knew I had become part of.

I was called in to see the case manager to discuss the letter. Of course they had read it, and had considered taking action. But their only segregation cell was occupied. During my conversation with him, I was able to assure him that I was okay and that I wouldn't cause any trouble. I had been through this before, I told him, and added that I felt it had strengthened me. He seemed convinced, and let me go.

I had watched other inmates go through similar "Dear John's," first on the telephone and then in their bunks or out in the yard, trying to cope with the loss of oftentimes the only thing that gave them any hope for a normal life on the outside. Anything is bearable as long as a loved one on the outside has faith in him. Having it snatched away in the midst of such hardship is yet another punishment that drives most of them deeper into lives of crime. More than a few strong men I knew broke under the pressure of such heartache. I wanted to die. I tried to bury myself in mindless effort, scraping meal trays, running for hours, playing chess—anything to get my mind off how miserable I was.

One day while lying on my bunk, I decided to work on a project to get my mind on something else. I had collected pictures of animals from magazines, and had planned to paste them into a picture book for one of my children. I took the pictures from my locker and spread them out on my bunk to sort them according to type and origin. As I did, I began to get an idea for a story. I arranged and rearranged the pictures as a story began to take form in my mind. The pictures were mostly of wild animals, many of them from articles I had read about Alaska.

Of those, the majority was of bald eagles and bears.

I sat down with my notebook and began to write a story about an eaglet that had lost his parents. It was my own version of "The Ugly Duckling," which I called "Tears of the Eagle." As I wrote, I felt a sense of excitement rising. Suddenly I had a purpose again. Writing and putting the pieces together in a way to form an actual book became a major undertaking. The more I worked on it, the more perfect I wanted it to be. I traded food and baked goods finagled from my friends in the bakery and the kitchen for materials with which to construct a large-size storybook, complete with beautiful pictures and even a binding as professional as if it were done in a print shop.

It was magnificent. It took me weeks to put it all together. I was so focused on writing the story and making the actual book that I gradually forgot about being miserable. By late January, I was largely clear of emotional upheaval. In a way, I was actually *glad* things had turned out the way they did. My work with the class by then had been taken over by the psychologist, but suddenly I felt inspired to rejoin the group. Sharing my experiences with the group opened up a whole new series of dialogs on how to deal with relationships while in prison….and how to handle break-ups.

In my effort to create the storybook, I spent a lot of time in the law library, which had three old typewriters I could use to type the story. On one of my visits there one day, I overheard a conversation between two inmates, one of whom was our "jailhouse lawyer." He had succeeded in getting several inmates favorable rulings in court cases and parole appeals, so I listened as he helped the other inmate file an appeal of his parole denial.

"It's easy," I heard him say. "You just fill in this form, write your reasons why you feel you deserve to be reconsidered, and send it off. It probably won't result in anything, but by law they have to at least look at it. They get so many of these, they usually just rubberstamp them, but they have been known to approve appeals on occasion. In any case, you have nothing to lose."

After they left the room, I sat there wondering. If the Commission has to look at the case, it wouldn't hurt to fill out one of the forms and send it in. I walked over to the counter where official forms were kept, and found the one I was looking for. I listed five major reasons why I should be reconsidered. I had the typewriter right there to make it look professional. Before the end of the day, my parole appeal was in the outgoing mail.

The next week I finished the storybook and felt so inspired, I kept on writing other stories. Three more weeks passed, and I was writing furiously. I got my old job back at the bakery, which allowed me to sit on my bunk and write in relative privacy while the rest of the inmates in the dorm were off to their various places of work.

Another week passed, and I was still writing. I became active in the Toastmasters' Club again, and won two awards in competition against other clubs in the region. The self-help group was running along smoothly without my having to come up with new material. Inspiration had taken over the class, and no one needed me or, for that matter, the Doc to guide them. They were making discoveries on their own, aided by new inmates who were far better qualified to assist them. The concept was working.

Almost as an afterthought, I remembered to request consideration for the upcoming parole hearings. Unbelievably, I nearly missed the deadline for applications, and the hearings were only five weeks away.

One morning soon after I had filed my request, I was summoned from my quiet perch on my bunk to the case manager's office. It was unusual to be summoned to his office for any reason, so I was more than a little uneasy as I waited outside his office, along with two other inmates who arrived after me. This had to be about the parole hearings coming up the following month, I thought. Inside the office, we could plainly hear that someone was angry, and shouting. Shortly afterward, an inmate I knew to be particularly hot-headed stormed out of the office, his face flushed with anger. I looked at the guy next to me and we both shrugged our shoulders. The case manager called "next," and I went in. He was busy writing in a file folder—no doubt his observations of the inmate who had just left. My attempt to lighten his mood with a little humor seemed to fall on deaf ears as he continued writing. When he looked up and saw me, a trace of a smile actually flashed across his face.

"Sit down," he said, as he began to search for something among the various files and documents spread out in front of him. "I've got some good news for you. Let me see, now...where did I put it?"

He shuffled through a stack of papers on his desk, then opened and closed each of three different desk drawers. At first I thought he might be toying with me, but then I began to realize he had really misplaced whatever he was referring to. I couldn't imagine what kind of "good news" he could possibly have for me, unless it was my clemency action finally getting some action. It was probably something mundane, like a new course to teach or a miniscule pay raise.

"So what's this 'good news'?" I yawned, as if bored with the whole thing. "Can't you just tell me? Okay, let me guess. I'm being transferred to a prison camp..."

"No, no," he responded as if I had asked him that question seriously. "This is really good news. But I want you to read it yourself. Now where the hell did I put it?"

Better news than a transfer to a prison camp ? That would be a Level One, minimum-security place. I had only been joking, but he was implying it was something better than that. *Could my clemency action have come through?*

Finally he gave up and called his secretary. Yes, she had the file he was looking for. Yes, she would bring it in right away. She came in and handed him a file that had obviously been handled a lot. It had more official markings and scribbled initials on it than anything I had seen on one of my files yet. He opened it and flipped through several pages.

"Evidently, you sent in an appeal on your parole denial."

I bolted upright in my chair. "Yes I did," I replied sharply. "But then I forgot all about it. That was several months ago. *You've heard from them?*"

"Yes, I have," he said as he pulled an official document from the file and handed it to me. "It seems we're supposed to have you out of here post-haste. According to this, you should have been out two months ago."

"*Whaaat?!?!?*" I exclaimed, grabbing the paper and pouring over every word on it. "Where does it say that? Are you serious?"

"Oh yes, I'm serious all right. I don't joke with inmates about things like that. It's down here in the lower right hand corner," he said as he stood up and leaned over his desk. He pointed upside down toward the appropriate place. "The first part is a bunch of legal gibberish that tells how they came to their ruling. But the number of months left to serve is right there in that corner. According to their ruling, you were technically eligible for a halfway house two months ago. You still have about four months to serve, but that puts you in the category of 'eligible for release' to community-based programs."

"What does that mean?" I shot back hungrily. "When can I leave? Where am I going? How do I get there?"

"Hold on, now. Just calm down a bit. I know this is a lot to take in so suddenly, but everything's working out. That's why Peggy had the file. She's already arranging space for you in a halfway house in Phoenix. It's still going to take us a few weeks to get you on your way, but it won't be long now."

"A few *weeks?!?* Why?"

"Well, we've got a lot of paperwork to get done before you can go. Technically, you'll still be in our custody even while you're on parole. There are BOP offices from here to Washington that have to officially approve our plan of release for you. If they want to, they can drag the process out for the entire time the Parole Commission has set for your actual parole to begin. Halfway houses are merely our way of transitioning prisoners back into their communities. It's not a 'right,' but a sort of an 'easing back' into the world, so to speak. We don't *have* to let you out, so you have to be real careful from here on."

"Okay, so what's the likelihood I'll be out of here like you said...'in a few weeks'?"

"Pretty good, actually. Peggy says they've got an opening in Phoenix, and I've got a friend in Washington who might just walk this through the right offices. Besides, the warden was pretty impressed with those two awards you won for the Toastmasters. He's been taking a lot of flack from the other Toastmasters' clubs in the area about how we've been getting weak. I think he's going to make a few calls, too. If I were you, I'd be wrapping things up pretty quick. But don't—I mean DO NOT—get too cocky, or change your attitude in any way. If you get a write-up for any reason...doesn't matter what...that will automatically delay your release while we investigate. I mean NO significant change in behavior. Got that?"

"Yeah, sure. I mean, can I smile a lot? That might be a significant change."

"Of course," he smiled. It was the first time I could remember seeing him actually break a smile. "I think you know what I mean. Just don't let me see you back in this office until the day you leave. I'll have your release papers to sign."

"Is that all? I just sit around and wait? Pace the floor? Bite my nails?"

"No, you'll be issued suitable civilian clothes, and the infirmary will want another AIDS test. The psychologist and the chaplain each have their required questions and release forms to deal with. Make sure you don't owe anything at the library, recreation department or the commissary. You'll be given a list of things to do. Just follow the list, get each thing initialed by each department head, and once the official papers come back from Washington, you're out of here. Now get out of here."

I was out the door like a rocket. For a moment, I didn't know which way to turn, what door to open, or whom to tell first. I wanted to call everyone I knew, but it was too early for the phones. They didn't come on until after chow. I would skip chow that night and get in line early. This was too much. My heart was beating like a racehorse. I was frantic, only this time with an explosion of thoughts, ideas and impressions in my brain, I couldn't think straight. I was going *home.* DAMN!!! *HOME!!!!*

I had to calm down...get hold of myself. I had to do something to release the pressure and excitement I felt. I thought maybe a few laps around the prison yard would help, so I went back to the dorm and pulled out my running clothes. Out on the exercise field, there was no one but me. I took off and fairly flew around the field. Around and around I went. I was *free*—or at least soon would be. I felt that if I stretched my arms out, I could lift off and fly out of there like the wrens and sparrows I had watched for two years and four months.

As I was halfway into the fifth lap around the field, I noticed one of the guards standing by the entrance to the field. Suddenly, a wave of panic swept over me. I had forgotten I was still in prison. In my sudden burst of elation, I had forgotten I was still just an inmate to the rest of the staff. What was worse, I hadn't bothered to get a pass.

My mind flooded with thoughts of what to say. As I slowed to a walk and headed toward him, I went weak in the knees. It was Officer Cantwell—one of the hardest, meanest guards on the entire staff. He loved to make life miserable for inmates. He had only been at Safford for six months, and already he had busted more guys for the pettiest things than guards who had been there for years. Rumor had it that he had been transferred to Safford from the federal penitentiary at Marion, Ohio. It was the absolute worst place in the entire federal system, and if the rumors about him were true, he *had been kicked out* for treating inmates so badly.

Now he stood waiting with his pad of D.R.'s for me to produce a pass I didn't have. I was in for a certain write-up, and automatic confinement in the hole. I had never been this vulnerable my entire time at Safford. There was no way out. He had me cold. Seeing him waiting in the sweltering heat, I knew I was in trouble. The case manager had just told me not an hour before to avoid any problems, and here I was about to get written up. My heart was pounding much more for what I was facing than it was from running laps. On the very day I get the news that I'm soon to be released, I violate the warden's own steadfast rule: Never be anywhere outside your work or living space without a pass.

My head was swimming. I was close enough to make out the veins bulging in his neck. I had to say something to disarm him before he wrote me up, but what?

Guards thrived on being able to write up an inmate. Some did it for the enjoyment of getting to us, and some of them did it just because it made them look like they were doing their jobs. This guy did it out of sheer spite.

Then I remembered the guard back in Pensacola—the one who had written me up for the telephone incident. I looked at Cantwell and felt the same sense of sadness and loneliness in him that the guard in Pensacola had shown. For an instant, I felt something shift in me, and I wondered what was eating him so much. Something awful had to have happened to him to drive him so. The fear and anger suddenly left me, and I saw him as a little boy left alone and hurting. Something had hurt that little boy terribly.

"Good afternoon," I initiated the exchange as I walked up to him, trying to catch my breath while I collected my thoughts. "It's pretty damn hot out here for only being April, don't you think?"

"Yes, it's hot. What are you doing out here?"

"Well, I just got some pretty good news. I'm being released in a few weeks. My parole appeal came through, and they just notified me to get my things in order. I was so excited about the news, I had to do something to calm down. Running seemed the only thing that would do it. But I forgot to get a pass. I didn't even think about it until I saw you standing there. Can you believe it? On the very day I get the news I've been waiting for two and a half years for, I screw up. What can I say?"

"Not much," he replied flatly, taking out his pad of official D.R. forms. My heart sank. He was going to do it. God*damn* if he wasn't going to write me up. He wasn't even going to discuss it. I wanted to tell him how I felt, what it might do to my release process…beg him, if need be, or plead with him. Tears welled up in my eyes, and I fought to hold them back. But something in me told me to just stand still and send him kind thoughts. No matter what it looked like, I knew that things weren't always as they seem at first.

He flipped through the thick pad of forms and pulled one out, scribbled on it and handed it to me. It wasn't a 'D.R.' at all…but a *pass*.

"What's this?" I questioned in disbelief.

"What's the matter?" he shot back at me as he walked away. "You've never seen a pass before?"

He turned and continued a few more steps down the pathway toward the compound, then stopped, turned around and looked back at me.

"Don't go home without it," he said, then grinned and walked away.

I couldn't believe my eyes or my ears. The meanest, baddest cop in the whole damn prison system had just passed up an opportunity to write me up, then gave me an unsolicited pass and actually made a joke about it. And a damn *good* joke, at that. All things considered, it seemed I had finally "re-written" my script.

Life suddenly looked marvelous. Decent. Joyous. Delicious. Everything was turning good. But I had to get myself grounded soon or I might get in trouble yet. I went back to the dorm and took a cold shower. Finally I was able to calm down. I lay on my bunk and let a rush of thoughts flood my mind. Where would I go, once I was through the halfway house? What would I do with my newfound freedom? Go back home, where the whole community knew about my prison time and about my fugitive years there? Or go someplace totally new and fresh? How did I want to create my soon-to-be-new life?

A few hours later, I woke up surprised to discover that I had actually drifted off to sleep. It was a few minutes after four, and the main head count was underway. All around me, inmates were shuffling and shouting, and typically antsy about mail call and chow time. Right after that would be TV programs, waiting in long lines for the telephones, chess, the weight pile or arts and crafts. Soon after would be "lights out" at the end of another typical day in our confined and secluded little world.

When the head count was done, I vaguely heard the muffled sounds of mail call as everyone crowded up to the front entrance, eagerly waiting for their names to be called. Suddenly I felt so detached from the whole thing, it was as if I wasn't even there. On my bunk was a body waiting to begin a whole new life back in the "real" world. I was merely a distant observer, watching a throng of inmates crowding around a white-shirted officer with a two-way radio and a set of keys jingling on his hip.

On an upper bunk midway along the right-hand side of Dormitory #4, was the shape and the substance of a man about to return from a journey through the darkness—*and* the light—of the human mind. It was the ending of one journey and the beginning of another—a continuing discovery of the mysteries of life and the power of the human spirit to become empowered by them in the face of apparently hopeless odds. It was a story as old as life itself—a story of the human heart and its inherent ability to overcome our own darkest shadows.

When the big day finally came two weeks later, it was almost anticlimactic. I was told to take my things, which amounted to three boxes of files and journal notes, to the "Receiving & Processing" room. There I found a set of civilian clothes waiting for me just like the ones Johnson had waiting for him when I first arrived at La Tuna. Before all the necessary release forms had come in from the warden's office, however, it was lunchtime. Unbelievably, the officer in charge coldly instructed me to step into the holding cell. I was scant minutes away from walking out the door to long-sought, well-deserved freedom, and this guy was going to lock me down like a new arrival to wait while he had lunch. With great restraint, I held my tongue and stepped into the tiny cell, dressed in my new "civilian" clothes as he turned the key in the lock and walked away as if nothing else mattered but his time in the staff lunchroom.

In the final moments of my release from my entire two and a half year journey, it came as no small twist of irony that before I would be permitted to walk out the door and down to the bus station, I had to wait in a holding cell for a guard to have his lunch.

As I sat there waiting in disbelief, however, I began to realize that he had unwittingly assisted me in completing an entirely different, and perhaps more important aspect of my journey—a ritual of closure, as it turned out. Feeling an old and very familiar urge to start pacing, I sat down, quieted myself, and considered what this most recent bit of irony might be about. Then it came to me.

A message had been imparted to me a long time back by an unknown, wise old soul that had carried me through the darkest moments of my journey. It needed to be passed along to someone else.

I looked around at the cinder block walls that had become such an integral part of my life, and I felt a smile come across my face as I felt the pen still in my hand from having signed my property release forms. Squatting down low and facing the wall next to the door where the guards wouldn't be likely to see it, I carefully and very precisely wrote ten little words that had come to me over and over again in all the jails and prisons and detention centers I had experienced since I had first read them.

In the tiniest, but still most legible words I could form with the pen, I wrote:

BE COOL   STAY CALM   IT'S ONLY A MATTER OF TIME.

Epilogue

More than ten years have passed since my exit from FCI Safford. The two weeks before my release seemed like the longest of my entire journey because of my intense anticipation and attempts on the part of some inmates to prod me into doing something rash. But the wait was well worth it. It forced me into a mode of objectivity and extreme care about what I said and what I did that has carried over into my life ever since. I listen more closely now, and I watch for motives and hidden agenda in my dealings with everyone. I pay a lot more attention to my intuition, and to the details of life that I used to overlook.

Prison changes one forever, no matter how resilient and adaptable one might be. The experience of it leaves scars that remain always in one's memory. For many, like Nick Murray and Big Jim Valentine, it also scars their bodies in ways that can never be erased. It haunts them in dreams that play out in endless combinations and forms, and in books and movies and over-dramatized stories meant to capture the public's fascination with the dark side of human behavior.

In a far more positive sense, however, I can emphasize that for those inmates and former prisoners who decide to make the best of their experiences, it can be an opportunity for enormous personal growth. For most of them, unfortunately, that's too difficult a challenge. Few have a decent education, and are often highly reactive to those who do. Most come from broken homes, and almost from birth know only the law of the streets. When they are released, they have no place to go but back to the same streets and neighborhoods from which they came. With no money, no job, no education, no car and, in many cases, no home, they're lost. Even the best, most determined among them are virtually forced to turn to their old contacts for even the most meager subsistence. And so the cycle repeats itself—over and over again.

With each incarceration, resentment and hostility builds to the point where many newly released inmates feel as if they are prisoners of war released behind enemy lines. With no sense of belonging to their communities, they are able to justify committing crimes against what they feel is an unfair and uncaring society of "haves," while they are "have-nots."

When I was released, it was with the ignorant comment from a newly arrived inmate processing officer, "See you in a couple of months." He had no idea about me, about my background or who I was. It never occurred to him that I might actually be going home with something meaningful to offer society, or that I would be a good father to my children. I was just another inmate to him, and that meant I was no good. Very few inmates ever will be, as far as many correctional officers and staff are concerned. That kind of attitude only causes more hostility and resentment on the part of even the best of former inmates who struggle to make sense of an otherwise hopeless situation.

For many, there is little or no hope for an end to the treadmill of jail and prison life. For them it's simply the dues one pays for having been born on the less fortunate side of life. But for those who have come to terms with themselves, and who have changed their attitude and outlook, there should be a way back. There should be a "bridge" home by being recognized as someone who has achieved a meaningful goal and who has value to the community in which they live. That can only come from individuals, groups and employers who are willing to lend a hand and assist them in getting on their feet. Sometimes that needn't be anything more than a warm welcome and encouragement that they belong there.

At this writing, there are several organizations which work to assist former prisoners, including one I have founded called "Society for Return to Honor," which facilitates the return of pre-selected, qualified men and women into their communities. Its principle aim is to assist communities and former prisoners to work together to not only reduce criminal behavior, but to address the conditions that cause it in the first place—particularly with juveniles.

There are other programs such as "Delancy Street," with facilities in San Francisco, Los Angeles, Chicago and other major cities, and others you can find on a simple Internet search. I encourage you to look into one or more of them...or inquire of your church, synagogue or other organization to see if it supports or would like to support a prison "after-care" or "community re-entry" program. There is much that can be done by simply caring enough to inquire. There is so much talent, skill and potential behind the bars and chainlink fences of America's prisons and jails that can be put to much better use once sentences are completed.

I urge you to look into the subject closely. Do some volunteer work in a jail or prison in your community. If you are willing to put in the time to demonstrate that you care, and don't have a superficial or self-righteous attitude, prisoners will listen. Even if they don't seem to at first, eventually they will. The breakthroughs can be powerful experiences for everyone involved.

There is very little to fear in contacts with prisoners, as long as you show respect rather than condescension or judgement. There are men and women who visit jails and prisons every day and never have a problem. If anything, you will be seen by inmates as someone who is willing to help, and you will be treated accordingly.

The man who helped me conceive of the idea for re-entry programs is confined to a wheelchair, yet for over fifteen years he administered educational programs to hundreds of inmates at BCDC in Albuquerque, NM. The inmates there, no matter how fierce and intimidating they appeared, would never harm him because he cared enough to offer them help and because he *respected* them. He didn't condone their negative behavior, nor did he ever debate the issues with them. Instead he offered them help to better understand themselves and how they could make a difference in their own lives.

You can make a difference. Get on a mailing list through your church, or a civic group, or through your state's Department of Corrections, and begin corresponding with agencies and individuals who know inmates who are soon to be released, and who have proven themselves worthy and honorable. Prison authorities at first may not appear to welcome your involvement, but if you persist, great opportunities are there. Correctional agencies are generally understaffed and are not always able to deal with the emotional and psychological issues that create criminal behavior in the first place. They know textbook solutions and the more obvious behavior patterns of inmates, but they don't seem to know or agree among themselves what causes men and women to keep coming back. If you take the time to read and experience what it's all about, you will be amazed at how basic the causes really are and how simple some of the solutions can be.

It will take enormous awareness and a high degree of compassion on society's part to change the system even a little. It's too big a business for those involved to want to change it. It's also job security for a major segment of the American workforce. But helping men and women *as they come out* won't affect that. Rather, it can make a huge difference in reducing repeat crime (recidivism), and restoring hope to thousands of people who have become trapped in the revolving doors of crime and punishment.

Like it or not, we're all in this together. Sooner or later, criminal behavior and its aftermath affects everyone. Positive involvement on the part of individuals and groups will ultimately benefit everyone.

For information on prison aftercare programs, contact your state Department of Corrections, the U.S. Bureau of Prisons Community Programs Office in your state capital, or:

Society for Return to Honor
P.O. 20931
Sedona, AZ 86341

For more interesting facts, information and history on the
actual people, places and events of this story, or on the
Return to Honor program, visit our Web site:
www.AMatterofTime.org

About the Author

Born in Lincoln, Nebraska, Don was raised with four sisters by a career U.S. Army officer and his wife. Graduating from high school in Greeley, Colorado in 1965, he attended Colorado State University in Ft. Collins, where he studied Business Administration and Pre-Law. Joining the U.S. Army in 1969, Don graduated from the U.S. Army Helicopter Flight School in Savannah, GA, and completed a tour of duty in Viet Nam as a combat helicopter pilot.

Most of Don's adult career has been involved in sales, marketing and small business development. He has owned his own restaurant, provided essential marketing efforts in the successful launching and/or expansion of numerous successful businesses in Arizona, Colorado and New Mexico, and has worked for twenty-five years as an freelance writer and marketing consultant.

Convicted in 1981 for his involvement with a marijuana smuggling operation in New Mexico, Don earned unprecedented commendations for his work in prison with other inmates, and established prisoner self-help and educational programs in several institutions. He also won the support of such notable authorities as the late U.S. Senator Barry S. Goldwater, U.S. Senator John McCain, and numerous other leaders in state and federal legislatures and Departments of Corrections and Justice. His first-hand experiences with inmates of all ages in federal prison inspired Don to address the desperate need for a support system for inmates upon release from prison. Within six months of his own release from federal prison in April of 1988, Don founded *The Society for Return to Honor* as an Arizona nonprofit corporation to facilitate the re-entry of former criminal offenders back into society.

Don has written extensively on the subject of prison reform and human redemption, has published numerous letters, essays and short stories, and is currently authoring a book for writers and artists on the subject of turning "creative passions into business."

He has two grown sons and a daughter, and currently lives in Sedona, Arizona.

The Story Continues...

Now that you've read about the past, we invite you to take a look at the present...and consider how you can help us create a better future—in real time.

No matter who you are, or what you do for a living,
there is something you can do to help this cause—and society as a whole.

You can help just for the sake of giving something of value to your community, or you can participate with us for more commercial purposes. We are growing a new business—a publishing and film production company that uplifts the human spirit. We promote stories that inspire people to achieve their full potential, and that make people feel good about themselves and about each other.

This book may be about prisons and the consequences of breaking the law, but it is far more about the prisons we create for ourselves by how we view the world and how we treat one another. We have created a cynical, competitive and impersonal society that tends not to respect individual needs and wants, but rather has us thinking that it's "us against the world." We are taught from a very young age not to trust anyone, not to talk to "strangers," and not to be kind or even considerate with each other. Yet that flies in the face of the greater teachings upon which this country was founded, and for which many thousands of lives have been sacrificed in order to defend and uphold the truest principles of democracy. Those principles are fundamentally based upon simple respect of one another. It also runs contrary in total to what I experienced in the bowels of darkness and depravity—in the midst of criminals doing time for all manner of crimes committed—in which I discovered that even the smallest acts of kindness brought positive results in every case.

These are hard times, to be certain...yet they could portend much better times ahead if we but simply change our way of thinking and acting toward one another. In spite of all the problems in the world today, these are times that future historians may well look back upon and declare, as Alvin Toffler once wrote,

"We are the dividing line between civilized and uncivilized humankind."

Just as some of the greatest breakthroughs in history took place just after the darkest times, so it may well be with present times. I believe it starts with and builds upon common human decency—the ability we have to treat one another with respect, regardless of race, creed, gender or culture. We don't have to agree with or condone the actions of others, but the degree to which we can respect others and treat them accordingly, will be the degree to which we can truly "modernize" our society and move into a more illuminated existence.

HIGH GROUND PRODUCTIONS, INC. was founded on such principles. Each of us *can* make a difference in the world if we believe enough in ourselves and if we are willing to respect others' right to their own "pursuit of happiness."

We have founded a company that promotes well-being and fosters the production and publication of stories that give people hope and promise of better times to come. We invite you to participate with us in any way you feel moved…by helping us promote this and succeeding books, and by spreading the word about us to others you know.

You can do this because it feels good to do so, and/or because there are financial and professional incentives. Recent box office smash hits and several best-selling books have achieved great success simply because people were encouraged to spread the word about them. You can do the same with this story, and succeeding ones, simply by urging others to buy the book and see the movie when it comes out. The result will be a rising sense of decency and goodwill between people that will have a ripple effect that will eventually come back around to you.

If you feel an interest in getting involved with us more professionally, there are many opportunities to do so by simply going to our Web site, or by contacting us at the below address and phone number for more information. Our Web site address is: www.AMatterofTime.org

We need research team members to help us find groups of people and organizations who might be willing to buy this and succeeding books. We also need sales representatives to help us find outlets for our books, and organizations to whom we can license the rights to the e-book or other versions of the book. Both positions earn commissions and a percentage of profits of the company, which can either be earned personally by you or designated to a charitable cause of your choice. In many cases, stock options may be available in quantity as well.

Whether you choose to work with us by merely referring our books to others, or by working with us as a volunteer or as a paid team member, we extend a hand of recognition to you and our voice of support and acknowledgment. Even with all the turmoil and crises in the world, we believe that this is a great time to be alive…and we invite you to join us in doing our part to make it so. Please contact us to find out how you can do that.

In the meantime, please know that we care about you. You matter. *Every single person matters.* **We are dedicated to bringing that realization to the world.**

There are few more effective ways we know of to accomplish that than through a best-selling book and a hit motion picture. Come and be a part of this with us.

For more information, contact us at:

HIGH GROUND PRODUCTIONS, INC.
P.O. Box 20931 • Sedona, AZ 86341
928-284-1898
www.AMatterofTime.org
info@AMatterofTime.org

WATCH FOR OUR UPCOMING NEXT BOOK:

Our next book, *Creating Working Capital: Turning Your Creative Passions Into Cashflow,* will be released early next spring. This will be a book that teaches writers, artists, performers and beginning entrepreneurs how to get off the "starving artist" treadmill and raise capital to do their dreams instead of doing everything else but that. This book will be released in conjunction with a series of weekend workshops that will teach participants the essentials of raising capital, and creating a healthy, functional business so that they can earn an income doing what they are most passionate about.

Resources For You

This story was completed in the summer of 1999, and was first released as a Print-on-Demand book in May of 2000. Since that time, we determined that getting a book published through more conventional means was virtually an impossible task. *Chicken Soup For The Soul,* as a prime example, was turned down by over a *hundred* publishers. Many other excellent, best-selling books experienced the same results. Since that time, we formed an Arizona Limited Liability Company, then later an Arizona C Corporation for the purpose of raising enough capital to form our own publishing company. Once we determined that we had a strong prospect for a film to come of it, we formed a film production company. We have to date raised a total of over $500,000 for both companies, have a film development contract with a known Hollywood producer, and a team of experts in business, film and publishing to guide us through the "minefields" that await the average entrepreneur starting his or her own business.

Many resources have been drawn upon in this overall effort, but none has contributed more powerfully to our success than Income Builders International…now known as "IBI GLOBAL." This thirteen-year-old organization with headquarters in Madison, Alabama, brings together five times a year expert "Fortune 500" business trainers and motivational speakers to assist people from all walks of life how to start, develop, manage and promote their own businesses, no matter what their backgrounds or dreams may be. Learning how to raise capital legally, then to manage it and turn it into positive cash flow, is among their more significant lessons.

I have watched with great delight people who had little more than "napkin" drawings, or a song to sing, a book to publish or a restaurant to build...virtually any kind of business venture conceivable...leave IBI Training Forums with a clear vision of what to do, how to do it and the tools with which to do so. Participants are taught principles of co-operation in business, rather than "dog-eat-dog" competition, and as a result find themselves able to draw upon the experiences, insights and even resources of hundreds of business development experts and successful entrepreneurs to help them succeed.

In the truest fashion of the old "pioneer" spirit, where everyone pitched in and helped build each others' homes and barns, IBI GLOBAL teaches people to help one another build their businesses and SUCCEED in a world where the Free Enterprise System—one of our most basic birthrights—has fallen victim to self-serving interests and corporate and bureaucratic mediocrity. I encourage...even urge...you to visit their website and consider attending one of their preview meetings in your area. If you have a dream you wish to pursue, you owe it to yourself to check out this organization and see for yourself what you might accomplish. If everyone did what these people teach in the business place, we would have had far fewer corporate collapses, and instead would have a business environment that is healthy, safe and enjoyable for everyone...not just for those at the top.

To find the IBI GLOBAL representative in your area, call their offices at 256-774-5444 x 10

Their Web site address is:

www.ibiglobal.com

FOR PUBLISHING ADVICE AND ASSISTANCE, there are few experts more knowlegible and up to date with the latest advances and methods than DAN POYNTER, whose Web site is www.Parapublishing.com. We rely on his wealth of knowledge and experience for all the latest techniques in publishing and marketing, and we attend his workshops as much as possible.

FOR PRINTING, there are few better and more reasonable sources than CENTRAL PLAINS BOOK MANUFACTURING, of Winfield, KS. This is a wholly employee-owned business which has a great story of their own, and has the best pricing and service of dozens we have researched. Contact Sharon Tully at 866-961-5456, or visit their Web site at www.centralplainsbook.com

There are other resources we have drawn upon over the years, the best of which we have listed on our Web site. These are businesses which we have determined to be the best, most reliable and trustworthy, all of which are free to you for the asking. Simply visit our Web site at www.AmatterofTime.org, and click on the "Resources" button for their contact information.

What people are saying about A Matter of Time . . .

"I don't know how to thank you for writing such a book. I felt I was actually experiencing what you were. Your insight into human nature is unbelievable. As I read, somewhere in the recesses of my mind I was thinking about how my life experiences in dealing with people have turned out and how I could have made them different if I had been able to think as you do. I wish everyone could read this book. It would give them hope and compassion for others in a way that is not taught, but learned. I can't express how much better I feel about myself as well as others because of reading this. . .If more people in this world had your philosophies and beliefs it would be a much better place. Thank you for taking the time and enduring the pain to write this. It has had a profound impact on me."
~Chris Rudell

"As a co-author of A Cup of Chicken Soup for the Soul, and founder of Let's Talk, a company dedicated to saving one million marriages, I feel safe in saying that you have a marvelous book in print that will have a dramatic impact on everyone who reads it. You have a passion for writing and for making a positive difference in the lives of others, and I commend you for it. Get ready, Don – it's your turn!"
~Barry Spilchuk

"Suffice it to say, your book has helped move me to a higher place... Thanks Don, for sharing this experience. It has served as my wake up call to continue my journey with my head held high and be actively involved in committing random acts of kindness."
~Alex Wilding

"I have been enjoying your book thoroughly – it's a doozy! Truly, I am anxious to see it come to life on the Silver Screen! I have to add that I am impressed at your bravery for sharing such personal experiences with the world...and that (miraculously) the baring of your soul makes your smile even brighter. Thank you so much for sharing your book with me. It was a major highlight and I will treasure it always."
~Chelsea Evenstar

"Once I started your book, I could hardly put it down. I am now emotionally driven to let you know the impact this story has had on me. I wanted to immediately pick up the phone and call the Department of Corrections and say, "Here am I, send me!" Thank you, Don. This book will be shared by many. It needs to be read by everyone. Have you sent a copy to our President?"
~Juana Price

"As you know, the IBI Free Enterprise Forum is the network and business boot camp that launched Jack Canfield and Mark Hansen's Chicken Soup for the Soul . Your book appeals to the same 70 million readers. We know you have film projects and sequels in mind, but as a stand alone, blockbuster best-seller, we are confident that A Matter of Time is a huge money making smash for everyone involved. Congratulations on a perfect project. Your team is amazing and your marketing superior. We can see warp drive success for you and for everyone involved in the project. Thank you for taking us into your VICTORY for the HUMAN SPIRIT."
~Bernhard Dohrmann, Founder, Income Builders International

BOARD OF COUNTY COMMISSIONERS
ESCAMBIA COUNTY, FLORIDA
223 PALAFOX PLACE
P.O. BOX 1591
PENSACOLA, FLORIDA 32597-1591
TEL. (904) 436-5783
(SUNCOM) 237-5783

PHILLIP M. (PHIL) WALTRIP
DISTRICT ONE

KENNETH J. KELSON
DISTRICT TWO

WILLIE J. JUNIOR
DISTRICT THREE

MURIEL WAGNER
DISTRICT FOUR

GRADY ALBRITTON
DISTRICT FIVE

April 24, 1987

AUGUST V. ELLIS, DPA
COUNTY ADMINISTRATOR

THOMAS R. SANTURRI
COUNTY ATTORNEY

TO WHOM IT MIGHT CONCERN

    Donald Eugene Kirchner, 19174-008 was an inmate at the Escambia County, Florida, jail during the later months of 1986 and until February 23, 1987. When he left our jail he asked me to forward some of my observations concerning his conduct and behavior while incarcerated.

    Mr. Kirchner was assigned in a sixteen (16) man pod of cells. He quickly recognized that a great number of his fellow inmates were school drop-outs or learning disability victims. Our GED program is relatively restricted because of classroom size and we cannot accomodate all candidates for educational enhancement. Mr. Kirchner approached me and requested basic educational material to be made available in the pod so that he could tutor the inmates. His unofficial "class" grew until he was working with almost half the inmates there. The motivation he provided was apparent in the change of behavior of the inmates after they became involved in the program.

    Because of Mr. Kirchner's maturity he also became a strong influence on his more youthful cell-mates in coping with the problems of living in confinement. They confided in him concerning family difficulties and sought his advice in many matters.

    Mr. Kirchner was exemplary in his own behavior and through his adherence to the regulations proved an ideal inmate to the correctional officers.

    I wish him well in his future endeavors, and hope that he will continue to share his knowledge and expertise in projects he may choose.

        Sincerely,

        Don H. Black
        Correctional Counselor
        Escambia County Jail

Department of Corrections—Detention
CITY OF ALBUQUERQUE - BERNALILLO COUNTY
415 Roma NW
Albuquerque, New Mexico 87102

City of Albuquerque

MICHAEL F. HANRAHAN
Director

Bernalillo County

PHONE:
(505) 842-8008

April 11, 1986

Donald Eugene Kirchner
415 Roma, N.W., (2NC10)
Albuquerque, N.M. 87102

Dear Mr. Kirchner:

The purpose of this letter is to express my appreciation for the assistance that you have been rendering the residents at the Bernalillo County Detention Center, Albuquerque, New Mexico. During the period of your incarceration (January 7, 1985, until present) you have served as a tutor/counselor for numerous other residents in a sincere effort to help them prepare for better education and improve themselves. You have also assisted several residents in the preparation for G.E.D. examinations.

I also want to commend you for your outstanding performance of duty as a bay orderly on your housing level and your outstanding conduct.

Once again thank you for your assistance.

Sincerely,

Michael F. Hanrahan,
Director

MFH:BC:pcc
0840A

cc. B. Chavez, CDM
     H. Howington, ACDM

FROM GORDON BERNELL
Bernalillo County Detention Center

In December of 1983, the average daily population in the Bernalillo County Detention Center was 435, including 12 women. Sixteen years later, the total was 1468, of which 241 were women. Nationwide, the numbers reveal the same disturbing trend. We now have more inmates than ever, more prisons and jails than ever, and unfortunately, more crime than ever.

As Programs Manager at the Detention Center, I direct academic, life skills, and substance abuse programs. While there is some success in the jail setting, total victory over criminal behavior can only be accomplished when effective, complimentary community programs continue the effort begun in jail.

One need not be a member of the Mensa Society to understand that incarceration alone is not the answer. Over 90% of all inmates will one day be released, most of them unprepared to re-enter the community. Allow me the opportunity to profile the average person who leaves our jail:

1. No job
2. No housing
3. Only the clothing on his or her back
4. Slightly more than a 5th grade education
5. No family support
6. A drug or alcohol problem
7. Under $1.00

Returning to honor is a difficult task. While just-released people may be eager to re-enter the community, is the community eager to accept them back? Not many employers will employ them. Very few landlords will rent to them. And how many parents will allow their children to socialize with them? Returning to dishonor is less difficult, less painful... and more dangerous.

Don Kirchner understood this, but he was not a typical inmate. While the anguish of his incarceration was apparent, and his frustration with the judicial system was obvious, he remained optimistic. He even took advantage of his circumstances to study the system, and develop his idea that a negative situation could someday have positive results. The day is here. The time is now. We either return to honor, or accept the unacceptable.

Like Don, I am an optimist, and I sense the appearance of an interesting coalition: altruists who want to save lives, and economists who want to save money. Jail programs and community programs do work. Our country incarcerated approximately 16 million people last year, and I am confident that effective programs can help at least 10% of them. If we are interested in saving lives, that's a lot of lives. If we are interested in saving money, that's a lot of money.

If we stand silently and let the world pass us by...it will.

JOHN McCAIN
ARIZONA

COMMITTEE ON ARMED SERVICES

COMMITTEE ON COMMERCE, SCIENCE,
AND TRANSPORTATION

SELECT COMMITTEE ON INDIAN AFFAIRS

SPECIAL COMMITTEE ON AGING

United States Senate

111 RUSSELL SENATE OFFICE BUILDING
WASHINGTON, DC 20510–0303
(202) 224–2235

TELEPHONE FOR HEARING IMPAIRED
(202) 224–7132

151 NORTH CENTENNIAL WAY
SUITE 1000
MESA, AZ 85201
(602) 835–8994

5353 NORTH 16TH STREET
SUITE 190
PHOENIX, AZ 85016
(602) 840–2567

5151 EAST BROADWAY
SUITE 170
TUCSON, AZ 85711
(602) 670–6334

May 8, 1991

Mr. Don Kirchner
Post Office Box 2731
Sedona, Arizona 86336

Dear Don:

    I wanted to take a moment to thank you for your recent correspondence regarding your organization, Return to Honor.

    As society is faced with ever increasing crime rates, the need for programs that assist in the re-entry of former convicts into society is becoming more apparent. I commend you for overcoming the difficulties you have faced in your life and taking the initiative to help others in similar situations.

    I have forwarded the information regarding your organization to Marta Aguirre of my Washington staff. Please do not hesitate to be in further contact with me, on this or any other matter of mutual concern.

    I enjoyed speaking to you in Sedona, and I hope we can do so again soon.

Sincerely,

John McCain
United States Senator

JM/ma/rt

U.S. Department of Justice

Office of Juvenile Justice and
Delinquency Prevention

Washington, D.C. 20531

JUL 30 1985

The Honorable Barry Goldwater
United States Senate
Washington, D.C. 20510

Dear Senator Goldwater:

This is in response to your letter on behalf of Mr. Roy W. Van
DeBogart concerning a proposal for a private sector juvenile
justice program drafted by Mr. Don Kirchner.

As you know, the Juvenile Justice and Delinquency Prevention Act
of 1974 established the Office of Juvenile Justice and
Delinquency Prevention to help states deal with the problems so
aptly described in Mr. Kirchner's proposal. Since that time,
the Office has awarded millions of dollars to the states to
support programs to prevent delinquency and treat juvenile
offenders, primarily through community-based facilities and
programs. In recent years, this Office has been interested in
the concept of private sector corrections for juveniles and has
funded and is evaluating a number of pilot projects around the
country.

I would suggest that Mr. Van DeBogart or Mr. Kirchner contact
the state agency that administers OJJDP funds in Arizona for
guidance on this proposal and for possible funding assistance.
The address is: Office of Economic Planning and Development,
1700 West Washington St., 4th Floor, Phoenix, Arizona 85007.
Mr. Rex Herron is the juvenile justice specialist there and his
telephone number is (602) 255-4952.

I am enclosing a fact sheet outlining the programs of OJJDP
which you may wish to send to Mr. Van DeBogart. Your interest
in this matter and the programs of the Office of Juvenile
Justice and Delinquency Prevention is greatly appreciated.

Sincerely,

Verne L. Spears
Acting Administrator

Enclosure

United States Senate

COMMITTEE ON ARMED SERVICES
WASHINGTON, DC 20510

August 13, 1986

Mr. Donald E. Kirchner
Post Office Box 2313
Sedona, Arizona   86336

Dear Mr. Kirchner:

Enclosed is the report I received from the Department of Justice
concerning your proposal for a private sector juvenile justice program.

The information contained in this report is self-explanatory. It is my
hope you will find this information useful in achieving your goals for
this program.   In addition, I am forwarding your most recent letter along
with your proposal to the Pardons Attorney at the Department of Justice.
As soon as I have heard from them, I will let you know.

Sincerely,

Barry Goldwater

NEF 2085 Mountain Road, Suite K2, Sedona, Arizona 86336-9800/520-204-1151

March 25, 1999

Don Kirchner
Executive Director
Society for the Return to Honor
P.O. Box 1822
Sedona, AZ   86339

Dear Don,

I am very pleased to inform you that the New Earth Foundation Board of Directors unanimously voted last night to approve for Return to Honor an emergency grant of $10,000. They also approved grantwriting efforts on your behalf for the amount of $25,000 to $75,000 to support the program in its first year. Everyone expressed their admiration for you and appreciation for your important work.

As you are well aware, the Foundation has been forced to write grants for its grantees due to an excess of giving from its endowment fund during the first two years. So you understand what a remarkable exception this is to the present policy! This is done in response not only to your neverending dedication to this project, but also to create the beginnings of a solution to this enormous problem we as a society face today.

You have told us that even the sum of $10,000 can make a world of difference, and we're going forward with the conviction that this is true. It is very heartening to see the large number of people that have responded so positively to this project. Certainly we here at New Earth feel the same way.

Thank you, Don, for following your guidance. God bless you in your quest for further funding and support. Perhaps at some point in time the entire nation will express its gratitude to you for the impact that Return to Honor will have on our society.

Sincerely,

John Pell
President

New Earth Foundation, Inc.
www.newearthfoundation.org